THE GIFTS
OF THE HOLY SPIRIT

THE GIFTS OF
THE HOLY SPIRIT

To unbelievers and believers

C. R. Vaughan, D.D.

THE BANNER OF TRUTH TRUST

THE BANNER OF TRUTH TRUST
3 *Murrayfield Road, Edinburgh* EH12 6EL
PO Box 621, *Carlisle, Pennsylvania* 17013, *USA*

*

First published 1894
First Banner of Truth Trust edition 1975
Reprinted 1984
Reprinted 1994
ISBN 0 85151 222 4

*

Printed in Finland by WSOY

TO

ROBERT LEWIS DABNEY, D. D., LL. D.,

THE EARNEST CHRISTIAN,

THE BRAVE AND FAITHFUL MINISTER OF THE GOSPEL, THE PROFOUND

THEOLOGIAN, THE DEEP PHILOSOPHER,

THE VERSATILE THINKER, THE ACCOMPLISHED WRITER,

THE INCORRUPTIBLE PATRIOT, THE BELOVED FRIEND OF MY YOUTH

AND AGE,

THIS VOLUME IS INSCRIBED,

A FAINT BUT TRUE TESTIMONY OF ESTEEM AND

AFFECTION,

FROM THE AUTHOR.

PREFACE.

IN these days when the issues of the press are so numerous, and the multitudes of readers are so greatly increased, it might be a sufficient apology for a fresh publication, to say it was a legitimate attempt to supply a possible public want, justifiable under the law of supply and demand. This vindication rests on the implied idea that for new works on old subjects, and, possibly, on new ones, apology is necessary. But this is absurd; it is an offence to the undoubted rights of authors and readers alike, to conceive that any legitimate attempt to supply any legitimate want of the human intellect needs any apology. Every man has a right to teach his views under his own responsibility, and every man to seek the information he may desire to possess on any legitimate subject of inquiry. This rule is specially applicable to any endeavor to aid in the extension of religious knowledge, or the increase of Christian activity, or the development of Christian experience. This last is the main object of the following treatise. It does not seek to enlarge the boundaries of Christian knowledge, unless the attempt to restate the old familiar truths of the gospel of grace in the forms they have assumed in a re-thinking of them under the current modes of thought in the passing era can be so called. The object is wholly practical. There are no new speculations here. The discussion only seeks to extend the application of some of these venerable truths to the practical experience of Christian people, and to restate the terms on which the Christian hope may be obtained by

5

those not yet entitled to indulge it. That there is need for some enlarged application of the glad tidings of great joy in order to the increase of Christian comfort among the servants of Christ, has long been clear to the writer. It has appeared in his intercourse with many Christians in the course of his work as a pastor in many parts of the church whose banner it has been his business and delight to carry for many chequered years. One of the most marked defects in the Christian character and experience of the present era is the want of legitimate and obligatory Christian joy. The standard of Christian activity is high, perhaps higher than it has ever been, except in some two or three periods during the nearly nineteen centuries of the Christian era. The energy of Christian work and the liberality of contribution to the revenues of the kingdom are commendably great in many directions. The work of missions at home and abroad, the private and associated labors of individual Christians, the formation of great voluntary societies, the extended work of evangelists, the various objects of special reforms, and the enormous activity of the Christian press, all warrant the assertion of a superior energy in the forces of the kingdom. This energy in work ought to be attended with a corresponding increase and prevalence of Christian comfort. In isolated instances it may be seen. But the result of years of observation directed to this very subject makes it clear, in the judgment of the writer, that there is grave defect in this regard in multitudes of modern believers, in those in whom the title of Christian appears to be vindicated by the fruits they bear in other directions. It is a sad deficiency. It not only saddens those whom the gracious Lord has not saddened, but disobeys and defeats the gracious will of him who has commanded his servants to "rejoice in the Lord always," and who has expressed his own solicitude that this command should be obeyed, by the emphatic reduplification of his order, "And again I say, rejoice." It is a grave discount of that holy faith which claims to be glad tidings of great joy, by showing how little substantial and abiding comfort it actually develops. What is more, this want of joy is want of strength; it brings not only a want of enjoyment, but a want of usefulness; for the joy of the Lord is pointedly declared to be the strength of his people. With the suitable development of this spirit of joy, the energies now in exercise would not only be elevated in tone, but redoubled in extent. Nothing would give such power to a proclaimed gospel as the universal prevalence of this deep and staunch spirit of real and habitual joy in the Lord. Nothing would quench the spirit of infidelity like this undeniable and priceless benefit to human happiness. Infidels, just like other men, feel the pressure of the stern conditions of human life. They are as eager for happiness as other men; and if they could see the practical demonstration of the power of the Christian faith in producing those effects on the human heart, on the scale of extent and degree which the gospel itself challenges its servants to test and realize, their attitude towards the gospel would be profoundly modified. They would become as keen as other men to share in a peace whose reality could no longer be questioned, whose value could no longer be disputed.

The causes of this defect in the Christian character of the age may not be far to seek, but it is now beside our purpose to seek them. It is enough to note the fact, for proof of which it is not unlikely the experience of the vast majority of Christian people might be safely challenged. Even those of whom it is least true will acknowledge that their highest and most durable joys fall far below the warrant for joy in the great Christian foundation for it. There can be no doubt that there have been few to share in the *exceeding joyfulness* of Paul, though the warrant of hope be the same, and the field of lawful endeavor to obtain it is open to every believer.

The object of this treatise, in the latter part of it especially, is to help the beloved of the Lord in the direction of this increase of the comfort of hope. But it does not seek to develop the whole gospel basis of it. It confines itself to the inward work of the Spirit. The great primary foundation of Christian joy is laid in that work of the Saviour of sinners which secures the actual justification of a sinning soul. To introduce a discussion of the forensic side of the great salvation would be to make a discussion designedly limited to the work of the Spirit embrace a treatise on the whole gospel. If the justification which is by faith is a real justification; if it not only exactly reverses all the effects of condemnation to which it is constantly opposed and contrasted in the Scriptures, but positively establishes the opposite effects in legal standing, then, beyond a doubt, a justified soul is a saved soul; a soul absolutely saved, so far as a sure title guaranteed by the veracity and power of God, in advance of a complete actual realization, can be said to secure safety. This affords a foundation for hope which cannot be equalled. Hope is the present expectation of a future good, and a sure hope cannot possibly be vindicated except on the basis of absolute certainty of the future good. The relation of the Redeemer's work to the joy of his people becomes clear; and assuredly no effort of the human mind to magnify the conception of the indebtedness of a guilty race to his grace could possibly overstate the case. But the *realization* of this and the other great results of the work of the Redeemer in the heart and consciousness of the individual is left to be wrought by the finger of the Holy Ghost. It is his allotted part to take of the things of Christ and show them unto us. It is his to unseal the full meaning of doctrine and promise, precept and prophecy. It is his to purge the inward vision, to quicken the intuitions of the mind, to soften and sweeten the affections that the heart may receive the just impress of the truth, to give that faith which is the substance of things hoped for, the evidence of things not seen, to restrain and eradicate the evil energies that obscure the vision and prevent the natural effects of the glad tidings of great joy. In a word, it is his office to give effect to the whole wonderful revelation of the divine mercy to a sinful race. Truth not rightly apprehended loses all its power. The mind of the learner must be opened to receive it. There must be a connection between the mind and its objects. All the power of the truth, whether to quicken, or comfort, or purify, is dependent upon this open apprehension. It is the office of the Blessed Spirit to control this essential communication by controlling the apprehensive mind of the seeker after safety. He guides the understanding; he moulds the heart into this capacity of rightly apprehending the truth. He does this in various ways; ways varied by the truth itself, by the relation of the individual to the covenant of grace as a believer or unbeliever, and by the object he may have it in hand to accomplish. Some truths are designed and adapted to produce certain effects; other truths, other effects. The Spirit works accordingly; this is true in both departments of his work, in the conversion of the unconverted, and in the sanctification of the converted. The work is done by distinct influences, producing distinct effects in both classes of persons, but in ways incomprehensible by us. The object of this discussion is to illustrate some of these influences, under the names appropriated to them in the sacred record, on both classes of their subjects.

Many years ago the mind of the writer was strongly drawn to a more special study of the general and special acts of the work of the Holy Spirit by a little treatise on the *Love of the Spirit*, by the Rev. Robert Phillip, Incumbent of Maberly Chapel, near the city of London. Mr. Phillip was one of those lovely and deeply-instructed ministers of the Lord Jesus who have illustrated the evangelical party in the

Church of England. His little book on the *Love of the
Spirit* was issued apparently about the year 1832. He was
also the author of several other treatises of an intensely
evangelical character, among which, *His Guides to Devotion*
have been reprinted in this country by the Carters, of New
York. The gem of his productions is the little treatise on
the grace of the Blessed Comforter; we would rather have
written that simple, but striking history of the dealings of
the Spirit than to have written *Hamlet* or *Othello*. The
work is now out of print; but it ought never to be allowed
to perish. Mr. Phillip illustrates the love of the Spirit in
his various broadly classified works in the soul, such as
awakening, conviction, conversion, and sanctification; and in
some of his special works in the soul of the believer, such as
sealing, unction, witness bearing, and calling to remembrance. Our own discussion follows closely in some particulars the series of topics, because essential to the development
of the subject; but the treatment is different under each, and
quite divergent under some, while necessarily similar in
some respects. Acknowledging gratefully our obligation to
his deep spiritual discernment, and grateful for the personal
benefit derived from his work, our more pronounced adhesion to the Calvinistic theology has compelled a more distinct tracery of the gifts of the Spirit to their fountain in the
distinguishing grace of the Father. Mr. Phillip was not a
Calvinist pronounced, but it is curious to see how his deep
spiritual intuitions and his rich experience of grace led him
to assert premises which he was not prepared to follow to
their conclusions. While the lines of thought in the two
discussions necessarily run parallel in treating the same
truths, the treatment will be found so different as to show
that the relation of a pupil to his master may be honorably
sustained, without servile imitation on one side, or unlawful
and unconfessed appropriation on the other. The two discussions may be well handled together; and if the gracious

work of the English preacher is destined to see the light no more, it will be a grateful reward to his Virginian follower to hope that his less valuable work may partially take its place, for a time, in helping the Master's pilgrims on their way to the Celestial City. Its highest aim is to be a *vade mecum* with some of the marching host.

The original design was simply to illustrate the gifts of the Spirit to believers. But on submitting the MSS. to one of the loveliest Christians he has ever known, who unites in a high degree the capacities of a profound thinker with the most attractive charms of popular eloquence, the suggestion was made that the discussion be extended to the dimensions of a treatise on the whole work of the Spirit. The suggestion has been followed to a certain extent; and the discussion on the gifts of the Spirit to unbelievers has been added. Neither pretends to be exhaustive. His valued encouragement to publish had been preceded by the requests of others. If our personal sense of independent and unqualified right to discharge the commission of a gospel teacher, both with pen and tongue, needed any such support as the desire of others, it might be justly claimed. Originally delivered as sermons in the ordinary discharge of pastoral duty, they were often followed by the request of elders, private Christians, and brother ministers of the gospel, to put them in a shape in which they could be permanently handled. So often and so earnestly was this done, it may have been a possible call of a higher authority to do it. At all events, these requests have created a boldness in attempting it which might never have sprung from a simple conviction of a right to do it. As the great desire of the writer was more completely to discharge his commission as a teacher of the gospel, and in a shape to do it after his lips are cold, he has sought to do it by honoring that blessed One to whose patient and tender grace he owes so much, through all the vicissitudes of a life not free from trial, both in his personal experience and in his official work.   The discussion itself will show that the author has sought no praise for learning or profundity of thought.   If, by the favor of God, the work can find its way to the hands of any class of inquiring sinners, and, as he originally designed and hoped, it shall prove ever so small an aid to the struggling saints of the Lord Jesus, by stimulating them to seek for larger and more abiding measures of the joy of his salvation, his dearest wish will be accomplished, and he will give hearty thanks to him who has commissioned his ministers to comfort his people.

C. R. V.

CONTENTS.

GIFTS TO BELIEVERS.

GIFTS TO UNBELIEVERS.

CHAPTER I.

RESTRAINT OF DEPRAVITY AND MOULDING OF THE MORAL NATURE.

"He turned their heart to hate his people, to deal subtilely with his servants."—*David in Psalms.*

"And the Lord hardened the heart of Pharaoh."—*Moses in Exodus.*

"God gave them over to a reprobate mind."—*Paul in Romans.*

1. THE doctrine of the influence of the Holy Spirit on the human heart is one of those doctrines of the inspired books towards which the carnal mind has always displayed the most uncompromising hostility. It has been denied as false; it has been scorned as fanatical; it has been assailed with positive hatred as an offence to the dignity and virtue of man. No weapon of argument or invective has been spared in the assault upon it. No restraint has been put on the virulent feeling it awakens in the open enemies of evangelical religion; and in the case of many who avow a general respect for the Christian faith there is a secret and strong contempt for the doctrine itself, for those who accept it, and especially for those who profess themselves to be actual subjects of this gracious influence. We do not propose, in a brief discussion, whose object is confined to the treatment of a single class of the influences of the Spirit, to vindicate at length the truth of this doctrine. We shall only briefly suggest one or two of the main points in the evidence. The word of God asserts it in the most

positive terms, and describes the various effects designed to be accomplished by it. The action is described as a secret touch on the soul, which does not interfere with the ordinary laws which regulate mental action. Its immediate effects are, therefore, not distinguishable usually from the usual manifestations of the operations of ordinary thought and feeling, and the real nature of the influence could, perhaps, never be known as a divine influence, except for the teachings of the Scriptures. But those teachings do afford a test of the truth of these operations, and of the source from which they come, of a most searching character. Not only the fact of the intervention of the Holy Ghost, but his detailed operations are asserted, and drawn out in their various consecutive and independent relations. This action and that are described; this object and another are asserted. This modification of thought and that manifestation of feeling are exhibited. These effects are said to be produced by the influence of the Spirit, and to be incapable of introduction into the mind when that influence is withdrawn. These effects are said to be exerted under certain conditions, and, if they are true, they will certainly be registered in human consciousness, and are consequently subject to inspection and report, just as any other mental modifications are subject to it.

The doctrine of the Spirit's influence, resting primarily on the testimony of God in his word, is thus brought secondarily under the jurisdiction of human experience and human testimony. As the record describes the consecutive mental states and the conditions under which they will arise, and under which alone they can arise, it is obvious that the complication and interdependence of these processes of thought and feeling will make up *an experimental test of the doctrine* sufficient to satisfy every rational demand. Inasmuch as many of these effects are claimed to be profound and permanent modifications of character, moral tastes, inclinations,

feelings, affections, principles of action, and sources of joy
and grief, and through these of the whole line of conduct in
the entire lives of men, it is obvious that human experience,
in long-protracted and varied forms, can be brought to test
this doctrine of the Holy Scriptures. To say that this experience, revealed in the testimony of living men, is not to be
received on such a subject, is absurd. Why may not a
series of mental modifications on the subject of religion be
as truly observed and reported as a series of mental modifications on any other subject ? Shall it be said that men are
so peculiarly liable to be deceived on this peculiar subject,
so open to the influences of enthusiasm, fanaticism, and the
misguidance of their own fancies, that their testimony is
worthless? Admitting the allegation would only impose the
obligation to make the test sufficiently stringent and diver-
sified to sift the testimony to any reasonable extent. If
some men are easily liable to imposition, there are others
who can be trusted to report the facts in their own consciousness, and the field of inquiry is so vast in this case as to
satisfy any demand possible to be made. Shall it be said
that the observation of mental phenomena and the tracing of
their mutual relations is a difficult thing for the disciplined
few, and an absolute impossibility for the untrained many?
The answer is obvious. The matter to be reported is a simple series of *facts* in consciousness, which does not require
profound capacities of mental analysis or trained habits of
mental introspection to report them. It would be intolerable
to impeach a plain man's assertion that he had a memory, or
that he remembered certain thoughts, and the feelings they
awakened. His attempt to explain the phenomena, of
which his consciousness and memory are perfect—to elaborate the laws and distinguish the interdependence of his
mental states—might be reasonably impeached ; but his report of simple facts lying in his consciousness is entirely
reliable. The human mind is no more liable to be deceived

in observing and reporting the current of conscious feeling
on the subject of religion than on any other subject. Nor
are the more recondite inter-relations and laws of religious
mental states any more incapable of just analysis by competent metaphysical talent than those of any other kind of
mental states. Suppose that one of these open enemies of
the Christian gospel were asked to state the real nature of
his feelings towards it. He would have no hesitation in saying *I dislike it;* and no profound mental investigation or
analysis of his mental states would be at all necessary to
enable him to report his feelings reliably. If this was demanded of him as a condition to his being believed, he
would at once see the absurdity of it. The state of his feeling would lie clear in his consciousness, and he would feel
himself seriously aggrieved if any one should doubt the truth
of his report.

Now, suppose a change should take place in this feeling,
and instead of dislike, he should learn to like the faith he
once despised. Would not this change be just as easily discerned in his consciousness, and be just as reliably reported,
as the original state of his feelings? No man can question
this; yet this simple and irresistible method of getting at
the facts of consciousness is the mode in which the testimony of the millions of evangelical Christians to the facts
of Christian experience is given, and proves that testimony
to be absolutely trustworthy. Perhaps this changed enemy
of the gospel may be a disciplined metaphysical thinker,
capable not only of observing the facts, but of tracing the
relations and interdependence of the facts in the changes he
reports. There is room for the exertion of the highest mental acumen in observing and discriminating the mental phenomena developed by the work of grace. This species of
human testimony would have its own peculiar value; but it
would not at all discount the value of the testimony given
by the mass of evangelical people. The simple and direct

testimony to the facts of consciousness may be even more valuable to many an investigator, who might rely on the report of the facts, and yet not altogether confide in the distinctions and relations between the facts as reported by the philosophic observer. But in point of fact, both of these classes of witnesses to the operations of the Holy Spirit are available; they can be found in every variety, from the highest and most profound metaphysical intellects, down along the whole scale of gradation, among minds not metaphysically trained, from the best of such minds to the humblest. They can be found in the literature of successive generations of Christians, in every age of the Christian era, and among many nationalities of the human race. The testimony is not merely sufficient, it is overwhelming, and the doctrine of the Spirit's influence stands impregnable; *first*, on the basis of a positive divine testimony; and *second*, on the basis of a human experience and testimony on a scale of magnitude and worthiness of confidence unapproached on any other similar subject in the annals of the world.

In plain truth, the doctrine of the Spirit's influence is an irresistible and not remote inference from the doctrine of the divine existence. How any one who admits the existence of a Deity at all can seriously balk at the doctrine of the possible contact of the Holy Ghost with the human soul, is one of those anomalies of human thought which passes the bounds of human comprehension. God exists; he is the maker of all other beings or things that exist; he has made them for a purpose; and to suppose an impassable barrier between him and his creatures, shutting him off from all communication with them adapted to their several natures, and thus abandoning the original end and purpose of their creation to absolute uncertainty of accomplishment, is inconsistent with the very notion of an intelligent and all-powerful being. Such a being under such conditions of restraint is impossible. The notion is absurd. The necessity of this ability to communicate with the creature grows more obvious in proportion to the degree in which the creature rises in the scale of being, and the ends to be accomplished by him increase in importance. Man stands at the head of the earthly scale; he is a being of endowments, absolutely grand and awful in the sublimity of his nature and the possibilities of his career. To say that God cannot come into contact and communion with such a being, to instruct and guide, to aid and defend, to control and mould him, so as to accomplish the possibilities of good and avert the possibilities of evil incident to his nature and the circumstances of his position, is to assert a proposition as cruel as it is absurd; as perilous in point of morals as it is foolish in point of sense.

If, then, it cannot be rationally denied that the Creator may come into effectual relations with his creatures, and emphatically with man, it is totally irrational to impeach the credibility of the influence of the Holy Ghost. That doctrine is only the specific statement and explanation of *the mode* in which this possible contact of God with man is realized. It differs from the general conception of the divine influence on this particular creature merely as *the specific* differs from *the general* on all subjects which admit of the distinction. The one proposition asserts a fact; the other, the mode of the fact. There is no inconsistency in saying a man traveled to a certain place, and in saying he traveled there on horseback, or in a carriage. The statement of a fact in general terms is not at all impeached or discredited by the additional statement of the mode or method in which it occurred. Everything that happens must happen in a certain way. If God communicates with any creature he has made, there must be a certain way in which he does it, and this way will be adjusted according to the nature of the creature. The power of God will be exerted in one way on a vegetable, in another way on an irrational animal, in another and altogether different way on a rational and accountable being. His intellect will be affected by some intelligent method; his moral nature will be affected by some moral influence; his faculties will all be appealed to by an adjustment suitable to each one of them. There is no denying the possible influence of the Holy Spirit but by denying the existence of God. To admit his existence is to admit the necessary attributes of his character; and to admit both of these and to deny the possibility of his communication with any work of his hands, and especially with the most important of them all, is an absolute contradiction. It is to deny the possibility of religion altogether. It is to render the unquenchable religious instincts of the human being absolute anomalies; to predicate faculties without any adjustments to them in the system of the universe. The existence of these religious proclivities of human nature is as absolutely unquestionable as the proclivities of his intellect towards knowledge, or of his appetites towards physical gratifications. The one may be as safely denied as the other. But all the adjustments of nature are truly made, and the religious instincts of the human soul point resistlessly to the existence of God and to his conversableness with man. If he is conversable with man, the influence of the Spirit on the human heart cannot be logically denied, since it is only the mode in which this conversableness is realized. If logically possible, the proof of the influence, as a matter of fact, may be safely left to rest on the evidence in the case, as already discussed, the testimony of God in the inspired books and in the experience of his servants.

2. The reality and the actual nature of the gifts of the Spirit to unbelieving men will be brought into view by considering the nature of sin and its inevitable natural tendencies on the nature of the violator of law. All the creatures of God are subjected to a law suitable to their natures; they are conditioned to live; and the well-being of each is abso-

lutely dependent on conformity to these conditions which
constitute the law of their being. The bird is conditioned
to live in the air, and the fish in the water. Let either of
them break these laws of their being; let the fish leave the
water and essay to live in the air; let the bird leave the air
and essay to live in the water, and the consequences will be
unavoidable. Suffering and death will ensue. If man vio-
lates the law of his being the same result will appear; his
nature will be injured; his strength and healthfulness will
be damaged; his comfort will be impaired; and as the final
effect death will emerge. If he violate the laws of his physical constitution, his physical nature will degenerate, and his
physical comfort will be destroyed. If he violate the law of
his intellectual nature, his intellectual power will be damaged,
and the operation of his faculties will be troublesome. If he
violate the law of his moral nature, the grandest and most
important department of his wonderful constitution, that
department of his nature will become morally corrupt, and
the peculiar distresses of such a disorder, coupled with the
peculiar sufferings of a guilty conscience, will follow. Sin
is the transgression of moral law; even the breach of a
positive divine statute is a breach of moral obligation to
obey God. The effects of sin inevitably appear more or less
directly in three directions—in the incurrence of guilt, in the
influx of depravity, and in the introduction of suffering.

Our attention is now drawn to the reaction of sin on the
nature of the transgressor. Sin is an energy of tremendous
power; it works towards all its natural effects with a swift,
relentless proclivity. Every sinful act recoils on the inward
nature of the actor, and stamps an indelible impression upon
it. Each act imprints its own likeness, and the varied forms
of sin develop a complicated and rapid picture of all evil on
the soul. Wicked men grow worse and worse. The law of
increase by exercise is all-powerful in things evil, as it is in
things good. There is also something contagious in moral

evil, which makes it peculiarly subject to this law of increase by indulgence. The great range of this influence of moral depravity is another distinct element to be considered in estimating the fearful character of its dominion. As the moral law covers every energy of every department of human nature, the moral energy of the soul which adjusts it to the law is incessantly called into play, and its reactionary effect on the moral nature is incessantly exerted. It affects the powers of the understanding, colors its perceptions, affects the judgment, pollutes the fancy, enfeebles the memory, weakens the capacity of invention, corrupts the sense of wit and humor, blunts the intuitions of right and wrong, and in the extreme cases of its deadly influence inverts that masterful distinction, and appears to annihilate the ability to discriminate it altogether. By its deadly reaction sin works an enormous deterioration in all the energies of the human heart, hardens the sensibilities, corrupts the affections, inflames the passions, distorts the positive volitions as well as the transient impulses of the will, and kindles all the energies of the moral nature into more and more dangerous instruments of fresh and progressive mischief. It not only perverts and deadens the intuitions of conscience, but weakens and often destroys to all appearance the authority and restraining power of conscience. Sin exerts a swift and inflexible influence to deprave the whole man, and, by necessary consequence, to affect his activities in every possible relation he can sustain to all other beings. It renders him more and more unfit to discharge the functions of every relation whatever. It makes him a worse father, husband, neighbor, citizen, soldier, or civilian. As its evil energies take effect and continually grow, he will become more unfit for duty, more and more dangerous as a factor in society. A certain degree of sensibility to the charms, and a certain practical regard to the positive obligations of truth, justice, kindness, and integrity, is essential to the very existence, to say nothing of the happy working, of society. The larger measures of them are indispensable to the higher developments of a genuine civilization. The perception and practical acknowledgment of the binding force, the equity, the wisdom, and the absolute necessity of the great moral conceptions, is essential to the peace of families, to the welfare of neighborhoods, to the safety of states, to the operations of commerce, to the progress of learning—in a word, to all the well-being of mankind. To the individual man a measure of compliance with the demands of personal integrity is indispensable to his safety and comfort. The unrestrained indulgence of his own passions will certainly and speedily work out his destruction. From this swift, relentless, unpausing, and universal tendency in sin to work out all its natural effects, and especially this tendency to corrupt the very nature and fountain of energy in the transgressor, the conclusion is irresistible, that unless some vast restraining power is introduced to check and hold under a competent restriction this enormous and deadly energy of sin, there would be no possible prevention of all the complicated evil consequences that would inevitably flow from it.

We are now at a point of view which will enable us to form some idea of the grand influence which the Holy Spirit of God exerts upon unbelieving and ungodly men for their personal and associated well-being. He exerts that grand restraining influence without which there can be no such things as home, society, government, civilization, or individual enjoyment anywhere among all the millions of the sinning human race. He restrains both the sinful acts and the natural tendencies of the acts within some tolerable bounds. He prevents these evil tendencies from running down into their extreme degrees, and thus secures all the great advantages which are dependent on some effective moral energies in the character and conduct of the individual and the associated man. The nature of this influence can only be described in general terms. The method of its exertion, like all the evangelic work of the Spirit, is wrapped in impenetrable mystery. It is mainly a restraining influence upon the evil energies it undertakes to combat. But there is also, no doubt, a communication of positive good on a lesser scale, a grant not of that saving grace which he gives under the limitations of God's eternal counsel where the gospel is preached, but an effective aid in the culture of the moral virtues in the pagan heroes, without which the natural effects of unrestrained sin would have made it impossible. But the the main action is *restraint upon sin.*

Let us look at some of the features of this vast benefit to an unholy world. By some few speculators, misinterpreting certain expressions in the word of God, he has been suspected of the gross dishonor of infusing moral evil by a positive communication into the hearts of those unhappy men who have brought themselves under God's judicial anger. It is supposed to be capable of vindication because it is judicially done, as the execution of a penal sentence. A few still more desperate speculators have affirmed it, as not only done, but sovereignly done, and apart from all judicial considerations whatever. But whether the conception is based on considerations of judgment or sovereignty, the idea of the Holy God positively infusing depravity into a creature's nature is utterly false, as false as it is blasphemous. God is in no sense the author of sin. It is an absurdity in itself; the very notion involves impossibility, not merely from the moral qualities of the divine nature, but in the nature of the thing supposed. Moral depravity is lodged in the human *will;* it is a manifestation of will in man, and the very nature of the case, as the manifestation of will in one being positively excludes it as founding in the will of all other beings. But, more than this, the desperate theory is excluded by the absolute superfluousness of the demand, even supposing it to be possible. There is no necessity for God to infuse depravity, even as the execution of a judicial sentence. All he need do is to withdraw restraint on the native impulse and energy of sin. If there is any just occasion for the interposition of judicial wrath, and in the exercise of his sovereign good pleasure in selecting the mode of executing the judicial decree, he pleases to allow the transgressor to run into more ruinous excesses, he has no need for any positive action. All he would have to do would be to withhold his restraining grace, which he is under no obligation to exert, and let loose the sin which he has hitherto dammed back in the unholy heart. This was the process by which he hardened Pharaoh's heart, and gave all the heathen world over to a reprobate mind. These instances illustrate two distinct points: *First*, the matter of fact of a removal of restraining grace in judicial cases; and *second*, this removal demonstrates the prior existence of the restraining grace before the parties were given over to the free play of their own wickedness. What was true of illustrative instances is true of the whole illustrated class. This is proved by the relentless tendency of sin towards its own natural effects—a proclivity to increase and intensify in the soul indefinitely, just like a virulent disease in the body to run to its extreme results. Both will inevitably, and with more or less rapidity, do this, unless checked by some opposing force. To cure in either case, an influence, not merely to check, but to reverse the course of the destructive tendencies, is indispensably necessary.

A brief citation of some of the gifts of the Spirit to ungodly men in heathen as in Christian lands can now be made. While the list shall be short, the blessings themselves are immeasurably great.

3. By his restraint on the growth of depravity in the human heart, the Holy Ghost preserves the moral element in human nature from running down into a complete paralysis and incapacity of any degree of good moral energy. The total depravity asserted in the Scriptures is a totality of ex-

tent, not of degree. A single sin extinguishes spiritual life, that holiness which is essential to the perfect integrity of moral action, but does not bring to perfection that evil energy which takes the place of the extinguished holiness. That evil energy increases with every evil act to which it leads. The loss of life is complete, but the corruption which ensues may exist in a limitless variety of degrees. Total depravity pervades all the powers of the soul; it excludes from the acts of the soul, and the character or habit formed by those acts, all absolute and perfect good; but it exists in a vast scale of degrees, and is capable of an endless succession and assortment of such varieties. An immortal being endlessly violating law will *never* reach a limit to his possible degradation. He will grow worse and worse in his nature the more he multiplies sin in his acts. He will grow worse and worse as long as he acts, which will be forever. But even in this world the moral nature in man is capable of a deterioration fearful to comtemplate. The restraints of the Spirit are designed merely to check, not to prevent, the growth of depravity. Particular instances in the case of individual men are often allowed to disclose the fearful results of a depraved will from which the restraints have been partially removed; for even in these instances the suspension of the blessed restraint is only partial. Particular instances on a larger scale, showing the effects on bodies of men, are sometimes disclosed in what are called the barbarous tribes of the human family. Among these degraded races the moral degradation proceeds to such extreme lengths as to almost efface the traits of human nature altogether, and develop a positive brute character, as much more dangerous than the fiercest of the original brutes as the improved ingenuity of a rational intellect exceeds the instincts of the mere animal being. Some are degraded until the very existence of any rational capacity is left disputable. Moral conceptions are found reduced to the lowest apparently possible scale among these miserable creatures, and the results are seen in the wretchedness and incessant perils which distinguish their ordinary lives. The influences of the Spirit restraining the natural progress of depravity leave the moral energies, not indeed capable of any activities really holy, but capable of an effective sense of justice and benevolence, civil wisdom and prudence, and the force of moral obligations generally. The moral intuitions of the understanding are preserved in some effective and useful degree. The sensibilities of the heart are left capable of impressions of humanity. The affections remain capable of domestic and social love, the sense of honor, the love of country, literature and art, capable not only of sympathy with noble ends and ideas, but of improvement on a vast scale. These valuable traits can be carried to a noble development by wise discipline and educational training, by the restraints and the stimulants of civil society, public opinion and private influence. The styptics of moral embalmment may long preserve the beauty of the dead from dissolving in the ultimate processes of corruption, though they can no more restore spiritual life to the soul than physical life to the body when either have departed. But that which is preserved for effective service in the present life is of inestimable value; it constitutes the main source of human happiness in this strange world. The debt of obligation to the gracious Spirit of the Lord for securing this inestimable benefit to unbelieving and disobedient men is supremely great. All the good effects of this retained efficiency of the moral energies are due to this gift of the Holy Spirit.

4. Among these good effects we may cite the preservation of moral knowledge, the just conception, as far as it goes, of the nature and authority of moral truth. Apart from the revealed word of God, this knowledge is very imperfect, and, with the Scriptures, the moral conceptions of vast multitudes are also gravely deficient. But still, the retraints of the Spirit on the growth of depravity, and per-

haps some positive aid to the moral intuitions, have left moral ideas to an effective influence of inestimable value. In the restrained moral nature, moral ideas spring up; moral obligation is felt in at least some measure of its authority; moral rules are discovered; moral principles, as impelling forces to action, are inculcated; moral speculations develop theories and schools of moral philosophy. Moral notions, regulating feeling, character, conduct, are felt to be the indispensable cement of the social structure, without which it could not exist. It comes to be seen, that without these conceptions no human relations could be supported. They, therefore, rise to a strong and invaluable ascendency, pervade every branch of advanced human society, and make possible all the sources of comfort, and all the noble enterprises for which society provides. For this effective knowledge of moral truth, even where the Christian records are unknown, and for all the good effects that knowledge secures, men are bound in gratitude to the Holy Spirit.

5. One more beneficial effect of the restraining influences of the Spirit on ungodly men, is the prevention of the dangerous prevalence of abnormal wickedness in individual men, and the prevention of particular crimes in men of the common standard of character, and less frequently, perhaps, but with even wider benefit, in nations and smaller communities. Allusion has been made to the fact that moral monsters are occasionally seen; any great prevalence of these characters would be a momentous calamity. What are called the vicious, or dangerous classes, are discoverable in the great cities of states highly civilized, in greater or less numbers, and in the regions occupied by half-civilized nomadic tribes. These classes are the terror of the communities in which they are found, and to the regions opened to the incursion of these lawless marauders. History samples both in the No Popery riots in London during the eighteenth century, and in the invasions of Attila and the Saracens. Un-

less these ruthless classes can be held under the terrors of
the law, civil or military, no security for life or property can
be found.   If the whole or the bulk of the population were
made up of such characters, all the ends of civil society
would be annihilated.   Even an occasional specimen of these
extreme cases of moral lawlessness is enough to destroy the
security of a whole neighborhood.   The occasional unloosing of the restraints which occasion these dangerous manifestations illustrates the value of the restrictions which
only allow them to appear unfrequently.   The more severe
operations of human law would be far oftener called into
action if it were not for the restraining agency of divine
power through the agency of the Holy Spirit.   Often, too,
beyond a doubt, the exasperated passions of individual
men are turned into safer channels by his secret touch.
The rage of Esau was thus averted from Jacob.   Often, too,
the violent counsels of national governments, or riotous
masses of seditious mobs, are turned aside.   The depraved
condition of human nature affords a perilous basis for particular temptations.   No one is exempt from the prudent
as well as holy obligation to pray, "lead us not into temptation, but deliver us from evil."   The sudden and violent influence of strong temptation has placed many a humane and
generous disposition on the verge of a criminal action which
would have darkened the whole future of life.   The secret
restraints of the Holy Spirit in the critical moment have
often averted crime and its calamities, and when this is done,
a great mercy is bestowed.   The counsels of nations are
sometimes as effectually modified.

6. To this grand restraining and modifying influence of
the Holy Spirit is due the development of civilization, the
safe accumulation of wealth, and all the vast benefits conditioned upon it, and all the conditions which make learning
and scientific investigations possible.   To it is it due that
there is such a thing as a respectable man in a depraved

race. To it is due the existence of that confidence which
makes trade and commerce possible. To it is due the protection of law, and the benefits of civil government. To it is
due the development of art in all its forms. To it is due the
existence of homes, and the refining and enjoyable influences
of refined society. In one word, *all earthly good* rests upon
it as its ultimate bases; for the natural tendencies of sin in
the human heart, left without restraint, would soon render
society impossible, and overwhelm the very existence of the
human race under the violence of its own lawlessness.

7. Among the gifts of the Spirit to unbelievers are found
all those evangelical influences, of every kind and degree,
brought to bear, previous to conversion, on the views and
character of unconverted men. Besides those special influences of divine grace in the positive awakening and effective
natural conviction, which will receive a special treatment in
the progress of this discussion, there are special positive as
well as restraining influences of the Holy Ghost, which are
brought to bear on ungodly men living under Christian
institutions. Effective religious education and training in
religious observances, the discipline of a Christian home,
the regular instructions of the pulpit, the example and direct
influence of pious friends, protection from dangerous associations, restraint from committing particular sins and entering scenes of special temptation, salutary impressions
from particular afflictions, are all brought to bear on multitudes of men previous to conversion. These influences
often work profound and permanent modifications of character stopping short of conversion; but their effectiveness
is due to the influences of the Spirit restraining the coun-
teracting energies of evil which otherwise would have
defeated them. Apart from his grace no means would
prove capable of permanent or efficient results. Without it
the ominous birds would pick up all the carefully chosen
and scattered seed. Those gracious influences are not

merely restraining, they are also active in making and re-straining the impression. There is nothing in the unmodi-fied state of an unregenerate heart to welcome or give healthy aid to evangelical truth. So far as such aid is given and abiding impressions are made in forming the conscience and moulding the judgment of Christian ideas, it is due to the influence of the Spirit. As in the communi-cation of his saving grace the influence of the truth employed must be accompanied by his positive power, it is in accord with this analogy to make all other moulding influences de-pendent on lesser measures of the same power. There is no room to question this from an evangelical point of view. This positive influence exerted on unregenerate men under gospel training renders it credible, to say the least, that, even among the unchristian populations of the world at large, the agency of the Spirit, while mainly restrictive, is not altogether confined to that species of action. It becomes credible, at least, that the moral ideas which became effec-tive in shaping the private and public virtues of some pagan heroes and other less distinguished individuals of pagan society, were aided in producing their effects by some posi-tive exertion of divine power and grace. It is evident that the afflictions of the great Babylonian prince, Nebuchad-nezzar, were so sanctified to him as to profoundly modify his views of the God of Israel, if they did not lead to his actual conversion. In the case of Cyrus the Great, a man raised up to accomplish great special purposes under the providence of God, it is most likely that his character was moulded by special influences to those virtues which were to be so necessary in accomplishing the work assigned him. Undoubtedly it would be an error to discount all effective, *natural* influences in the moral discipline of the heathen mind. But it is certainly in keeping with the analogy of Christian truth, and the necessity of the Spirit to give it saving effect, to suppose some similar, though less effective

influences of the same blessed agent to give effect to the
moral ideas which moulded the virtues of a pagan community. If this speculation is true, it is obvious that unbelievers do receive gifts of the Holy Spirit, stopping short of
regeneration, which are, nevertheless, of great value, and
that these gifts are something more than merely salutary
restraints. They are positive grants, which exert a commanding influence in the development and maintenance of
the virtues which secure the private happiness and the public usefulness of a heathen community.

The notion that the *intellectual* achievements of the great
pagan minds, the philosophy of Socrates, or the poetry of
Homer, are to be attributed, as much as their moral virtues,
to the secret influences of the Holy Spirit, is not so clear or
credible. Doubtless these great intellectual works are indirectly attributable to his restraining power; for had the
depravity in these great men, as in all other men, been
allowed to work out without restraint along the lines of sin's
inevitable tendency, the great lights of their immortal genius
would never have shone out on the track of the advancing
ages. But that their great intellectual work was positively
due to any positive grants of the Spirit, is another and a less
credible thing. There is no evidence to prove it. It would,
in fact, be an injury to the doctrine of the obligations of an
ungodly world to the grace of the Holy Ghost to discount
all real and effective energy in the gifts of the Creator in the
sphere of nature. All gifts of body, mind, and heart are
from him, acting in the sphere of creation, and to him is due
the praise and gratitude for giving such valuable gifts; but
the praise is due to him as Creator, and to ascribe the
efficiency of these gifts to a secret divine influence in the
sphere of grace is to discount his glory in the sphere of
nature. There is real intrinsic efficiency in the physical and
intellectual gifts bestowed by the Creator. But this is only
true of the physical and intellectual divisions of his creative

work, and only true of them in part; for both of them have been grievously injured by the moral decadence of human nature. In the moral sphere it is different, for the obvious reason that in the moral sphere man has destroyed his original endowments for perfect moral action, and needs the interposition of the power that gave them to restore them again. But his physical and intellectual endowments, though greatly injured by the ruin of his moral and spiritual gifts, have not been destroyed altogether, and may, therefore, be fairly credited with the praise they may deserve. Homer, as a great intellect, reflects praise on the being who created him. Homer, as a transgressor of law, is indebted to the grace of the Holy Spirit for so restraining the natural tendencies of the sin that was in him as to give free play to his glorious genius.

8. There is something inexpressibly grand and heart-moving in the conception of the work of the Spirit of God in this strange world. It is a scene in which evil is everywhere intermingled with good, and good with evil. This condition of things is altogether anomalous, and indicates a very peculiar operation in the causes that produce and account for it. On the regular principles of moral government, the violation of law is at once followed by the stroke of its penalties, and the scene presented is a scene of unqualified misery. But when actual good appears intermingled with evil in an admitted scene of violated law, it indicates the introduction of another cause, and a peculiar modification of the regular administration of a moral government. The Scriptures explain it by the revelation of the wonderful purpose of God to save sinners, to dispute the dominion of the fallen world with the powers of darkness. To carry out this strange conception, the scene of revolt has been placed under the regulation of grace, as well as under the operation of law. Hence the chequered scene of human existence. The evils which prevail are due to the violation of law, and all the good that

prevails is due to the operation of grace. Hence the strange anomalies of disease and health, death and life, joy and grief. Hence the still stronger anomaly of pleasures in sin, and sinners having more than heart can wish. Hence the paradox of joy in tribulation, of the righteous in trouble, the faithful servants of the revealed will of God perplexed, but not in despair, cast down, but not destroyed, persecuted, but not forsaken. Hence many a blessing bestowed on those who abuse them, long years of prosperity given to the ungodly and the ungrateful. Hence the strangest anomaly of all, of high but qualified private and public virtues, respect, ability, and just claims to esteem, in beings whose hearts are alienated from God, in whose natures the power of sin is entrenched with an energy which no force can dislodge except the power of God himself. To support this conflict of the good against the evil is the purpose and work of the Holy Spirit.

As the dispute between the contending elements is literally co-extensive with the race, and as the objects of the disputed supremacy are literally every object of human pursuit, the benignant influences of the blessed agent of the divine goodness extend literally over the whole extent of the human race. He guards the happiness of families, and the peace of communities. He keeps his hand on all the sources of human well-being. In the cottages of the poor, in the halls of the rich, in the tents of the wandering nomad, in the homes of the refined, in the wigwam of the savage, in the palaces of the great, wherever any measure or degree of good affections are found qualifying the universal intrusion of evil, there the traces of his benignant restraints and positive helps to what is good are to be found. He thus qualifies the policies of governments in peace and war, according to his own sovereign good pleasure, softening the rough usages of military conflict with the gentle influences of humanity, and throwing the regards of melting sympathy over

the sufferings and deficiencies of the poor in peace. Whatever advance in science and the arts of invention can be
turned to the good of the human family are more or less
directly due to his goodness. It is not unreasonable or unscriptural to suppose that in all the discoveries which have
increased the supplies of human food, in the enlarged trans-
portation which has made them available to millions of the
poor in distant quarters of the earth, in the discovery of
remedies for disease, in all the inventions that tend to elevate
and improve the condition of human life, that his hand has
been somewhere concerned.

It is altogether probable that the great supporter of the
good, in its conflict with the evil, will aid in everything
which can contribute to the increased power and the final
supremacy of the cause which he champions. Then under
the institutions of the gospel, through which his main work
is to be done, his mighty energies are incessantly employed.
He sustains and invigorates the spiritual life of every believer. He secures the kind of prayer that conditions the
life-giving power. He secures the right knowledge and
proclamation of the truth. He checks the spread of errors
in doctrine and practice in the church according to his own
wise will. He maintains the godly example of the saints, and
the spread of the kingdom over the earth. All this reveals
one vast department of his work. He applies the truth to
the hearts and consciences of the ungodly. He restrains
and overcomes the subtle influences that impede their return
to their allegiance. He regulates the views and feelings
which tend to lead to permanent reconciliation. He effectually awakens the dull sleepers to their danger, and convinces them sufficiently of their sin to make them seek with
all their heart for the way of salvation. He executes that
final crowning wonder, the raising of a dead soul to life, and
then takes up his abode within to complete the purification
he has begun. Here his gifts to the unbeliever cease, and

his gifts to the believer begin. All this discloses another grand department of his work. Brooding unceasingly over the lost world, entering with more or less energy, with more or less permanence into every lost soul, ruling the depraved millions of its inhabitants, guiding its progress, concerned about all that affects its well-being, this subject of the gifts of the Holy Spirit to unbelieving and rebel men expands our conceptions of the divine benignity, until we feel that the enterprise is worthy of the infinite and loving character of the Lord God Almighty.

This wonderful encounter of grace with sin is peculiar to this world. The King is busy in hell, dealing with the felons of the abyss; hopeless of good to them, he deals with their sin only to execute justice. Busy in heaven in raising the saved sinners along an endless scale of elevation, he has there no sin to encounter. But on earth he is busy with sin and misery to deliver from both; he is here working out an enterprise which will crown the long series of his glorious works with the most splendid of them all; an enterprise in which *grace*, the sweetest modification of infinite love, shall win the loftiest trophy of all his infinite excellences. What are called the "common operations" of the Holy Ghost are embraced in these incessant and universal movements to restrain the sin of the world, and to bring those sinners who are favored with gospel ordinances to lay hold on eternal life. These effects on the ungodly under gospel influences are indicated by periods of thoughtfulness about the issues of human existence, by restlessness of conscience, by sensibility to the appeals of the truth and providences of God, by half-formed resolutions to repent, and by the earlier motions of the soul in awakening and conviction. The operations of the Spirit, of which we have spoken as wrought over the whole human race in the restraint of sin and in the development of such relative good as may be found, are truly his common operations. The value of them cannot be adequately apprehended. If they were altogether suspended, even for the briefest period of time, the consequences would be fearful. All that is good in this life and earthly sphere, and all that is promising of more immeasurable good in preparing a lost immortal to receive the gospel and to become an heir of everlasting life, is due to the vast, rich gifts of the Holy Spirit to unbelieving and disobedient men.

CHAPTER II.

AWAKENING INFLUENCE.

"WHEREFORE he saith, Awake, thou that sleepest, and arise from the dead, and Christ shall give thee light."—*Paul to the Ephesians.*

THE relations of the Holy Spirit to the unconverted, in the administration of the covenant of grace, are of inexpressible importance. It is his function to reprove the world of sin, and of righteousness, and of judgment; and until he does this work there is no prospect of salvation. This preliminary work of grace is generally divided into two classifications, which, although in some aspects of the case interlocked with each other, present differences sufficiently marked to justify the distinct classification employed in delineating them. One of these embraces what are called the *awakening* influences of the Holy Spirit, and the other, the *convicting* influences of the same gracious agent. There are two forms of conviction of sin, one previous to conversion, and the other subsequent to it. With the first of these, awakening is always and closely connected, so that it is not easy to consider them apart, even in thought. Awakening has its chief reference to the *danger* which sin has entailed; but this cause of the danger necessarily comes under view in considering the danger itself. The awakening, then, is really an awakening to sin as well as to danger, although the reference to sin is secondary to the apprehension of the peril it has induced. This apprehension of both may exist on a wide scale of degrees, from mere uneasiness to a tragic intensity of feeling; but in all its degrees it is the result of those awakening and partially convictive influences of the Holy Ghost which precede regeneration. Leaving any fur-

41

ther attempt to draw the distinction between the apprehension of sin which does not lead to salvation and that which does, at the present, we design to call attention to the state of the human mind which makes an *awakening* necessary as a preliminary process in the work of grace.

The Scripture accounts of the mental states of a soul born under the existing conditions of human nature in this world describe them in strange terms, as "asleep," "blind," "unconscious," and in still stranger terms, as "dead," "dead in trespasses and sins," and "needing to rise from the dead." Still more strangely, they are commanded and exhorted "to rise from the dead," and to awaken themselves in the very grasp of their deadly sleep. The strangeness of these terms is partly due to, and at the same time partly explained by, the unquestionable fact that these dead and sleeping souls are alive, intelligent, active, full of curiosity, full of strong passions, energetic, resolute, and wide awake to all the demands of the present life. In the face of such a fact, the sleep and the deadness must have reference to some peculiar insensibility and incapacity of action which is entirely consistent because co-existent with this acknowledged activity. It must refer to a particular disability in a certain direction and towards a particular object. Such a partial and particular mental disablement may be compatible with activity towards certain other objects. This is a condition of things not at all uncommon There are many things which are true, and known to be true, which excite the strongest interest of some minds and never enter the thoughts nor awaken the smallest concern in others. The common laborer passes by a hundred weeds and wild flowers without anything more than a bare recognition of their presence and their obtrusive qualities, without any thought of the wonderful mysteries that are involved in them. To these he is blind or dead. Everything that exists is full of hidden significances which never excite a thought, and to which many an active and energetic mind is as dead and insensible as if there was no subject of discovery or thought involved. A man may be *color blind,* and at the same time possess a very active and intelligent understanding. But under that singular disability, with all his mental activity he is as completely dead to all the glories of color as if no splendor of hue was incorporated in the works of nature. These instances show us that the paradox is, notwithstanding the appearance of contradiction, true in fact; that the view may be perceptive and yet insensible, and, therefore, it is altogether possible for a man to be intellectually intelligent and yet spiritually blind; that he may be active in some things yet dead in others; that he may know many a fact, and yet be utterly insensible to the real significance and force of the fact. If, now, this insensibility is the result of moral causes, the product of sin, the datum of a depraved state of the faculties which condition responsibility, there is no escaping the conclusion that man is justly accountable for the spiritual death that is in him. This is the general scope of the Scripture doctrine about the *sleep* and *death* of a sinful soul. It refers to a certain insensibility which co-exists with every, even the highest, degree of mental energy, and is found in every soul of the human race without exception. It is a natural trait in every fallen moral agent. It does not assert that man has not and cannot have any idea of God at all, but that he has no just conception of what he is.

In the higher grades of this corrupt and misguiding influence, the very idea of God may become obscured and obliterated. Nay, the understanding, under a correct education, may form the conceptions of the divine attributes intellectually just, but no process of mere culture can unveil the real quality of those attributes, and render them agreeable to the affections of an unrenewed heart. A man may know that God is just, and have a grave and deep conviction of the essential value of such a quality in the Governor of the universe; and yet that very quality may make him uneasy, and excite his fears instead of his affections, under the conscious-ness of his own sin. If he saw God as he is, he would de-light in his glorious qualities; he would love him. But an unholy heart perverts his discernment, and he remains blind and dead to the real character of God. Nor does this doc-trine of spiritual blindness mean that man has no ideas, and even correct conceptions, as far as they go, of the law and the government of God; but it means that feelings and affec-tions, alienated from holiness, obscure to his view the real quality and excellence of those two grand expressions of the divine nature. If he was not blind to them, he would love them. The Bible doctrine of the spiritual slumber and the spiritual death of a fallen soul affirms a similar effect of in-sensibility to the real force and significance of all the grand facts and doctrines of man's spiritual condition. Some of these are discovered in the Bible; some of them lie in the open sphere of experience and consciousness; yet all are more or less oppressed and sunk out of view by the same deadly state of the mind as colored by the carnal heart. Take the melancholy conditions of human existence in this world, death and the uncertain tenure of life. No man is more certain that he lives than he is that he will die. Nothing is more sure than the uncertainty of life. Yet prac-tically, these facts make little or no impression on the masses of mankind; the mind is dead to them. In like manner, the disquiet of conscience, and the consciousness of habitual wrong-doing, are recognized and disabled of their genuine weight and impressiveness. The sense of accountability is similarly disabled and deadened. All the great doctrines of the Christian faith are thus disabled in millions of minds which have never had or harbored a doubt of their truth. The facts in human nature and in human life, as well as the doctrines of religion, are so apprehended that the mind re-mains as insensible to their real force and meaning as if it were rendered insensible by death or deep sleep. This insensibility remains in the natural mind even when the recognition of them in their purely intellectual aspects may lead to very active religious service, to the building of churches, to the support of a costly religious ritual, and to the fierce polemic defence of religious dogmas. The real difficulty is not removed, the blindness and the deadness remain, until the Holy Spirit begins his marvelous work.

2. The *awakening* of the Spirit is just the *breaking up of this insensibility to a certain extent*. It is not regeneration, which is the actual giving of life, a passing from death to life. It is a restoration of sensibility within the bounds of that natural energy of the intellect, heart, and conscience which we have seen to co-exist with the spiritual death and sleep induced by sin. It stops short of spiritual life. The understanding is quickened to apprehend something more of the facts than it ever did before, though not to the full comprehension of them. The conscience is quickened to feel more of what is involved in the facts, yet under the same limitation. The heart is correspondingly affected. No new truth is revealed to the understanding, but new and more just views of old ideas are introduced, though still short of what is necessary to be known; and instead of the absolute want, or of a totally insufficient degree of feeling suitable to the facts, some approximately suitable feeling is awakened, though not yet altogether suitable. Awakening and conviction are generally treated together, and this is altogether proper in reference to that species of conviction which precedes conversion, because there is a most intimate relation between them, and they generally, in greater or less degree, appear in the consciousness at the same time. But there is a marked difference between awakening and that species of conviction which accompanies, or, more accurately, flows from conversion. Awakening, and the conviction which generally attends it, is not saving; many a soul has been awak-

ened and made subject to mere natural convictions of guilt, and thus aroused to intense anxiety and active effort to obtain deliverance, and yet has again subsided into utter unconcern. A partial or imperfect, or, as we have called it, natural conviction of guilt, differs from that full or perfect conviction of sin which always leads to genuine repentance, and thus to safety. This difference will be more fully developed hereafter; for the present we note one or two of the leading distinctions.

There is such a thing as a natural conviction of sin, and although dependent more or less on the common operations of the Spirit, appears frequently on the commission of the higher crimes, especially in the early career of a criminal. A detected thief or adulterer feels guilty. A murderer often feels keenly the guilt of his bloody deed; conscience protests with stern fidelity, and the sense of guilt provokes the feeling of remorse, and 'often a bitter wish that the deed had not been done. This conviction yields a species of repentance, the sorrow of the world that worketh death. Its leading ear-marks are that it is altogether selfish; it is confined to one or two criminal actions; it is strongly qualified by the fear of detection; it is greatly intensified by detection; it is disposed to self-defence or self-justification, and it only produces a limited reform of conduct when occasion allows. True and full conviction stands opposed to mere natural conviction on these and on several others.

Now, this natural conviction of sin is generally, though not always, in the earlier stages of awakening, associated with that state of the mind. Awakening is *the break-up*, in a varying scale of degrees in the energy of the feeling, of that stupor and insensibility to spiritual things which is one of the distinguishing traits of the carnal mind, and its main reference is *to the peril* in which the discovery of those spiritual things has involved the soul. The *justice* of this exposure to danger is not considered, or, if recognized at all, is so faintly recognized as to be thrust far into the background. *The fact of exposure and the apprehension of danger* constitute the leading characteristics of the awakening of the Holy Ghost. The mind becomes alive to the reality and solemnity of death and the uncertain tenure of life; to the claims of Almighty God, which have been hitherto neglected and forgotten; to the accountability the soul is to meet, and to the great doctrines of the word of God about the peril of unpardoned sin and the way of salvation. These facts begin to *reveal* something of the *power* that is in them. They all hint of *danger*. It is conceivable that this quickened sense of spiritual realities might exist in the mind without any special movement of the sense of personal guilt in natural conviction. It may exist for a time, a brief time, as a mere becoming sensible of this species of realities, without consideration of personal guilt; and this fact will justify the distinction between awakening and that natural conviction with which it is always associated ultimately. The severance is never long and not always apparent; the sense of danger roused by awakening speedily connects itself *with its cause;* that appears in the consciousness of sin ; and thus awakening and natural conviction soon become merged in the consciousness. Neither element in this joint apprehension of spiritual realities and the consciousness of sin can lead to any saving result by themselves. They breed *remorse,* but stop short of *repentance;* they breed the sorrow of the world that worketh death, but not the godly sorrow that worketh repentance unto life. The mere presentment of spiritual facts in life-like, real form before the mind, and the sense of personal peril, which are the distinctive features of mere awakening, have no virtue in themselves; they are valuable in view of that to which they lead. Mere natural conviction of personal guilt lays no ground to warrant escape from it. Consequently, all conviction of sin previous to conversion is defective, and its results are defective. It is true as far as it

goes, but it does not go far enough ; it discloses a part of the
case, but not the whole of it.   If shows the *danger* and the
criminality of sin to a certain extent, but not enough to alter
the tastes and affections of the heart towards it, and therefore stops short of repentance and pardon.   Natural conviction, even as far as it recognizes the guilt of a sin, as in the
case of a detected liar or thief, looks mainly to the peril involved ; and if the danger were removed, the consciousness
of the criminality would be greatly qualified, though not, in
all cases, entirely removed.   It is strongly colored by the
datum of awakening, which is a sense of danger.   This illustrates the propriety of treating awakening and natural conviction together ; they are not only generally found in prox-
imity in the consciousness, but are generally intermixed together.

As our attention is now limited to the study of *awakening*
by the Spirit, we remit all consideration of a full conviction
in its contrast with natural conviction, and for the present
look only to the characteristics of the awakening produced
by the Holy Ghost.

3. The first thing we note about this peculiar state of the
mind is, that it does not create, but only reveals, the perilous
and painful facts in this strange world, and in the conditions
of existence in its strange denizen, man.   The history of
every individual human being, comprehending the end with
the intervening hazards and events of his life, is a tragedy.
The aggregate history of the race needs a new term of terror
to express it.   Born in an agony, man universally lives in
danger of a thousand perils, and finally sinks a victim to the
most terrible of them all.   The passing joys that are inter-
spersed with these overshadowing evils, the pleasant days,
the delights of home and gratified affections, the triumphs
of human genius and energy, the sports of the field, the
delights of art, the profits of knowledge, the accumulations
and enjoyments of wealth, disguise to the thoughtless mind

the never-shifting eternal cloud of woe and death that over-hangs the awful scene. The pathos and terror of a world in which evil reigns with such universal and tragic supremacy, never seems to pierce the veil of hallucination which covers the ordinary mind. A few grim thinkers have cut through the shams; and the vision, unchecked by the palliations of gospel hope, has withered them into lunatics or devils. Man himself is the most awful and pathetic object on the accursed planet. A body subject to disease, pain and death; a mind enfeebled by ignorance and distorted by prejudice; a heart full of depraved impulses, disordered affections, and ill-regulated passions; his relations to others fountains of possible evil as well as good, he stands a most pathetic and awful figure. Then, as the lights of divine revelation are poured upon them, the colors of the picture are immeasurably heightened. Accountable for every breach of the divine law which he is constantly violating; already condemned; the slave of sin, led captive by a fearful hierarchy of fallen angels; already under the penal claims of violated law; with an essential immortality in his spirit holding him to an endless duration of these conditions, he is emphatically *a lost soul!* No wonder he shrinks from any open vision of such a state! To see it in its full force would bankrupt human reason and fill the air all round the whole earth with threnes of despair. God is merciful in holding back the vision of the facts from its full impression.

But that utter forgetfulness and ignoring of all recognition whatever of these awful realities, as they concern the individual self, is fraught with the immeasurable woe of barring all escape out of the terrible ruin, and subjecting the lost transgressor to the greater ultimate hazards of his position. Hence he needs to be awakened; he needs the awakening of that Holy Spirit who is able to temper his cognition of the awful ruin into safe conditions. He can show enough of it to rouse up a suitable and enduring effort to escape, and at the same time prevent it from going into a dangerous excess. There is a large class of minds which deprecates any lifting of the veil which obscures the ruin and curse on the world. They openly blame the religious system and its followers which seeks wisely to disturb this fatal insensibility in order to remedy it. This deprecation would be wise but for two things: if there was no remedy, no escape for the individual from under the curse; and if there was no necessity to break up his slumber in order to secure this remedy, then it would be both wise and kind not to disturb his insensibility. It should be distinctly noted by these benevolent friends of human peace, that the conditions which vacate their argument do exist. Let it also be distinctly apprehended that the awakening influence, needful to rouse up the needful effort to escape, does not create the evils which it reveals. Those evils would remain exactly the same if no notice should ever be taken of them. Death and sin, the perils of life, and human accountability, do not depend for their reality or their awfulness on talking about them. The talk does not create them; they are facts in the life and nature of man, grave and perilous realities, which cannot be extinguished by shutting the eyes and refusing to recognize their existence. As admitted, if no good could come out of an awakening to the facts, then there would be no use and only needless mischief in any breach of his dull peace. But if there is good to be done by it; if deliverance is conditioned upon it, then both the necessity and the kindness of rousing the endangered sleeper is obvious enough. To refuse to attempt to awaken him under these conditions would involve a guilty participation in his coming destruction. The unbeliever who censures all attempts to rouse sinners to repentance cannot justly lay blame on the servants of Christ as creating needless anxieties and alarms The peril is in the facts, and not in the talk about them, and the object of the endeavor is to secure escape and compliance with the inexorable condition of making it.

4. The next thing to be noted in this awakening is, that it is due to the influence of the Holy Spirit. The tendency of sin is always in one direction—to work out all its natural effects with a swift and cumulative effect. Any arrest on any one of these tendencies shows the presence of a restraining power. Any remnant of good moral energy, then, left in the intuitions of the understanding or the feelings of the heart shows the presence of this restraining power. Without this, the blinding and hardening influence of sin would have long ago worked out its natural results in the utter extinction of all good moral energies of every sort in a fallen soul. This effect has been seen in some of the extreme barbarous tribes of the human race. To inflict his judicial curse, then, on incorrigible offenders, God has only to withdraw this restraining influence, and sin will swiftly work out its natural effects. It is by this process of withdrawal that God is said "to give the spirit of slumber," "to blind the eyes, and harden the heart." Any reversal of the spirit of slumber, then, must be due to the reverse action of the same agent, the Holy Spirit. That he is the agent by whom the conviction of sin is wrought is asserted in so many words; and as he is the universal agent of all gracious effects on the soul, to him is to be attributed all the effects of awakening and natural conviction. This truth is illustrated in the experience of men. The spiritual realities of human life are indisputable facts. But though sin, death, and moral accountability are facts confessed, they are facts very imperfectly apprehended, and very insufficiently allowed their legitimate influence in the conduct of life. They are admitted, but not realized; they are, with studied intent, held in the background; they are repelled when they intrude into the mind in their personal bearings. So complete is the effect in many cases that death, although one of the most unquestionable and universal incidents of every human existence, is positively and completely eliminated out of all the thoughts. It is not recognized at

all in these cases. An actual instance of the mysterious and
dreadful mischief in some one else, especially in one nearly
related, may excite a momentary remembrance of one's own
mortality; but it soon passes, and the false lights of an assumed exemption from the fatal law of human nature again
fall on the field of view. In the majority of cases this extreme insensibility does not prevail, but a scarcely less fatal
degree of it is literally universal.

Death and sin are sometimes recognized, but they are at
once ordered to retire. Their legitimate and natural tendency to turn the thoughts upon a serious canvas of any
possible remedy is so promptly and powerfully repelled that
they soon depart, and leave the soul to drift. No mere didac-
tic or personal influence can hope to contend with the
mighty impulse to silence consideration of these inevitable
and painful incidents. Unless some effectual foreign or outside influence can be brought to bear, the repulse will be
complete, and no thought, no feeling, no care would ever enter the mind; and the man would live insensible, and die just
as if he were flung from a precipice a thousand feet into a
midnight sea, when locked fast in a natural or artificial sleep.
Besides this dread of death, sin is a species of evil which
involves positive criminality and guilt. Consequently, every
man flinches from the actual knowledge and realization of
sin as eagerly as he does from death itself. He would as
soon meet a sheeted ghost, fresh from the realms of shadows,
as confront his own sin, unveiled in the full awfulness of its
criminal nature. Conscience, roused up to do its office of
accuser, treads the trembling soul, like the angel with the
trumpet of the judgment treads the trembling skies. No
wonder the heart unacquainted with any other refuge cries
out to be allowed to forget, and seeks eagerly to sink into
sleep. He must exorcise these dreadful visions of sin and
guilt. In the same manner, and on the same broad ground
of conscious exposure, he shrinks from the thought of God,

from his revealed character, and from the essential and unalterable nature of his relations to all intelligent and responsible creatures. The conception of a being infinitely holy, inflexibly just, sitting on the place of universal dominion administering law, with a perfect knowledge of the facts in every individual case, with absolute integrity to uphold the right and to condemn the wrong, hating all evil with infinite intensity, such a conception is overpowering. Sleep and utter insensibility are the chosen refuge of a soul conscious of personal peril under such an administration. Yet further, sin has a blinding and deadening influence on mind and heart, and this natural effect, combined with the intense voluntary and personal effort to extinguish all sensibility to the alarming facts, result in such a state of mind that no power in the mind itself could overcome it. A power from without must interfere; and the only power competent to control a resistance so powerful is the power of God himself.

Hence the Scripture doctrine of the awakening influences of the Holy Ghost. If he did not interpose, no motion of regard to its spiritual condition would ever cross the surface of the sin-deadened soul. It would live on, keenly alive to the transitory interests of this life, but dead as a stone to all the higher relations which bind an immortal being, and point him to a state of existence beyond this present scene. The absolute nature of the dependence on the Spirit is demonstrated by the phenomena of his occasional and intermittent interpositions. He sometimes works in this way, he comes and goes. The movement of the affected human spirit exactly corresponds. When the Spirit strives, the soul wakes out of its deadly slumber. As he quickens the apprehension of death and sin, God, and immortality, the awakened soul fears and trembles. But, alas! the inevitable combat with the Holy Ghost at once ensues, and he yields the ground; he suspends his influence; he takes his departure. Immediately the deep sleep returns,

and the awakened soul is at ease once more. Again the
Spirit returns, and again the sinner awakes; again he retires,
and the sinner slumbers again. When, in his sovereign
good pleasure, the blessed giver of life resolves to win the
struggle, his influence is not remitted; it becomes steady,
constant, more and more powerful and pointed. The corresponding effects are seen in the soul; it awakes and keeps
awake; it yields more and more to the demands of the
Spirit; it conforms more and more to the leadings of his
influence, until the actual work of giving life is accomplished,
and the soul passes permanently out of the grasp of sleep
and death. The Holy Ghost alone can awaken any sinner
out of his fatal security.

5. Another peculiarity is to be found in the awakening of
the Spirit: there are *various degrees* in the energy of his
awakening influence. The range of these variations is wide,
extending through every grade of feeling, from a calm state
of sincere and settled sensibility to the grand facts in the
condition of an unpardoned soul, up to an unbearable measure of mental distress. It not unfrequently happens that
persons discount the reality and sufficiency of their mental
exercises, as being so completely out of proportion to the
evils of their condition. Their judgments tell them these
evils are very great, and that any suitable sensibility to
them must involve much stronger emotions than they are
conscious of feeling; and therefore they discount the sufficiency of their exercises of mind. But this is often a mistake
in experience; it is always erroneous in theory. It is
frequently the case that these calmer views are more effective,
and produce far more valuable results, than states of feeling
far more poignant and powerful. The question is, do these
calm states of feeling lead to action, to a calm but steadfast
effort to find the way of peace. The test of all degrees of
awakened sensibility is in the abiding results they produce.

The calmer apprehension often leads to obedience to the drawings of the Holy Spirit, and to the full acceptance of the gospel offers, while the keener feeling wears out and leaves no permanent result behind it. A calm, steady apprehension of the evils in the human lot, which leads to full compliance with the terms on which God has promised to forgive, is generally, in point of fact, the prevailing experience; the more intense realization is the exception rather than the rule. The value of both is in the effects they cause. None need depreciate the exercises of their minds because they are moderate in degree and sensibly out of proportion to the evils which occasion them. If they lead steadily forward to the feet of the Saviour, they are serving their purpose, and do not deserve to be depreciated as useless.

6. The resistance which is invariably made to the benevolent and most merciful awakening of the Holy Ghost is ungrateful and unwise to a degree which defies any adequate description. It is natural enough for men to shrink from what will give them pain, either of body or mind; but for all that, it is often absolute madness for them to do it. The operations of surgery give pain, but they are often necessary to save life. If a skilled surgeon, in the kindness of his heart, offers to do what is essential to life, it is ingratitude, as well as folly, to shrink from the suffering and to refuse his offer. There is no royal road to repentance; sin is an evil, and to know sin is to discern the evil that is in it. The great enemy of God and man has a tremendous advantage in this natural aversion to suffering, when he would persuade sinners to sleep on now and take their ease. They have only to do this to accomplish his ends. There is a startling warning in the fact that God only can awaken sinners to any effective purpose. All that he need do to bring them to the retribution of their sin is just to let them alone; it is just to co-operate with themselves in their own policy and effort to

sleep in peace. He need do nothing positive; he has only to restrain his effort to awaken them, only to allow them their own way. There is boundless mercy in his awakening grace. This grace is one of the gifts of the Holy Spirit to unbelievers, the value of which cannot be fully comprehended.

CHAPTER III.

CONVICTING INFLUENCE.

"And when he is come, he will reprove the world of sin, and of right-eousness, and of judgment."—*John in his Gospel.*

1. THERE are shades of difference in the meaning of the words used to express the idea of conviction of sin, but the general notion conveyed by them is the same. They all carry the idea of sin charged, proved, apprehended, and acknowledged, at least in the secret thoughts of the transgressor. To "reprove" is to charge a fault, and to rebuke for it. To "convince" is to persuade and satisfy touching the truth of a thing, whether good or bad. To "convict" always implies that the thing charged and proved is a wrong thing. Applied to sin, to *convince*, or to *convict* of sin mean exactly the same; but inasmuch as the word *convince* may be applied to things good as well as evil, it is better to use the word *convict* in connection with sin, because it carries the notion of something wrong or erroneous. To convict of sin not only means that the fact is proved, but that the wrong in the fact is also revealed, and the transgressor is discovered. No one is convicted of sin unless he is satisfied that the fact is true, that it involves wrong, and that he himself is truly charged with it. This is equally, though in different manners, true of natural and saving conviction of sin. A detected liar or thief recognizes that the fact of his crime is true; that it involves guilt, and that he has committed it. True and full conviction of sin involves the recognition of each of these incidents, but with marked differences in the method of the recognition, which can be more effectively brought out by a detailed contrast than by

57

a single definition. These intuitions are certified by *the feeling* they produce.

2. The basis of all conviction of sin is *the law of God.* "Sin is the transgression of the law," and consequently "by the law is the knowledge of sin." It is only when we know the law that it is possible to discover what is the violation of it. We must know what the law actually prescribes or prohibits, that we may tell what is a violation of law as a matter of fact. We must understand the *nature* of the requirements of the law, whether they are reasonable and right, or unreasonable and wrong, before we can estimate the real nature of a violation of it as right or wrong. We must understand *the extent* of the law, as reaching only to the outward conduct, or as embracing the thoughts, feelings, and motives of the inward fountain of moral energy, before we can estimate *the extent* of violations of it. If the law only prescribes duties to man, sin can only be against man. If it prescribes duties to God, sin will be discovered as against God. This makes clear the saying, "by the law is the knowledge of sin."

There is another feature in the law besides its prescriptions, it is enforced *by a penalty.* Penalty is of the essence of all law; without a power to enforce them, its precepts cease to be *law* and sink into *advice.* Authority is the right to give law; but without power to enforce, authority is rendered entirely nugatory. Penalty is essential to enforce law, to sustain authority, and to preserve the very nature of law from decay. It is very obvious that these two elements of law—precept and penalty, prescription and power—give room for two very different kinds of consideration in looking at the law from the ground of a violation of it. The transgressor cannot avoid *some* consideration of both of its essential elements, but they may be very differently regarded in the view taken. If he looks mainly at the *nature* of the particular precept he has broken, he will be more impressed with the nature of his sin, with the injustice involved in the violation of a just requirement, or the unreasonableness of a violation of a reasonable requirement. His reference to the penalty will be subordinate to his reference to the precept he has broken. On the contrary, if he has the penalty chiefly before his eyes, he will be far more concerned for the risk he has encountered than for the wrong he has done. He must have a certain recognition of the precept in order to feel any degree of guilt, such as the detected thief feels; but as the penalty is his main concern, he will be far more sensible of his danger than of his guilt. It is obvious that the feelings created by these two varying views of the law—the one looking mainly to the precept, and the other to the penalty—will have a very different moral value, and will exert very different effects. The one looks more to the nature of sin, the other, to its risks. The one lays the basis for repentance, the other, for remorse. The one opens the way for a true conviction of sin, the other, for a mere natural conviction of sin.

3. Conviction of sin under both of its modes has certain generic qualities inhering in both. Both involve an action in the understanding. Both produce feeling and affection in the heart. Both produce effects on conduct. Both have a regard to God as well as to self. But in all these points they are more or less strongly distinguished. They are more at one in the nature of the mental energy evoked in producing them than in any other point. All conviction of sin is an intuitive action of the understanding. The mind simply *sees* the evil opened up to its view. It is an act of the understanding, like that which is put forth when the mind discerns colors and forms. When a man sees the green of the grass, or the red of the rose, he sees them by a direct intuition or act of sight. There is nothing between the mind and the object to enable the discernment. Argument and illustration may present the character of sin, but fail to enable the intuition of it. If the mind is so corrupted by vice, it will fail to see the wickedness of even a gross crime, and no explana-

tion of it will enable the perception of it. The mind has been made to see certain things in themselves, and if this intuitive power has been injured or entirely disabled, the power must be restored, or no mere exposition will enable discernment. Hence the need of the Spirit's influence in the just discernment of sin. In natural conviction the perception of criminality in sin is imperfect, but the mental energy is the same. In both it is an intuitive act of the understanding; but in the one the power of intuition is injured, and only in part, if at all, aided by grace; in the other, the power is so far influenced by the Spirit as to see with a degree of justness and completeness of vision sufficient to work out the desired effect. Conviction of sin is a simple *seeing* the guiltiness of sin; in natural conviction, partial and defective; in spiritual conviction, measurably just and full. The man in both cases may not be able to tell you why the sin he sees is evil, but he sees it to be so. This perception is immediately followed by a strong *belief* that the thing is what the mind sees it to be. A man who sees a tree, or the form and color of a flower, cannot be persuaded that the tree and the flower are not what he sees them to be. This belief and perception are followed by *a feeling* suitable to the thing seen. If a man sees a beautiful thing, his perception and belief in it are instantly followed by a feeling of pleasure. If the thing is evil, the perception will be followed by a feeling of fear or dislike. In like manner the conviction of sin will be followed by feelings determined by the kind of conviction which produces it.

Sin has two elements of evil in it corresponding to the two grand divisions of the law: the precept and the penalty; its criminality and its danger; its intrinsic wrongfulness and its mischievous effects. According as the mind of the criminal is directed mainly to the one or the other of these will be the feeling which will follow it. To see the danger mainly, and the badness of sin only partially, is to have an imperfect view of sin, and the feeling that follows will partake of that imperfection. To see both elements of the evil in sin in a due proportion is to have a view of sin relatively perfect, and the feeling that follows will be qualified accordingly.

Here, then, is the first point in which the contrast between natural and spiritual conviction begins, in the difference of the view taken of the nature and the hazard of sin. Natural conviction discerns the danger of sin as the chief object of its concern, and is, therefore, true as far as it goes. It perceives the péril of the soul, but has little or no sense of the justice of the exposure to it. In this lies one of the leading distinctions between it and a spiritual apprehension of sin. It has a certain sense of criminality in it, although it looks chiefly to the danger involved. But this sense of criminality is not based on a true judgment of the real excellence of the law, and consequently is not based on a true discernment of the evil nature of sin. It sees very imperfectly, if at all, the criminality in the act itself. It sees that the act has been prohibited by the law, under peril of consequences, but does not see that the law ought to have prohibited it. Consequently, when the act is committed, he knows he has violated the law, and is, therefore, criminal in the eye of the law. He feels guilty to this extent. At the very same time he may feel that the law was hard and unreasonable in prohibiting the act. He is, therefore, disposed to carp at the law. In doing this it is evident that he is disposed to defend the act, and himself for doing it, in spite of his vague sense of criminality. His feeling of criminality is clearly a very limited and imperfect thing. He does not see the propriety of the law he has broken; on the contrary, he thinks it unreasonable. He recognizes that he has broken it; he discerns the risks he has encountered, and feels the qualified sense of criminality growing out of the fact that he has voluntarily broken it, and has brought on himself the hazards involved.

Even in the case of the higher crimes, the criminal feels that it would be hard to punish him; he is selfish even when conscious of guilt. Even in those rare cases where remorse drives a criminal to surrender himself to the law, he is seeking a selfish relief from a more intolerable evil by surrendering himself to a lesser one.

On the contrary, a just and full conviction of sin sees the evil in the act itself, as well as the danger it has involved. It sees the justice of the peril in the evil of the act. It looks to the precept of the law as well as to the penalty. It sees the exact propriety and excellence of the violated precept. It sees the true personal blameworthiness of the person who has voluntarily broken it. It sees the danger, but also *the badness* of the act. It sees the danger is the just consequent and the direct effect of this badness. Not only the *fact*, but *the righteousness* of personal responsibility for the criminal deed is clearly discerned. It sees the criminality in the act, and not merely in the inhibition of the law. Guilt involves two distinct elements: one arising from the precept of the law, marking *desert* of punishment; the other, arising from the penalty of the law, marking *liability* to punishment. Genuine or spiritual conviction of sin is chiefly concerned about the first; mere natural conviction about the last. While a saving conviction of sin is thus chiefly discriminated by this element of badness in the act, it must not be forgotten that it also apprehends the danger of sin; it sees the element of liability in its guilt, as well as the ill-desert. It often happens that persons whose claim to the character of Christians cannot be disputed are perplexed by this distinction, and write hard things against themselves, because they are very distinctly conscious of their sensibility to the *danger* of sin, and not so distinctly conscious of their discernment of the *badness* or *wickedness* of it. But such persons ought to keep steadily in mind, that inasmuch as true conviction embraces both elements of the evil of sin, it

embraces the *fear* of the consequences of sin; and, therefore, the mental exercises of no one are to be discounted as
fatally defective, because conscious of this fear; it is a part
of the mental state of which they are suspicious. The question really turns on the matter of fact, whether, in addition
to this fear, there is also a real discernment of the intrinsic
badness of sin, no matter how feeble it may be in comparison with the vigor of the fear which is felt. How, then, are
we to know when we do really see the intrinsic evil of sin?
It will disclose itself in a variety of ways.

In the first place, it will be indicated *by the absence of all
disposition or wish to excuse or defend ourselves* against the
charge of sin, or to belittle or extenuate the fault. In true
conviction, as we have seen, there is an intuition of the intrinsic badness of sin. It recognizes this part of the evil in
sin, and knowing that it is rightfully charged against self,
the sense of personal culpability at once springs up, and
silences all pleas in abatement. The intrinsic nature of sin
is found in its *wrongfulness;* it involves the essence of wrong.
The voluntary doing of wrong carries the notion of *culpability;* the two notions always go together and are inseparable. The distinction of right and wrong is founded in the
very nature of things; it is eternal and unchangeable; it
carries invariably a sense of obligation; it has the force of
an eternal and unchangeable law. Each of these notions,
defined by this eternal distinction, carries its own inseparable
feeling: right, the feeling of approval when it is done, and
wrong, the feeling of condemnation. The notion of wrong,
and its inseparable correlated feeling of culpability or blame-
worthiness in the doer of it, necessarily exclude all justification, extenuation, or excuse. If any part of it admits of
excuse or defence, that part of it is proved not to be wrong.
True and full conviction of sin is then ear-marked by this
peculiarity, that it extinguishes all disposition or thought of
self-excuse or self-defence. It lays the hand upon the

mouth, and the mouth in dust.   On the contrary, there is a
consciousness that the sense of guilt in the mind is not adequate to the evil which has been done, and consequently
there is a desire for deeper and clearer convictions, and for
a more profound feeling of self-condemnation.   Instead of
hunting for excuses and extenuating circumstances, the
desire and the effort is to see more of the evil in order to a
deeper and more definite repentance.   Any one who is conscious of this humility and condemnation of self, conscious
of no wish to excuse himself or to extenuate his sin, conscious of these habitual desires for a deeper and clearer
intuition of his own guilt and for a more profound repentance, and who is conscious that this is a permanent and
abiding state of his mind, has no need to suspect the sufficiency of his own convictions of sin, just because he is conscious that his dread of the consequences of sin is more
definitely clear in his consciousness than his intuitions of its
nature.   The weakness, ignorance and spiritual disorder in
a soul in which the law of sin in the members is perpetually
struggling with the law of grace in the soul, is sufficient to
account for these disorders and disproportions in the exercises of a regenerate heart.

Another mark of discrimination in our knowledge of sin,
disclosing the intuition of its intrinsic evil, closely allied to
this intuition of its culpability, is *the laying of the blame on
self*.   This strongly discriminates it from a mere natural and
incompetent conviction, which is always *selfish*.   The sin of
a man is *his sin*, and not the imputable fault of any one else.
Where two or more persons are combined together in a
criminal deed, the share which each takes in it constitutes
his own sin, and cannot possibly be construed as the sin of
another.   What belongs to each is altogether his own.   True
conviction of sin distinctly recognizes sin not only to be sin,
and not a mere misfortune, but to be the fault of *self*, and
not of another.   False conviction, or, more accurately, im-

perfect conviction, for it is true as far as it goes, apprehending the *danger* but not the real evil of sin, will be disposed to throw the blame on some thing or some person outside of self. Even when it is impossible to extricate self altogether, it will seek to share the responsibility with others, or to qualify personal concern in the transaction by reference to circumstances, as more highly answerable for misleading influences. This trait appeared when sin first entered the world. Adam laid the blame on Eve, and Eve laid it on the serpent. Instead of seeing and feeling the excellency of the law in the precept which has been broken, and consequently the evil nature of the deed done, it is disposed to cavil at the law and to accuse it in some way. It will lay stress on unfavorable providences; it will seek for alleviating circumstances in poverty, or health, or domestic troubles, or absorbing occupations. It will recite the defects and shortcomings of others, and in their sins find an excuse, if not a justification, of its own. Not seeing sin as it is, and self in its true and exclusive relation to it, as something which is its own, it seeks relief from the accusations of conscience, and the peril incurred, by throwing accusations around in every direction, and *defending self*. Saving conviction works in just the opposite way. It accuses self, and no one else. It sees sin in its true relation to self, and has no one to accuse but self for what has been done by self. It recognizes that no one is called upon to repent of his neighbor's sin, but to repent of his own. It sees irresistibly that self only is involved in the sins of self, and puts the blame where it ought to be—on self, and self only. It sees the true responsibility of self, and makes no effort to hide, alter, or unfairly qualify the exact nature of what self has done. It calls a spade a spade, even if it is its own. The necessary consequence of this state of mind is humility, not fawning obsequiousness; repentance, not mere remorse; and dependence on the gospel remedy

for sin, and not recourse to excuses, or extenuations, or false
constructions of sin, in order to find relief from it.

Another proof of a true conviction and knowledge of sin,
by which it is strongly distinguished from a mere natural
conviction, is the discovery of it *as against God* as well as
against one's own soul or against one's neighbor.   Natural
conviction also has a reference to God, but of a very different character.   It recognizes God as the source of the
danger which it apprehends.   It recognizes him as the
•maker of the law which has been broken; as the executive
magistrate who is set to see after the execution of the law,
and therefore, as concerned, to inquire into all offences, and
deal with them as the law directs.   It recognizes him, as an
arrested thief or murderer recognizes the magistracy of the
state, as the power which is to deal with his crime and himself.   Such a criminal has no thought or care for the rights
or the interests of the government.   He never dreams that
he has injured the sanctity of the great institute set for the
protection of the people by the administration of the public
law and justice of the commonwealth.   Neither does the
natural conviction of sin dictate any regard for God, save as
the power which imperils his safety.   God is the giver of the
whole law, and when that part of the law which prescribes
duties to others besides himself is violated, he is sinned
against, as well as those whom he has legislated to protect;
for it is his authority which is defied.   So far as the law
defines duties to himself, the violation of the law sins more
immediately, but not more really, against him.   All sin, then,
is against God.   All sin involves, in some way and to some
degree, the element of *wrong*.   All the qualities of the nature
of God, and all his claims, are essentially and infinitely right.
All sin, then, is in direct moral antagonism to the very nature
of God.   It is the destruction of the quality of the good
that is in him.   Injustice is in itself, and as far as it goes,

the absolute destruction of justice. Cruelty is the absolute destruction of kindness.

Sin would kill every quality of moral excellence it can reach. It would kill it in God if it could reach him. It cannot do this, only because it is weak in its malignity; but it is none the less malignant on that account. It is to be judged by what it would do, if it could, and not merely by what it accomplishes under the limitations and restraints which, either in its own weakness or from other causes, put bounds to its native destructiveness. Sin is against God because it so completely antagonizes his very nature; it would kill him if it could. Sin is against God as an universally opposing force to his nature, his law, his administration, and his designs. It is an injury to his dominions, an offence to his person, an insult to his majesty, an outrage on his authority, a trespass on his rights, an opposition to his character, a reflection on his qualities, an impeachment of his law, and of himself as a law-giver, an interference with his purposes in their primary design, a disgust to his tastes, a contempt of his dignity, and an outrage on his feelings. It has filled his fair domains with infinite pollution, agony, and confusion. It has revolted against his control, and set up the awful dominion of ungovernable evil in its place. If it were only strong enough it would abolish him as a nuisance in his own universe, and draw a winding-sheet over the vacant throne of Jehovah. Spiritual conviction sees something—often feebly and confusedly—but something of sin as against God, and this leads to repentance towards him, not less than on account of self. False conviction has no idea of sin against God, except as the power to which the transgressor is accountable. It has no conception of sin as against God himself as distinguished from his law, or as subject to any personal damage or offence from sin. It knows that sin breaks no bones—inflicts no agony on the serene King in his infinite elevation. It is fully satisfied that he would

take no harm if sin was allowed perfect impunity. It sees
no reason why a thing so agreeable to the natural heart in
man should not be allowed free range, or why the supreme
Power should be so jealous of it. If it is in some respects
an evil, it sees no reason why he should not good-humoredly
overlook it. It sees no ground for that awful dispensation
of atonement by the blood of God's own Son. Sin only
endangers man; it cannot possibly hurt God; and, therefore, the only concern dictated by mere natural conviction is
for the safety of self, the sinner. Sin is against self; it imperils personal interests; and all the feeling kindled by this
species of conviction terminates on self. The remorse it
breeds is selfish; and if self could only be made secure, all
solicitude about sin would vanish. Natural conviction has
no care for God, or for his interests and concern in the matter of sin.

True conviction works opposite to this selfish resort against
sin at every point. It sees that sin is a true act of self
against God, as well as against self. It sees it antago-
nizing God along the whole line of the relations of the creature to him. It sees sin as a violation of just law, and a rebellion against just authority. It sees it as essentially and
necessarily warring on God's rights and honor, making small
of his importance to his own creation. It sees sin as an
offence to his tastes, and absolutely antagonistic to his essential qualities. It consequently feels a keen desire that all of
its endangered interests should be fully protected in any
accommodation with sin, and bound up in a full and honorable satisfaction with its own safety. Sin must be atoned
for as well as repented of, and God honored, while the sinner
is saved. True conviction is distinguished by this just recognition of sin as an evil towards God not less than towards man.

A final distinction between true and false conviction of sin
is found in a *broad series of contrasts in their consequences.*

Their effects are strongly discriminated. They are distinguished in the point of *permanence*. As a general rule, in countries where the pure gospel is preached, the effects of a mere natural conviction of sin are generally evanescent; they soon pass away, and leave no trace behind. In Popish countries where the deadly travesties of Popery are the prevailing views, false convictions of sin often have very powerful and abiding effects, sending the misguided, awakened sinner into the long routine of penances, scourging of the body, fasting, wearing of hair-cloth, and all manner of self-torture. The people are taught to believe that this sort of penitence is available to salvation, and hence the pertinacity with which it is practiced. In gospel lands, too, many a deceived soul lives quietly for years in the communion of the church, thinking that the troubled exercises of their early religious career were true repentance. But this class of persons generally pass their days in no trouble about their sins; for the effects of their early convictions, not being sufficient to lead to genuine repentance, have long ago worn out, and the peace of insensibility is mistaken for the peace of pardon But effects of a true conviction are known by their abiding influence. Sin never loses its interest to those under its control; they are as afraid of it, and as keen to overcome it twenty or fifty years after the outset of their religious career as they were at the beginning. The impression of this species of conviction never wears out. It may lose something of its liveliness; it may be more keen sometimes than at others; but it exerts an habitual and controlling force on the heart, and on the whole character and career.

The two species of conviction are also distinguished in their *purifying effects*. Both lead to reformation and the effort to get rid of sin. Natural conviction leads to a limited reform—to the giving up of particular sins, the danger of which it has learned to dread; but it confines its surrender to certain specific sins, gives them up with something of regret, and generally only for a time. There is a secret regret at the necessity of having to do it, and this unchanged preference for the sin itself, though given up to avoid its perils, is almost sure to lead back to its indulgence. Even when sound instruction informs the sinner that the thoughts and feelings must be purified, the effort to control them is confined to the specific evil thoughts which are accused, and little care is taken for the unholy tastes and affections which lie back of these specific mental manifestations and originate them. On the other hand, true conviction leads to the willing surrender of all sin as soon as it is recognized to be sin. When sin is committed, it is committed with a greater or less degree of conflict with the resisting forces implanted by grace. It is committed with many a pang mixed up with the unlawful indulgence, and is always followed, more or less quickly, by an honest sorrow and regret leading to better obedience in the future. The struggle of the true convict of sin against the sins which rise up in the inward consciousness is more determined, more indiscriminate, and more constant than the struggle of the natural convict. Paul describes the effects of a true repentance following a just conviction of sin: "What carefulness it wrought in you; yea, what purifying of yourselves; yea, what indignation; yea, what zeal; yea, what revenge." Imperfect conviction never works such results.

The difference between the two species of conviction is strongly marked by the *scope* of the purifying and reforming effects determined by each of them. The natural conviction is confined almost entirely to outward actions, and these the specific actions which it has come to dread for their dangerous consequences upon the interests of this life. It has no reference to the great fountain head of sin, the unholy heart, and the inward sinfulness determined by it. If it refers to the heart at all, it is apt to do so more as an excuse or extenuation of outward sins than as the unholy source from which they spring and the aggravation of their guilt. But under the light of an effective and full conviction of sin this unholy heart, this depraved nature, this inward proclivity of affection and will to sin, becomes in no long time the chief object of solicitude. Outward sins are seen to be but the expression of this inward sin. The outward act is soon done and finished; but an unholy heart is a perpetual fountain of such acts. The cry of the truly and fully convicted sinner is, "Create in me a clean heart, and renew a right spirit within me." He learns to mistrust his own heart; "he has no confidence in the flesh." He watches the upspring of evil thought and feeling in his soul, and not only becomes prompt to repress, but carries his indignant and painful effort at resistance down back of these troublesome thoughts to the more troublesome heart that lies below them. This permanent suspicion and discontent with his own heart leads to steady efforts to overcome sin, not only in the secret spring of thought and feeling, but in all its outward expression, in word or deed. No false conviction ever leads to such reforms as these.

The two species of conviction produce also different species of *humility*, and are thereby distinguished from each other. Both produce a feeling of self-abasement. A detected thief feels mean. This feeling may be so strong as to produce an abject, fawning demeanor; but there is not an atom of genuine humiliation in his feelings or his conduct. True conviction breeds genuine humility; it produces a true and honest self-abasement. False conviction often breeds the bitterness of mortified pride, and awakens sullen and resentful feelings. The one leads to self-defence; the other, to self-accusation. The one leads to tenderness and the spirit of forgiveness and forbearance; the other, to hardness of heart. The one leads to great endurance; the other, to retaliation on others, and revenge on all accusers and punishers of the criminal conduct. The one leads to general and particular confession; the other dreads detection, and is greatly aggravated by detection. True conviction breeds an invincible desire for the mercy of God, followed by a similar unwearied effort to attain it. False conviction breeds desires which are soon discouraged by difficulties, and pass away. The one justifies God in the condemnation of sin; the other tends to charge him foolishly. False conviction never leads of itself to the acceptance of offered grace; true conviction always does. The one leads to repentance; the other, only to remorse. The one takes hold on the atonement and the great High Priest; the other, on a thousand refuges of lies. The loving, free forgiveness of gospel grace enables true conviction to see with special energy of intuitive insight the aggravated sin of unbelief, which refuses to accept it, and always learns to cleave to Christ as the sinner's Saviour. False conviction never leads to faith, and leaves the soul to perish at last, in spite of all the bitter exercises of remorse and self-condemnation which may attend its selfish and self-seeking motions in a guilty conscience.

CHAPTER IV.

REPENTANCE.

"Him hath God exalted with his right hand to be a Prince and Saviour, for to give repentance to Israel, and forgiveness of sins."—*Luke in Acts.*

"For godly sorrow worketh repentance to salvation, not to be repented of; but the sorrow of the world worketh death."—*Paul to the Corinthians.*

THE gift of conviction by the Holy Spirit is followed by repentance. Every cognition of an evil is followed by some answerable movement of feeling. Natural or false conviction will be followed by remorse in various degrees; true conviction will be followed by true repentance. That there are two kinds of sorrow for sin, leading to two different kinds of repentance, is evident, not only from the two kinds of conviction, but from the distinction taken by the sacred writers between the godly sorrow, which worketh repentance unto salvation, and the sorrow of the world, which worketh death. Obviously, then, it is a matter of the most supreme importance not to confound these two species of sorrow, and the two species of repentance to which they lead, either in our knowledge or in our practical experience. To confound them is to die. To lead those who only sorrow for sin with the sorrow of the world to call and construe themselves as *penitents*, and as such entitled to eternal life, is to delude them to their ruin.

The importance of this discrimination in knowledge and in experience is due to the fact that a real repentance is necessary to salvation. As we propose at present a comparison between the two kinds of repentance in their essential *nature*, we shall state the main reasons which make genuine repentance a necessity as briefly as possible.

73

In the first place, the *evil nature of sin* requires repentance altogether apart from the question of its bearing on the deliverance of the transgressor from the consequences of his sin; even although it should have no effect whatever on his relief he is bound to repent of his sin. Sin is essential evil; it is condemnable in itself; to do justice to it is necessarily to condemn and repudiate it. Every moral being is bound to do justice; the sinner in any particular case is as much bound to do justice as any one else—to do justice to his own act, as to the act of any one else. He is consequently bound to condemn and repudiate his own sin, or, in other words, to repent. The obligation of justice is independent of consequences. For a transgressor to refuse to repent is to double his guilt; it is to endorse and stand by the wrong he has done; and this deliberate reëndorsement of an evil done is to redouble the guilt of the wrong doing.

In the second place, the necessity of repentance without regard to its effects is created by *the continued obligation of the law*. The breach of a law never works the abrogation of a law; it continues to bind the transgressor as fully after his sin as it did before it. One violation leaves the law still demanding obedience. If that obedience is rendered, its necessary effect is to prevent a repetition of the wrong; it creates resistance and cessation of sin. Repentance, which is a turning away from sin, is manifestly the very thing which the law requires, and which a return to obedience would produce. This obedience to the law leading to repentance is obligatory, without regard to consequences, and repentance is a moral necessity, irrespective of its bearing on the release of the transgressor from the liabilities of his sin.

In the third place, on the supposition that the sinner is to be saved, the necessity of repentance is still more conspicuously asserted. Salvation *in sin* is a contradiction in terms. It is as truly an impossibility in the nature of things as health in disease, or ease in suffering, or reason in insanity.

Sin is in itself polluting, and, therefore, incompatible with purity. It is a natural fountain of pain, and incompatible with peace. One must give place to the other, and salvation must be salvation from sin, or it is nothing. Many other reasons support this conclusion, but these are sufficient to prove, beyond all doubt, the necessity of repentance to the salvation of a sinner, and the supreme importance of a real repentance, for no other species of it can possibly avail to accomplish that end.

The indispensable necessity of a true repentance having been illustrated, it becomes a matter of the last importance to understand what it is—what is the real nature of an effectual repentance. Repentance for sin will be necessarily controlled by the view taken of sin itself; true repentance will be based on a true view of sin—that is, a view answering to the real elements of evil in it. We have already seen that there are two distinct elements of evil in sin determined by the two grand divisions of the law of which sin is the violation, its precept and its penalty, the one yielding the intrinsic evil in sin, the other its consequential evil ; the one its criminality, the other its danger.

The nature of the repentance following the cognition of an evil will be controlled by the evil which is chiefly seen. If the intrinsic evil in sin occupies the view, the repentance that follows will be repentance for sin in itself. If the consequential evil is chiefly apprehended, the repentance that follows will be repentance for its consequences, and for sin merely on account of its consequences. Calamity will excite regret; pain will produce distress; prospective danger will produce fear; but a sense of criminality and wrong-doing alone can lead to repentance. Nay, only a sense of criminality based upon a just and approximately complete view of sin can lead to *a true* as distinguished from *a false* repentance. A man suffering under a fever is distressed; but he does not charge himself with criminality; he has no self-condemnation however much of regret he may have.   But if he is in trouble as the result of a criminal act, his grief is modified by a sense of personal blame-worthiness and responsibility.   But in all criminal acts there are always two elements, *the wrong* and *the danger*, involved in the act; and the grief occasioned by the act will be essentially modified in its moral quality according as the one or the other of these two elements holds the attention.   One view may look mainly to the substance of the act, and another, to its effects.   The one may look mainly at the wrong done, and only incidentally to the danger involved.   The other may look mainly to the danger, and only partially to the wrong.   In both there is a certain sense of criminality; but in the one case the sense of criminality is altogether secondary to the sense of danger, and terminates on self and the interests of self.   In the other case the sense of criminality is far deeper, broader, and truer to the fact; it terminates on the moral pollution and the condemnable nature of the wrong done, as the chief object of solicitude, and secondarily, on the peril incurred.   The grief produced by the one view is a just grief; the grief produced by the other is a selfish grief.   In the one case exemption from the danger would annihilate the concern felt; in the other, exemption from the danger by a gracious pardon will make the sorrow and self-reproach for the wrong itself only the more intense and lasting.   "Then shalt thou remember and be ashamed for all thine iniquities, when I am pacified towards thee, saith the Lord."

It is clear, then, that there is a foundation, in the nature of the case, for the distinction drawn in the Scriptures between a true and a false repentance.   Yet a necessary distinction must be made just here to prevent an unhappy misconstruction by some tender consciences.   As sin involves danger, a just view of sin will recognize this fact, and consequently, in true repentance there is a distinct modification of feeling produced by this element in sin; and so far forth, there is an element in genuine repentance of a sense of danger, and terminating on self. Christians sometimes discount their penitent exercises as insufficient and unreliable, because they are distinctly conscious that they dread the results of sin. This is evidently a mistake, because a complete view of sin, as a *danger* as well as a *wrong*, must produce this dread of its consequences. The question really is, whether this view of sin is the only view of it, or the chief and controlling view of it. If the other element of wrong, or essential criminality in sin, is apprehended truly, and in addition to the apprehension of its danger, then it is manifest that the emotions excited will be radically different from those excited by an exclusive, or mainly apprehended, view of the danger of transgression. As the *danger* solely concerns self, the emotions created will be directed upon self, and will be morally unsound, or otherwise, according to circumstances. Self-love is not necessarily selfishness. A certain regard to self-wellbeing is altogether proper; it is nothing more nor less than that desire of happiness which is essential to the constitution of every rational and moral being. Selfishness is the corrupt excess of self-love. Many a vice is the mere excess of a virtue. Consequently, a regard to the well-being of one's own self may properly mingle with the repentance of sin, and does not make it suspicious. False repentance is selfish, regardful only of self, regardless of others, even of God himself and his rightful claims. True repentance involves a just self-love, which is altogether consistent with the claims of others, and of the offended sovereign especially.

Hence, we may deduce the distinctive natures of the two species of repentance, and the marks which distinguish the one from the other, and reveal which is colored by a just self-regard, and which is animated by mere selfishness. The one is *selfish;* the other is *just.* The one terminates on self alone; the other terminates on God as well as on self, and on self within the limits of a lawful regard to self-well-being. This regard to God and this lawful regard to self both constitute the discriminating feature of a true, as distinguished from a false, repentance, and shows itself in all the effects produced by them. Both species of repentance produce general effects, which are similar in some respects, but with vital differences yet involved. Both result in a sorrow for sin, in a sense of shame, pollution, self-condemnation, hatred to sin, self-abasement, and the abandonment of sin; yet the radical elements of selfishness or godliness run through all these effects, and radically modify the nature of each, determining the one as morally evil, and the other as morally good, as each is the result, respectively, of a selfish or a godly repentance. The qualifying influence of selfishness, or a just self-love, on all of these effects will enable any one to decide whether his own repentance is true or false.

1. The leading emotion created by a sense of criminality is *shame*. Sin is instinctively felt to be polluting and debasing. The sinner feels degraded. The thief feels that he is mean, and especially so when detected. The man caught in any vice is ashamed when discovered. He feels a certain degree of shame on account of his conscious meanness, previous to any other person's knowledge of his fault; but this is comparatively feeble, and the capacity of feeling this secret shame rapidly gives way under repeated acts of transgression. It gains an immense accession of strength, however, from the discovery and contempt of other persons. So long as his vice remains a secret of his own, his sense of shame is bearable; but let it be disclosed, and the sense of shame becomes poignant, and perhaps, for a time, almost intolerable. It may awaken a high degree of the sorrow of the world, which worketh death. But this sense of shame for personal meanness and detected vice terminates on self; it is altogether selfish. There is no sense of wrong towards a pure law and the God who gave it. The criminal

feels that he has sacrificed himself. He has forfeited his claim to self-respect and to the respect of others. Here the difference between the shame of a false repentance and the shame of a true repentance begins to appear. His pride and self-conceit are wounded, and he is at once thrown into the attitude and effort at self-defence or self-extenuation. Resentment and the spirit of bitterness, and even of revenge, towards those who are acquainted with his fault begin to emerge. This shame is entirely compatible with a violent and haughty self-assertion, and also with the opposite manifestation of an abject deprecation of censure and exposure at the hands of others. This shame is entirely compatible with a heart unsubdued in its rebellion against moral law, and with the continued practice of other vices, and even of the very vice which produced it. The bitter consciousness of personal degradation produced by it is a dreadful scourge to a transgressor. But it is all selfish; it terminates wholly on self, and always looks more to the *effects* than to the intrinsic wrongfulness of the transgression.

There is an element of *shame* in true repentance. There is something degrading in sin, and when sin is discerned in a just approximation to the whole evil that is in it, this quality will produce its effect; and when the transgressor sees that he has incorporated this debasing element in his own responsible activities, it will be impossible for him to escape a feeling of degradation and consequent shame. This sentiment may often be less keen and powerful than the shame of detected vice; but it is more complete in its insight into the evil of sin, and more conscious of the evil done to others—notably to God himself as well as to self. It is not occupied solely with one act or a few associated acts of a single vice, as is the case in a false repentance. It sees sin more or less in all the acts of the life, as far as memory recalls them. More than this, it interprets these acts as they really are, the fruits and the disclosures of the evil proclivities in the soul itself, and its attention is mainly concentrated upon this ever-flowing fountain of sinful energies. The shame of true repentance springs mainly from this recognition of the sin in the soul, the evil heart, the permanent dispositions of the will to evil, the capability of all kinds of sin in the soul itself. The shame of false repentance is confined to one act of vice, or, if it looks back of the act at all, to one recognized capability of one mean action. But the shame of true repentance is based on the recognized moral deficiency in all its acts, even its best, and on that universally controlling element of evil in the heart itself from which the universal defect in all its expressions comes.

Moreover, it is distinguished by the recognition of God and his sacred claims. It is a shame for having so completely eliminated God out of all the thoughts and regards of the soul. It sees sin as rebellion against an authority infinitely entitled, not only to regard, but to reverence. It sees sin as naturally and inveterately opposed to holiness, just as injustice is in its very essence opposed to justice. It thus recognizes its love for sin as opposition and discontent with the very nature of God. It is ashamed of the degradation involved in this distaste for infinite excellence. It sees God, as the lawful owner of his creatures, robbed of his property and his right to control it. It sees a Father robbed of his honor by the disobedience of his children; a lawful King deprived of his right by the renunciation of the allegiance due to him; a Benefactor requited by ingratitude. All this is involved *in sin as against God*. When the human heart is led to genuine repentance, and sees the intrinsic evil in sin, it recognizes it as mainly against God in his nature, law, and lawful claims, and it repents towards God. It is ashamed of such a fixed discrepancy of moral traits and affections with infinite purity. A feeling of universal defect and pollution comes to the front, and *breeds shame* for all its actions as far they are recognized, and especially for the polluted thoughts

and feelings which fill the consciousness, and still more especially from the polluted soul from which they spring. When
sin as against God is recognized, it cannot fail to produce a
feeling of meanness and criminality, which will create a sense
of shame just in proportion to the energy with which sin is
so revealed to the sanctified intuitions of the mind. All the
expressions of penitent feeling delineated in the Scriptures
are full of this sense of shame. "Thou shalt be ashamed and
confounded because of thy iniquities." "O Lord, righteousness belongeth unto thee, but unto us confusion of faces, as
at this day."

2. This feeling of shame is followed by its natural consequent, the feeling of *self-abasement*. This feeling, under
mere natural conviction of criminality, is a sense of degradation purely selfish, and is strongly discriminated from the
self-abasement of a true and gracious sense of sinfulness.
The convict feels that he himself is degraded, but he does
not consent to it as a just consequent of his crime. He does
not abase himself; his abasement is something enforced on
him from without. It is attended by wounded pride, by irri-
tated temper, by the disposition to excuse or defend the
criminal conduct, and by feelings of revenge towards all who
may know or allude to it. It will lead to self-assertion, or a
cringing abjectness of demeanor. True conviction leads to
genuine humility; the shame it produces leads to a just and
candid recognition of the degradation involved, and the man
abases himself; he consents to a feeling of degradation as
just. Instead of endeavoring to throw it off, he desires to
feel more of it, to be more and more humbled. He takes
the blame of his evil-doing, and looking back of his act sees
the evil disposition in himself from which it sprung. There
is no wounded pride, no irritation of temper, no wish to excuse or defend self, no disposition to revenge. Pride is
truly humbled, sin is honestly confessed; he condemns himself, and feels that the censures of others, even when unchar-

itably rendered, are true to the facts, and instead of resistance to their judgment, or revengeful feelings towards themselves, feels that he is justly condemned. He condemns himself; he is humbled; he abases himself, and he is not excited to self-extenuation, or feelings of bitterness and revenge.

3. This feeling of self-abasement leads to *sorrow for sin*. Natural conviction produces sorrow, frequently an intensely bitter grief. There is verily a sorrow of the world that worketh death. It is regret for the criminal conduct which has brought peril to himself, and, it may be, affliction to those dear to him or to others whom he had no wish or intention to harm. But even this partial sense of unselfishness is only partial; it is at bottom selfish; the criminal grieves because the undesigned injury to others has only added to personal responsibility. He laments the folly which has betrayed his own interests. But the sorrow of spiritual conviction reaches further than this, and its moral quality is totally different. The true convict sorrows for the consequences of his sin, but also for something else. He sees the evil he has done, and grieves for it. He grieves for the criminal nature of his act. He grieves for the evil condition of his own heart, from which his positive evil ways have come. He grieves for the injury done to the authority, the honor, and the gracious kindness of God. He grieves for his disregard for the wise and right requirements of the law. He grieves for his indefensible treatment of the grace of the gospel. He grieves most when the danger is past; the natural convict ceases to grieve when he conceives the danger is past. The sorrow of the true penitent is deepest and purest when God is pacified for sin through the power of the atonement. The more the divine mercy is realized, the more the sorrow for sin melts into sweeter and more purifying emotions. "Then shalt thou remember and be ashamed for all thine iniquities, when I am pacified towards thee, saith the Lord."

4. The mingled senses of the shame, self-pollution, sorrow-breeding force in sin unite to produce a *hatred for sin*. Natural conviction produces often a real hatred for sin; but it is confined to only the one sin, or a few sins, which have produced losses to the sinner. The drunkard often hates and dreads the particular crime of drunkenness, which has overwhelmed him time after time with distress. The gambler often hates the vice which has ruined his fortune. This kind of hatred for sin is discriminated by its selfishness and by its limited range of application; it is confined to the special sins which have imperiled self. The hatred of sin which springs from a true intuition of its evil nature is based on a discernment of its essential criminality, its essential wickedness against God, as a violation of a right law, as a natural polluting influence, and as a fountain of universal destruction to the nature and the interests of the transgressor. It is not limited to a few special sins; it is not confined to the forms of transgression revealed as dangerous, and therefore hateful, to the alarmed selfishness of the heart by an experimental realization of their power to distress. It recognizes all sin as transgression of law, and as such, an offence to the great Lawgiver. As such, it discerns it to be a criminal thing, no matter how pleasing; as a danger, no matter how apparently harmless. It sees offence to God, and both pollution and peril to self, wherever it sees sin at all. The result is a disgust, a dread, and a hatred of all sin indiscriminately, although on a scale of degrees suitable to different grades of the evil wherever it is fairly discerned.

5. This hatred and shame leads to self-abhorrence and self-condemnation. "Now mine eye seeth thee; wherefore I abhor myself and repent in dust and ashes." The distinct and definite development of all the emotions leading to repentance for sin is more or less gradual, as a general rule. As the renewed man becomes more and more acquainted with the intractable spiritual disorders of the heart; as he

realizes more and more its hardness, its proclivity to all evil, its treachery to good, its readiness to sin, he grows steadily in a profound disgust and distrust towards himself. As self-abasement springs mainly from the sense of positive criminal energies, self-abhorrence springs mainly from the conscious-ness of the permanent depraved states of the soul itself As the stubborn wickedness of the heart is more fully disclosed, he abhors this state of things; he abhors himself; he shrinks from it with a mixture of terror and disgust. He is ready to join Paul in the cry: "O wretched man that I am! who shall deliver me from the body of this death?" Under the united views of his guilt and depravity, he *condemns* himself. He realizes that God is just in condemning him. He sees that any just judgment formed of himself or of his acts must condemn both. He sees the justice of the censures of the law so plainly that he is unable to see how the condemnation of the law can be escaped, and there is no relief from this difficulty until he can realize the redemption of grace. At this point of contrast one of the leading distinctions between a true and a false repentance emerges to view. The one sees a single act, or a short series of specific criminal acts, disclosing, it may be, a specific degrading tendency in the character, which it often endeavors to offset by a claim to virtues of act and character in other respects. The sense of guilt, however keen, does not prevent the feeling that God might overlook the fault if he just chose to do it. No atone-ment is recognized as necessary to free his integrity from the obligation to do justice. But true repentance distrusts the perfect purity of its best actions; it sees defect in all its manifested energies; it sees the taint on all the inward powers of the soul. It sees its condemnation to be so just and inevitable under the natural operation of the law, that it realizes the necessity of an atonement, and a redemption, if it be possible. Under this sense of guilt and depravity, this soul feels itself to be vile, and abhors itself; it condemns itself. It lays its hand upon its mouth, and its mouth in the dust. It cries, Unclean! unclean! So masterful becomes this consciousness of pollution, as time passes and the years mature experience, that the mind comparatively ceases its attention to the peril of sin, and even the sinfulness of specific acts.

The great source of constant anxiety is the felt consciousness of a living spring of iniquity in the soul itself, that law of sin in the members, whose tyranny made even the great apostle compare it to a decaying dead body chained fast to his living limbs. The most passionate and permanent desire is for the cleansing of this unholy fountain of energy within, knowing that such a purification is indispensable to purify the life as well as the abiding elements of the personal nature. The attention is fascinated by the working of this law of sin. It watches the uprising of unholy thoughts, fancies and wishes, evil feelings, desires, and stable affections, which, like flocks of obscene and ominous birds, drift in dense, incessantly moving masses out of the dark caverns of an unholy nature. It sighs for deliverance; and the few brief periods of temporary victory, and the occasional brief supremacy of holy emotions which now and then temper the stern struggle of the spiritual warfare, remain in the memory of the comforted saint like the memories of spring-time, sweet with scented air, the bloom of early flowers, and the glad lyrics of joyful birds. The sweetest vision of heaven itself is not the rose-embossed gold of its gorgeous avenues, the white splendor of the palaces and colonnaded halls, where the kings and priests of God forever dwell, nor the waving trees on the banks of the broad river of life, but the freedom of the soul from sin, the true and ready answer of a holy heart to the beauty of the Lord God, the ordered harmony of thought, feeling and will with all the divine requirements, the rest, never again to be disturbed, from all evil. The grand charm of heaven is *holiness*. This quality is to

the soul what health is to the body—a mysterious, indefinable, all-pervading condition of strength, beauty, exhilaration, and usefulness.   Depravity is just the opposite quality,
and lays a necessary foundation for self-abhorrence, self-
condemnation, and all the conditions of repentance.

6. Finally, to this series of perceptions and emotions leading to godly repentance, one grand distinction between it and
the sorrow of the world is found in the realization of the
goodness of God.   "Know ye not that the goodness of God
leadeth thee to repentance?"   That goodness is only realized
in the forgiveness of sin, when God is pacified towards the
sinner.   No such perception enters into the sorrow that
worketh death; that unfruitful remorse springs exclusively
from a sense of the justice of God and the terrors of his administration.   Release the natural convict from his danger,
and his care is extinguished.   His mourning is all selfish.
Not so with him whom godly sorrow is leading to the repentance which is unto life.   The goodness of God has laid
its white hand upon him, and is leading him to an unselfish
and generous sorrow for his sin.   The cross of the Redeemer
has revealed its infinite tender compassion and its power of
saving the lost; and as the lips drink eagerly the first deep
draught from the stream of forgiving love, the heart breaks
down into a sorrow for sinning against a being so gracious,
far deeper and more effectual in its abiding influences than
the bitterest emotions which spring from the view of sin
apart from the grace which takes it away.   It is an unselfish
sorrow, and, mingled with its grief, there is a distinct ruling
element of sweetness, love and hope, which makes the sorrow
which leads to true repentance sweeter than many a joy of an
unpardoned soul.   There is no such element of sweet emotion qualifying the unmingled bitterness of a false repentance.

7. These precedent perceptions and emotions, the just views
of the divine law and of sin, and the emotions which follow

them—the shame, the self-abasement, the sorrow, the hatred, the self-abhorrence, the self-condemnation, and the grateful sense of the divine goodness, *all unite to work the act of repentance unto life.* The emotions which lead to repentance are often confounded with the act of repentance, and while they are inseparably connected with it, they are not only distinguishable in thought, but are distinguished from it in so many words of the Holy Ghost. Paul clearly discriminates between "the godly sorrow that worketh repentance unto salvation," and the repentance itself. The sorrow works the act: the one is precedent, as cause, the other consequent, as effect. "Repentance unto life is a saving grace, whereby a sinner, out of a true sense of his sin and apprehension of the mercy of God in Christ, doth, with grief and hatred of his sin, turn from it unto God, with a full purpose of and endeavor after new obedience." The essence of repentance is in this act of turning from sin. Luther defined repentance as ceasing to sin. It is the act of the whole soul, mind and heart, taste and volition, all consenting in a revolt from sin, with a fixed purpose by the grace of God to do it no more with consent and free acquiescence. It is the fruit of regeneration, the issue of a change of heart. The word translated repentance means, literally, change of mind; and it is contradictory to predicate change of mind without change of mind. If repentance takes effect on the heart as well as on the mind, it is equally contradictory to predicate a change of heart without a change of heart. Repentance implies a change of feeling as well as a change of view. False repentance implies a change of feeling towards a sin, or some sins, as identified with its effects; but the very circumstance which distinguishes it from true repentance is that the latter implies a real change of feeling and affection towards all sin, not merely as identified with its dangerous consequences, but on account of its intrinsic criminal nature. Such a change is only another name for that change of heart which is involved in regeneration. Repentance is a right-about movement, reversing the direction in which the energies of the whole soul are acting, not merely in the governing purpose, but in the views of the understanding, in the affections of the heart, in the supremacy of the conscience, in all the forces which color and control character and conduct. It is an instant act of revolt against all sin, growing out into ten thousand repeated acts, and thus into a steady work and habit of resistance to all sin, and for the whole life. The emotions leading to repentance may be at times more or less difficult to discriminate from the similar emotions of false repentance; but if the acts and habit of resisting sin are clear in the consciousness, there can be little difficulty in deciding the question. If the soul is conscious of this constant aversion and dread towards sin; if this fixed purpose and habit, and this fixed but anxious and solicitous determination to overcome it, is clear in experience, such a soul hath good reason to believe that he who has been exalted as a Prince and a Saviour to give repentance unto life and the forgiveness of sins, hath already granted unto him repentance and the good hope it insures.

To sum up in a specific and detailed contrast between the two species of repentance—one springing from the godly sorrow that worketh salvation; the other, from the sorrow of the world that worketh death. The one is selfish, controlled by selfishness; the other is prudent, controlled by a lawful regard to well-being. The one is confined to special sins; the other extends to all sin, whenever recognized as such. One is embittered; the other is humble. One is afraid of detection; the other is free to confess. One is disposed to extenuation and self-defence; the other is anxious to see more of its own evil. The one is revengeful to others; the other is revengeful towards itself. The one leads to a limited reform of faults in conduct, and to little or none in heart; the other seeks an unlimited reform, and most eagerly in the inward parts. The one refers to God, only as the source of danger; the other to God as rightly offended. The one produces effects not often permanent, even in their limited range; the other does produce permanent effects of general improvement. The effects of the one are not purifying; the effects of the other are purifying, especially in the heart. The effects of the one are not humility, but self-assertion; the effect of the other is self-condemnation. The desire of salvation produced by the one is soon discouraged; the desire of salvation produced by the other is permanent and inextinguishable. The effort to escape produced by the one soon ceases; the effort to escape produced by the other never ceases. The one never leads to the acceptance of gospel mercy; the other always does. The one sorrow leads to remorse, and ends in death; the other leads to godly repentance, and works out salvation. The one is the datum of natural conscience restrained from the paralysis of its functions by sin, and enabled to do its work by the restraining and supporting influences of the Holy Spirit; the other is the gift of Christ, the Prince and Saviour exalted to give repentance and forgiveness of sins through the agency of the Spirit, and is the exercise of a regenerate heart.

The fundamental notion of all repentance is *change* of mind. If the repentance is a real repentance of the heart, it is necessarily in itself a change of the heart towards sin. All exercises of sorrow for sin, previous to a real change of the heart from the love to the honest hatred of sin, are *selfish*, and belong to the sorrow that worketh death. This selfish sorrow from awakening and natural conviction, under gospel influences, is not useless, as it always precedes a genuine repentance, and tends to lead to it; but it is dangerous and misleading to speak of persons in this state of mind as *penitents;* they are more properly designated as "mourners," or "seekers," or 'inquirers." False repentance is not for sin separated from its effects, and only seeks to comply with the terms of grace to escape destruction. True repentance is repentance for sin, and wages war on it in all its known forms, "to escape its pollution as well as its danger." False repentance may lead sometimes to the repair of wrongs and the restitution of injuries, under stress of remorse, and as an inducement to mercy; but it is all selfish. True repentance leads to restitution, because it is just, and because it has learned to abhor the crime which has injured others. False repentance seeks reform in the inward parts, whenever it does seek it at all, merely as the recognized path away from peril. True repentance leads to an habitual and eager universal purification, because it is not only essential to safety, but because it has learned to abhor the law of sin in the members. "What carefulness it wrought in you; yea, what zeal, yea, what indignation, yea, what revenge," is said of it. It leads to an universal and permanent reform of heart and life. Not discouraged by a thousand failures and falls, weeping and ashamed of its want of fidelity in duty, the grace-supported heart of a true penitent sends back evermore the heroic battle-cry of the weary but unconquered soldier of Christ, "Rejoice not against me, O mine enemy; though I weep, I shall rejoice; though I am weak, yet am I strong; though I sit in darkness, the light shall arise unto me; though I fall, I shall rise again; though he slay me, yet will I trust in him." True repentance leads to life eternal.

CHAPTER V.

FAITH.

"For by grace are ye saved through faith; and that not of yourselves; it is the gift of God."—*Paul to the Ephesians.*

ON *faith* turns the issue of eternal life according to the gospel of grace. It is of faith that it may be of grace. To know what it is to believe is to know the way of life; to exercise faith is to obtain it. Faith in itself is the simplest of conceptions; but to describe it in the completeness of its nature, its offices in the scheme of redemption, and its relations to other truths and graces, is not easy. The movement of the arm is very simple, but to describe in full the movement of every muscle, tendon, and nervous energy brought into play, would not answer to the simplicity of the movement analyzed. Every guide of an anxious inquirer knows how impossible it is to convey any satisfactory notion of faith when the soul is trying to exercise it. It becomes very clear that the saying is true, faith is the gift of God, and he alone can enable it. Yet the truth must be taught, for only through the truth does God put forth his saving power, and there are so many difficulties, not pertaining to the real cause of the seeker's disability, which are made occasions of resistance, and which may be quelled by instruction, to render it hopeless of effect to teach the real nature of saving faith in the Saviour and his truth.

All faith in its generic nature is the same; it is belief of testimony; it is the credit of evidence. To believe a thing is to accept it as *true.* But this generic nature of faith may be so qualified by both intellectual and moral qualities as to make it entirely different, and thus to create different kinds of faith, more or less entitled to respect. To accept a thing as true on insufficient or unjustifiable evidence is *credulity*, or *rash confidence*. To construe the evidence and thus accept as true, under the coloring influence of pride, prejudice, perverted moral tastes, or false rules of judgment, is to create a faith intellectually mistaken and morally corrupt. The nature of all faith is strongly qualified as judicious or injudicious, by the intellectual qualities that enter into it, and equally qualified as morally censurable or otherwise by the moral qualities that color it. This is the great principle by which all kinds of faith are to be judged and their real nature discovered, *by the qualities, intellectual and moral, that enter into their composition.* The rule rests, as its basis, on the great fact of human nature, that its moral energies are called into play in the formation of its views; and the particular kind of moral feeling or energy which is controlling in that formation, or which enters into it, although not sufficient to be controlling, will modify the final result. Ignorance, carelessness in dealing with the evidence, prejudice in construing it, perverted habits, affections, or tastes perverting the final conclusion, taint the faith which accepts, mars the conclusion itself, and irresistibly discloses the responsibility of the actor for his accepted belief.

It is not, therefore, at all strange that the Scriptures describe at least *four species* of faith: *historical* faith, *temporary* faith, the *faith of devils*, and the *faith which saves.* Each of these is an acceptance of something as true, modified by the presence of evil qualities which ought not to have entered into the faith which is exercised, or by the absence or the presence of some good quality which ought to have entered into it. With this clue, we may form some approximately just notion of each of them.

1. *Historical faith* is the faith of the masses of the people generally in all Christian countries. It stands discriminated from all kinds of infidelity, on the one side, and from **saving**

faith in the gospel, on the other. It is the settled intellectual conviction of the truth of the whole Christian system,
and thus stands opposed to infidelity, which rejects it. It
not only believes in the existence of God and in his government in the world, but in Christianity as a divinely revealed
and supernatural system, in the Bible as inspired, and in
Christ as a Saviour. It is a real, honest, calm, intellectual
conviction; but it is not incorporated with the feelings of
the heart to any great extent, and those feelings are not the
right and justly due feelings which ought to enter into such
a conviction. It enlists strong feeling as to the necessity of
religion as a political and social restraint. It may be associated with family ties and hereditary honors. But it does
not take hold of individual affections, except to a certain
extent, or excite the anxieties of the mind, and certainly fails
to awaken the pleasing affections and to establish a law of
habitual personal conduct, steadfastly authoritative over the
conscience and delightful to the heart. In this grave defect
it stands opposed to saving faith. It is a real and honest
faith, but entirely wanting in those moral qualities essential to
do justice to the truth as a whole. It, therefore, cannot save.
This sad result is proved by the sadder fact that many such
believers are not saved—a result conclusively shown by the
ungodly tenor of their lives. Historical faith, so far as it
goes, does justice to the truth, and to the evidence which
supports it; but it does justice to the truth only in part, and
its exclusively intellectual character makes no room for those
exercises of the heart which give the complexion of moral
or spiritual excellence to the faith which is indulged.

2. *Temporary* faith, or an acceptance of a certain class of
truths—the joyful truths of revealed mercy—for a time, is
portrayed in the stony-ground hearers of the parable of the
seed-sower. They are said to have received the word with
joy, but not having sufficient depth of earth, they fell away
when the time of persecution and affliction came. This

faith is supposed by some to be saving, because a certain degree of joyful feeling was mixed up with it. It is thus construed to be the saving faith of the heart. That it was not saving is proved by the strongest of all proof, it did not save them. That it excited some feeling does not necessarily show that it was the right feeling—the feeling and affection of the whole heart, the feeling necessary to qualify a faith as it ought, and is required, to be. It has just been seen that the real nature of any species of faith is regulated by the kind of moral and intellectual feeling that enters into it. It is not enough to show that some feeling enters into it, but also what *kind* of feeling. There is a certain kind of feeling, often strong and decisive, a feeling of political importance, or hereditary or social pride, that is mixed up with historical faith. The faith of devils is mixed with strong feelings. But that does not make those species of faith saving. What, then, is the nature of this feeling in the stony-ground hearers? It is evident, in the first place, that it was a joyful feeling; it is not said to be attended by any other kind of feeling. It was based on the joyful truths of the Saviour's teaching, and on that only. It was consequently based on an incomplete foundation. It was a faith *without repentance.* It was the joy which springs up on the presentment of a hopeful prospect without paying just regard to the conditions and preliminary steps to secure it. Moreover, and most conclusively, it was a movement in a part of the heart only, in the desire of well-being, but not in its moral tastes and affections. It was the dread of danger, breeding hope of escape on the presentment of pleasing truths; but not the revolt of the whole heart, affections, tastes, desires, and fixed purposes, *against sin*, leading to the assured hope of escape on the presentment of the gospel remedies. Any heart, no matter how thoroughly ungodly, would rejoice under a strong, no matter how delusive, if yet an actual, hope of everlasting well-being. But the joyful feeling in such a heart would by no means prove it to be a right heart, and its cheerful emotions, though strongly qualifying his faith, would by no means guarantee his faith. The feelings of the heart which determine the nature of true faith, and the absence of which disqualify any faith, are the real moral tastes, inclinations, and affections of the heart, and not any merely passing sensibilities of hope or joy bred by a prospect of advantage without any sound or reliable foundation. This joy of the stony-ground hearers was like the joy of a child at the prospect of a new gift; it excites a temporary influence; but it soon passes away, and makes no abiding impression on the tastes and desires of the heart. The ground on which it sprang up was still *stony;* there was no depth of earth to receive the seed; the plough had not passed over it. The law must do its work to prepare the heart for the reception of the gospel; carnal security must be broken up; the awakening and convicting influences of the Holy Spirit must bring the sinner to see he is actually lost before he can appreciate truly the glad tidings of great joy. There may be religious joy before this takes place, from some mistaken apprehension of the good news; but this is the joy of the stony-ground hearer, which soon passes away.

There are many exercises about religion which are not truly religious. Every false religion the world has ever seen has its exhilarating considerations, which, when realized by the devotee, produce a kind of joy, but it is none the less delusive and ruinous. Faith must be qualified by feelings and affections far deeper than mere selfish appetencies awakened by mistaken views of partial truth, and soon passing away.

3. The classification of *the faith of devils* is justified by the Scripture declaration, "the devils also believe and tremble." The lost angels have no room for skepticism of God's existence, or his government, or the truth of his promises. Their own knowledge acquaints them with his existence and

his character. Their own awful experience, past and present, acquaints them with his government and law. Their own experience and knowledge combined acquaints them with the certain overthrow of their usurped dominion on earth, and of their own final segregation from the possibility of re-establishing it, and of their own final subjection to the full penalty of their crimes. They believe these things, and they tremble under the assurance. Their faith is no cold and impassive historical faith. It is a faith which reaches their hearts, not in the sense of a loving and joyful assent and consent to the things believed, but in the sense of a bitter, malignant, and terrified repulsion and discontent with the things believed. It is substantially identical with the remorse which sometimes seizes a human criminal and awakes the assured conviction within him that the retribution of his crime is unavoidable. The expression, *believing with the heart*, needs to be discriminated to express the saving faith of the elect of God. There is *a faith of the heart* which is not saving—a faith which receives the truth and hates it; accepts it, because it cannot disbelieve it, but accepts it unwillingly, with the revolt of feeling, with intense opposition of will. This is often seen in men; it is identical with the faith of devils, and seems to indicate that the faith of devils is not altogether confined to the hierarchs of the abyss. There are phases of human unbelief which have no place in the infernal regions. There are no atheists there to deny the existence of God. There are no skeptics to doubt, no agnostics to be ignorant of, the realities of the divine administration. There are no pantheists among the devils to construe themselves as parts of God, and not personal and distinct existencies in their own wicked and miserable selves. There are no cool and unmoved historical believers among them, honestly accepting the revelation of the divine will, and not caring a bawbee about it. They believe and they hate; they believe with intense and unrestricted convictions, and they tremble with awful foreboding of the sure wrath which is to come. There is no peace, hope, or salvation in the faith of devils; it breeds in them, and perhaps in certain classes of men, "a fearful looking for of judgment and fiery indignation which shall consume the adversaries."

4. Saving faith is the last discrimination of faith to which we shall allude, and the most important. The generic nature of all faith is the same; it is the acceptance of anything as true; but the entry of different intellectual and moral elements into its generic nature results in producing different kinds of faith of vastly differing moral and intellectual values, and, as such, exerting answerable differences in the effects they produce. Saving faith is qualified by certain intellectual and spiritual affections which constitute its peculiar character, and under the arrangements of the covenant of grace enable it to secure that immeasurable result, the salvation of the lost soul. But inasmuch as this species of faith in its generic nature possesses some features in common with all other species of faith, and the consideration of these features will tend powerfully to vindicate the faith that saves from some assaults that have been made upon it, it will be advisable to discuss these generic features of all belief before entering on the detail of the special and distinguishing peculiarities of this belief which is the instrument of salvation in the Christian system.

1. All kinds of faith have certain generic or general features in common. Faith, under all kinds, is the acceptance of a thing as true. Whenever anything is believed, it is meant that that thing is received as true. But in order to the reception of a thing as true, there must be something *to show* that it is true; that is, there must be evidence or testimony to the thing in order to its being accepted as true. Belief, then, is a confidence in testimony. But the dealing with the evidence at once calls into play the active powers of the mind; this calls into play the energies of the will, and

throws open the sphere of feeling, passion, and prejudice, and this at once draws the authority of moral law over the scene of action, and determines responsibility for the final resulting belief. As moral law and the voluntary and moral powers of the human spirit are thus inevitably involved in the genesis of belief, the right formation and exercise of belief may be properly required and commanded. There are features in the Christian doctrine of faith which have excited opposition to it, but they are the generic features of all faiths recognized by the common-sense judgments of all mankind, and it is, therefore, altogether nugatory to cite them as objections to the gospel doctrine of saving faith. Test these several generic features of faith by the universal requirements and usages of mankind, and the fact will undoubtedly appear, that in the teachings of the gospel about faith, it has displayed no subtlety of its own, exclusively, but has proceeded on grounds common to all forms of belief recognized among men. These universal grounds vindicate its generic features, and its special peculiarities are vindicated by their own special evidence.

(1.) As to the first generic feature of all beliefs there will be no dispute. Faith or belief is the simple acceptance of a thing *as true*. Accepting as true is the very nature of the thing and the very meaning of the word *belief*. This is the primary and essential conception of faith. About this there will be no dispute. However true or false the thing believed may be, if believed, it is taken to be true.

(2.) But to the acceptance of a thing as true there must be something to show it to be true; otherwise its truth cannot be conceived either as probable or known, and, therefore, cannot be properly asserted to be or believed to be. To assert a thing to be true, without any sufficient reason, or any reason at all to believe it to be true, is to assert a falsehood; it is a breach of the law of veracity. Let any man do this about any secular matter, and the common-sense judgments of men at once hold him responsible and condemn him as wanting in integrity. If he accepts any statement on insufficient, or extravagant, or superstitious, or incompetent evidence of any sort, the same inexorable common-sense judgment ascertains his responsibility, and sets him down as credulous, or superstitious, or rash, or foolish in his belief. On the contrary, if the evidence is clear and powerful, and yet it is refused, and the thing proved is rejected as false, the very same common-sense judgment will ascertain responsibility, and ascribe the refusal to see and recognize the truth to passion, prejudice, ignorance, or to some cause resting in the will and feelings of the man. Without competent evidence no man can be required to believe anything. To deny this is to say that a man can be required to believe or accept a thing as true in the absence of everything that could show it to be true; in other words, to affirm as true what he has *no reason* to believe is true, which is only another way of saying he is bound to tell a lie. Evidence is the only rational basis of belief. It is not only the basis, but for that very reason the measure, of assent. If the evidence is decisive, belief ought to be decisive. If the evidence is only probable, the assent of the mind ought to be graduated accordingly. The degree of assent ought to be determined by the degree of the evidence. The relation of evidence to faith is all-important.

From this relation between evidence and belief two of the greatest thinkers of the age drew the conclusion that there was no responsibility for belief. If the evidence was clear, it compelled assent; and if the evidence was incomplete, no one could be required to believe. In this they have been followed by the great bulk of the scientific world, the infidel section of which, especially, are eager to repel all responsibility for their rejection of the Christian faith, and hold all the censures of the Christian world as the unjust expressions of ignorance and bigotry. They regard the commands of the gospel to believe, and its grave censures of unbelief, as absurd; evidence controls belief, and to command belief and to censure the want of it is as unjust and ridiculous as to command a man chilled with cold to be warm without fire, and to censure him for continuing to be cold. But the common-sense judgments of mankind coincide with the teachings of the gospel in rejecting this view, and in holding men responsible for their beliefs. They require unprejudiced and just judgments of men and things of each other in the ordinary transactions of life; they require them of judges on the bench, of statesmen in council, of all who are endowed with trust powers. The reason is plain: The view of Sir James McIntosh and Lord Brougham proceeded on the supposition that belief was the product of *one factor alone;* that is, the evidence in the case. But the common-sense judgments of mankind are grounded on the clear perception that belief is the product of *two factors* instead of one; that is, *evidence,* and the *action of human faculties upon it.* The presentation of the evidence at once calls the human faculties into action. This calls into play the energies of the will, throws open the space for the activity of the moral feelings of fairness or unfairness in judging of the evidence, and thus imposes the authority of moral law over the formation of the judgment. Consequently, obedience to moral law may be justly required in the treatment of the evidence, and in the consequent genesis of faith. The common sense of mankind does not disable the effect, or dislocate the relation, of evidence to belief, but it does at the same time rightly construe the influence of the *will,* and rightly estimate the influence of pride, passion, prejudice, and of all the moral feelings, good or bad, in construing the evidence. It sees clearly the coloring influence of the will and of all its affections in the genesis of all kinds of faith, and hence does not hesitate to hold all men responsible for their beliefs on all subjects whatever. To subject the Christian religion to contemptuous censure because it does the very same thing, censures men for unbelief, and commands them to believe the gospel, is silly. The Christian faith and the common-sense judgments of mankind proceed on the same great underlying principles, and coincide in these five great generic features of all just and true beliefs. They construe all belief as the *acceptance of truth;* they demand *evidence* as *the basis and measure* of faith; they recognize the inevitable concern of the *will* and its *affections* in the construction and estimate of the evidence, and in the genesis of belief; they recognize *the supremacy of moral law* over this genesis or production, and the obligation to form just judgments on the impartial consideration of all the evidence on both sides; and they unite in holding men responsible for their beliefs on all subjects whatever.

There is another point falling as a subdivision of one of the five great generic features of belief, in which the general judgments of mankind and the demands of the Christian system coincide. Both require evidence as the basis and measure of assent, and both admit the full claims of legitimate *personal* testimony as one species of lawful evidence. Both admit that the testimony of a reliable personal witness is entitled to be believed. Both admit the right and the obligation to test his trustworthiness to any extent that may be necessary. Both recognize the lawful limits and qualifications which rationally guard the reception of such testimony, and either reduce or enhance its claims to credit. A just and honorable man feels that he is entitled to confidence, and that as he speaks the truth he is entitled to be believed. He recognizes the right of full inquiry into his trustworthiness in general and in every particular case. But injustice is done when the veracity of a true man is impeached; injustice is a breach of moral law; men are universally bound to do justice; and consequently the rejection of personal testimony when really trustworthy is a wrong. Preliminary investigation as to integrity, soundness of mind, opportunity of knowing, and all other elements of credibility is not only allowable, but obligatory. But when trustworthiness is ascertained, the common-sense judgments of mankind and the teachings of the word of God unite in affirming that personal testimony carries all the weight of any other evidence in creating an *obligation to believe*.

We may now proceed to investigate the Scripture account of the faith which saves the soul. The account given in the Scriptures of the nature and offices of faith is drawn out into a great variety of particulars, which can only be alluded to, and not fully discussed, in a limited treatise. The offices assigned it in the economy of redemption are manifold. It is absolutely necessary to give effect to the great redemption for the benefit of any individual soul. It is the principle that unites to Christ and secures his functions as a Saviour. It is the instrument by which all grace is received. It is the instrument of justification. It develops the power of the truth by giving evidence to things unseen, and thus makes it the instrument of sanctification. It animates all the graces of the renewed soul. It is the principle which regulates the visible walk and conversation. It gives power to prayer; it inspires zeal; it develops comfort; it overcomes the world; it triumphs over death; it crowns with full accomplishment that promise of salvation which it sealed the first moment of its exercise.

The teaching of the Scriptures touching *the nature* of saving faith is equally elaborate, and in some of its features apparently strange and paradoxical. Faith in its generic form is the acceptance of anything as true on a sufficient evidence; it is belief of testimony. Saving faith is the acceptance of all the truth revealed in his word on the testimony of God himself. It is confined to the holy Scriptures alone as containing the testimony. It is confined to God alone as the witness. It is described as morally obliga-

tory, and is, therefore, required of all persons to whom the
testimony comes. It is grounded on evidence sufficient to
create a just moral obligation to believe. It is also described
as a datum of *the will*, an exercise of the heart in man, and
not merely the issue of activity in the intellectual powers.
It is described, with an apparent paradox, as a gift of God as
fully as it is affirmed to be a duty in man. It is described
as a belief of truth mediated through tastes, inclinations,
and affections in sympathy with the truth. It is also emphatically described *as a trust*, which is always an exercise
of the will—a trust *in a person*, in his truth and faithfulness,
in his love and power. It is a trust in the *words* and in the
works of this person. Another paradoxical feature is, that
while this faith is morally obligatory, and, therefore, required
under peril of guilty accountability, it is plainly and
positively pronounced to be beyond the native personal
ability of those required to exercise it. It is said to be the
great regulating force over the character and life of the
Christian. It is described as the acceptance merely of an
offered gift, a drink of freely-given and refreshing water, a
gift to one asking, as well as the reception of a gift from one
giving it. Finally, it is described as a moral and intellectual
energy in a soul peculiarly energized, and with all the wonderful effects it has been organized or appointed to accomplish, possessing no special merit in itself. All its power is
not in itself, but in something else to which it is related; it is
simply the correlated adjustment of *grace*, to which all the
power of faith is due. "It is of faith that it might be of
grace," and, therefore, faith is only considerable as the instrument of effective grace. These are the leading characteristic marks which distinguish the nature of saving faith.
All these marks have been more or less perverted in the
endless vagaries of human speculation. A brief expansion
of them on their scriptural foundation will expose some of
the more important of these misconstructions, and put us

in possession of a truth which no man can afford to mistake.

1. Saving faith is the acceptance of the truth on the testimony of God in his word. This exclusive sphere and warranty of saving faith as found in the testimony of God in his word is clearly set forth in the word itself. "Abraham believed God, and it was accounted to him for righteousness." "Faith cometh by hearing, and hearing by the word of God." "Blessed are they that keep his testimonies." "Thy word have I hid in my heart, that I might not sin against thee." "He that believeth not God hath made him a liar, because he believeth not the record that God gave of his Son." The whole Bible is full of admonitions to trust in God, and of warnings against trust in any other being. In the Old Testament the requisition is to trust in Jehovah our righteousness as the God of the covenant; in the New Testament, to trust only in Jesus; and unless two radically different religions are taught in the two parts of the inspired record, the Jehovah of the Old and the Jesus of the New Testament are one and the same person. The testimony of God is found in the record he has made, and nowhere else. Consequently, saving faith in his testimony is confined to that record exclusively; it cannot be required to extend its confidence beyond that record, while it is required to give full confidence to all that is in it. This truth is full of important consequences. It not only rebukes the dangerous resort to tradition outside of the record, or to deliverances of the church not based upon the record, but discounts many an error based on the misguided experiences of his professed people. Yet further, this peculiar character of saving faith rests all its confidence in the testimony on the divine witness himself. All the confidence it gives to the secondary grounds of confidence in the testimony of men, miracle, prophecy, or the wonderful accuracy and concatenation of the statements of the record, runs back into this confidence in God himself. True believers

confide in inspired men because God has inspired them; in miracles, because God was the worker of them; in prophecy, because God has spoken it; in the unity and harmony of Scripture, because the mind of God was the source of the revelation. Men may honestly believe in these secondary grounds of confidence, but their faith is not saving; it is the honest but ineffectual historic faith which does not save. They do not see the divine witness back of the mere proofs, and trust in him. It is belief in a communication from him, but not a trust in himself, nor in the words he has spoken. The insufficiency of this faith will be more fully illustrated hereafter. Real faith in God, the divine witness, is not only a trust in his promises, but a trust in himself. That faith is "a fruit of the Spirit," and when exercised specifically on the record as his word, it alone can convey *the full impression* that it is indeed the very word of God.*

This mark of saving faith, its confinement to the inspired record, exposes some practical and some theoretical errors which obtain even among evangelical believers. It exposes an error of practice among some who overstrain or abuse the duty of self-examination. These are, for the most part, perhaps altogether, the true children of God, anxious to be clear in their professed claim to the character they profess, and who, obedient to the command to examine themselves, seek the proof of their faith in the records of their own consciousness and experience. To a certain extent, this is a legitimate proceeding, but it is easily abused. Faith is exercised on things out of us, not on things within us. Its objects are the record and the being who has made it, the promises, and the Saviour. Faith is required in the testimony and in the testifier. The traveler who comes to a bridge on the highway, does not pause at the bridge-head and turn his thoughts inward on his own mind to see if he has faith in the bridge; he never thinks of his own mental states; he looks outward

---

* Larger Catechism, Question 4.

at the bridge, and as he discovers the strength of its timbers, confidence in the roadway over it insensibly springs up. So long as faith is sought *out of* the testimony, and apart from the glorious witness; so long as it is sought merely in experience and consciousness, just so long will doubt and perplexity ensue. Experience is often complicated and perplexed, consciousness is often difficult to decipher, and if it actually yields confidence, it is primarily confidence in ourselves, in what grace has given us, in our own piety, but it is only secondarily faith in the testimony. While trust in our own graces as disclosed in experience will often be doubtful, trust in the great legitimate and primary basis of saving faith, in the word of God and in the Saviour it presents, may always be clear and absolute. "The word of faith is nigh thee, even in thy mouth and in thy heart." To believe it is to trust the word and him who spoke it. It is not to trust in self, or in what has been given to self. Saving faith is not an inference from experience. It may be certified and confirmed by experience after faith has done its work and displayed its fruits. The confidence in the reality and soundness of tested faith is, morally valued, only the same with the confidence bred by the satisfactory proof of anything else which is esteemed to be valuable. But the saving faith itself is confidence in the testimony and in the witness, not confidence in itself, no matter how sound it may be. This faith is not yielded by experience, but by the word under the illumination of the Spirit. Faith precedes and introduces experience. Manifestly, then, the original acts of faith are grounded on something else than experience, and all the acts of faith through the whole Christian life, down to the end, are grounded on the original basis upon which they began. They are based all along on the testimony of God in his word. Resting always on that alone, the experience of his servants will be freed from many a harassing perplexity which will and ought to grow out of the change, however unconsciously effected, of the basis of confidence from the sure word of the testimony to the complications of experience.

This principle of saving faith being grounded only on the word of the testimony corrects another dangerous misconception of faith. It is supposed that saving faith is simply a persuasion of ourselves that we are saved—a conviction of our own minds that things are, or will be, as we wish them to be. This misconception of faith springs from a misapprehension of the words of Jesus, "what things soever ye desire, when ye pray, believe that ye receive them, and ye shall have them." It is very clear that these words convey the common doctrine of the New Testament touching the relation of faith to the blessings of grace. They mean *believe in order that you may receive.* It is the doctrine of James, "let him ask in faith, nothing wavering: for he that wavereth is like a wave of the sea driven with the wind and tossed; let not that man think that he shall receive anything of the Lord." The error in question may be construed in two ways, one referring to time present, and the other to time future. In the first, it teaches that if a person persuades himself that he actually possesses the grace he desires, he will actually possess it in fact. In the second, it teaches that, if he can persuade himself *that he will* possess the desired grace, he will assuredly come into possession of it. In reference to the first, it is obvious to see that to persuade one's self that he is in actual present possession in order that he may come into possession, involves either a persuasion of what is not true or of what is superfluous. In reference to the second, it is also obvious to be seen that the belief that the grace *will be given,* unless based on a promise previously made, is a mere presumption, without a warrant for the confidence. If the expectation is grounded on a promise, this is faith in the testimony and in the testifier. It is obvious that faith in a promise is one thing, and confidence in something not in the record is another. All men are bound to give credit to every declaration God has made in his word; but no man has a right to persuade himself of anything not in the record. It is a dangerous delusion to teach men to persuade themselves that things will be, just because they may successfully delude themselves into the belief that they will be. Saving faith is not a presumptuous assurance concerning *any unrevealed thing*, such as the time, place, and circumstance in the fulfilment of prophecy, in which such incidents are not foretold; or personal salvation, or the salvation of particular persons, or the final triumph of any particular creed or system. The discriminating feature of true faith is rest on the word, and on God who has given his testimony in it and nowhere else. Self-persuasion is bottomed on something discovered, or which is supposed will be discovered, in self as its main basis.

This feature of saving faith discounts a variety of errors of different sorts. It shows the folly of some anxious and tender consciences which refuse to be comforted because they can see no allusion which they can construe to be personal to themselves in the divine record. But even if their very names were in it the circumstance would only enhance the anxiety to be assured that another person of the same name was not mentioned. The assurance of hope, which is the assurance of personal salvation, is altogether practicable *under the record just as it stands.* Belief of that record will soon warrant the conclusion of personal safety, for the promise is to the believer. Faith raised to the degree warranted by the mighty ground on which it is invited to rest, would soon disclose itself and all that it warranted to hope. The error of interpreting visions, voices, dreams, and peculiar experiences as assurances of salvation is cut up by the roots by this quality of saving faith as grounded and measured only on the testimony of God in his word.

A more dangerous and common error is equally annihilated by it, the error of trust in church connections and sacraments,

in the merits of other beside the only name given under heaven
whereby we can be saved, in personal virtues, and in other
kinds of faith. Trust in these is not trust in the only
Saviour, and want of trust in him is want of trust in the recorded testimony which God has given of his Son. This
essential quality of saving faith, trust in the testimony of
God, and the trust in God himself as the witness, stands like
a granite light-house throwing back the waves of all possible
error that assail it on every side, or may ever assail it.

2. The Scriptures teach concerning the faith that saves
that *it is morally obligatory* in the highest possible degree on
all to whom the testimony comes. This teaching assumes as
its basis several considerations of the greatest importance,
each of which is essential to a just moral obligation to
believe.

(1.) First, it assumes and asserts that the claim rests on
a mass of evidence all-sufficient to sustain the truth of it,
and thus to create an obligation to receive it as true. This
evidence falls under two classifications generally contemplated: first, the proof that God has testified; and secondly,
the proof of the truth of what he has said. The first is opposed by that species of unbelief which is called *infidelity*
in its various forms; the second, by the species of unbelief
which is characteristic of those who admit the historical
verity of the gospel system, and yet *reject its offers, and refuse to come under its bonds of obedience.* An old, yet simple
and effective, illustration will bring out the distinctions in
these kinds of faith with clearness and precision Suppose a
man to be in prison for a debt which he is utterly unable to
pay. He receives a note from a friend offering to pay the
debt and to release him from imprisonment. He is at once
called upon to deal with the proposition. It is a free proposal, and must be simply accepted or rejected. The imprisoned debtor may deal with it in one or two modes, both of
which carry the rejection of, or refusal to accept, the offer. He

may question whether his friend is the author of the writing containing the proposal, and may refuse to accept it as a reliable expression of his friend's views and purposes. This will be the species of unbelief called *infidelity*. This is the procedure of all kinds of infidelity in dealing with the testimony of God. It does not *primarily*, in its own consciousness and intent, deny what God has said, but only that he has said anything. But let it be noted, that this species of unbelief effectually disposes of the offer made, and leaves the prisoner in the full stress of his unfortunate circumstances. But he may also deal with the proposition in a different way, yet with the same effect of no relief from his trouble. He may be fully convinced that his friend did write the note; he recognizes the handwriting, the signature, and the seal, and is satisfied that the offer was made by the person from whom it purports to come. This is the ordinary historical faith of the people of Christian countries: they accept the gospel as a divinely-given religion. But now the prisoner begins to question and doubt in his own thoughts. He may question whether his friend is really *able* to pay his debt; or, holding him perfectly able, from his known resources, to pay, doubts whether he is really *willing* to do what he offers to do. This is the modification of unbelief which coëxists with historical faith in the record, yet rejects the proposals it contains. It is a refusal to trust in the *person* who presents himself in the testimony of the note. On the other hand, the imprisoned debtor may deal with the note sent him in a way to secure the benefit offered to his acceptance. He not only accepts the note as genuine, but, believing his friend to be fully able and willing to do what he offers to do, immediately closes with the proposal; he accepts the offer. His faith is not merely *a belief in the note, but a trust in a person.* The effect is an immediate relief to his mental anxieties; he will not wait to have the debt actually paid, and to walk out of the prison walls, before he will rejoice. His mind will be instantly filled with the joy of an assured, anticipated relief, before it is realized in the fact. His faith in the note and in the person who wrote its generous proposals will give him immediate peace. This *trust or faith* is the saving faith of the glad tidings of great joy.

Now suppose this letter to the debtor in prison comes from a stranger to himself, every consideration of candor and prudence would warrant him in demanding evidence that the paper containing such generous offers should be proved to be authentic, and the person proposing in the offer should be proved to be absolutely trustworthy. Suppose that a sufficient number of personal witnesses thoroughly acquainted with the handwriting, signature and seal of the writer, gives him full assurance that the note is authentic. Suppose an equally trustworthy set of witnesses should assure him of the great resources of the generous offerer, and of many a similar act of kindness done for many prisoners in the same harassing circumstances. What would be the obligation created by this posture of affairs? Obviously, in advance of all testimony to the reliability of the note and its contained offer, the prisoner would not be justified in at once and finally repudiating the whole matter as a piece of incredible nonsense. A degree of skepticism in the outset that so unusual a proposal could be authentic might be justified so far as to make the prisoner at least *raise the inquiry*. But as soon as the testimony began to accumulate, vindicating the proposal as probably true, the obligation to inquire would rapidly increase in force; and as the evidence grew into irresistible demonstration this obligation would merge into the full obligation to accept the testimony and to close with the offered kindness. Any imprisoned debtor dealing otherwise with such an offer would be held responsible by every sound understanding as guilty of reckless disregard of his own interests, and of gross ingratitude, in questioning the veracity and in refusing the kindness of

an unmerited benefactor.   No doubt of the evidence would
excuse his course; he has had full liberty to inquire; plenty
of evidence has been offered him; yet because some feeling
has been roused up in his heart, some pride in not accepting
a gratuitous relief, his mind is so biased that the testimony
loses all its weight in his judgment.   He is dependent on the
witnesses, for the writer of the note is a stranger to himself;
and the testimony of these witnesses is conclusive; yet, from
a secret disgust at the substance of the offer, he refuses to
accept the testimony and persists in construing the offer as
a mere nullity.   Is he not morally responsible and morally
guilty for doing it?   It is clear that he has violated an obligation to believe the testimony of the witnesses on one side,
and an obligation of gratitude and confidence in a generous
benefactor on the other.   His right to test both the witnesses
and the trustworthiness of the maker of the offer has been
abused in the interests of his own pride or disgusted feelings,
to the sacrifice of the interests of his freedom from imprisonment and his freedom from indebtedness.

The application of this parable to both species of unbelief—infidelity, and rejection of the offered mercy of God
in the gospel—is obvious.   So far as the first species is
concerned—the proof of the note—the evidence of the
divine authority of the Christian records is abundant and
complete.   The steady progress and the wide and ever-increasing prevalence of a system so severe in its construction
of human character, and so hostile to the indulgence of the
cherished inclinations of the human heart, over the most enlightened portions of the human race, in the face of the most
determined opposition of the strongest influences that can
operate on human opinion, is proof demonstrative of a force
in the supports of the system of the most extraordinary
character.   The evidences of Christianity constitute by
themselves a branch of knowledge which, in width, variety,
and valuable qualities, will compare favorably with any

other. No records of the past have come down from so venerable a remoteness of history, so interlocked with the legislation and the annals of nations, and so sustained by proofs of authenticity, as the records known as the Scriptures. Prophecies extending over thousands of years, over the affairs of many different nationalities and the histories of individuals, appeal boldly to events to justify their claims to a true foreknowledge. Miracles, showing the finger of God along a long line of messengers charged with his commission, have defied the resistance of the most consummate abilities at various stages of its progress, and commanded the confidence of the highest minds of every age. The traces of a super-human insight into the principles of the divine administration, the facts of the universe, the nature of God, the conditions of human existence, and the relief of human necessities, are to be found in the wonderful writings which bear the name and the signature of the infinite God. Personal testimony, of a species irresistible by any unbiased understanding, affirms them as no other records are affirmed. The delineation of the chief figure in its great galleries of historic characters is by itself a vindication of its subordinate official witnesses. These men, judged by the fair application of all the rules for testing the trustworthiness of personal witnesses, are vindicated as entitled to the absolute confidence of mankind. But apart from all consideration of their claim from character, their work in the record itself demonstrates the truth of their narrative. The delineation of the character and history of Jesus of Nazareth is as real a work of literary art as any character of Shakespeare, or a description of a great mediæval church by John Ruskin. It was as impossible to several unlettered Jewish peasants as the delineation of Hamlet by a village idiot, or the description of St. Mark's by a child in his primer.

The sketch of the Christ is true, because it was impossible unless it was true. The only way in which such men as the

authors of the Gospels could have drawn a character so simple, so grand, so beautiful, so absolutely unique in human
history, is that they simply told what they had seen a living person do, and what they had heard him say. This
wonderful person has been endorsed as no other being ever
was or ever will be. Not only the millions who have risked
their eternal future upon his words and works, but great
statesmen, soldiers, philosophers, and even the great infidel
leaders of the opposition to his system, have endorsed him as
no other member of the human race has ever been. Napo-
leon, the greatest genius for action the world has probably ever
produced, has given the most remarkable testimony of modern times. A king and the founder of a kingdom alone can
fully appreciate a king and the founder of a kingdom. The
great emperor, comparing himself, Cæsar, Alexander, and
Charlemagne, as founders of empires, with Jesus of Nazareth, is amazed at the brief standing of the most remarkable
kingdoms founded upon force, compared with the long duration and the ever-increasing vitality of a kingdom founded
upon love. The judgment was just. Already the kingdom
of Messiah has lasted more than six hundred and fifty years
longer than the most stable of all earthly states, the old Roman republic and empire. Not one penny now flows into
the treasury of the Cæsars; ever-increasing millions flow into
the treasury of the Nazarene every year. Not one human
being now stretches a limb to obey the orders of a prince
whose word would once have set in motion a hundred millions of men, from the border of Scotland to the Euphrates in
Asia. Thousands of faithful men, and gentle women too, go
out over all the seas and tempt the rage of all barbarous
tribes, in obedience to the words, "Go ye into all the world
and preach the gospel to every creature." No wonder Napo-
leon said to his suite in St. Helena, "I know men, and I
tell you, Jesus is not a man." If any one ever knew what
man can do, it was the man who had done perhaps more than

any one man had ever done before, and this was his judgment of the Messiah of the kingdom. But more striking still is the endorsement of the great infidel leaders of our own day. Strauss, the leader of the modern infidels, speaks of him "as the highest object we can possibly imagine with respect to religion, the being without whose presence in the mind perfect piety is impossible." Hegel sees in him "the union between the human and divine." At an earlier day, Spinoza sees in him "the best and truest symbol of heavenly wisdom." Kant discovers in him "ideal perfection." Rousseau strains his wonderful eloquence to exalt him. Even the sneering spirit of Voltaire is awed in his presence. His worst enemies fall upon their knees as they gaze at him. This is the great personal witness of the gospel. The notion that the only personal witnesses of the facts lying at the base of the Christian system are the apostles, is wholly mistaken. They are worthy of the highest confidence, but they are not the only witnesses. The Christ himself, this grand embodiment of all purity and truth, testifies to his own gospel: "I tell you the truth." Endorsed more highly by the infidels themselves than any other witness was ever endorsed, his clear and positive testimony creates an obligation to believe, than which no similar obligation can be conceived to be higher. If unimpeachable evidence can create such a bond, the evidence of the Christian faith creates it in its highest form. The common-sense intuitions of all men pronounce that competent proof creates obligation to believe, which no man can refuse to obey without guilt. The gospel only confirms that decision.

(2.) A second element of obvious responsibility in saving faith is the fact that it is a datum of will; it is an issue of the heart in man. "With the heart man believeth unto righteousness." Unbelief is the outcome of "an evil heart of unbelief." This assertion is resented by the infidels of the day, who pride themselves on the philosophic candor of their judgments, and their rigorous obedience to the laws of scientific investigation. That they are consciously so, we have no disposition to deny of any; we are sure of the truth of this claim on the part of many of them. But we are also sure that there is such a thing as honest self-deception. We are even more certain that these speculators are not emancipated from the universal law, recognized by the common-sense judgments of men as well as by the Scriptures, which binds the *human will* in an unchangeable relation to evidence on all subjects whatever. It cannot be expected, then, that any fair analyst of the genesis of beliefs should exempt them from responsibility for the implication of their voluntary faculties in their opinions and from the obligation of that grand moral law called into play whenever the voluntary and moral energies of the human spirit are exerted, and preside over the formation of the resulting judgments. It is vain to attempt to obscure, much less to destroy, the relation of *faith to evidence*, the relation of *evidence to will*, the relation of *moral law to will* dealing with the evidence, and the consequent responsibility for belief. If men are responsible for their beliefs on all subjects whatever, these skeptical and infidel thinkers are not just in claiming an exemption from full responsibility for their accepted conclusions.

That the saving faith of the gospel is to a grave extent a datum of the will or heart in man is shown by more than one proof. It has been shown already that the action of the will in the formation of beliefs is recognized as universally true of all judgments whatever by the common-sense of mankind. It is not strange that the saving faith of the gospel should be qualified by an element recognized as universally prevalent; it would be strange if it were not. Every one of the three species of faith in the Christian system already described as historical, temporary, and the faith of devils, is strongly colored by the influence of the voluntary and moral powers; it would be an unaccountable anomaly if the fourth species of saving faith were not similarly qualified.

But more than this, the moral tastes, affections, emotions and permanent dispositions, which are all characteristic determinations of the voluntary powers of the soul, are *directly concerned* in the genesis of the unbelief and the saving faith which determine the issues of the Christian gospel for good or ill. This inevitably determines obligation and responsibility at every step of the processes of both these opposite conclusions, unbelief and faith. A brief detail of those processes, showing the coloring influence of the prevailing tastes and inclinations of the will, will make this plain.

Faith is the belief of testimony; unbelief is the refusal to believe it. The testimony may be either personal or impersonal. Impersonal testimony may be the force of reasoning, the power in facts, the concurrence of circumstances, or the adhesion of a system. If either of these species of proof are clearly and powerfully developed, they create an obligation to believe, proportionate to their own conclusiveness, which cannot be resisted without a corresponding responsibility. Personal testimony is the declaration of a person, and both of these classes allow the strong influence of the voluntary and moral energies in the production of the conclusions reached. A person testifies concerning the character of another person, and declares that he is a wise and good man. Suppose, now, this testimony is fully believed, what is the effect? In the first place it *approves the witness;* it relies upon him as at once competent in intelligence to discern, and morally trustworthy to report character in men. In the second place, belief in the testimony not only approves the witness, but approves *the subject-matter* of the testimony, and accepts the person referred to as a wise and good man. But suppose, now, there are strong and fixed feelings of hostility in the heart of him to whom the testimony is given, against the person referred to, the opposite conclusions would be reached, and would be altogether due to the hostile feelings which qualified the testimony of the witness. The witness himself would be impeached, either as mistaken or false, and the subject-matter of the testimony, instead of being approved as wise and good, would be assailed by the unbelief of the testimony as neither wise nor good. Unbelief not only impeaches the witness, but strikes directly at the subject of the testimony. To say we do not believe one to be wise is the same thing as to say he is foolish. To say we do not believe him to be good or honest is to say he is bad or dishonest. This is a sample of personal testimony. Take one of impersonal testimony. The Scriptures and the just intuitions of the human understanding assert that sin is a hateful, and holiness a lovely and lovable thing. To believe that asseveration to be true is to approve the testimony which asserts it, and to endorse the subject-matter of the testimony as being actually what the testimony asserts it to be, to really accept sin as hateful and holiness as lovely. But now suppose the heart is in love with sin and sees it as agreeable; suppose the heart is opposed to holiness and sees it as a needless puritanical precision, what would be the effect? Certainly the testimony would be rejected; and the unbelief generated directly by the state of the depraved affections would leave the mind fully possessed with the conviction that sin was not hateful but pleasing, that holiness was not lovely but disagreeable. The direct cause of this fatal unbelief is the state of the heart. The sample illustrates the whole. The conclusion is resistless that, inasmuch as the tastes and inclinations of the voluntary powers of the soul do enter so greatly and control so powerfully the genesis of faith, that grace is properly brought under the obligation of moral law, and men are lawfully commanded to obey it when it requires men to believe aright.

The analysis also discloses the awful sinfulness of unbelief when applied to the testimony of God in his word. It as-

sails the divine witness in the first instance. It is in vain
for the infidel to protest that he does not assail God, but
only the witnesses who have pretended to impart his testimony. They assail the testimony; if that testimony is only
the testimony of Paul and John, then truly only Paul and
John are assailed; but if they really did speak as moved by
the Holy Ghost, and as the mere mouth-pieces of Almighty
God, it is impossible to avoid the conclusion that they
assail the divine witness and make him a liar. Yet further,
as unbelief not only assails the witness, but strikes, through
the dishonored testimony, at the matter it contains, unbelief
of the records which God has given is really one sublime
energy of wickedness assailing all the matter contained in
the testimony. That testimony contains all the grand principles of his moral administration in nature and in grace.
It asserts the rightful authority, the wisdom, and the equity
of his laws. It asserts all the grand excellences of his personal character. It affirms the beauty and blessedness of
his service. It asserts the wonders of his love in the redemption of grace. It declares the existence of heaven and
hell; it offers the one; it warns against the other. It un-
covers the history of the past; it foretells of the future. It
warns and entreats; it threatens and pleads. To all this
unbelief gives a negative. It denies all, and by this denial
not only assails the witness, but assails the whole subject-
matter of his testimony. It assails the authority and excellence of the law. It assails the character of God. It assails his grace and renounces his redemption. It denies
heaven; it denies hell. It will have nothing as God would
have it. It would reverse all the matter of the testimony *if
its power could realize its tendencies.* It is weak in its malignity, but it is none the less malignant for that. It is to be
judged by what it would do if it could. This effect, however,
it does accomplish. While unbelief in the excellence of the
divine law, for example, does not make that law a bad law,

it does make it a bad law *to him* who indulges this unbelief. While powerless in its malignant tendencies on all the truth it assails, outwardly considered, it does succeed in transmuting all the truth it denies to the mind of the individual who disbelieves. To him the law of God is a harsh and unreasonable bond; the character of God only an occasion of hate and fear; his grace is a dream, and his wrath a bug-bear. It reverses every item in the matter of the testimony, denies and assails all, and fills him who indulges the wicked and destructive principle with an immeasurable and most guilty responsibility. To prohibit such a principle, and to command men to yield to the principle opposed to it, and to believe the testimony of God, is too conspicuously right to admit of any rational denial. To command men to believe the gospel, with the usual notions of moral responsibility for obedience to the command, appears an incomprehensible piece of folly to the skeptics of the day. This is due to the fact that they are accustomed to regard belief as the determination of the intellect alone, unaffected by any energy of the will, as a result of evidence alone, which they are accustomed to consider omnipotent over belief. The notion is absurd and impossible, contradicted by the universal common-sense judgments of mankind, and repudiated in all the scenes of intellectual activity among men. The influence of the will, and the moral tastes and dispositions grounded in the will, in the genesis of faith of every kind, imposes the authority of moral law over the whole process, and requires *just* judgments to be formed. It thus becomes absolutely proper to command men to believe, and to hold them answerable for their beliefs.

(3.) Another element in the obligatory and responsible character of saving faith is that it is a *trust*, and a *trust in a person*. A trust is an act of the will, which always carries responsibility. It is an act of committal to an agent to act for us, the choice of a person to whom grave interests are committed to be administered. It is an act of choice. It is an act of confidence which must be vindicated in order to justify the trust. If events show the confidence was misplaced, the chooser and maker of the trust will stand responsible for his choice as truly as if he had had no agent, and had acted for himself. The degrees of this responsibility admit of wide variations, from mere misfortune to positive criminality in risking grave concerns without due caution. But responsibility is involved in the very nature of a trust-responsibility on both parties to it—on him who makes it and on him who undertakes it.

In our initial illustration, bringing out distinctly the difference between belief in a record and faith in a person, this notion of a trust was clearly involved. In the Scripture lessons about saving faith, this notion of a trust is often expressed and always implied. "Trust ye in the Lord forever," "who first trusted in Christ," are specimen instances from both of the Testaments. To believe in a person is, in general form, to confide in him, which is only another name for trusting in him. This species of trust may exist where nothing is expected of the trusted person. It is another and a more pointed form of a trust, when, confiding in his integrity, some valued interest is committed to his charge. In our parallel of the imprisoned debtor, supposing him resolved to accept the generous offer of his friend, it is plain that the second act of his faith was a trust in his friend as a person. The first act was to accept the note containing the offer as truly a communication from his friend. But while believing this, he was not satisfied at first of the ability of his friend to pay his debt, or, satisfied of his ability, felt suspicious of his willingness to do an action of such transcendent generosity. This state of mind indicated belief in the authenticity of the letter, and a want of confidence in the person. But now supposing this want of confidence to give way, and a thorough conviction of both the ability and willingness of his friend to do what he offered to do, this new state of mind indicates more than one change. It reveals not only belief in the authenticity of the letter, but confidence in the words it contains; not only confidence in the words spoken, but a confidence in the person who spoke them; and not only a confidence in the person, but a consent to his proposal, an acceptance of his offer, and a *trust* in the person to do what he offered to do. This trust is an act of the will, a motion of the heart, committing freely to his friend the doing of all the acts necessary to be done in order to free him from his debt, and to deliver him from the prison. This trust in a person is a trust in his own words, and also in his works, in his veracity as well as in his kindness, in his ability as well as in his good will. It is immediately followed by peace of mind, and this is the peace of saving faith; it is due only to this trust in a person. Then, when all is done, the debt paid, the necessary papers of the prison authorities signed, and the prisoner, leaving his cell, begins to pass along the prison corridors to liberty at the gate, his exultation is renewed; and this is the joy of experience which follows the saving faith in the person of the Redeemer. This is the peace of the whole Christian life in part, until the gate is opened and the trusting soul is admitted into the full liberty of the state of glory. In part, the peace of that period of progress towards the completed deliverance rests still on the offer, the promise, the kindness, ability, and faithfulness of the glorious person who has undertaken to deliver. A mere persuasion that Christ will save, without a distinct acceptance of his offer, without definite reference to his own words, and confidence in them, and without a definite trust in himself and a definite committal of the work of saving into his hands, is a travesity of this saving faith, which is dangerous. The trust and acceptance logically precede the persuasion that he will save, and the two are not to be confounded.

It is obvious that this trust in the person of the offered

deliverer was obligatory on the imprisoned debtor. He would have been guilty in a high degree to have failed to confide in his generous friend, to accept his offer, and to trust in his person, his words, his ability and willingness to redeem his pledge, and his pledged activity in doing all the work necessary to redeem it. Every conceivable obligation of gratitude, love, and confidence bound the act of trust and demanded it. The prisoner might have been properly exhorted and commanded to do it. An appeal to will, grounded upon such grave obligatory considerations created a profound obligation to believe and live. Such is saving faith as directed upon the Saviour as a person. It is a trust in himself as a person, as a living Saviour now administering his grace on the throne of heaven. It also implies a trust in his works, already finished, as well as in his work yet to be done in carrying out his pledge to save. It is a trust in his work as a dying Saviour—in the efficacy of his atonement. It is a trust in his words as already spoken; for they contain the offer of his grace, the promise of his saving intervention, and all the grand truths he proposes to the faith of his people for their comfort in their pilgrimage. It is a trust in his works as a living Saviour working out the everlasting righteousness which grounds all his positive gifts to his saints. This was done during his earthly life, and is found among the things which he triumphantly proclaimed complete on the cross. Saving faith is not only a belief that these works were done, and that these gracious words were spoken, but a trust in both words and works themselves.

(4.) Saving faith, as directed not only on the Saviour as a person, but upon all the truths which God has been pleased to reveal in his word, is a *double energy of moral and intellectual qualities, and yet has no special merit in itself considered.* Let us endeavor to understand each of these three predications concerning faith.

Faith contains definite moral qualities, as must result from

its being a product of the heart and will, obedient to the
moral laws imposed upon the process of its production. It
works by love; it purifies the heart; it overcomes the world.
The exposition of faith as a product of the will and the moral
expressions of the will, has shown how the heart is concerned in the genesis, and modifies the nature of faith. It
has been seen how hostile feelings towards the person referred to would mar the testimony to his wisdom and goodness. It has been seen how love to sin and aversion to
holiness would balk the testimony to the hatefulness of the
one, and the loveliness of the other. All moral and religious
truth is subject to the same hostile and transfiguring
influence of an unholy heart. The character of God, the
nature of his law, the sovereignty, the freedom, and infinite
magnanimity and tenderness of his grace; every statement of
fact, every exposition of doctrine, every truth, whatever he
has declared, has been distorted from their true significance
by this deadly energy of depraved feeling. The field of
view in the intellect has been discolored by this disturbing influence, and all that is seen through it is not seen as it
is. As the green leaves of a tree seen through the deep
crimson surface of a colored glass will be seen in foreign
and not in their real colours, so all moral and religious
truth will be more or less warped out of its real meaning by
the influence of the unholy heart. The seer will see, but
not perceive; he will be as blind to the true significance of
the truth as if he could not see at all. This is what is meant
by the spiritual blindness of the mind, which is represented
by the Scriptures as coëxisting and entirely compatible with
any amount of intellectual energy. When the record asserts
the beauty of holiness, the unbelief of the depraved heart
will deny it and assert the contrary. When it asserts any
truth which crosses the inclinations and tastes of a perverted
will, unbelief, determined by the depraved affections, will impeach the conclusion.

It is manifest, then, that to enable faith really to accept the whole testimony of God in his word, *the depraved heart must be changed.* Until this is done the misguiding crimson in the glass will make the leaves of the tree appear in similar colors, and the seer will never believe the leaves are green or anything but what he sees them to be. Does he not see they are crimson and not green? Is he not perfectly honest in so seeing, and in so saying? He is entirely unconscious that he is looking through a perverted medium of depraved feeling, and until he is awakened to the discernment of his sin, he will see no error in his views. But if his heart can be changed, then he will be able to see and believe aright, and according to the real nature of the truth. Saving faith, then, is strongly qualified by the right moral apprehensions of a heart rightly qualified by the grace of regeneration, and without this qualification of this particular grace it can never exist in a human soul. "With the heart man believeth unto righteousness," and this faith works by love. If the principle by which it works is love, it can only exist in a carnal heart by the precedent implanting of the force which moves it. Unbelief is the datum of an unholy heart, and saving faith is the datum of a regenerate and holy heart.

Saving faith is also qualified by the intellectual qualities which enter into all faiths; but in this species of faith these intellectual qualities are given *by a mind peculiarly energized.* All faiths are in part the issues of mental activity. Faith is the belief of testimony and the acceptance of things as true. This implies the action of the understanding in judging the testimony and in apprehending the thing to be believed. There is no dispute about this point. Incompetent mental action will result in credulity and in error, and men are not slow to see and censure the intellectual work which falls short of a rational standard. But the intellectual energies which enter into saving faith spring from a mind itself under peculiar influences. This is evident from what has already been said touching the influence of the perverted will on the views of the understanding, and the necessity of a change of heart in order to justness of view and rightness of belief. This effect on the mind is called in the Scriptures "enlightening the eyes," and "opening the eyes of the blind." That extraordinary effect which moral evil has produced on the discernment of the understanding, by which it sees, yet does not perceive, presents one of the most extraordinary of all the phenomena of mind. There is no doubt in any human intellect, for example, of the certainty of the fact, and the uncertainty of the period, of that strange mystery of death. Men walk perpetually under a liability of the most strange and striking character; they know it absolutely; yet practically it is apprehended only as a distant possibility, and under colors which disguise the grandeur and pathos of the situation. It is seen, yet not perceived. Sin is intellectually apprehended as an evil, yet is felt to be agreeable, and the evil is not discerned. This disablement of the power of perception by the influence of the depraved will can only be removed by a peculiar power exerted upon the disordered faculty which produces the disability in question; and when this is done, the power of perception is restored to the understanding, and the eyes of the blind are opened. The influence of this restored energy of the intellect in the production of saving faith will then be felt.

Saving faith, however, in spite of the moral and intellectual qualities in it, and although it is "the fruit of the Spirit," has no *special* merit or excellence in itself. It performs high offices in the scheme of redemption: we are justified by faith, we walk by faith, faith gives power to prayer, and leads into the comforts of hope; yet it does all this merely as an instrument, and not by any virtue of its own. Faith is powerful only because it mediates the grace by which all the wonders of faith are accomplished. There is a righteousness of faith, not because faith constitutes or creates it, but

because it *conveys* it. Faith works by *love*, but is distinct
from the love that impels it. Faith is distinctly pronounced
to be less than charity. Faith believes God and trusts in
him ; but while the refusal to do this would involve great
guilt, doing it is only compliance with strong obligation, and
involves no special merit. Faith, in a word, has been appointed as the mere instrument for the action of grace ; it is
of faith that it might be of grace ; and all the triumphs of
faith are due to the grace it conveys, and not to itself. It
appeals to power outside of itself, and thus confesses its own
weakness. It appeals to the righteousness of Christ, and
thus confesses the want of it in itself. It appeals for all
things to an outward source, and thus confesses its own barrenness. It is merely the empty hand stretched out to receive all the gifts needed to save an impoverished soul. It
is not without a measure of spiritual excellence, for no gift
of the Spirit is utterly wanting in it; but it is mainly considerable from the values it conveys, not in its own. As the
main instrument of grace, it ranks in value chief of the graces;
as an intrinsic value, it is below love, and in the same rank
with hope, joy, gentleness, and other fruits of the Spirit.

(5.) Saving faith is described in the Scriptures as a principle
by means of which the power of different kinds of truth is
drawn out, and thus becomes an instrument of sanctification
of the second remove, and a regulating force over character
and action. The grace of the Spirit is the efficient of sanctification ; the truth is the instrument nearest to the effect;
and faith, which elicits the force of the truth, is the second
instrumentality in producing it. Faith is defined as "the
substance of things hoped for, the evidence of things not
seen." If a man is informed that his house has been burned
and his family destroyed, if he did not believe it, he would
feel no distress, even though the report might be true. On
the other hand, if he did believe it, he would be overwhelmed
with grief, even though the report might be false. Faith in

the one case would give substance and reality to what is *false;* in the other, unbelief would strip *truth* of its power. It is evident that such a principle is full of power in this direction, however undistinguished for moral merit. This capacity of realizing truth and bringing out its force will operate different effects, according to the nature of the truth thus realized by faith. Threatening truth thus apprehended will produce fear; hopeful truth will produce joy; promises will yield expectation; commands will produce obedience. Faith thus will cause offers to be accepted, a person to be trusted, sins to be surrendered, and warnings to be taken. Faith will energize and produce all the various passions of the heart. Noah was moved by fear to the building of the ark. Abraham, by hope to look for a city with foundations. Joseph made his bones the seal of a promise of deliverance to his people. It is powerful to mould character and animate activity; to breed hope, and throw wide open the realities of the eternal state revealed in the record. Faith thus becomes the instrument of all Christian comfort, as well as of all progress in the conformity of character to the divine image, and of conduct to the divine will.

(6.) This saving faith is represented under some aspects so apparently paradoxical as to create a feeling of perplexity and sometimes of irritation in constraining it. But the paradox is only in appearance, and the consistency with truth and justice can easily be made to appear. It has already been seen that the absurdity, as it appears to many, of a command and requirement to believe in spite of the strong dependence of faith upon evidence, is vindicated from the charge, and shown to be exactly appropriate from the relation of the will to evidence, and from the relation of moral law to will. The paradox is only apparent, not real. In like manner, this faith is declared to be beyond the capacity of the soul in its natural condition, and yet it is justly required to be exercised. This statement appears, not only to be paradoxical, but unjust. The vindication is very simple. There are two kinds of inability to action, one of which does exempt from responsibility, and the other actually increases it. The one is the inability of a paralytic to walk; the other is the inability of a drunkard to keep sober. The one inability lies outside of the will, and is not subject to its control, or to the jurisdiction of moral law, to command or prohibition. The other lies in the will, and consists in its depravity, and is, therefore, under the jurisdiction of law, and subject to command. One man may not be able to attend to his business because he is sick, and another because he is drunk. The common-sense of mankind adjudges one to be blameless, and the other to be blameworthy; it sees the incapacity of one is the proper object of pity, the incapacity of the other the just object of censure. The incapacity of the carnal mind to exercise faith is of the latter kind; it lies in the will, and not out of it; it consists in the strength of the perverted affections of the will, which disable the strength of the evidence and the power of the truth. The stronger the evidence, the more censurable the perversity of feeling which disables it. Since it has been abundantly shown that the will is deeply involved in the genesis of faith, according to the common judgments of mankind as well as of Scripture, it is perfectly useless to impeach the decision, that when faith is disabled by the power of perverted affections in the will, responsibility is properly imputed for unbelief or misbelief.

When this aversion of the will is so strong as to defy control, the notion of responsibility increases in proportion to the strength of this aversion, and cannot possibly be diminished, much less destroyed by it. When that aversion is so powerful as to defy the control of the man himself, and no power but the power of God himself can govern it, and that, too, in some of the highest acts of almighty power, the notion of responsibility is carried to the highest conceivable point, instead of being destroyed. The obligation of duty remains unimpaired by the disability of a perverted will to obey it. This apparent paradoxy may receive another expression. Faith is the gift of God, and yet the duty of man. It is the gift of God because he alone can break down the resistance of the perverted will. It is the duty of man because no moral obligation is broken down by any amount of vigor in the aversion to discharge it. Faith being an issue of will, and under just obligation of moral propriety, cannot possibly be discharged from full responsibility, because of aversion in the will to accept the truth, that is, to *believe.* The more powerful that aversion, the more complete the inability it creates and constitutes, the higher the responsibility is carried, instead of being weakened, and much less of being destroyed. The two teachings of the Christ are both true, both consistent, and one true because the other is true; "ye will not come unto me that ye might have life ;" and "no man can come unto me except the Father which hath sent me draw him." He alone can "make us willing in the day of his power."

(7.) Saving faith is represented under a variety of forms in the testimony of God. It is called a *looking.* "Look unto me all ye ends of the earth, and be ye saved, saith the Lord; for I am God, and there is none else." Looking is a common expression of reliance or trust; a servant looks to his master, a soldier to his commander, a patient to his physician, a client to his counsel. "I look to you to do it," is an ordinary expression of holding to responsibility for a trust committed. It is called a *coming.* "Come unto me all ye who are weary and are heavy laden." The same notion of applying for help and going for assistance, appealing to the power and good-will of another, is expressed by this phrase. Faith is called acceptance, the *receiving of a gift*: "take the water of life freely." It is spoken of as *the giving of a gift*: "my son, give my thy heart." Confidence is often spoken of as something *given*. It is described as eating, as drinking, as going, as resting, as learning, all of which carry the notion of resorting to something apart from self for strength and comfort. Saving faith is the act of the whole human soul accepting all the truths contained in the testimony of God, with a realizing sense of their truth, and trusting in that glorious person who is the grand centre of all the truth thus revealed. It is the fruit of the Spirit, the gift of God in the exercise of his sovereign and distinguishing grace, the greatest of all his inward gifts to a lost sinner. It is the gift of eternal life. "He that believeth shall be saved."

CHAPTER VI.

THE NECESSITY OF REGENERATION.

"Marvel not that I said unto thee, ye must be born again."—*Jesus of Nazareth.*

1. THESE words introduce us to one of the great peculiar doctrines of the Christian faith. They were spoken by the great founder of that faith, and carry all the weight of his character and authority in the establishment of the doctrine taught. Nicodemus, an officer of high rank in the religious orders of the temple system, had been profoundly impressed by the wonderful works done by the Nazarene prophet. His intellectual convictions had been determined by them, that Jesus was a teacher sent from God. He became eager to inquire more fully into the nature of the message which had been sent by him to the people of Israel. But knowing the intense prejudice, which even at that early stage of the prophet's ministry had taken possession of the religious leaders of the nation, and not yet having come under the power of the truth, he sought a secret interview with the great teacher. This secrecy indicated the imperfection of his faith; his coming at all showed the strength and sincerity of his convictions. His introductory words reveal no hesitation or doubt in the judgment he had formed on the evidence of the miracles. "Rabbi, we know that thou art a teacher come from God: for no man can do these miracles that thou doest except God be with him." The intellectual conviction was absolute; it was actual knowledge, not any inferior grade of belief. The reasoning which led to this conviction was both sound and irresistible; miracle was demonstration of a divine commission. The reply

of Jesus, on a first inspection, seems to be somewhat irrelevant, or its relevancy is not immediately apparent. "Verily, verily, I say unto thee, except a man be born again, he cannot see the kingdom of God." But in point of fact the reply was not only to the point, but happily led forward into a further development of the ideas involved in his mission, and opened the way to settle the principal purpose which the Jewish ruler had in view.

At that time the Jewish mind was in a feverish ferment about the coming of Messiah, and the kingdom which he was about to establish. The time indicated in the prophecies was universally understood to be at hand; and to find out what this demonstrated messenger of God had to say in relation to these intensely exciting facts was the end sought by Nicodemus. The reply of Messiah was, then, substantially this: your conclusion is rightly drawn; the wonderful exhibition of divine power does prove me to be a teacher come from God; but a similar exhibition of the same power is necessary to enable any man to understand the nature, or perceive the advent, of the kingdom he is about to set up. Nicodemus was astounded; in common with all other Jews he expected a kingdom as cognizable by the unaided natural faculties of men as the kingdom of David had been in the life-time of the royal soldier and poet, who was the pride of Israel. He was confounded to have his unspoken inquiry about the kingdom of Messiah answered by an assertion that made a miraculous or similar exertion of divine power necessary to see it when it came, or to enter into its privileges. He rejoined in vague confusion, "How can a man be born when he is old?" His conceptions were altogether below the plane on which Jesus was leading him up. Jesus went on to explain, prefacing his explanation and defence with an expression of wonder on his own part, that one who held the high official position of the master or chief of the ruling teachers of Israel should be utterly unacquainted with

the spiritual nature of that kingdom of God whose necessary first foundation and form was to be laid in the very
soul—in the thoughts and affections of man. Nicodemus
had suggested the intolerable mystery of the doctrine involved in the impossibility of the case. Messiah at once
replied, It is indeed mysterious, but not impossible; mystery
attaches to many a thing which is nevertheless real; the
wind is an example; but although no man can tell the spot
where it rises in the vast sea of the surrounding air, nor the
line where it stops, no man ever questions its reality. He
then goes on to explain that the kingdom of God laid its
foundations in the inward nature of man; no one could be a
true servant and subject of the King who did not serve him
with the heart, and, therefore, the evil heart must be changed
if it ever sees the nature of the kingdom, or becomes a true
servant of the King Messiah. The alleged impossibility is
set aside by a reiteration of the fact, and the positive assertion of the absolute necessity for it.

2. This teaching of our Lord sets at rest all rational doubt
about this wonderful doctrine of Christianity. The astonish-
ment of Nicodemus, and the firm assent of Christ to the
fact, both demonstrate the assertion of something marvelous
as necessary to the true apprehension of the kingdom. No
attempt is made to disguise the fact, and all human attempts
to obscure the teaching will be in vain. It plainly affirms an
effect must be exerted on the soul, which can only be adequately described as a *new birth, a being born again.* It is
elsewhere described as a *new creation,* and as *a resurrection
from the dead.* It is positively assigned as the exclusive effect of *divine will and power ;* it is a being born, *not of man,
nor of the will of man, but of God.* It is ascribed solely to
the energy of the Holy Ghost. The very term, *born of the
Spirit,* points clearly both to the agent of the change and the
radical nature of his work. As the word *born,* descriptive of
the mode of man's creation and introduction to the condi-

tions of his existence in the present life, is used to describe the effect, something equally radical in its nature and effects must be involved in the analogous change. The natural birth puts the human being into the full possession of his nature as such a being. If not born, all the preliminary constituents of his being are nullified, and his nature is not only not completed and put into his possession in order to serve its purposes, but it is absolutely prohibited and destroyed. The *new birth* also involves the creation and the grant of a new nature adjusted to its own uses and ends. Natural birth introduces to new conditions of life, new laws of action, new responsibilities, new associations, new possibilities of both pleasure and pain, new powers of action, and new capabilities of influence. It makes a new man. It not only makes a new being, but introduces him into the adjustments for its action. In like manner, the effects of the *new birth* are equally radical and pervading, giving a new nature, making a new man, as an apostle calls it, and introducing this new nature into a new life adjusted to it, to new views, new feelings, new affections and desires, new hopes, new fears, new energies, new rules of conduct, new objects of endeavor, and new results of the new action determined by this great change.

It is obvious from these positive and most peculiar statements that all attempts to construe the Christian doctrine of regeneration out of all its high mysterious and spiritual significance must be altogether incompetent interpretations of the language used to describe it in the sacred record. To construe it as nothing more than the modifying influence exerted upon thought and feeling by the written words of the Scriptures, identical in nature with the influence exerted by the written words of any other author, is not only inadequate as an explanation of the terms used, but is positively refuted by the assertion that the gospel must come, not in word only, but in power and in the Holy Ghost. To say it

is only the change in the external relations effected by a
visible rite, which not only can be administered by man, but
which in point of fact can be administered by no one
but man, is not only absolutely in contravention of the positive ascription of the effect exclusively to the will and power
of God, but it is to convict the terms used in Scripture to
define it of a want of candor or of clearness in making the
definition.   All attempts to identify this change with the
mere ordinance of baptism, or with the mere modifications
of thought and feeling produced by the influence of written
words, are useless.   All attempts to construe it as a mere
change in any outward or merely legal relations of a man
are failures, complete in abortiveness.   It is a change inward, not outward, a change of nature, not of relations.   It
is not a change of mere *state*, defined by relations to an
outward order or law of action.   Even when contemplated as
an inward change, it is not merely a change of *habits*, or
even of some modifications of *character ;* for these may be
effected by human energies and associations, by human
will and moral culture.   It goes deeper than any such influences can reach.   It is a profound movement on that inner
moral energy which determines thought and feeling—which
forms character, which dictates action, and thus creates
habits.   It goes to the bottom of the deep radical disorder
of the human heart.

To define *the nature* of anything is not easy, because it is
one of those primitive conceptions given by the intuitive
energy of the mind, easily enough apprehended as existing,
but not comprehensible to define.   We readily understand
that it is the *nature* of a fruit tree which determines the
kind of fruit it produces.   From this it is easy to discern
that it is due to difference in the nature of the trees that one
produces one kind of fruit, and the other another kind.   But
what the nature in each of the trees actually is, or what constitutes the difference in their nature, no wit has ever dis-

covered or will ever discover. The fact is known; the method or the causative quality called the nature of the tree is beyond analysis and definition. All we know is, that the nature of a fruit tree is an indefinable force in the tree, which results in the production of a certain fruit. The nature of an animal is a certain characteristic force or disposition which dictates certain modes of action peculiar to the animal. Nature is a force which grounds and regulates energy. There is thus a nature in man which determines certain results, variously modified as that nature itself is modified. Man has a physical nature which determines certain physical functions in his life. He has an intellectual nature which determines certain intellectual functions and activities. He has as the chief distinction and the master principle of his whole being, a *moral nature*, which yields moral results. To control the manifestations of his nature, physical, mental, or moral, that nature in its characteristic marks must be controlled. The stream of energy must be regulated by regulating the fountain from which it flows. The grand doctrine of Christ, then, touching the regeneration of man's moral nature, is in strict accordance with the laws and analogies of nature, in all its various departments. There is nothing strange or eccentric in it.

3. The incompetence of any other view of the real meaning of regeneration will be still more clearly demonstrated by an examination into the nature of the evil to be removed. This will prove the absolute necessity of a profound change in the moral condition of the human soul. The declaration of our Lord is, *Ye must be born again.* This affirms a necessity absolutely uncompromising. A view of the difficulty which grounds this necessity will vindicate his words, and show the utter folly of any conception of regeneration less radical than a total change in the very nature of a sinning being in order to his salvation.

The first fact which illustrates the nature of the evil to be

removed before man can be saved is, that every creature or
form of existence in the universe must conform *to the law*
of its being in order to meet the ends and offices of its being.
In non-sensitive existence, non-conformity to the law of its
nature must produce disorder and confusion. In sensitive
beings, non-conformity must produce disease and suffering.
A fish in the air, or a bird in the water must suffer and ultimately die. In beings conditioned to conform to the moral
distinction, non-conformity·must result in moral corruption
as well as in suffering. The law is universal. Man as a
moral being has been adjusted to moral law, just as an intellectual being he has been adjusted to the laws of mind, and as
a physical being he has been adjusted to physical law. The
moral law which has been established over the moral creature, man, is not merely confined to his positive transient
actions, but extends its jurisdiction over all the interior and
seminal energies from which his actions flow. It extends
over all feelings, motives, passions, purposes, affections, and
desires, and over all the permanent states of moral feeling
which constitute what is called character, and which, as permanent expressions of the will, involve moral responsibility
as truly and justly as a determined purpose or any other
transient act of the voluntary faculty. In order that man,
then, should conform to the law of his being, it is not merely
necessary he should conform to it in his outward actions,
but that he should conform to it in his whole interior nature,
in the ground of all those interior energies of his spirit which
are embraced in the requisitions of the law, and are capable of a moral complexion, either good or bad. There is no
such thing as securing the well-being of man unless he is
brought up to conformity with the grand law which asserts
its supremacy over him in every particular in which that law
claims his conformity, whether in his acts or in his nature.
The law requires him to be good as well as to do right; its
jurisdiction is over his nature in all that constitutes it, as

well as over his actions; and if his nature has become morally corrupt it must be purified.

The next proof of the necessity of regeneration is found in the actual condition of his moral nature. Man has sinned; he sins continually. That is to say, he has transgressed the grand law of his being, and lives in the constant transgression of it with the disastrous effects that might have been expected. One of the most disastrous of these effects is the actual result produced on his *own moral* nature. This result is a fact in human nature, proceeding under the operation of a regular law of cause and effect, and admits of no more doubt than any other fact observed and ascertained in the nature of the human being. It is one of the old and long established facts in the nature of man, that criminal action of every species exerts a reactionary influence on the nature of the criminal actor himself, corrupting his feelings and rendering him more liable to repeat the criminal act than he was before its commission. He grows worse and worse the more his criminal acts are multiplied, the particular kind of criminal act increasing the inward criminal tendency to that species of evil. Sin in act breeds sin in the soul, and a depraving influence on the moral nature within keeps step with all the active uses of the depraved impulses of the unholy will. This peculiarity of human nature is a datum, not merely of the word of God, but of ordinary observation and experience, which can no more be questioned or denied than that a man will be burnt if he applies fire to his flesh, or be fouled if he falls into a cess-pool. The teachings of Scripture are identical with the teachings of experience, as far as the latter are able to go. The difference lies in the fact that the Scriptures go farther in the explanation of the evil, analyze it more deeply, and point out more fully the extent, nature, and final results of those effects which criminal action has upon the moral nature of the criminal actor. The lesson of experience is enough of itself to disclose the abso-

lute necessity for a vital change of some sort in the depraved
moral nature. The teaching of the Scriptures only makes
that necessity reveal itself in a still more impressive form.
The moral element in human nature pervades the whole intellectual structure of man, just as color pervades the transparency of glass or a pure fluid, and thus regulates its
quality and the view of all that is seen through it. This all-
pervading moral energy is that which adjusts man to that
eternal distinction of right and wrong which determines the
great moral law under which he is bound. That distinction
inhering in his acts makes them good or bad; inhering in
his inward moral energies makes them and him either good
or bad. This judgment, that the actor himself must be either
good or bad, is one of those universal common-sense judgments which men always form of each other from the manifestations of their conduct. Men always go back of a moral
act, whether good or bad, and look at the disposition, temper, and moral character which gave origin to the act. The
act is attributed to a moral energy within, and is accepted as
a revelation of the energy from which it springs. An ex-
plosion of temper is taken to reveal a permanent characteristic in the nature of the man, and he is judged to be a hot-
tempered man. All acts are judged in the same way; they
are held to disclose a trait or capacity in the fixed moral
energies, answerable in moral quality to the moral quality of
the act that springs from them. The law holds of all acts or
energies whatever; it is equally true of good and evil acts;
all are held to be the expression of an answerable quality in
the permanent characteristics of the man. Now if this intuitive judgment of a moral nature in man, lying back of his
acts, and regulating their moral complexion as true expressions of itself, is a true diagnosis of human nature, the inference is irresistible, that any effectual reform of man as an evil-
doer necessarily requires the reform and purification of the
permanent moral energies which determine the character of

his outward conduct. This is the invincible decision of logic and common sense. To purify the stream the fountain must be purified; the stream can never be effectually cleansed as long as a polluted head-spring is perpetually pouring polluted water into the channel. The teachings of Messiah coincide with this conclusion of reason and experience. Man cannot gather grapes of thorns, nor figs of thistles. It is vain to purify a cup or a platter unless the inside, as well as the outside, is cleansed.

But the Scriptures go deeper in their discernment of the effects of sin on the nature of the sinner. They speak of a *spiritual life*. Life is a capacity to exert certain energies, distinctive of the kind of life in view. Spiritual life is a capability of moral energies, embracing *the whole* sphere of moral obligations; not merely the moral obligations which embrace the present life, and all the relations of man to his fellow-man, but moral obligations as they embrace every degree and possibility of moral energy, and man's relations to God as well as to his fellow-creatures. This implies a far broader and higher form and degree of moral energy than is disclosed by the lower system of relations limited to the creature. *Holiness* is but another name for this spiritual life. Morality, or the moral quality, in common parlance is usually confined to the relations between creatures. Holiness in the same usage of language is applied to the relations between God and the creature. Holiness is, in fact, moral excellence in its completed form, developed by a right state of all the relations and affections of the creature to God, and flowing over from this right state towards God upon all the relations and affections towards all other beings, raising the moral quality determined by those relations into a higher and purer form. This state of relation and feeling towards God is the supreme controlling moral force over all the moral states and feelings of the creature. It is the key-stone of the arch which holds all other moral states in their proper place.

It is the controlling light which alone gives the proper coloring and complexion to all other states, feelings, and determinations of the moral element of the human soul. Without
holiness all moral quality is more or less depraved. All the
cultured moral virtues of the moral element in human nature
are fatally defective without this all-important coloring of
genuine holiness. Holiness is the principle of real life,
beauty and power in all moral quality. Abolish holiness
and the arch is broken, the beautifying light is withdrawn,
the principle of life is destroyed, and a spiritual death, the
ruin of the capacity to energize purely, at once ensues.
There may be a certain grade or degree of moral excellence
in human character, determined by culture in his relations
to his fellow-men; but it is wretchedly incomplete in its best
development, and wanting in that element which is essential
to its completeness. It is somewhat like what painting
would be if the red ray in the coloring was annihilated; its
perfection as a thing of beauty would be gone. This is the
character of all moral excellence in the natural man; it is
divorced from that element which alone gives life and perfection to moral energy. A figure may be moulded in wax
or carved in marble to a degree of ideal excellence, superior
in charm to any living being; but it wants life; and a living
dog is better than a dead lion. Such is the diagnosis of the
moral nature, and the laws that regulate it, as given in the
Scriptures. They teach the absolute essentiality of holiness
to all true and sound moral energy.

They follow up this teaching by a necessary corollary;
they teach that the effect of one single criminal act is to
destroy this principle of spiritual life. This does not mean
that the moral energy in the soul is destroyed, but depraved.
It does not mean that man becomes incapable of any moral
act, incapable of any moral perceptions, or feelings, or volitions, or deeds, but it does mean that he becomes incapable
of any moral view, feeling, or action which is not defective

in some degree. The vital element of *holiness* is eliminated, and that ingredient being wanting, even the very highest form of natural virtue is essentially defective in obligatory moral excellence, and is, therefore, a species of actual sin. That lofty element which springs from the right state of the relations and feelings towards God-holiness necessarily dies under the reaction of one criminal act. The reason of it is, that even one sin, as a breach of divine law, casts off his authority, insults his sacred claim to obedience and respect, and necessarily arms his justice to uphold them all. One sin breaks all kindly relations between God and the offender; both parties are thrown apart; the transgressor is alienated from God, and God is angry with the wicked doer. The necessary and inevitable result is the loss of holiness, the distinction of the spiritual life, which, as we have seen, is the determination of right relations and feelings of the crea-ture towards God. This is the only element which can give real and complete moral excellence to any basis of moral quality, whether thought, word, deed, or inward moral faculty. The only capability of moral act which is left in the transgressor is of an inferior degree, from which the necessary ingredient of all true and complete moral excel-lence has passed away, without the possibility of its restora-tion by any means within the reach of man's own competency. Hence it is that the loss of holiness, which results even from a single criminal act, is called *spiritual death;* it is the loss of spiritual life, the capacity of spiritual energies which condi-tions all the moral powers of the soul in the same way in which other kinds of life condition the energies peculiar to each of those kinds of life. Moral depravity in its higher degrees results from repeated criminal acts. Holiness is at once destroyed by a single criminal act.

The relation between holiness or spiritual life and mo-rality, and the dependence of both on right relations to God, may be illustrated by the relation between the principle of life and the substance of vegetable existence. Take a tree, for example, as it stands growing on its stock, it has two distinct elements in it, the substance of its matter, and a certain mysterious principle in it which we call its *life*. This life in the wood is dependent on its connection with the living roots and stock in the ground. All *life*, whether in a vegetable or. animal, is an impenetrable mystery. It seems to be an incomprehensible force which creates certain capabilities which are entirely dependent upon it. So long as its mystic life abides in it, it is capable of growth and of putting forth the leaves and fruits peculiar to its nature as a tree. Cut it away from its stock, and the wood becomes *dead*. It ceases to be capable of growth or bearing, and at once becomes subject to a reverse law which will bring it through many a state of change down to decay and final ruin. For a time its usefulness is not destroyed; it can be used as fuel, or wrought into many useful and beautiful forms, *for a time*. But only for a time. The principle of decay was introduced the very moment when its life was destroyed by severance from its vital stock, and it can only end in final destruction. In like manner holiness is the life principle of all moral excellence, and this principle has its vital connection in God. If that connection is severed, it dies instantly, and can never recover it, any more than the mass of noble matter in some great leaf and nut-bearing tree can recover itself after the axe has passed between it and the vital stock on which it grew. It may exist for a time in noble and beautiful shapes; it may be made useful to an extent absolutely inestimable in the domestic and mechanical uses of earthly society. But it is dead; its noblest manifestations are "dead works." Morality without holiness has lost the principle of its *peculiar life*. It has no longer the vital energy which made it capable of spontaneous growth; it can only develop at all under patient and protracted culture. It is still capable of use, change into happy modifications, great polish and cultured beauty, like the dead wood of its analogue; but it is dead; it is under the law of decay from the moment when its peculiar life departed by its severance from God; and however it may be saved to its uses by careful processes for its protection, it will go to decay at last. Mere morality is developed out of the relations between the creatures; it seeks for justice and well-being for them; but makes no provision to secure justice for God. All regard for him and his interests is left out, and thus the very life and saving element of its peculiar nature is destroyed. The noblest exhibit of unsanctified virtues is fatally defective for this reason. A son is commanded by a noble father to go do some noble work; he does the work; but deliberately repudiates all regard to his father's authority in doing it, and does it from the mere sense of his own dignity. All cultured human sentiment will pronounce the noble work marred by selfishness, pride, and repudiation of just authority. Morality without holiness is morality without perfection, and this perfection is dependent wholly on right relations to God, the source of all life.

Thus the invincible necessity for regeneration, a profound moral and spiritual change in the very nature of man as a moral and spiritual being, is revealed. Holiness must be restored to his nature; the principle which is essential to give essential and perfect excellence to every basis of the moral quality in him must be restored, or he can never be delivered from the power of moral evil. Not only must the moral depravity of his moral nature, as it is disclosed to observation and experience, be removed, but in order to this deliverance, and also on account of its own intrinsic value and necessity, *holiness* must be restored. If sinning man is ever to be saved, he must be saved from all the effects of his sin, not only from its effects on his relations to the law, but its inward effects on his own soul. Salvation without regeneration is a contradiction in terms. To talk of saving a sinner, and yet leaving the depraved fountain of his moral energies, a **spring** which must necessarily control the whole current of his energies as long as it exists, unregenerated and unpurified, is to talk of doing that which is absurd and impossible. *Ye must be born again.* The declaration of Christ rests on impregnable grounds.

A second line of investigation will more broadly illustrate this necessity. A more specific inspection of the particular effects of this depraved moral condition of the moral element in human nature will confirm the doctrine of this necessity beyond all rational doubt. This moral element, pervading, as it does, the whole mental structure, will, as a matter of course, exert its influence, *first,* on the views of the *mind; second,* on the affections and desires of the heart; *third,* on the determinations of the will; *fourth,* on the perceptions and power of the conscience; *fifth,* on the action of all the faculties of the mind, on the imagination and the fancy, on the sense of wit and humor, on the processes of reason and judgment; and *sixth,* on the positive actions of the conduct. In a word, it will regulate all the activities of human nature, and color them with its own complexion to a greater or less degree. A depraved moral nature will more or less pollute the views of the mind and the affections of the heart on all kinds of subjects, even on those considered remote from morals and religion. It will taint the sense of wit and humor, the play of fancy, the action of memory, the perceptions and authority of conscience, the positive determinations of the will, and the actions of the life. A pure moral nature will exert the opposite effects on all these various faculties and energies of the soul.

Take the first of these specifications—the perverting influence exerted on *the views of the understanding* by an unholy moral nature, and then inquire how such perverted views are compatible with the idea of salvation. Under such a deadly influence the character of God is necessarily misconceived;

it appears to be an object of dread and dislike. His holiness
seems to be oppressive; his justice, severity. His law is distorted to view, and instead of appearing, as it is, the consummate expression of all wisdom, purity and goodness—the
embodiment of the broad and fruitful distinction of *right*—it
seems to be the harsh and hateful expression of an almighty
tyranny and injustice. To this perverted understanding, the
grace of the gospel, the love of the great Messiah, the infinite patience and benignity of the Holy Ghost, and the rich
provisions of the covenant of redemption, seem to be the fan-
tastic creations of a dreamy fanaticism—utterly without attraction to a rational understanding. All the grand evidences
which support this fabric of revealed religion are utterly
empty of force to such a mind, and all the peculiarities of
doctrine and prescribed service are construed as legitimate
objects of unsparing scorn. The feverish temper of the hate
with which the whole system is regarded is clear in the consciousness of every such sin-misguided intellect. How can
such a system be embraced by a genuine and hearty acceptance? How can the character of God awaken love in a
mind so perverted? How can salvation—which in part signifies communion and friendship with God, and in part, conformity to his law—be a possible thing without a change, a
radical change, in such views, and in the perverted moral
qualities of the soul which originates and determines such
views? It is simply impossible.

Take, again, the influence of a perverted moral nature upon
the *affections of the heart*. They are all more or less depraved, and just so far forth are disabled from performing
their true functions and working out their true ends. They
become eccentric, exaggerated, and unsafe to indulge. They
love what they ought not to love; they hate what they ought
not to hate. They thus come under the rebuke of conscience,
and that indulgence results only in mischief, in enhancing the
moral corruption from which they spring, and in producing

a misery which is the natural outcome of perverted nature and violated law. A corrupt heart is the greatest source of evil in the universe of God. The heart is omnipotent over conduct, character and happiness. It dictates action. It controls character. It determines happiness or misery. As a man loves, so will he act in seeking the gratification of his desires. As a man loves so is he; his character is determined by his affections. If he loves war, his character is construed as warlike; if he loves money, his character is construed as avaricious; if he loves pleasure or idleness, his character is construed as frivolous. The influence of the heart is all-powerful over happiness. If all he likes is removed out of his reach, his misery is secured. If he is able to indulge his attachments, his satisfaction is secured. With a heart opposed to the character of God and the employments of his service it would be impossible to be happy, even in heaven and in the beatific vision of God and his glory. To make heaven itself endurable to a sinful soul is an absolute impossibility; hell itself would be more tolerable. The bold French infidel who said he had rather spend eternity in hell than in eternal sing-song in heaven, was true in the expression of the necessary demands of an unholy heart. Nothing could illustrate the necessity of a change of heart with more irresistible energy of demonstration than the fact that the almightiness of God himself could not contrive to make even heaven endurable to a sinful soul. Even infinite power cannot control an essential impossibility.

The same line of investigation pursued through all the applications of a depraved moral nature, to the reasoning powers, the judgment, the fancy, the sense of humor, the perceptions of conscience, and the positive volitions and actions of a man, would bring out the same result. To rescue all the powers of human nature from perverted uses, it is indispensable that the great ruling cause of their perverted action should be removed by regenerating grace. Salvation is a contradictory predicate to a conscience perverted, a mind blinded, a heart depraved, a will debauched, and a life full of those activities which are necessarily determined by a polluted moral nature. It is as perfectly a contradiction to talk of salvation in sin as to talk of ease to one in agony, or breath to one in the very fever of a deadly disease. All the evidence procurable from the nature of man, and the laws that regulate it, proves the absolute truth of the declaration of our Lord, *Ye must be born again.*

4. The necessity of the thorough purification of the depraved moral nature of man, by a real regeneration, is demonstrated by another line of proofs, separate altogether from man himself. It is shown by the essential implication of the interests and peace of other beings beside himself. The Scriptures reveal to us the existence of a holy and most noble race of creatures who dwell in the presence of God, and do their faultless service before his throne. It is necessary to the safety and interests of this grand race of angelic intelligences that man should be purified, if he is to be admitted into their society when the mystery of death is accomplished upon him. The same great law of moral and social influence which makes man here so powerful in moulding the character of his fellow, seems to pervade the universe. The angels are subject to this law; they are naturally liable to fall, as we know from the fatal history of the fallen members of that great fraternity. Their safety would be imperiled by unholy associations in their regular existence. Their happiness, too, like ours, is strongly dependent upon their social relations. The character of their companions must be congenial, or their peace would be disturbed. If no regeneration could be gained, and if man with his low instincts, polluted passions, and tendencies ever reaching downward, should be introduced into their holy society, disgust and horror would soon banish every sentiment of satisfaction. The music of the rejoicing host would be marred by

the discords of the unholy rabble. The feelings of the
stately seraphim would be kindled into horror by the rude
greeting of some debauched and distempered villain reeling
along the streets of the celestial city. If God cares aught
for the integrity and comfort of that brilliant and holy host,
who have served him for ages, without fault or flaw in their
service, it will be absolutely necessary to do one of two
things: either to keep unholy souls out of their company, or
else to purify their polluted natures, and thus fit them for
this glorious society. The very sight of a depraved being
there would be a signal of distress, and silence would reign
in every celestial group until the unclean spirit had gone by
and disappeared. It is not wonderful that the Lord of
heaven said to the sinners on the earth, *Ye must be born
again.*

5. If anything more were wanting to vindicate the declaration of the text, it will be found in the culminating fact
that not only the honor of God himself as a holy moral
being, and the interests of his moral government, but his
own personal blessedness and peace, are involved in this
issue of the purification of man as the essential condition of
his salvation. In every conceivable way God has given expression to his intense abhorrence of all moral evil. Sin is
the abominable thing which he hates. Now suppose him to
receive into his presence and unalterable favor a creature
covered with this unendurable pollution. What would be
the judgment formed of a holiness which, after all its manifestations of invincible aversion to sin, could still receive an
uncleansed sinner into abiding favor? What would be
thought of his veracity in declaring that aversion? The
very integrity of infinite perfection stands as the guarantee
and pledge of the necessity of regeneration. One grand aim
of the divine administration is the restraint and punishment
of moral evil. Consequently salvation, without regeneration
of an unholy nature, would overthrow the fundamental prin-

ciples and purposes of the government of God. Not only his personal integrity, but the essential principles of his administration, affirm the necessity of regeneration. But further still, if any additional assurance could be given, it can be found in the fact that the very peace and personal blessedness of the infinite God are dependent on the purification of a sinful soul, on the supposition that it is saved. He is infinitely holy, and his joy is grounded on the free and unembarrassed action of his own personal qualities and affections. The presence of sin is an offence in his eyes; and the only circumstance which makes sin endurable in his presence is his liberty to deal with it as it deserves. Sin is in his presence here in this world, and in the regions of the lost; but in both places he is dealing with it in consistency with his own character and his own claims. He is not fettered or embarrassed by it; his own nature has free play in his relations to the evil. But for sin to exist and run riot in his presence under a perpetual guarantee of immunity, and God himself be placed under the necessity of eternally curbing the natural and free action of his own character in dealing with it, would ruin his peace forevermore. What more do we need to impress the awful, inexorable necessity of regeneration, than the conception that without it the serene and unassailable peace of the infinite Lord must give way, and he, the author of all good, must become blasted with misery. The alternatives are, the misery of the sin-fettered soul, or the misery of God, or the reconciliation of the contending issues by regeneration. *Ye must be born again.*

6. From this view of the absolute necessity of the new birth, how inexpressibly dangerous are any mistaken views of the nature of regeneration! In view of the intrinsic and all-comprehensive necessity of a real and fundamental change in the moral element of human nature, how fearful is the error and the peril of any mistake on a matter so vital! To make regeneration synonymous with baptism, or as depend-

ent only on this visible ordinance; to construe it as a mere change of relations, and not of intrinsic moral character; to make it a mere modification of thought and feeling, produced by the words of Scripture, after a manner exactly analogous to the influence of any other written composition, is to err in a vital point. To object to the doctrine as visionary, or fanatical, or enthusiastic, or absurd, is to cut the very ground away on which all rational or scriptural hope of eternal life rests. In the progress of this discussion we hope to make satisfactory explanation of every objection to the doctrine of regeneration, and to vindicate the solid ground of hope in the gospel assurances of the possibility and actual reality of a true and effective spiritual regeneration. But inasmuch as the main purpose of this little treatise is not so much the guidance of the opinions as the movement of the heart to practical action, let us, in the meanwhile, search our own hearts, test our own experiences, sound the depths of our own hopes, affections, and fears. Let us seek by humble and fervent prayer the blessing of God in the gift of his Spirit. It is very certain that if any of us can gain what Paul rejoiced had been given to him, the real illumination of the Holy Ghost, there will be no room to question the reality of his control over the thoughts and feelings of the soul, and his consequent demonstrated power to produce the change, the necessity of which is asserted by our Lord in terms so clear and solemn, and demonstrated by considerations too obvious to be denied, and too powerful to be rationally resisted.

CHAPTER VII.

THE NATURE OF REGENERATION.

"Therefore, if any man be in Christ, he is a new creature: old things are passed away; behold, all things are become new."—*Paul to the Corinthians.*

THE nature of the change, called the new birth, the new creation, regeneration, conversion, and the spiritual resurrection from the dead, may be inferred in general terms from the nature of the mischief which makes it a necessity. The necessity of the change is grounded in the depraved condition of the moral nature of a sinning being. Generally defined, the nature of regeneration is a change of this depraved condition into an opposite or holy condition of this moral nature in sinning man. The specific consideration of the itemized features and distinctions of the change will furnish us with a special definition, or, at least, a more exact and comprehensive knowledge of what is involved in it. The teachings of the word of God are full and clear on the subject; they describe its nature, specify its precedent changes, delineate its effects, explain its evidences, and definitely affirm the agent by whose power it is effected. In the progressive development of these teachings, the various misconceptions which exist touching this vital point of the Christian faith may be corrected. These misconceptions vary in different, and even opposite, directions, from a purely rationalistic to a ritualistic, and to a fanatical construction of the doctrine; all of which will stand exposed by the display of the real doctrine of the Scriptures. The radical nature of the change is logically involved in the radical nature of the evil to be removed; and salvation to a sinner is a contradiction in terms, unless all the effects of his sin

153

are removed. To save him from one, and leave him to the
unchanged operation of another, is to still leave him to destruction. To qualify the legal effects of his violation of
law, and rescue him from its penalty, and yet leave him to the
unchecked effect of sin on his own soul, is not to save, but to
insure his ruin. The redemption work of Christ is designed
to control the one; the offices and work of the Holy Spirit to
control the other.

To enable us to form a clear notion of the nature of regeneration, we must first attempt to form a clear notion of
the real nature of the mischief it is intended to cure. The
general conception of moral depravity, and its effects on the
different faculties of the soul, must be reduced to its actual
contents before a just notion of it can be formed.

There is a distinction in the nature of things, called *true
and false*, which is irresistibly recognized by the intuitive
energy of the human understanding. When the distinction
of *true* is discerned in a thing, it is accepted as a reality, a
something that is. When the distinction of *false* is discerned, it is accepted as something that is not. There is a
distinction in things, which is named *right and wrong*, which
is also intuitively discerned. This distinction is apprehended
differently from the distinction between true and false. The
distinction between right and wrong, which we call the *moral*
distinction, is felt to be obligatory; it has the force of law.
If it is disregarded, the notion of criminality at once springs
up. If it is not disregarded, but obeyed, the notion of rightness in conduct emerges, and a sentiment of approval. The
nature of man is adjusted to these distinctions. His nature
is threefold: it has a physical, an intellectual, and a moral
department. By his physical nature he is adjusted to the material condition of his existence. By his intellectual nature
he is adjusted to the grand distinction of *true and false;* when
he sees a thing to be true he is furnished *quod hoc* with

knowledge; when he sees a thing to be false he knows that that thing is no subject or matter of knowledge. The vast powers and attainments of understanding are all adjusted to the distinction between *the true and the false.* By his moral nature he is adjusted to the great fundamental and all-powerful distinction between *right and wrong.* He is able to see it, to feel its obligatory force, to impress it on his own active energies of every sort, and what is still more startling, on the fixed elements of his own nature. When he impresses the distinction of right, he feels a sentiment of complacency and approval. But when he impresses the distinction of wrong, a feeling of disapproval and criminality irresistibly emerges. This judgment of *criminality* is always the datum of *wrong.* No matter to what basis it may attach, a wrong word, a wrong act, a wrong desire, or a wrong permanent disposition is always a criminal word, a criminal act, a criminal desire, a criminal disposition. No other judgment of wrong is possible but a judgment of criminality. Sin is moral wrong, and always involves criminalit, The ground of regeneration is then disclosed in its true nature. A depraved moral nature is that essential and permanent moral energy in man which adjusts him to the great moral distinction *infected with wrong,* and therefore *essentially criminal,* and making the man *a criminal being.* Regeneration is the alteration of this wrong-tainted moral nature, making it *right,* changing its essentially *criminal* quality into a quality *commanding approval,* inspiring *holiness* into it in the place of *sin.*

Regeneration takes effect on the very nature of the man, on the permanent moral energy that is in him. The ascription of sin, or corrupt moral quality, to the nature of man is disputed as an impossible predication by some. These theorists restrict sin to positive acts, on the ground that the will must be concerned in sin, and that the volitions of the voluntary faculty can only be implicated in action. This view is repudiated by the intuitions of the understanding, and by the universal experience and judgments of mankind. The theory assumes that there is no action of the will except the positive determined purposes which precede action. But the intuitions of the mind discern a scale of actions in the will, rising from mere impulse to desires and to more stable affections, and then to determined volitions, or positive purposes to act. To each of these expressions of will responsibility attaches on a variable scale of degrees. An unholy desire may never be followed by the positive determination to gratify it, but it involves moral responsibility, because it is an expression of will-desiring wrong. This judgment, ascribing moral quality to acts of will other than positive actions, is alike the doctrine of Scripture and the doctrine of common sense.

The denial of moral quality, carrying the notion of responsibility to the fixed moral elements in the nature of man, is equally repudiated by these two great authorities. The will conditions moral quality in an agent; but all forms of voluntary energy do it, and the moral element in human nature is *the will in its fixed quality and stable disposition.* That there are such permanent states or habits of the will is affirmed by the word of God, and by the experience and the consciousness of mankind; and because they are true energies of the will, the fixed complexion of those energies, even when in repose, the universal judgments of mankind confirm the award of the Scriptures in attaching a true moral responsibility to them. Men are pronounced to be "by nature children of wrath." "The heart is said to be deceitful above all things, and desperately wicked." Such is the judgment of God in the case. The testimony of the human intellect on it can be evoked by an inspection of the fact that men do ascribe permanent moral characteristics to each other, and of the method by which they discover what they call these permanent traits of *character* in their fellows.

It is a simple fact of common experience that men do con-

strue each other according to the moral distinction of right
and wrong—as being good or bad men; not merely as doing
good or bad acts, but as being themselves good or bad—as
having good or bad characters; by which they mean permanent traits of disposition and feeling. The mode of expression shows that they regard the imputed traits as modifications of *the will*, and therefore they do not hesitate to hold
men responsible for their characters—for these permanent
traits of their dispositions. Men reach the conception of
these fixed and stable traits of the personal nature of their
fellows by an inspection of acts or other visible expressions
of the spirit within. They go back of the act, or other outward expression of thought and feeling, and judge the moral
complexion of the energy from which that act or expression
flowed. An exhibit of hot or malicious temper is held to
reveal a hot or malicious temper in the man, and he is
judged to be such a man even in his unexcited moments.
The evil energy is known to be in him, even when not in exercise. A dishonest man is so construed even when he is
dealing fairly; men know that the disposition to take advantage when he can is a permanent quality in him, even though
in a given case he may be acting honestly. The confidence
in *character* is always demanded in confiding trusts, because
men well know that the permanent traits of the disposition
are constant sources of corresponding actions. The judgment of mankind is a matter of common experience, that men
are good or bad in themselves, as well as that they do good
or bad things—good or bad in character—in the fixed qualities of their disposition as well as in their acts. This judgment of character is in fact the most important thing in
forming our moral estimates of men. Acts are of use in one
main line of their utility as disclosures and proofs of the
permanent traits. The full significance of acts is not always
immediate; they are sometimes studiously disguised to con-
ceal the real character. They sometimes depend upon char-

acter previously disclosed for their full significance.   An
act regarded as springing from a sudden temptation, or an
unusual impulse, is never so seriously condemned, or graded
so high in guilt, as an act which is regarded as the product
of a fixed quality in the actor.   This superior regard to character rather than to acts is rightly felt; for an act done is a
thing of the past; it can never be repeated; but a permanent disposition to such acts is a perpetual fountain of them.
This fixed moral quality in the nature of man, lying back of
his acts and determining their complexion, is *the object of
regeneration*.   This depraved moral nature in which that evil
quality inheres is the substratum on which the regenerating
energy of divine grace is exerted.   To save a bad man—bad
in his nature as well as in his acts, he must be purified in
his inward being, in order that all his energies may be rightly
ordered.

This moral element in human nature pervades every part
of his spiritual and intellectual being, just as a coloring pervades the transparency of glass or a pure fluid.   Take a
simple illustration, which may give some conception of the
interaction created, and of the mode in which regeneration
will affect all the powers that are implicated.   A vase of
clear glass filled with pure water may be taken as an analogue of the intellectual and moral elements of human nature
in their mutual relations to each other.   The light passes
through the untainted medium unaltered in its native hue;
its flavor is pure and sweet; it is at once healthful and pleasant to drink.   The transparency represents the intellectual
part of human nature.   The bright uncolored sheen of the
pure fluid represents the *moral* element pervading the intellectual in all its parts, in a state of sinless purity.   But now
infuse a coloring matter into the water.   The crimson stain
pervades the entire mass of the fluid; it has become totally
depraved; not that the color has become as deep in its shade
as it can be; but that it pervades every part of the altered

element, and changes all its qualities. The nature of the water as a fluid is still the same; it remains a fluid; but its nature as a wholesome and untainted fluid is altered, and its utilities have altered with it. The light still passes through it; its transparency is still in it; objects can still be seen through it; but under different aspects from before. The light as it passes through the transparency has caught the hue of the coloring which pervades the medium, and all the objects seen through it are covered with these altered colors. The value and uses of the fluid have changed; its taste is no longer sweet; it is no longer safe to drink; it has become bitter and poisonous. Now, to restore that water what would be necessary? Simply to withdraw the coloring matter which has depraved it, if that be possible. That being done, the stainless brightness returns to the fluid; its sweetness is restored; its healthful qualities are renewed, and recover it to all its uses; the light passes through it in its natural hues; all objects are seen through it in their natural colors; *the water is regenerated.*

Now, we may conceive something of the intellectual and moral elements in human nature, in their relation to each other. The moral pervades the whole intellectual structure and modifies it in every faculty and in all its energies, just as the pure colorless sheen or the depraved crimson coloring pervades the transparency of glass or water, and controls all that is seen through it. This pervading moral force not only controls absolutely the powers of conscience and the will, but qualifies strongly memory, judgment, imagination, fancy, the powers of intuition and reasoning, and the sense of wit and humor. It pervades the whole mind, and qualifies the activity and the uses of every part of it. So long as this moral element remains sinlessly holy, and measurably as it does not descend into the graver degrees of depravity, the light of truth passes clear and straight through the understanding. The heart is pure; its affections are rightly

ordered; it loves only what it ought to love; it hates only
what it ought to hate. All the energies of the will, from
simple desire to determined purpose, are rightly ordered and
guided. The conscience performs its functions perfectly. The
memory is as tenacious of moral and religious notions as of
any other notions. The judgment and the powers of reasoning are not disturbed by any misguided intuitions, nor enfeebled by any depraving habits. The play of the fancy, and
the sense of humor are all instinctively pure. The whole energies of the man are regulated into holy action by the influence
of this all-pervading moral element in a state of sinless purity.

But now suppose that pervasive moral element is become
depraved. Its relation to the intellectual element remains,
and its influence is still controlling over all its energies. The
only difference is, that it was once pure in itself, determining
purity in its effects; now, it is bad, determining badness in its
effects. Just according to its own degree of badness it will
determine an answerable degree of badness in its effects on
all things subject to its influence. Just as an added strength
or degree in the coloring matter which pervaded the water
in our illustration will increase its power over the light that
passes through it, over the bitterness of its taste, and the
virulence of its poison, so will increased degrees of depravity
in the moral nature of man control more strongly the whole
intellectual and active powers of the soul. The perception
of truth, especially of moral and religious truth, will be qualified by it. All the functions of conscience will be affected
by it. The memory of moral and religious concepts will be
enfeebled by it. The sense of wit and humor will be modified by it; a low debased type of man will see wit and humor
in relations the coarseness of which would nullify all sense
of these pleasing suggestions in a higher type of moral character. The affections of the heart, in a word, all the degrees
and manifestations of the will, are more directly qualified by
moral evil, and all the positive external actions of the con-

duct are determined in sin by the depraved quality of this
regulating moral element of human nature. That element
must be purified, or all hope of purifying the man himself or
the course of his career must be abandoned. Upon this depraved condition of the moral nature the energies of divine
grace, as revealed in the offices of the Holy Ghost, are
exerted. Regeneration is simply the change of quality in
this ruling moral nature of the soul; it is the renewal of the
will; it is the change of the heart; it is the new creation of
the nature of a sinning creature. If there is no such thing
as a regeneration of just this sort, man is hopelessly lost.
One of the grandest and most disastrous effects of his sin is,
on this theory, irredeemable. The light thrown by this stern
fact in the very nature of man, upon all other theories of
regeneration than that of a new creation by the power of
God, is overwhelming. Any scheme of religion, looking to
the salvation of the soul, which does not provide for the real
purification of the depraved moral nature is worse than
worthless; it is destructive.

It will be seen at once from this view of the evil to be removed, that some change as radical as that which the Bible
declares to be necessary must be accomplished. How shall
it be done? But that same word of God which declares the
necessity of the change provides for it. It points out the
change as it is actually wrought, and the great agent by
which it is accomplished. It tells us there is such a thing
as being "born of the Spirit," as being "created anew in
Christ Jesus," as being "made alive from the dead." It de-
lineates the wonderful transformation, lays down its conditions, describes its effects on the consciousness and on the
character, marks out its evidences, and portrays its influence
on the peace and comfort of its subject. We propose to follow up the teachings of the Scriptures, and the corresponding testimonies of Christian experience, on some of the leading features of this great gospel doctrine of regeneration.

We shall endeavor to illustrate it, *first*, as a *moral*, not a *physical* change; *second*, as a *real*, and not a *supposititious* or *imaginary* change; *third*, as a *supernatural* effect by the power of the Holy Ghost, and not a *natural* change by the mere force of ideas, or a mere *ritual* change by the force of observed rights, administered by official men; *fourth*, not a change of *faculties* themselves, but a change of *capabilities* in faculties already existing; and *fifth*, as an *universal* change, affecting the views of the understanding, the affections of the heart, the energies of the conscience, the activities of the will, the imagination, judgment, the sense of humor, memory, and the powers of reasoning; in a word, affecting the whole man, and every expression of the energies in him, in accordance with the declarations in the sacred record, "old things are passed away; behold, all things have become new." This wide result is produced by affecting the quality of that radical moral force which pervades the whole mental structure, and determines its energies for good or evil, just as it is itself holy or depraved. This moral force, *seated as it is in the will, in the permanent, yet responsible, states of its affections*, shows how thoroughly responsibility for this status of the heart is grounded in the very nature of the case. When this moral element is depraved, this universality of its supremacy disclosed the range, and explains the meaning of the terms *total depravity*, which are used to describe it. They do not mean that man is as bad as he can be, for no limit to the possible degree of moral corruption has or can ever be defined in words, or reached in fact; they mean that, under infinite varieties of degree in the coloring, the whole moral element in human nature is depraved, producing an answerable influence on every faculty and energy of the soul in variant measures.

First, in illustration of the nature of regeneration as a *moral*, not a *physical* change, we need not spend time after what has been said in explanation already. The evil to be removed is *moral;* the change effecting that removal must be necessarily also moral. The coloring in the transparency is to be altered, not the transparency itself. The understanding remains the same, only the disturbing elements in it are removed. The capacity of affection remains in the heart, only the nature of its capacity is altered, so that it now loves what once it hated, and hates what it once loved. The testimony of the Scriptures is uniform, that the purpose of the inward application of grace to the human soul is to purify the evils found in it. It is the *washing* of regeneration; it is the *renewal* of the Holy Ghost; it is the creation of a new heart; it is the destroying of the dominion of sin. If reference is had in the reproach of regeneration as a change wrought by *physical* power on the part of God, it is only necessary to say, we cannot comprehend the *methods* of God's power in any of its exercises; but we do know that he did originally create man upright and pure, and there does not appear any reason to impeach the exercise of the same power to create man anew unto holiness. The same power may be exerted again, no matter what name you may give it, for the same purpose. The one case is as conceivable as the other, and if there was no impossibility in the one, there can be none in the other. The notion that it is impossible to create holiness is a foolish confusion of the exercises of a holy nature with that nature itself. God does not directly produce the intellectual exercises of an intellect created by him; but that does not impeach his ability to create the intellect itself. In the same manner he can create a soul with a holy nature, with a capacity of holy exercises, with a holy principle in it, capable of energizing in holiness; and this is all that is necessary in the regeneration of the soul. In the regeneration, or new creation, he uses a secondary instrument—the truth— the word of God, which liveth and abideth forever. Dealing with a nature already existent, he respects its fundamental constitution; but while using the truth, he exerts a power which is described in the strongest terms as the exceeding greatness of his power towards those who believe. Perhaps to create anew, without jar or trespass on the existing powers of the creature, may be even a higher energy of power than an original creation conferring powers. At all events they are equal; the power employed is creative power; and that is fully competent to God, call it physical power or what not, and may be equally employed in an old or new creation. In what manner he puts the new spiritual life into the soul dead in trespasses and sins, none can possibly tell. The manner in which he creates a holy nature is as mysterious as the manner in which he creates any kind of nature, whether animal or vegetable, but not one whit more so. It is enough for the human soul, anxious to know how to get rid of the deadly stain upon the moral nature, to know that God can create him anew in Christ Jesus, and restore the lost image of his own glory. As to the manner in which the grace of God will do this, the receiver of its wonderful deliverance is content to be ignorant; he is content with *the fact;* and he is fully satisfied to leave the mode of the fact to him who probably alone can comprehend it. It is the grandest and most joyous of all thoughts, to a mind conscious of the nature and the awful energy of its own inward sinfulness, to know that in Christ, the Saviour of sinners, the almighty power of God is actually available as an agency of human purification and as the guarantee of human integrity.

The *second* point which we wish to illustrate is, that regeneration is *a real, and not a supposititious or imaginary change.* The value of this wonderful work of divine grace is conditioned absolutely on its reality; and that reality, if demonstrable, possesses another value additional to its value as a ground of hope to the individual soul sighing under its conscious defects—in its force as a perpetual demonstration of the truth of the whole system of Christianity. This is a species of evidence, distinct from prophecy and visible miracle, reproduced in innumerable instances in every successive generation of men. The gospel claims to be not only a system to be believed, but *a power to be felt*, and as such it is a power to be manifested. It claims to produce certain effects. These effects are described; the conditions on which they occur are stated; and the effects, their antecedent conditions, and their subsequent manifestations, constitute a strong test of the claim which is asserted. Suppose it had asserted that a certain physical effect, visible to the eye, should be exerted on the body of every one who accepted its terms—say that a golden glory should illuminate the face, or play as an aureole of lambent fire around the head of every one who experienced its power. Such a claim would be an irresistible test of its truth. If it were true, we should see the golden glory in the face, or the pale splendor of the aureole encircling the head. If a single instance were seen, it would not only prove the individual to be a Christian, but it would demonstrate the whole claim of the gospel. If those instances were multiplied into thousands and millions, they would only intensify the demonstration. Now it is unquestionable that mental phenomena are as real and as capable of proof on their own peculiar evidence as any material phenomena whatever; the facts of consciousness are as true and as demonstrable as any other facts. The fact that man has a memory is as true and as capable of proof as the fact that he has a nose or a mouth. The fact that man suffers or enjoys, that he likes and dislikes, is as true and provable as that he has hands and feet, and is capable of using them. The existence and the connections of mental facts, their conditions and laws of existence and succession, are as capable of observation and description as the conditions and regulating laws of any other facts.

Bearing this in mind, let us remember that the gospel does distinctly claim to exert a profound influence on the human spirit—to produce a radical and permanent change on its controlling forces. It not only describes the nature of this change, but the conditions under which it will arise, and under which *alone* it will arise. It describes its antecedent and consequent peculiarities. It discriminates its characteristic features, points out its effects in a variety of ways, and details its evidences. Now, if there is any truth in this claim of power to produce these results in this order and connection, under these terms and conditions, it is certainly capable of demonstration. If there is no truth in the claim, that, too, can be demonstrated. Here is a bold and audacious claim of power, of living and practical power, on the minds and radical energies of living men, which challenges investigation and proof. The case affords the fairest of opportunities to test its reality that any reasonable inquirer can desire. There is the record of Scripture, specifying its claim, with all its connected terms and the characteristic marks of its asserted work. The Christian claimants to an experience of this power are to be found by thousands everywhere the gospel has been preached. The seal and its impressions can be coördinated and compared without difficulty. Let the inquirer take up the investigation and search for the verification or non-verification of the claim in the facts of human experience. It has been justly considered a triumph of skilled scientific knowledge, when an astronomer affirmed that a planet, hitherto unseen and unsuspected, must be found in a certain quarter of the heavens, and when search was made it was found. In this case the fact verified the record. A like challenge is made in regard to this claim of the great Christian faith. The witnesses can be found of every character, in every Christian nation, in every generation, of every rank, age, and sex, of every degree of intellect, from the humblest to the highest grade of talent—from the plainest observers of facts in their own minds to the highest and most profoundly disciplined metaphysical intellects which ever scrutinized the phenomena of the mind.

Many skeptical minds deride this grand doctrine of spiritual regeneration as a mere delusion. But surely they must admit that a Christian is just as competent as any one else to notice the changes in his own consciousness, to observe the movements of his own thoughts and feelings, and to report his observations. It is certainly difficult to imagine why observations cannot be as accurately made, and as truly reported, upon religious feelings as on any other feelings. If one of these objectors should candidly confess that his feelings were opposed to these peculiarities of the gospel, he would take it hard if any one should refuse to believe his report upon the states of his own mind. Now, supposing that an entire change should take place in his feelings, and instead of disliking he should learn to love and admire these peculiarities, why should not his report of his feelings in this case be as reliable as his report in the other? If this be so, why may he not take the reports of others to be as reliable as his own? The change is registered more or less clearly and distinctly in the consciousness; why cannot a Christian reliably report it? If he can accept as true the statement of the facts, and the formulation of the laws of the association of ideas, or of the more recondite phenomena of mental action from a metaphysical philosopher, why not the observation and statement of the facts and laws of religious feeling by such Christian philosophers as Baxter, and John Howe, Archbishop Leighton, and Charles Simeon, Jonathan Edwards, Luther, and Archibald Alexander? If he would accept the facts, not an explanation of the facts, of their parental affections from plain men and women, why not take the facts of their religious affections with equal credit as true to their felt consciousness and experience? The *fact* of a thorough change of thought, feeling, desire, and affection, hope and fear, motive and rule of action, can be reliably attested by any plain mind, as well as by minds of a higher grade, and there are millions of all grades to attest the reality of regeneration on the terms specified to condition it.   The formulation of the phenomena, the coördination of the facts, the evolution of the order, connections, and conditions of the facts, have been made over and over again by many of the highest minds of the human species.   The demonstration of the reality of a true regeneration of the human heart on the terms and conditions of the gospel cannot admit of a question in the face of the experience of the church of God, multiplied to the contentment of any possible conditions of human inquiry.   The claim of *power* in the gospel is demonstrated to the highest degree by the proof of *its exercise*, according to its own specified conditions.   Regeneration, according to those conditions, is a *real, and not an imaginary, change*.

The *third* point to be illustrated is, that it is *a supernatural change effected by the power of the Holy Ghost*.   The method of proof will be the combination of the evidence as given in the Christian experience with that given in the Scriptures. The experience of Christians shows that the change is effected by a power from without, and the Scriptures inform us what agent exerts it.   We think it can undoubtedly be shown that the results reported in consciousness, and certified by the appointed tests, are wrought by some agency independent of the mind itself; and if this independent agency can be shown to act, it will be easy to accept the testimony of the sacred record that this agency is the Spirit of God.   The phenomena occurring according to the recorded account of the Spirit's procedure will definitely prove, not only the externality of the agent, but who he is.   We affirm this supernatural origin of regeneration, *first*, as against the theory of it as a mere natural change wrought by the force of mere religious ideas, just as other written or spoken thoughts modify character, on the one side, and on the other, as against the theory of it as a mere ritual change wrought by the sacraments administered by human agents in an official character.

The testimony of the Scriptures is clear and positive that it is not wrought by the will of the flesh, or the will of man, but of God. As against the theory of a mere natural change produced by the modifying power of the mere truth revealed in the word of God, the testimony is clear and positive that the gospel must come, not in word only, but in demonstration of the Spirit and of power. As against the theory of this grace as given by the sacraments, it is clear that, so far as adults are concerned, neither of the two sacraments can be lawfully administered until this change has already taken place—until repentance and faith, the fruit and proof of regenerating grace, have been credibly evinced. The sacraments, then, cannot be credited with producing the change. The declaration that our Lord made to Nicodemus, that we must be born of water and of the Spirit, clearly settles a distinction between what is effected by the water and what is effected by the Spirit; in the birth as determined by the one, and the birth as determined by the other. There are various constructions put upon the word *water* as used in this remarkable passage. Some construe it as referring to the sacrament of baptism; others, as referring to the word or truth which is the instrument employed by the Holy Ghost in sanctification of the soul. This last is borne out to a certain reliable degree by the phrase "washing with water by the word," and by Jewish usage. That baptism is referred to is also sustained to a certain probable degree by its recognized relation to the visible church as the ordinance of admission to its privileges. But neither of these constructions gives any support to the theory of regeneration by the sacraments carrying grace as fire carries heat or ice carries cold. That the truth in itself, and by itself, carries no effectual saving influence is definitely settled by the decisive statement, "the gospel must come, not in word only." The truth is the instrument in the hand of the Spirit, who ordinarily never acts without the word; and hence we are said to

be born of the word of God which liveth and abideth forever.   Hence the word is all-important to the regeneration
of the soul, not because the word carries the power, but because
the power never acts without the word.   Hence it is very
probable that the word was alluded to under the metaphor of
water in the words of Messiah to the Jewish ruler.   There is,
however, no insuperable difficulty in supposing an allusion
in the phrase to both the truth of the word and the sacrament of baptism.   But if so, this does not by any means
link the effective power of saving grace to the sacrament, for
the decisive reason already given, that the lawful administration of the sacrament to any one capable of faith pre-
supposes the grace of regeneration already bestowed.   Faith
precedes baptism according to the well-recognized law of the
gospel in relation to all capable of faith; and regeneration
precedes faith by the necessity of the existence of any kind
of life to precede the acts of such life.   Baptism is, then,
certainly not designed to carry the grace of regeneration.
But its relation to the visible church is imperative; and no
one can see the inside of that visible kingdom, or share its
privileges, until admitted by the rite of baptism.   This application of water is necessary to the grand change of visible
relations between the kingdom of Satan and the kingdom of
Messiah.   This change, according to the old Jewish modes
of thought, may be called a new birth; but to confound this
with the new birth by the power of the Holy Ghost is
absurd.   The difference is clearly discriminiated by the two-
or rather several-fold nature of Messiah's kingdom.   As a
visible organization it can only be entered by baptism, a met-
aphorical birth by water.   As a kingdom within you, it can
only be entered by a conversion of a rebellious will into true
obedience to the King; this kingdom can only be seen,
known, or entered by an effectual new birth of the Holy
Spirit.   It is thus literally true, "Except a man be born
of water and of the Spirit he cannot see the kingdom of

heaven." This is also true of that form of the glorious kingdom called heaven.

This setting aside of the dangerous and fascinating theory of regeneration by the sacraments will be more effectively demolished by the presentation of the positive proof from Christian experience of the independent, external, or supernatural origin of the manifested phases of regeneration. The digression on sacramental grace was too important to be omitted, and the facts and phenomena of Christian experience demonstrate the falsity of the perilous theory. Let us see.

Religious experience is nothing more nor less than the answer and accord of our consciousness to the teachings of the word of God. The relation between them is the relation between a seal and its impression. One of the most striking parts of the diagnosis of human nature in the Scriptures is, that it is *spiritually blind*. This is a conception hard for the natural mind to form with any precision or distinctness. Conscious of mental vigor, the power of perception, and the functions of understanding generally, it cannot take in the charge of a spiritual blindness, an incompetence of spiritual intuition. But as soon as it begins to deal practically with the terms of the gospel, and seeks to comply with them, it soon becomes aware that these terms as rules of action, spiritual action, are of all things the most mysterious. Faith is simple enough; it is simplicity itself, as a mere idea or speculative thought; but when the man *tries to do it*—to embody it in an energy of the heart, it becomes incomprehensible; and the mind may struggle for days and months together in the vain attempt to comprehend faith as an actual movement of the soul. He learns at length that he is blind, and that the Bible told him the truth about himself when it told him he was *blind*. Another statement the Bible makes in its itemized description of the spiritual condition of the soul is, that the *heart is hard*, harder than the nether mill-stone—

hardened by sin.   This, too, is mysterious, especially **incom**-prehensible by persons of a gentle and compassionate nature. But the charge is on all men, on the sympathetic as well as on the visibly hard and unfeeling.   One of these gentler spirits is particularly puzzled to comprehend the imputation; but when he begins to try and repent, he soon finds he *cannot feel* as he knows he ought to feel, as he wishes to feel, and as he tries to feel.   The most advanced Christian never outgrows all of this conscious hardness of heart; the more his views of the evil of sin expand, the more incompetent his feelings towards it appear to himself.   The seeker for grace suddenly awakes to the consciousness that the Bible told him the truth about himself when it told him his heart was hard.

Another statement the Scriptures make about the spiritual condition of a sinner is that he is altogether *helpless*, unable to do anything effectual to extricate himself, and that relief will only come when he ceases the impossible effort at self-deliverance, and relies on another, *trusts in Christ* to save him.   The awakened sinner always, at first, struggles resolutely to comply with the terms of the gospel, repentance and faith; but as he proceeds with the effort to save himself, the blindness and hardness prove too much for him, and at last he realizes it is true as the Bible said, he is a helpless sinner.   He now realizes, what the same deep-searching witness declared, that he is *a lost sinner*.   All his efforts at self-help have failed; the terrible peril of his state presses keenly; and he *feels* that he is really a lost sinner.   He has been now brought to the point where he can appreciate the need of a *Saviour;* and now as, by the further proceeding of sovereign grace, his mind opens to the conception of Christ as a sinner's Saviour, his present helper in his time of need, the old familiar notion opens with the force of a new revelation.   He at once ceases the effort to serve himself; he accepts the offer of Christ to save him; he trusts in him to do it; his only appeal is to this outside resource; and at once he is at peace. Relief has come to him. Now note the bearing of all this on the supernatural origin of regeneration. Put the facts together: the experimental and well-tried conviction of his blindness, hardness, and helplessness, which has come to him in his struggle to save himself; his conscious inability to break his bonds; his distinct cessation of the effort to do it; his appeal to the power of another; and then the fact that relief comes. The inference is irresistible, that he has been helped to this relief *by some external and independent agency.* Where did it come from except from without? He is fully conscious of his helplessness; he ceases his exertions, not in the use of means, but as endeavoring to save himself; he trusts in another to do it for him, and he gets what he wanted. The conclusion is irresistible, that he has been helped to it, and is in full accord with the great gospel doctrine that we are saved by a "faith in Christ," which is "the fruit of the Spirit." The facts disclose a power external to the soul as the origin of its spiritual life in regeneration; the Bible tells who the agent putting forth this power really is; and the two lines of testimony converge on the same conclusion. Christ saves through the agency of the Holy Spirit quickening the spiritually dead into spiritual life, regenerating the unholy and rebellious heart, and through this marvelous achievement implanting the germ of all the fruits of the Spirit. We must be born again by the awful energy of the Holy Ghost, or *perish!*

CHAPTER VIII.

THE NATURE OF REGENERATION.

"Therefore, if any man be in Christ, he is a new creature; old things are passed away; behold, all things are become new."—*Paul to the Corinthians.*

IT is probably expedient to throw the discussion of the nature of regeneration into two sections, not to weary by too great a protraction of a single exposition. We resume at the point under treatment at the close of the last chapter, and proceed to vindicate the position taken from some possible exceptions to it. That position was, that the facts of consciousness in Christian experience plainly disclosed the relief of the struggling soul in some external agency. It may be excepted to this testimony of the facts of the Christian consciousness, that perhaps this realization of *helplessness* was a mistake, that the man possessed more power than he supposed, that he failed at first to relieve himself because his powers were not in a propitious condition for exertion, and that, as in many other cases, a renewed effort, under more favorable conditions, secured success, and consequently that a new exertion of his own abilities, at a happier moment, was the real cause of the change in his consciousness. It is obvious that this exception proceeds on the supposition that the consciousness of helplessness was a mistake. But if it is true in point of fact, the relief finally experienced points directly to some independent agency. Proof of the reality of this spiritual disability, then, will establish the argument and the conclusion. Now, there are two lines of evidence which prove the reality of this disablement The Scriptures are plain and positive in the assertion of it as one of the invariable effects of transgression. "Dead in sin" is one mode of assertion in reference to it, and death excludes the notion of life and energy. "Without me, ye can do nothing" says Christ in another mode of assertion, conclusive on the subject. No stream can of itself ascend higher than its source; no nature can transcend itself in the manifestation of its energies, and if man is really dead in trespasses and sins, he can put forth no energy containing in it the element of real holiness, or true spiritual life. But the testimony of consciousness is also resistless on the point, and cannot be overborne by any imputation of delusion. Since Christian experience is nothing but the answer of our consciousness to the teaching of the Scriptures, any true discovery of his own spiritual state will lead to the discovery and distinct consciousness of this helplessness in the soul. In every truly awakened sinner this consciousness does become clear; he feels, as the result of many an abortive effort, that he is unable to extricate himself from the difficulties which surround him, and is really lost if help cannot be gained. The inability is true in itself; it is asserted in the sacred record; it is distinctly recognized in the consciousness. Its reality cannot be denied. When, therefore, the relief comes, this inability to achieve it points clearly to some independent agency for its origin.

But even if it should be admitted that this conscious sense of spiritual weakness was a delusion or a mistake, this will not bar the inference of the independent origin of the experienced relief. It is certain that the sinner never experiences this relief until he ceases to exert himself, and relies upon the assistance of another; and it comes to the same thing to have no power, or not to exert it. This is the invariable law of those peculiar operations of the mind which we call religious experience; they only manifest themselves through a *trust in Christ*. Now, if we admit that this consciousness of utter helplessness is a delusion, if yet the relief never comes until the person ceases to exert himself and trusts in another power altogether, the conclusion will still be irresistible, that this relief comes from some independent agency; because it amounts to the same thing in the production of an effect, to say that the alleged cause had no power to produce it, or that it did not exert what power it had. In this case both warranties of the inference are true; the sinner is both unable to effect the result, and ceases to attempt it. He relies upon another to do it; and the actual gain of the relief points to an independent origin of it, under a warrant under either of these compulsions to the inference, sufficient under one and resistless under both.

It may also be objected, that this asserted relief may be only the quiet and repose of the soul following a period of exertion, as a necessary consequence of the cessation of its efforts. This, however, is fully refuted by the fact demonstrated by too many instances to admit of any question, that the consequences flowing from that conscious relief of felt difficulties in the soul are not merely *negative, but positive;* they are something more than a mere change from agitation to repose. They affect character; they take hold on the deepest and most effective impelling forces in the inner man. The immediate effects on the consciousness are often very striking; they are sometimes gradual, almost imperceptible in their growth. The immediate emotions excited are very animated in some cases; they are very quiet in others. In some instances the notion of *faith,* which was wrapped in impenetrable mystery, becomes so clear in its utter simplicity that the mind is amazed that it was unable to catch a conception so plain and easy. In other instances the growth of this intuition of faith is slow and progressive, just as the Scriptures describe it in the figure of the early dawn with its indefinite shades, growing more and more unto the perfect day. But independent of these immediate effects on the consciousness, varying in degree and proportion in every case, the relief that is experienced is not merely a change in the immediate consciousness, but develops profound and permanent modifications of character, disposition, feeling, affections, views, principles, and outward conduct. It produces effects at once too broad, too powerful, and too permanent to result from a mere cessation of mental struggle. The result is not merely repose of mind, but profound and far-reaching modifications of character. The inference is irresistible from the facts, not only that the change is *real* and very profound in its force, but also that it originates in an independent agency. That agency is defined for us in the Bible as the Spirit of God. The effect is ascribed to an origin not only supernatural, but divine. The facts of consciousness clearly reveal an independent origin without the soul, and distinct from its own energies, but can give no account of the nature of the power whose benefits it experiences as divine, or distinguished from divine. The Scriptures alone settle that; but the facts of consciousness warrant the acceptance of its testimony; perhaps, more deeply investigated, may confirm the description of the power as divine.

Not only does the word of God assert this power to be divine, but it is singularly emphatic in the assertion that the regeneration of the human heart is the result of a very peculiar manifestation of divine power. It strains the energies of one of the richest and most powerful of human languages to carry the assertion that it is *by the exceeding greatness of his power that men believe.* It is reckoned to be an exercise of divine power fully equal to that by which he raised Christ from the dead.* No outward sign of it is given; all proceeds in the silence of the soul. All its laws are respected; none of its faculties are jostled out of place. The power exerted is supreme omnipotence. All exercises of infinite power are, by the very perfection of the energy employed, free from the signs and throes of exertion. The movement is noiseless; there is no convulsion or open dis-

---

* Ephesians i. 19, 20.

turbance; the effect is displayed without any other sign of the energy employed than the effect itself. The regeneration of a human soul, though it involves possibly one of the highest exertions of infinite power, occurs without any violent shock or disturbance of human consciousness. The effect is plainly registered in the consciousness, and developed in its profound influences on the character and life, on the thoughts and feelings; but no sign of the energy employed, different either from the ordinary workings of human thought and feeling, or the regular characteristics of the working of infinite power, is displayed. It is only inferior power, struggling with difficulties which tax its energies to the uttermost, which yields the signs of its exertion in violent throes and convulsions of effort. Occasionally reports are made of extraordinary convulsive movements on the consciousness, producing similar disturbances in the body, in connection with the work of grace. But wherever this occurs it is not due to the power of the Holy Ghost, which works with swift and silent energy, and always in accord with the written law, let all things be done decently and in order. These strong displays of mental disturbance are due to the infirmities of human nature itself; they may exist in connection with the smooth, swift energy with which the competent power of the Holy Ghost does its regenerating work; but they are not due to it.

The *fourth* point which we made in the enumerated list of the peculiar characteristics of regeneration was, that it was not a fundamental change in the faculties of the soul themselves, but in some of the capabilities of those faculties, such capabilities as are affected by the pervading moral element of human nature. This discrimination is made in order to meet an objection to the Scripture doctrine, as involving a positive alteration of the physical constitution of the soul itself. We have already met one part of this objection in attributing the change to the physical power of God, by showing that we cannot discern the nature of the divine power in any of its workings, and that whether the power employed in originally creating man holy was designated physical power or not, the same power might be employed in a new creation of a depraved nature unto holiness, without giving any legitimate ground for complaint. We shall now attempt to show that the change itself as wrought by this power is not a change in the natural constitution of any human faculty, but only in the moral complexion of that constitution, superinduced by sin, and ingrained into the moral energies of the soul. As we have repeatedly stated, the moral element of the soul, seated in the will or heart, which is the subject of regenerating grace, pervades the whole mental structure in a manner analogous to that in which a color pervades the transparency of glass or a fluid. It consequently modifies everything seen through it. A man looking at a landscape through a crimson glass will see every object in it, every house, tree, hill, and meadow, just as if they were seen through a clear, uncolored glass, only with this plain difference: in one case, the objects will be seen in their own natural colors; in the other, they will be seen covered with crimson hues, yielded by the medium through which they are observed. In a similar way the moral elements in the soul, considered as pure or depraved, will control the view of the very same truths when brought under inspection. It is too well known to be disputed, that the affections of the will, the passions, affections, and prejudices, which are all the direct expressions of the will or heart in man, do control the views of the understanding, and create the responsibility which is universally attached to all the effects of prejudice and passion. To extract and remove the influence of such feelings will inevitably modify the judgments of the understanding and the feelings growing out of them.

We may now understand what was meant by the expression, that regeneration effected a change, not in faculties, but

in certain capabilities of faculty. The removal of a prejudice disabling correct views in the understanding is not the
creation of that understanding, but the mere restoration of a
capability of a correct view which had been destroyed by
the modifying prejudice. We are also enabled to conceive
a little more clearly what is meant by *spiritual blindness*. It
is not a destruction of the intellect, but the destruction of a
certain capability in the intellect produced by sin, by the
coloring influence of moral depravity. Just as we see the
objects in a landscape under the colors yielded by the colored medium through which we look, and do not see the
natural and real colors of those objects, we are as truly *blind*
to those colors as if we did not see them at all. The leaves
on a tree in summer are green, but seen through a crimson
glass they appear red, and we are as incapable of seeing the
real colors, we are as truly blind to them, as if we did not see
them at all. We see, but do not perceive. Just so the mind,
blinded by sin, can in one sense see the truths of the gospel,
and yet, in another, be utterly *blind* to their true significance.
This is the explanation of the gospel paradox, "seeing they
shall see and not perceive." The illustration and the fact
illustrated show the worthlessness of the cavil, that there is
a hopeless paradox, if not a positive contradiction, in the gospel, when it speaks of an understanding perceptive and yet
insensible. There are other facts which show the same thing.
It is proved under the analogous case of color blindness, or
the want of musical perception, or the want of the artistic
sense of the beautiful in art or nature, that there is such a
thing as a mind perceptive *and yet blind*. Color blindness is
a singular incompetence to discern colors, which is sometimes
found in particular individuals. It is not want of eyesight;
these persons can see, but they are not able to see colors, or
to distinguish one from another. Some individuals of the
class can see some difference between a thing colored and a
thing uncolored, but they are utterly blind to the actual hues

and to the distinctions between them. Here is an instance of a mind perceptive and yet blind. We frequently hear that one has no ear for music. There are two senses in which this is true, but in neither does it mean that the person is deaf. But in one of the senses it means that the person has no capacity to make music himself, although he may hear and enjoy it. In the other of the two senses it means that the person has no capacity to perceive the melody and charm of music; music is often positively disagreeable to him. In this case we have a striking instance of a mind seeing and yet blind, perceptive yet insensible. Such a person is not deaf; every note in a strain of music comes clearly to the ear; but he has no perception of the melody and charm in it. A man totally wanting in the artistic sense of the beautiful in nature and in art may stand before a glorious landscape or a beautiful painting; he may see every object in the one, and every form, color, and combination in the other, and yet be totally blind to the beauty in both. In view of these facts, why should any one question the fact that the mind may be intellectually perceptive of religious truth, and yet spiritually blind to its real significance?

In the spiritual blindness which the word of God attributes to the fallen human soul the same general characteristics prevail. The understanding is able to see the truth concerning God, the law, and the gospel, by an intellectual operation, just as it sees other truths; but inasmuch as the field of vision in the intellect is transfused with the influence of a depraved moral nature, it fails to see the true significance—the real color of these truths. Hence the character of God is misjudged, his law is misapprehended; the excellence of both is discounted; his grace is misconstrued; and all his glorious claims to affection present an aspect of offence instead of attraction.

When, then, we take in the full meaning of the fact that this misguiding element in the mental vision is *moral*—that

it is seated in the will, and all its misguiding power is an expression of the will—that this moral element is *morally bad*,
not only as it is the result of sin, and as such involves
responsibility, but as it is in itself a bad or depraved moral
energy, necessarily determining both responsibility and condemnation, we can understand why the Scriptures hold
men accountable, not merely in spite of their spiritual blindness, but on account of it. The incapacity to see the truth
is directly due to the badness, the moral evil, which is in the
moral nature of the man. To the color in the glass is due
the blindness to the real nature of the objects seen. The
responsibility for spiritual blindness is absolutely demonstrated when we remember that the seat of the incapacity is
in the will itself—in the permanent states and disposition of
the very faculty which chiefly conditions responsibility.

Regeneration acting directly on this depraved moral element in the heart, changing it from the morally bad to the
morally good, altering the crimson color which regulates all
the activities of the mental structure, will necessarily affect
the views of the understanding. But it is not a change of
faculty; it is only a change in the capability of a faculty.
The color does not confer the transparency on the glass
through which objects are seen; it only modifies it. The
grace of regeneration does not create an understanding; it
only purges an existing power of perception into a capacity
to see aright. This view of the function of grace in regeneration also corrects a fanatical misapprehension of it, as
involving *the revelation of new facts to the mind*. The blindness it is designed to remove is not an ignorance of facts,
but merely an insensibility to the true significance of facts
already known. We are sure, therefore, that all who claim
to have a new revelation from God, and appeal to the illuminating office of the Holy Ghost in proof of the assertion, are
altogether mistaken, simply *because the revelation of new
truth is not the object of that illumination*. The effect of

regeneration on the understanding is to enable it to see
moral and religious truth, with more or less completeness, in
its true colors. The character of God, instead of appearing
offensive, begins to reveal its intrinsic beauty. The law of God,
instead of appearing harsh, overstrained, an object of disgust and terror, begins to appear as the venerable bond of
all justice, wisdom, and goodness. The nature of sin is revealed as only evil, and worthy of universal condemnation
and resistance. The nature of holiness is revealed as worthy
of all reverence and love, and conformity to its dictates, the
eternal obligation of all wisdom and righteousness. The
grace and glory of the gospel begin to reveal their real
aspects. This is what is meant by opening the eyes of the
understanding to see wonders in the law of the Lord.

In the *fifth* and last place, the change involved in regeneration does not stop with its effects on the perceptive
powers of the understanding; it is *universal in its influence.*
Such is the positive assertion of the apostle : *old things are
passed away; behold, all things are become new.* It affects
the *heart* as well as the understanding. The man still loves
and hates ; but the things he once loved now lose their attraction, and the things he once hated put on an attraction
they never had before. The heart has been changed; its
moral tastes have been altered. Sin, instead of being an
object of delight, now excites disgust, anxiety, and distress.
The idea of God and Christ, instead of exciting fear and dislike, now becomes welcome to the thoughts, the object of
an affectionate consideration, more or less powerful in degree. The law of God is approved as wise, just, and good.
The soul discovers a pleasure in prayer, and delights in its
exercise. The Bible becomes precious, and there is a sensible satisfaction in reading it, and in meditation on the high
things of religion and the future life. As the aversion of the
heart once banished such reflections, the change of the heart
invites them. The whole moral tone of the soul is purified

and elevated. It can no longer find the delight it once did in books, companionships, and pleasures in which sinful elements constituted the controlling complexion. There is an elevation and refinement of the whole moral energy of the soul in true regeneration. The heart is brought into sympathy with good men and good things. The spirit and temper of the whole heart is purified and refined to a degree measured accurately by the degree of the grace given and the definiteness with which the work of regeneration is accomplished and revealed in the consciousness. It creates new fears and new hopes, new desires and new aversions. The old dread of religious ideas, and of sensibility to the meaning of them, gives way to the dread of a want of them. The influence of the Holy Ghost, once resisted, is now invited and cherished. The hope of being left to sin in peace is now exchanged for the fear of being left to sin in peace. The society of Christians, once dreaded, is now welcomed, and that, too, in proportion to the vigor of their spiritual character as affording both pleasure and help to one's own religious life by the association. Temptations are no longer sought for or welcomed, but are dreaded and shunned; restraint from wrong-doing is eagerly desired instead of being resisted.

The grace of regeneration affects all the energies of the man. It will regulate the whole series of the distinct energies of the will, from mere impulse to positive volitions, the determined purposes which have passed from desire and stable affections to settled resolves. It draws the authority of the divine law over all these manifestations of will, and gives effect to that authority. It controls the positive volitions as they pass on further and go over into actions, the last and highest expression of the moral energy. It regulates the use of language, and teaches a man to refine his vocabulary, and clear it of all impure or unholy words in epithet or argument. It affects his whole conduct, making him regardful of the rights and interests of others. It establishes the supreme obligation of justice, candor, integrity, and kindness over all his positive acts. It controls his *habits* as well as his feelings; his *passions* as well as his *acts*. It pervades every *relation* he sustains; it makes him a better husband and father, a better child or servant, a better citizen and friend. It makes him more vigilant and careful to be what he ought to be in every relation and office of human life. It controls a man's whole view of this earthly scene of existence, gives evidence to the unseen things of the life to come, and substance to the things of hope in the revelations of the Scriptures. It gives him practical estimates of the relative value of the things that are seen and the things that are unseen, which exert a powerful control over his endeavor to secure them.

The grace of regeneration exerts a profound influence on the human *memory*, keeping it awake to the truths which concern the higher interests of the soul. The memory has become seriously affected in its hold upon moral and religious ideas. Under the undisturbed influence of the depravity of the heart, the faculty has become singularly treacherous to the impression of these truths. This impression is hard to make, and easy to erase. This is due to the secret reluctance of the will to entertain these ideas, and the secret repulsion thus given to their presence in the mind. The impression is described by a prophet to be as evanescent as the morning cloud or the early dew. The influence of even a thorough religious training is frequently very faint to all appearances. The memory of God, sin, death, and responsibility, unsupported by the grace of the Holy Spirit, will be unwelcome, swift in passing out of the mind, resisted and soon obliterated altogether. There is nothing more important for a sinner, if he only knew it, than intense and constant prayer that God would keep alive the recollection of his spiritual relations in the deadly atmosphere of an unholy moral nature. Regeneration corrects this fatal tendency in memory to let go its hold on these all-important thoughts. These ideas become welcome; they are no longer repelled, but cherished; they return easily; they remain more constantly. God, instead of "not being in all their thoughts," is now in daily remembrance, and in many cases is literally in all their thoughts. The mind learns to cleave to these spiritual ideas as the very strength and solace of life. The deadly paralysis of memory on its spiritual side is overcome by the grace of regeneration.

It also profoundly affects that wonderful faculty called *conscience*. It purifies and intensifies its intuitions of right and wrong. It becomes more delicate and refined in its perceptions. This is the reason why Christians often see improprieties in things in which the less delicate intuitions of a merely cultivated conscience can see none. It also gives more authority to conscience, making its requirements more effective. It sets up conscience, guided by the word of God, the master principle of action, as distinguished from expediency, especially in cases where there is no bond of civil law or effective public opinion which can be brought to bear to secure right action. This master principle, the vice-royalty of God in the soul, is endued by regenerating grace with a higher fitness for its great functions, and established in a wider and stronger, as well as a more constant, exercise of its peculiar dominion.

Regeneration also affects the play of *the fancy* and the energies of the *imaginative faculty*. It trains the imagination by constant reference to the unseen realities of the future state, and leads it to higher conceptions, and thus imparts a more vivid force to the apprehension of the grand truths revealed to faith. It tends to quell those licentious combinations of images which are so pleasing to an unholy heart, and which throng on the unregenerate fancy without any suspicion of their degrading and ruinous effects on the purity and dignity of the character. It restrains the less odious, yet dangerous, indulgence of unchastened desires and hopes, the useless dreams of impossible self-exaltation. It brings every imagination of the thoughts of the heart under the obedience of Christ. It sets a force to watch and resist the entry and entertainment of all polluting visions and all misguiding fancies, and will finally quench them altogether.

It affects also the *sense of wit and humor*. These charming faculties have felt deeply the influence of the depravity in the moral nature. They have been led to the discernment of the witty and humorous relations, peculiar to their own nature, in things foul and wicked, and have thus been betrayed into becoming ministers of iniquitous influence, often to such an extent as to make some good men, more sensitive to wrong than competent in judgment, suspicious of the lawfulness of these faculties themselves. It is certain that these faculties in a low type of moral character often obliterate their own uses, and destroy their own charm, by the coarseness to which they are determined by the low type of the ruling moral element which breeds it. It is also certain they are often used to destroy reverence for sacred things, and to discredit the truth and service of God. The purgation of that corrupt element which distorts them would not destroy these fascinating faculties, but would emancipate them to a legitimate use, bring them under the influence of holiness, and make them the ministers of its ends. They assuredly have a legitimate use; they are parts of the human understanding as God has made it, and to discount them as essentially wrong would be to charge him foolishly. Indeed, the question has been raised, whether there will be any place in heaven for the use of these brilliant powers of the soul. Without pretending to dogmatize on the subject, we, at least, have no hesitation in expressing the opinion that there will be. These faculties belong to the actual constitution of the soul, as much as reason or memory. The Scriptures nowhere intimate that any essential faculty of the mind will be obliterated by the full redemption of heaven. The redeemed man will be a man still, unshorn of any essential power of his intellectual nature; and if these faculties of wit and humor should remain, we can conceive no reason why the faculties should be retained, and their employment should be forbidden. It adds a new zest to the conception of the higher and more sacred employments of that region of serene and holy peace, to conceive its intervals of relaxation enlivened by the joyous merriment of its holy and happy inhabitants rejoicing in each other's society. There are no tears in heaven; it is nowhere said there is no laughter.

It would be interesting and perhaps profitable to trace the influence of moral depravity, and the counter-influence of divine grace, on those more recondite parts of the soul which are not usually considered in discussions of this great doctrine. The study of the human spirit, both on its intellectual and ethical side, must be more or less complete as the states of the mind and heart, as affected by sin and by regenerating grace, are more or less perfectly apprehended. But we must pass this inquiry by.

We may now form some conception of that great change which must be wrought in us before we can see either that kingdom of God which is *within the soul*, or that kingdom where God unseals his full glory to the view of his rejoicing creatures. It is a profound and radical change in the whole existing moral nature of the man. It makes him a new creature in Christ; it renews his nature; it re-colors his character; it transforms his will; it re-moulds his whole system of thinking, feeling, and acting. It gives him new objects to live for; new rules to live by; new principles to impel to action; and new sensibilities to success or failure in the progress and development of that new life. Regeneration works through that faith which gives evidence to things unseen, and substance to things of hope. It thus gives reality to all the grand doctrines and facts of the gospel revelation. It gives substance to heaven and hell, to God and angels, to the perils of the pilgrimage through this world, and to the grand guarantees of safety to the child of God in the covenant of his grace. It will tear open the crystal vault of the sky, with its studded stars, and display to the eye of faith, above and beyond the visible creation, a crystal city, more glorious than the most splendid creation of Grecian genius, overspread by a serener sky and more glorious stars, crowded and piled high with the gemmed walls and columns of the palaces and temples of the kings and priests unto God. Yea, this mighty change will draw down over this visible creation all the realities of eternity; they will settle down upon it, pervading, but not disturbing it, as a cloud comes down with its light veil upon a mountain. It will develop a grand existence even in this world for any soul which is bold enough to develop the full force of that faith which gives evidence and force to invisible things. We are all walking in a state closely allied to somnambulism under the grand things of this life and of the life to come, under the effects of sin and revealed grace, under the realities of an immortal state. But we are moving as a man walks under the columns and arches of some mighty temple with a veil upon his face or a dimness in his eyes. Regeneration will break that deadly stupor. Faith, as the organ of the new regenerate nature, tears off the veil and lets in the grandeur and glory of the surrounding and the overhanging truth. Faith seldom leads to its more pronounced and positive effects, simply because it is so feebly developed. But to every bold, meek seeker after attainable grace, the warrant of great boldness in the faith is given; and to every such an one regeneration, and the living faith which is the fruit of the Spirit, will open fountains, not only of holy joy and energy, but visions of glory, even in this life, more beautiful than the curly clouds which swing in amber and gold on the western arch at evening. It is possible for a regenerate soul, even here on the dusty and hot highway of the pilgrimage, even here in the very heat and grapple of heady conflict, to rejoice in the Lord—yes, to rejoice with a joy that is inexpressible and full of glory. Thanks be unto the Father for the grace of the Spirit, not less than for the gift of the Son.

CHAPTER IX.

THE EVIDENCES OF REGENERATION.

"Hereby know we that we dwell in him and he in us, because he hath given us of his Spirit."—*John in his Epistles.*

THE discussion of regeneration will be made sufficiently complete for the purposes of this little treatise by an exposition of its evidences. The reality of the change cannot be disputed, either as a doctrine of the Scriptures or as a matter of experience. But the reality and soundness of any particular instance of professed conversion is an issue which is to be proved, and hence the importance of a clear understanding of the scriptural evidences which prove it. The necessity of this proof arises from the fact that the *nature* of the change is a question of *inference* and not of consciousness. The *fact* of a change of some sort is a matter of consciousness, but the real nature of that conscious change is necessarily a question of inference by a comparison of the marks of a genuine conversion as laid down in the word of God, and the facts as reported by self-examination into the conscious experiences of the soul. It is a favorite doctrine with some, that as the testimony of consciousness is direct, it must be clear and correct; that consequently a man always *knows* when he is converted; that any doubt is only a form of unbelief; and that every true Christian is necessarily in a state of assurance. Hence the boldest and most confident language is used; all modesty and caution in the estimate of one's spiritual standing is discounted, all necessity for the warning, " be not high-minded, but fear," for self-distrust, and self-examination to see if we be in the faith, is set aside ; and the absolute assurance that we have passed from death unto life is accepted on the bare consciousness of a change in the feelings—a consciousness assuredly reliable as to a change of some sort, but by no means giving assurance that the change is regeneration. The mind may undergo many changes on the subject of religion, each one of which may be reliably certified by consciousness; but whether the conscious and certified change is the saving change of the heart, the *real nature* of the change is still to be ascertained; and this is to be done by comparing the altered mental phenomena with the Scripture marks of conversion, and *the conclusion inferred from their agreement.*

It is a question of *inference,* not of *mere consciousness;* an inference to be cautiously and deliberately drawn, and not hurried to a conclusion. As the facts in the consciousness which constitute one premise from which the conclusion is drawn, are, in many cases, not so strongly and definitely developed as to warrant an instant judgment of their real nature, the need for caution is obvious. The facts may and do reveal themselves with varying degrees of distinctness; and while, in some cases, a quick and confident decision upon them may be warranted, yet, in many others, a wide scale of modest judgments is not only warranted, but demanded. The stony-ground hearers in the parable teach us that there is such a thing as receiving the word with joy, yet soon giving way to a withered condition of experience and hope. They bring the blade, but no grain; leaves, but no fruit; and by their fruits they are known. Satan has made a counterfeit of every coin in the currency of the kingdom. There is a false faith and a false joy. That deceitfulness of the heart, which is pronounced more deceitful than anything else, gives space for a vast series of spurious religious affections. There is often, especially in high and wide-spread scenes of religious excitement, an honest, but mistaken, conviction in many minds that they do comply with the terms of salvation; this breeds the equally honest, but equally mistaken, conviction that they have passed from death unto life; this, again, persuades them that they are saved; and this, again, produces a feeling of joy and sympathy with holy men and things. But it soon passes away, and the conviction of being deceived takes permanent possession of the mind. All this possibility of deception, the existence of false affections, the deceitfulness of sin, the art and cunning of the adversary, lift a warning finger, and emphasize the command of Paul, "Examine yourselves," "Prove your own selves."

In making the test, one premise of the inference is always clear, that is, the scriptural signs and evidences of conversion; but the other premise, the facts in the consciousness, are often far from clear. In all these cases the conclusion cannot be rationally and scripturally drawn with clearness and decision. Upon this state of facts rest the apostolic injunctions to cautious self-inspection. In those cases where the personal experiences of grace are exceptionally definite and distinct, a more decisive and rapid inference is altogether warrantable; but it is very certain that, even in these cases, in the long conflict of the spiritual warfare which is before them if life is prolonged, these more fortunate children of grace will find a plentiful occasion for the wise caution of the sacred writers. The test of regeneration is found in the conformity of the facts in consciousness with the marks which discriminate the saving work of the Spirit, and not merely or only in the consciousness of a change of some kind. It is all-important, then, to ascertain these discriminating marks as they are delineated in the word of God.

1. One testimony in reference to these tests tells us, "Hereby know we that we dwell in him and he in us, because he hath given us of his Spirit"; and we know that he has given us of his Spirit by one infallible test, "the fruit of the Spirit" in us. These fruits of the Spirit are clearly defined for us; they are "love, joy, peace, long-suffering, gentleness, goodness, faith, meekness, temperance." The presence of these

affections and qualities in the mind is proof of the saving
energy of the Holy Ghost in regenerating the human soul;
the absence of them proves the want of it.   The feeble and
doubtful development of these graces, throwing the existence
of them into question, makes the saving grant of the Spirit
in regeneration a matter of doubt.   The prevalence of these
qualities, clear and unquestionable in the consciousness,
leaves the question of regeneration settled beyond a doubt.
The presence of the opposite qualities, " hatred, misery, restlessness, impatience under trial and provocation, badness,
roughness, unbelief, pride, and perpetual self-assertion, and
the want of restraint upon unholy and selfish impulses and
passions," indicates the want of the Spirit in his saving power.
A steady resistance to these evil qualities, a sincere aversion
to their presence, a persistent grief for their intrusion, while
a proof that they do exist in the heart, is also a proof that
the Holy Ghost is there also, animating and sustaining an
irreconcilable conflict with them, which will surely issue in
full victory over them in the end.   Let us follow the series
of the fruits of the Spirit in the order in which they are described.

2. The series begins *with love.*   It has been explained at
length how the ruling moral element in the human spirit, like
the crimson or golden coloring in glass or a transparent
fluid, regulates or modifies every power of the understanding
and every feeling of the heart, to a greater or less degree.
When this moral energy is *holy,* it determines every power
which it influences *in holiness;* when *depraved,* it determines
them *in sin, or in the effects of sin.*   When we segregate in
thought, and consider the influence exerted on *the heart,* we
see a powerful control exerted over all *the affections.*   When
the modifying element is depraved, we see its manifestations
in depraved affections.   The carnal mind is seen to be at enmity against God; his character is disliked; his law is dis-
tasteful; his claims are resisted; his service is discounted as

unpleasant; all his asserted relations to man are regarded with invincible aversion. But when the pervading moral energy which conditions these dreadful results is purified by regenerating grace, a change, corresponding in the energy of its manifestations to the degree of the purifying grace given, at once appears *in the affections* towards God, and towards all the revelations and expressions of his will, character, and supremacy in the universe. Leading up to the manifestation of the change in the heart is a preliminary and corresponding change in the views of the understanding. As the depraved moral element, whose seat is in the will or heart itself, determines warped and distorted views of God, and all his manifested will, so the purification of this modifying force determines a change in the views of the understanding, giving it just views of God and his manifested will. The regeneration of the heart secures this change in the views of the mind, and this change in the mind leads directly to the manifestations of change in the heart itself. The revolution begins in the seat of the mischief, and thence transmits its altering force over the whole circle of the energies subject to its influence. Without dwelling on the relation between the heart and the understanding in this mutual interaction in regeneration, let us trace out the practical modifications in the governing love of the soul as delineated in the Scriptures.

The *first* change we notice is towards *Christ as the Saviour of sinners.* "To you which believe he is precious." "We are the circumcision, which worship God in the spirit, and rejoice in Christ Jesus, and have no confidence in the flesh." To every natural mind, capable of understanding and appreciating the unique and unparalleled personal character of Jesus of Nazareth, there appears such an assemblage of personal excellences as to extort the tribute of unbounded admiration, even from infidels and errorists of every class. This species of natural good feeling towards him is the travesty of genuine love to him, the counterfeit of the saving

affection of love to him; and in those who rely upon the
mere culture of the religious nature may be easily mistaken
for it.   But when he is presented and pressed upon the conscience in his grand comprehensive character and function
as the Saviour of sinners, these lovers turn away in aversion,
and no trace of love to him is discoverable.   The implication
of their own character, *as sinners*—the very terms of his deliverance—*free grace*, deepening and adding intensity to the
implied charge of guilt and helplessness, is more than they
can stand.   Consequently all men at first, and always, unless
moved by the grace of the Holy Spirit, turn away from
Christ as a sinner's free and gracious Saviour with fixed
aversion.   Yet this office of Christ is the chief glory of his
character, personal and official; it is the very object of his
advent on earth; it is the very thing which constitutes his
priceless value to the human race, and this is the very thing
which discriminates *the love to him* which is the fruit of the
Spirit in regeneration, and distinguishes it from all the
merely natural affection towards him, bred in the natural
mind by the unique perfection of his personal character.
The freedom of his grace is the very crown and summit of
his value to a race of lost and helpless sinners.   It is this
office and this grace which adjusts him to the miseries, the
sins, the fears, and the yearning hopes of the human soul.
It is this which adjusts him to the felt wants of every individual who becomes acquainted with his own spiritual condition.   It is the discovery of him in this character as a
sinner's Saviour which awakens the love of such a soul.
Just as soon as grace triumphs in regeneration, *this* insight
into Christ comes to the front, and that very notion of him
as a Saviour of sinners, saving them *by free grace*, which was
once the chief occasion of offence in him, becomes the chief
cause of all the joy and peace of the regenerated and saved
sinner.   There is no more striking and reliable proof of regeneration than this change of feeling and affection towards

Christ as a *sinner's Saviour*. Hence the test as laid down by the apostle: "To you which believe he is precious." That *love* to Christ as the friend and deliverer of sinners is demonstration of regenerating grace.

This *love* implanted by the Spirit manifests itself suitably on occasion towards every revelation of the nature and will of God. It is love towards the Father as well as to the Son; it brings to view that glorious fatherhood restored to his reconciled rebel by the grace of redemption. It is love to the Holy Spirit, the sweet, benignant dweller in the unholy heart, to develop the regenerate life he has given, and unfold all the comfort and glory of the covenant of grace and the things of Christ. As that enmity to God which marked and distinguished the carnal mind showed itself in the judgments and feelings excited by every display of his will, whether in his word, law, ordinances, and the events of his providence, the change of this enmity into *genuine love towards himself* will exert a corresponding change in the views and feelings *towards his will*, however disclosed.

The *second* manifestation in the altered love of the heart, which we note, is the affection which springs up towards *the followers of Christ*. "We know that we have passed from death unto life, because we love the brethren." One of the most remarkable traits of the true Christian nature is the sympathy created for all men indiscriminately as lost souls, and the peculiar sympathy and affection for all who love and trust the Saviour. One of the earliest impulses of the renewed soul is to bring others to share in forgiving mercy. The same principle in which this feeling is rooted determines a strong sympathy for all who do share in it. The desire that the gracious giver of hopes so sweet should be suitably loved and honored is delighted when it finds those who do so love and honor him. Often in some darkened mood, when his own love to his Saviour appears to his own jealous heart to be doubtful, there is a sensible satisfaction in the thought that

others do love and do him justice.   This sympathy leads to
delight in the society of Christians, to the desire to talk with
them, to open the heart to them, to learn of their experiences,
to a sense of joy and safety in such communion with them.
As the carnal mind found no pleasure in the society of believers as such, the regenerate mind does find a real delight
in the communion of saints.

Another expression of this altered love of the soul is
towards *the law of God.*   " Oh, *how love* I thy law; it is my
meditation all the day."   The law of God may be considered under the specific notion of the moral law, or under
the notion of his positive and statutory legislation, or under
the more general notion of the Holy Scriptures at large, in
which all his revealed will is set forth.   Under each of these
notions the love of the regenerate heart is elicited.   It no
longer finds discontent in the pure and lofty spiritual holiness embodied in the moral law and required in the obedience of every creature.   It sees in the moral law only the
formal articulation into definite requirements of that eternal
distinction of *right* which is felt to be essentially obligatory.
Holiness has become sweet to the taste of the regenerate
heart, and it exults in the law which requires, and, when
obeyed, develops it.   The law which once seemed the harsh
bond of an impracticable purity has become the embodiment of all justice, wisdom, purity, and goodness, the noble
standard to define and stimulate every attainment in excellence.   It is the universal bond of *right.*   Its very penalty
is felt to be the indispensable sanction of a law for creatures
who are to exist forever, and its execution the necessary and
natural, and altogether righteous, consequence of law eternally violated.   Under its positive aspects it regards the
statutes of the Lord as always right and wise, adapted to
the conditions of mankind, when ordered to be observed,
and to the purposes of the divine Lawgiver in making them.
But under its broader aspect as the word of God, the regen-

erate heart finds an inexhaustible fountain of strength and comfort in its grand doctrines of covenanted grace; in its promises, which animate faith and obedience to ardent energy; in its assurances of divine love, which fill the soul with grateful joy; and in its prophecies of the triumph and coming glory of the kingdom, which fill hope with exultant visions of glory, honor, and immortality. In its lessons of covenanted grace, in its histories of the kingdom, in its biographies of the saints, in its wise and faithful warnings, in its firm pledges of all the grace needful for every emergency of the Christian career, the renewed heart finds an abundance of priceless truth; and the word of God becomes inexpressibly dear. It is the daily counsellor and companion, the guide in all activity, the solace in every affliction, of the Christian soul. Nothing could be in stronger contrast to the feelings of the unregenerate heart towards the word of God.

Another striking expression of this changed affection is towards the *ordinance of prayer.* The renewed soul delights to pray; it feels a necessity for prayer so imperious that the command and broad warrant to pray seems not so much to define a duty as to secure and exalt an immeasurable privilege. The old carnal reluctance and disgust at prayer has given way to a delighted appreciation of a boundless franchise, which makes its employment at once the necessity and joy of daily existence. There is now no need to drive him, as before, to a reluctant and joyless observance. He has learned to love to pray, and he delights to draw near to the throne where grace is reigning through righteousness unto eternal life.

Yet another manifestation of this new love in the heart is a similar valuation and delight in all the ordinances of the house of God. The regenerated man has learned to love the church of Christ, not only in its worship, but in its work; not only in its ordinances, but in its organization. The preaching of the gospel, the sacraments, the songs of praise, the whole appointed service of the sanctuary, the Sabbath, and all the active demands of the Christian sacrifice and service, now give him a noble satisfaction. The growth and extension of the organized church, all that involves its honor, purity, and successful accomplishment of its grand ends in the spread of the gospel, and its establishment in the whole world, concern him; he takes a share and a delight in it all.

Yet another display of this new affection is the delight it creates *in meditation* on the things of grace.   Love delights in thoughts and reveries about the object loved.   To the unholy heart the thought of God is unpleasing; it remembers him, and is troubled, as a guilty conscience even in a believer will be.   The remembrance of him is banished as soon as may be; God is not in all his thoughts; often for long periods literally forgotten, and always unwelcome when the recollection returns.   This form of atheism is the direct result of that carnal mind which is enmity against God; but when that unnatural feeling is subdued by regenerating grace, he lives in the thoughts of the purified soul—often, literally, in all his thoughts—because the meditation of him, bitter to hatred, has become sweet to love.   It also embraces Christ as the Saviour, the Spirit as the Paraclete, and all the truth in which his grace has revealed itself to human hope.

The same renewed affection shows its noble regenerate energy in its disposition and dealings with the will of God, as manifested in *the orderings of his providence*.   It shows itself in contentment with the orderings of his allotments in life.   It shows itself in patient and trustful endurance of sorrow and affliction.   It animates the heart by an unfaltering confidence in Christ, and in the pledges of his grace; in the love of the Spirit and in his fidelity to his trust; in the fatherhood of God, and in the assurances of his protection. When the storm of providential trial is so sore as apparently to sweep the breaking heart from the rock of its salvation, it will still patiently struggle to regain its foothold, and will always blame its own weakness and unbelief rather than to charge God foolishly. The renewed heart clings to God in Christ as its only safety and hope. It spoke out in Job's grand confession and vow of faithfulness, "Though he slay me, yet will I trust in him."

This same renewed affection determines also a new set of *dislikes as well as likes*, and in this, too, its reality and its true nature appear. It determines an honest hatred to sin. It dreads temptation. It shrinks from the fascinations of an unholy world. It dreads everything that may obscure its view of Christ and the plan of salvation. It hates its own unbelief, its own hardness of heart, its own pride, selfishness, and self-righteousness, its own ingratitude and coldness of affection. It abhors its own sinful tendencies and its own imperfect efforts at obedience. It is full of self-distrust. It determines repentance for sin. The regenerate heart is the contrite and broken heart. Such are some of the leading manifestations and proofs of that fruit of the Spirit the apostle designates as *love*.

3. The *second* member of the fruits of the Spirit as given in the Scriptures is *joy*. The gospel is glad tidings of great joy. When the gospel is realized by that faith which is the substance of things hoped for and the evidence of things not seen, the necessary effect of its intrinsic gladness is to produce joy. The absence of joy at any time in a Christian soul is due solely to the fact that his faith for the time being, and during all that time of paralyzed comfort, is not doing justice to the truth of the glad gospel of infinite grace. The command is, "Rejoice in the Lord," not in one's self, not in what has been given and made ours, either by nature or grace, but in the Lord. "Rejoice in the Lord always," and with emphatic reduplication, "again I say unto you, Rejoice." Rejoice in the Lord; for all safety and comfort are in him. Rejoice in him at all times; for at no time does his grace fail.

Rejoice in times of sorrow; for the presence of the good Physician is a comfort even in sickness. Rejoice in times of trial; for trouble does not grow out of the ground, and he presides over all the remedial afflictions which he sends. Rejoice in him at all times; for he is never absent, never forgetful, never indifferent, and always bound by his gracious promise to make all things work together for good to them that love God and are the called according to his purpose. The absence of joy at any time ought to set every regenerate soul to diligent endeavor to bring back this dear fruit of the Spirit. Why should a regenerate soul go mourning all the day long?

4. The next of the series is *peace*. "Being justified by faith, we have peace with God." The cause of controversy between him and man is sin; that necessarily produces the condemnation of the King, and the hazard of the law. Peace can only come by taking away sin. The atonement of Christ is the only thing that can take sin away; and the necessary effect of the application of his blood is *peace with God*. This peace, based on the absolute extinction of all threatening claims, reflects itself on the mind of the forgiven sinner, and there is peace within him as well as without him, peace of conscience as well as peace in law. Fresh transgression may disturb this peace, but the way is always open to restore it; fresh repentance and fresh application to the atoning blood will yield fresh peace. As transgression will disturb, obedience will increase, this peace, and as it is the function of regenerating grace to secure obedience, that grace has more than one channel through which it brings peace. All regenerate souls should seek for the habitual presence of this fruit of the Spirit. Peace and joy are not merely to be prized as pleasant companions to our thoughts; but because they do to a most important extent condition our ability, zeal, and faithfulness in our service. "The joy of the Lord is our strength."

5. The next fruit of the Spirit in the test of the apostle *is long-suffering*. There is abundant occasion for this grace in any world like this. Selfishness reigns in it; injustice and open violence are the fruits of selfishness. Breaches of faith, treachery and fraud, insolence and unjust aggression, unkindness and want of sympathy justly due, make many a demand on the resentful passions. The natural heart yields freely to these impulses, and all the more freely because it commonly feels justified in doing it. But such yielding generally makes matters worse, instead of healing them. The regenerate heart, whenever grace is allowed a fair chance to assert its real quality, is full of sensibility to its own faults and infirmities, and is, therefore, more forbearing towards the faults and infirmities of others. As by the tender love of God its own sins are forgiven, it is all the more ready to forgive. The spirit of forbearance is this spirit of forgiveness in a certain relation to offences; it refuses to retaliate; and its presence, ruling the instincts of resentment and revenge, is a fruit of regenerating grace, and a noble proof of its power and beauty. Coming into open conflict, as it does, with the pride and pugnacious instincts of an unholy nature, this grace of long-suffering under injury and insult is often misjudged and subjected to opprobrious names in the passionate and blind judgments of men; but it is, nevertheless, a noble sample and proof of the regenerating grace of God. The indulgence of the opposite spirit will bring protracted and bitter sorrow into any Christian life. The high estimate put on this noble self-control in the word of God is the standard by which to judge it.

6. The next specification of the series is *gentleness*. One of the most prominent and dangerous developments produced by the depraving of the moral nature in man is found in the corruption and dangerous exasperation of a sensibility natural to every moral as well as to every animal being—the natural provision to secure self-protection and to repel un-

lawful aggression upon vested rights. Anger is not essentially and necessarily a wicked feeling. Christ was said to be angry on two occasions in his sinless life. But as affected by the corrupt condition of the human heart, superinduced by sin, it has become one of the most dangerous energies in human nature. Gentleness stands opposed to all sinful manifestations of anger in word or in deed, or in the secret motions of the silent soul. It prevents all hasty and unjust uprising of angry feelings; it controls speech into mildness and courtesy; it restrains the hand from violence. It breeds the spirit of kindness in lieu of the spirit of harshness; it breeds patience instead of irritability. It throws the sweet, subduing power of love and kindness over the provocations, even the just provocations, of life. It reduces anger to its proper place, and only allows it in the defence of just rights, the repulse of unlawful aggression, and when the honor of God demands it. No ornament of character is more beautitiful than that fruit of the Spirit and that proof of regenerating grace, the gentleness of an humble and good heart, ruling all the stormy impulses of the soul, refining the manners, and coloring with its noble beauty the words, acts, and character of a regenerate man. When combined with courage, fortitude, and strength of will, it presents the noblest combination possible to human nature.

7. Yet another fruit of the Spirit and evidence of regeneration *is goodness*. Sin mars the sympathies natural to the common nature and brotherhood of the human kind. Amid the wreck and ruin wrought on the moral nature of fallen man, enough of the quality of his original make has survived in a damaged condition to make even the culture of natural means effective in developing the virtues of benevolence, humanity, and kindness. Even this is indirectly due to the influence of the Holy Spirit in holding back the natural tendency of moral evil to rush steadily along the line of perpetual declension from one degree of

evil to another. Hence the possibility of civilization and
the ties of society among the heathen and the ungodly
masses of Christian lands. These virtues of humanity,
wherever found, show a marvelous beauty to the admiring
eye. But regenerating grace develops them into nobler forms
than moral culture can ever do. It leads to, and yet beyond,
those occasions for their exercise which are found in the
evils of this present life, and which limit benevolence in its
mere natural and cultivated form. It carries the unselfish
and generous sympathies to the relief of the higher spiritual
evils which threaten a far deeper disaster than any mere
earthly calamities. It produces not only the asylums and
other contrivances for the care of the orphan and the suffering poor, in which mere humanity may take a part, but all
the grand works of Christian enterprise for the salvation of
the world, in which mere humanity, however cultured, takes
no general interest. This goodness, which is the fruit of
the Spirit, qualifies the whole character; it sweetens the
sympathies; it refines the manners; it makes charitable the
social judgments, and chastens the social relations of men
into sources of safety and comfort. It tends to make men
good in every relation of life—good fathers and mothers,
good husbands and wives, good friends and neighbors. It
throws the sweet sympathies of a purified heart over all the
connections and events of this strange world. If any man
hopes and believes that the regenerating grace of God has
displayed its power upon his soul, without making him a
better man, more honest, more just, more pure, more kind,
more obedient to God, more useful to man, he may subject
his hope and confidence of grace to very serious discount.
Grace breeds goodness in all its forms; the fruit of the
Spirit carries always a betterment to man, both in himself,
and in all his relations. This is its necessary effect.

8. The next fruit of the Spirit in the enumeration of the
apostle is *faith*. Saving faith is everywhere described in

the Scriptures as "the fruit of the Spirit," and the "gift of God." It manifests itself in renouncing absolutely all other grounds of hope towards God but the merits and grace of Christ. It is conspicuously faith in Christ, a personal trust in his redeeming work, in his personal love, power, and faithfulness, in his promises, in all the statements of fact and doctrine he has made. It accepts the whole word of God; it admits the laws it prescribes; and obeys because it believes. It relies upon the pledged word and promise of grace, and expects the fulfilment of every pledge. It trusts in his administration of events, and, no matter how dark and mysterious his providences may seem, relies unshaken on his wisdom, love, and faithfulness. It gives evidence to things unseen, and substance to things of hope, and thus sees the gleam of heaven far in the dim clouds of the mystic future. It brings peace and hope; it renews strength; it animates patience; it impels obedience; it saves the soul. Wherever faith is seen in its effects, it demonstrates a regenerate heart.

9. The next item in the series is *meekness*. This opposes the pride and self-righteousness of the unrenewed soul. Pride is undue self-esteem; self-righteousness; a claim to integrity of life and character. When the spiritual illumination of regeneration takes effect, both of these feelings perish in the awful consciousness of inward pollution and personal guilt, and meekness and humility take their place.

10. The last specification is *temperance*. This does not mean merely sobriety; it is a far broader term; it means *restraint*, and covers all the passions and evil impulses of the soul. Regeneration does not at once make the regenerate soul completely holy; but it does fill it, not only with positive impelling forces towards holiness, but with powerful principles of restraint upon all the evil still left within the soul—upon the workings of the law of sin in the members.

A character and life which claims to be regenerate must show a restraint on evil impulses, generally effective, or the claim is nothing worth.

11. We must rapidly condense the remaining tests of regeneration; but as these have already been substantially discussed in the exposition of the nature of this wonderful work of divine grace, this brevity will not be unfaithfulness to the truth. As the ruling moral element, when depraved, affected the memory, conscience, judgment, and all the actions of the outward conduct, so will the same moral element when purified by regenerating grace. Conscience will become more clear-sighted, more delicate in its discriminations, and more masterful in its authority. Memory will become more tenacious of moral and religious ideas. The judgment will become more accurate in its discernment of moral and religious truth. The sense of wit and humor will be purified. All the powers of the human spirit will feel more or less directly the effect of grace in the heart. The whole external life will feel its controlling energy, and all will testify to the reality and the power of this great spiritual movement. "Old things will pass away; behold, all things will become new."

GIFTS TO BELIEVERS.

GIFTS TO BELIEVERS.

CHAPTER I.

THE SPECIAL GIFT OF THE HOLY SPIRIT HIMSELF TO BELIEVERS.

"Wherefore I also, after I heard of your faith in the Lord Jesus, and love unto all the saints, cease not to give thanks for you, making mention of you in my prayers, that the God of our Lord Jesus Christ, the Father of glory, may give unto you the spirit of wisdom and revelation in the knowledge of him; the eyes of your understanding being enlightened, that ye may know what is the hope of his calling, and what the riches of the glory of his inheritance in the saints, and what is the exceeding greatness of his power to usward who believe, according to the working of his mighty power."—*Paul to the Ephesians.*

1. THESE words of the apostle carry the statement of a great gospel truth which has suffered something of an eclipse in the apprehension of the church of our day, a truth, the absence of which is sorely felt in the experience, in the diminished comfort and efficiency of believers. That truth is the gift of the Holy Spirit to believers as such. It is not to be confounded with the gift of the Spirit in regeneration, and in the grant of that saving faith which is emphatically said to be "the fruit of the Spirit" and "the gift of God." Paul gives thanks for the faith and love to all the saints which he had heard was in these Ephesian Christians. He fully recognized them as already believers, as already animated with that love of the brethren which is one of the proofs of a regenerate heart.* He then goes on to tell them how he prayed unceasingly that the God and Father of the

---

*1 John iii. 14.

Lord Jesus would give to them *another gift*, special influences
of the Holy Spirit, who was already dwelling in them, by
which another measure of spiritual illumination would be
imparted to them, and by which they might be led unto
higher and sweeter views of the hope of their calling, of the
inheritance of the Father in them, and of the greatness of
power pledged to their salvation.   There can be no doubt of
the peculiarity of the gift to which he alludes.   It is not regeneration; for it is to be given to the regenerate.   It is not
faith; for it is sought for those who already believe.   It is
not one of the miraculous gifts of the Holy Spirit peculiar to
the apostolic age; for it was sought for those who are recognized simply by their faith and love to the brethren.   Nor is
it the gift of inspiration peculiar to the apostles and certain
apostolic men; for it is sought in the prayers of Paul for the
whole body of the Ephesian Christians, merely as Christians.
The effects ascribed to it, the increased vigor of spiritual enlightenment, and the consequent improved apprehension of
the truths of the gospel, clearly indicate that the gift was not
miraculous, or confined to any special class of Christians,
but was designed to minister to the spiritual graces of all
who believe.   Nor is it to be confounded with the indwelling
of the Spirit, which is already begun in every believer.   Yet
it is called a gift of the Spirit to believers.   The Spirit in one
sense being already given and already dwelling in the believer, this gift must refer to some special manifestation of
the Spirit's power, which may be properly designated as a
distinct gift of the Spirit himself.   This suggests the last
negative distinction of this peculiar gift of the Spirit to believers: it is not to be confounded with the process of sanctification.   It is rather a means of sanctification than the
result in sanctification, though the result always follows it,
and is the ultimate end sought in granting the gift.   It seems
to be designed to keep the attention of the body of believers
fixed on their dependence, their incessant dependence, on

fresh energies of the indwelling Spirit, constantly put forth and repeated to secure the sanctification of the soul. It is in the apprehension of the necessity for these ever-fresh and renewed manifestations of the Spirit's grace that the eclipse in the apprehension of the truth to which we alluded takes place. There is no decay in the full recognition of the necessity and nature of sanctification; the faith that every believing soul will ultimately be perfectly purified is intact. But the defect lies here: sanctification is rather expected than worked for; rather anticipated as the necessary growth of the germ implanted in regeneration than a development dependent on positive cultivation on the part of man, and on positive energies distinctly and designedly put forth on the part of the great efficient agent, the Holy Ghost. More dangerous still, even when sought in the active use of appointed means and service, sanctification is looked for as a result to be expected as the consequence of a certain steadiness and fidelity in this use of means, rather than as a work to be accomplished really by the Holy Ghost, and by as distinct and definite a series of actions in accomplishing the work of sanctification as is necessary in doing every sustained and constant work. The work of the Spirit is to be accomplished by the acts of the Spirit, and while the steady use of means is rigorously demanded by the divine rule, the mind is with equal imperativeness required not to rest at all in these means, but always to look beyond them for the effective power. There is an intense force and precision in the gospel doctrine that sanctification is *by the Spirit*. It is his work, to be accomplished by his special acts. These special actions of the indwelling Spirit are his gifts to believers, and being dependent on special energies manifested by the Spirit, are warrantably described as the gift of the Spirit himself to believers. The prayer of Paul for the Christians of Ephesus instructs us that we must look to a definite gift of the Holy Ghost, and to definite acts of that gracious giver, as well as gifts, to work out our deliverance from the inward power of sin, and our inward endowment with the power of holiness. The apostle here teaches what is abundantly taught in other Scriptures, the inexpressibly cheering and comforting doctrine that there is a special gift of the Holy Ghost as the Comforter, or, more exactly, the Paraclete, provided for the saint in the covenant of God's wonderful grace, a gift different from regenerating grace, yet working to the same end, and designed to make him acquainted with all the strength, the moral beauty, and the glorious comfort of the true believer in the Son of God.

2. These special acts of the Holy Spirit in carrying out the work of sanctification are manifold : he *seals*, he *anoints*, he *bears witness*, he gives *assurance* as an *earnest*, he *leads*, he *intercedes*, he *comforts*, he *brings to mind*, he expresses a *peculiar affection*, and he animates *the private and public worship of the believer in all its acts*,—in the songs of praise, in reading the Scriptures, in listening to the preaching of the word, in the offering of gifts, and in the use of the sacraments. The inexpressible grace and value of these gifts of the Holy Spirit will appear in the exposition of them, and emphatically through the prior consideration of the necessity for them, as it appears in the defects of the Christian experience of believers in our day. That experience, in spite of many advantages peculiar to the present age, and of many trials well suited to improve the graces of a regenerate heart, does not seem to differ advantageously from that of other times in many important respects. In some respects the Christian activity of this age is greatly in advance of the activity of most of the previous ages of the Christian era, and no doubt the immediate agents in this improved activity do enjoy an answerable degree of inward grace and comfort, certainly a large percentage of them. Yet, considering the bulk of the members of the Christian church, it will not be unwarranted to say that they do not exhibit an experience

in keeping with the recognized character and privileges of a
Christian as these are delineated and authorized in the
Scriptures.   So far as a long pastoral experience has unveiled the facts in typical instances, it is unquestionable that
the bulk of modern Christians are living far below the grade
of both character and comfort to which they are not only
authorized, but required, to aspire and attain.   The prevailing measure of activity in Christian work is not attended
with an answerable measure of Christian joy,—a state of
things which discloses a defect in the work as well as in the
comfort.   Look at the elements involved in the case.   Every
Christian is rightly recognized, according to the positive
statements of the Christian gospel, as a sinner actually
saved.   An actual salvation is positively pledged to the exercise of faith.   By the supposition that he is a Christian,
he has complied with the terms on which the promise of deliverance binds, and he is, therefore, secured by the integrity
of a God whose faithfulness is like the great mountains.   His
state has changed from one of infinite disaster to one of
infinite advantage.   His sins are pardoned; he is delivered
from the hazards of violated law.   A positive righteousness
has been imputed to him, which carries a sure title to eternal life.   He has been adopted into the family of God, and
has become his child.   The Holy Ghost has taken up his
abode in his soul to secure his integrity, and to make good
the promise to faith, "Sin shall not have dominion over you."
His salvation is assured; it is already begun; its progress
and ultimate completion are guaranteed by the pledge that
he who has begun the good work will complete it.   The engagement to faith is absolute.   The truth and power of the
infinite and infallible God stand guard over his hope.   He
has the promise of the life that now is as well as of that
which is to come.   Grace sufficient for him is positively covenanted.   He is by position the most fortunate and blest
of mortals; a true Christian can look down from an infinite

elevation on the most favored station of mere earthly advantage. He that believeth hath eternal life. This is his actual state by grace and covenant. Unquestionably he ought to be *in feeling* what he is *in law and in fact*, the happiest of mortals. But what is he in reality, so far as the states of his mind are concerned? As a rule, he is a prey to anxiety; he goes in bondage to fear. The idea of death is full of pain. Sin is a constant menace to his peace. The way of life through the mediation of Christ lies confused and cloudy in his thoughts. His graces are so incompetently developed that he hardly knows how to construe them, whether as sound or unsound. Now a grace will seem hopeful, and then it changes into an appearance which is untrustworthy. He knows not how far to confide in his faith, or hope, or love, or any part of his experience. He clings to his hope, but has little comfort in it. He shrinks from trials, though he knows that they come as proofs of divine love and fidelity. His obedience is steadily rendered, for the most part, but without conscious joy or sweetness in rendering it. He has often more dread of God than hope and affection to him. His religion, honestly judged, is more a source of trouble than of satisfaction. He is timid and uncertain in claiming the character of Christian, which, nevertheless, he would not give up for his life; and he frequently thinks it a commendable humility not to aspire to the joy and comfort of the Christian's hope, professing himself content to be without these if he can only be satisfied that he is a true Christian, although not happy. He fails to appreciate the suspicion thrown on the claim to the Christian character by the absence of the Christian comfort. He is actually drawing consolation from the defects and diseases of his spirit. The contrast between his state under the covenant and the state of his consciousness is wonderful, and as criminal as it is amazing.

3. The causes of this unhappy condition of things are

many and various. It springs in chief part from *unbelief;* from a want of confidence in Christ—in his teachings, in his promises, in the real power of his blood and righteousness. This lack of confidence is a defect in the degree and a weakness in the exercise of faith—not a total want of the principle of faith; for the existence of the germ of faith and spiritual life is presupposed in the character of Christian. When our Lord upbraided the twelve for their unbelief and hardness of heart he brought to light the paradox which appears in the experience of all his saints: of faith and unbelief co-existing and contending in the same heart. It is but one manifestation of the perpetual conflict between the law of grace in the mind and the law of sin in the members. When the faith is weak, unbelief is strong, and when unbelief prevails, the whole arrangement of the covenant loses its consolatory energy; the power of the atonement ceases to control the bitterness of sin; the ordinances lose their power to awaken hope; and the trials of faith, which are real strains upon its strength, often appear to have destroyed it altogether. Prayer has been so often disappointed that a general suspicion of its efficacy is bred, and then prayer continues to be offered more from a sense of duty, or a vague dread of neglecting it, than from any lively sense of its power or real value. Expectation of answers to it is thus blunted, and the ordinance is effectually nullified. What is true of prayer is true of all the rest of the ordinances, and the whole series is dishonored by this undisguised triumph of unbelief and the law of sin in the members.

Another cause of the prevalent anxiety is carelessness in living; sin indulged in many forms; acting from selfish impulses instead of regard to the will of God; transgressions growing out of heedlessness; absorption in business; engagement in improper pleasures; languor of spiritual desire; unsteadiness and the want of engaged and earnest feeling in using the means of grace. Such things are sufficient to account for defeated prayer and poverty of comfort. David knew that if he regarded iniquity in his heart the Lord would not hear him.

Another cause is found in ignorance, or at least in incompetent conceptions of the *great gospel grounds of hope*. The range of this cause of defects in Christian experience is so wide and varied that it will be impossible to expound it in its full extent. There is one of constant prevalence, the often unconscious substitution of the legal spirit of obedience for the free and gracious spirit of evangelical service. *The spirit of obedience to the law of works is applied to the terms of gospel grace.* The maxim of legal obedience is, *do and live*, comply with the demands of the established law, and then hope for life. The maxim of evangelical service is, *believe and then do*, accept the free gifts of a gracious salvation, and then go on to obey. The spirit of these two rules of action is widely different by the necessity of the case. The spirit of the law necessarily breeds dependence *on self;* something is to be done, and we are to do it. The spirit of free service breeds dependence on a basis of hope *out of self*, and the energy it creates looks for its support to that foundation out of self. The spirit of legal obedience unavoidably breeds endless anxiety, through fear of failure in complying with the conditions prescribed. The spirit of evangelical obedience accepts a full salvation as the free gift of infinite grace; anxieties are thus forestalled by faith; and the obedience secured by it is unselfish, free, affectionate, and hopeful. But there is such a thing as applying in our ignorance the spirit of legal obedience to the terms of grace, and where this is done the terms of grace will yield the same anxieties and the same *appeals to self-help* with the conditions of law. Faith is the instrument by which salvation is secured, the eye that sees the Saviour, the hand that takes hold of him, and it is, therefore, easily construed as a strict legal condition precedent of salvation. Under this view of it the whole

effort will be directed to comply with it in exactly the same
spirit as would be developed by a real legal antecedent to
the blessing.   Instead of looking outward to the Saviour and
to his great work, the mind is turned inward on what is going
on within itself.   Instead of fixing attention on the free full
offer of the gift of eternal life, and construing faith as the
simple acceptance of that offer, faith is looked upon as becoming a part of the offer itself, and as so conditioning and
qualifying it that the condition must be complied with before
it can be accepted.   This is to say, it must be accepted
before it is accepted.   Instead of looking out to the proposal
of infinite love, the attention is turned inward to scrutinize
the faith of the soul itself, and until that faith is certified all
the uncertainties and anxieties of the legal spirit are turned
loose in the heart.   It is as absurd as it would be for a traveler
to stop at the head of a bridge and turn his thoughts inward
on his own mind to see if he had confidence in the bridge,
instead of looking outward at the bridge itself to see if it was
worthy of his confidence.   This grave folly in construing the
plan of salvation accounts for a large measure of the anxieties of Christian people.   They have unconsciously passed
from a trust in the Saviour to a trust in their own faith.   No
wonder they are troubled.   The gift of the Holy Spirit to
guide them away from such an error, and to keep the way of
life clear in their thoughts, is an invaluable blessing.

Another cause of Christian anxieties is in the incompetent
views of the breadth and power of the redemptive work of
Christ the Saviour of sinners.   It is a marked feature in the
administration of grace, that while it pledges an absolute
salvation to every believer, from his sin as well as from its
effects, it does not undertake to do this completely and at
once.   The promise which takes effect at the beginning of
the exercise of faith is, "Sin shall not have dominion over
you."   That means that sin shall not be the ruling or master
principle in the regenerate soul.   But the promise also im-

plies that sin shall have *a standing*, and exert a certain measure
of influence in every such soul. This is universally admitted
of the great mass of average Christians, at least by all classes
of Christian interpreters. Saints are therefore not sinless;
they continually come short of their real duties; the law of
sin in the members is in constant conflict with the law of
grace in their minds. Now sin is a natural and necessary
fountain of suffering, and when the believer sins he may
expect to suffer. The consolations of a good hope of final
deliverance, while they will powerfully modify the suffering
of sin, will not absolutely extinguish it. But as a matter of
fact, his suffering is needlessly intensified and prolonged by
his ignorance and incompetent views of the redemption
wrought out for him.

There are two distinct elements of evil in sin: its essential
evil, and the danger it provokes. The one calls for repentance; the other is to be met by the energy of the atonement.
It is healthful to the soul to repent, and the suffering which
is involved in repentance may be so qualified by grace that
the exercises of a contrite heart may have an element of
positive delight intermingled with its grief. In this appears
one form of the gospel paradox, or apparent contradiction
in terms, "rejoicing in tribulation," and this ought to be the
regular and permanent state of feeling in a Christian soul in
view of his sin. But in reference to the other element of
sin—*the danger* it involves—however he may suffer from
certain effects of his faults, he is entitled to peace, because
his sin has been forgiven him, and the salvation which has
been pledged to him gives him assurance of deliverance, both
from sin and its dangers. By the very supposition that he
is a Christian, he is a sinner justified by grace, "justified
from all things," as it is stated; and being justified by faith,
through the blood and righteousness of Christ, he has peace
with God. If this blood and righteousness are really imbued
with a power to give real peace, beyond all question the

want of peace is proof beyond a doubt that that power is incompetently apprehended.   The anxiety of the Christian
heart would always be quelled *by a competent view of this
great gospel ground of hope.*   The anxiety of believers, growing out of their many infirmities and faults, is chiefly on two
accounts: they fear either that their sin demonstrates the
unsoundness of their claim to the character of a Christian,
or that it exposes them to the judgments of God.   The
acknowledged fact that a saint is not sinless is of itself proof
that all sin is not a proof of radical unsoundness.   The
power of the atonement made by the great High Priest
is utterly discounted if it cannot arrest the judicial expressions of divine wrath.   The presumptuous sin of a believer
will be sure of chastisement.   The disciplinary cure of all
his sins, whether distinctively presumptuous or not, will call
for chastening, but this will be done all in love.   The power
of the blood of Christ is complete.

To suppose his blood competent to take away sins that are
past, and to suspend its efficacy over sins subsequent to the
original period of justification, is to discount its value
altogether.   If it saves a man only from the sins of the past,
and leaves him to perish under the sins of the future, it cannot be said to save him at all.   In that case there can be no
such thing as Christian hope.   Hope is the effect of things
surely promised, yet not actually given into possession, and
it is intended for the present comfort of the future possessor.
But if there is no assurance, covering the future, in the promise given, the expectation of possession would be presumption, but not a basis of rational hope.   The legal spirit of the
carnal mind, and the self-righteous spirit of the unillumined
natural heart, will say that this assurance of forgiveness to
future sin will breed presumption and carelessness in living.
This has always been the cavil of the carnal mind against
the redemption of grace; but it utterly forgets or disregards
the fact that the grace which freely forgives, at the same

time renews and purifies the heart; and the justified sinner so decisively revolts against sin, that nothing delights him so much as to be delivered from it. In becoming alive unto holiness he becomes dead to sin; and as Paul puts it, "How can he that is dead to sin live any longer therein?" The objection also disregards the fact that the Holy Ghost dwells in every justified sinner for the very purpose of making good the promise, "Sin shall not have dominion over you." The sinner, then, who is justified by faith, is commanded to go boldly to the throne of grace, that he may find mercy, and obtain grace to help in time of need.

Whenever, therefore, he is overtaken in a fault, he ought not to discount the power of the atonement, nor discredit the sure promise of God; but always go at once and confess it to the great High Priest and sue out his pardon afresh. Trusting in Jesus he can be sure of pardon. The great mistake of Christians when overtaken in a fault is, that they think it necessary to keep away from the great loving Priest of the covenant until they have gone through some self-righteous series of duties, or some penance, or self-punishment, until they have suffered something of the pain they know they have deserved to suffer. By these self-saving expedients their distress is needlessly prolonged; and in their complacent sense of self-righteous behavior they discount the power of the saving blood and the tender pity of a sinner's Saviour. No wonder they suffer; no wonder they suffer more than was originally necessary. He who has any adequate spiritual discernment of the real power and scope of the great redemption will feel abundant encouragement to go at once with the heartfelt confession of his sins, and will speedily return realizing the blessed paradox of sorrow for his sin and peace in his Redeemer. No sin, however truly and rightfully it may give occasion to repentance, can long overpower the peace and hope of him who, adequately conceiving the power of the great redemption, humbly trusts

in the mediation of the great High Priest.   Inadequate conceptions of his work and his grace will leave the heart a
prey to fear, and accounts in large degree for the anxieties of
Christians.

Another cause of the prevailing want of settled peace and
liberty in the experience of believers is found in their incompetent views of the gospel doctrine of the Holy Spirit.   The
sadness of the believer is greatly due to the conscious failure
of his struggle against sin.   In a true Christian soul there is
maintained from the beginning of his spiritual life a conflict
with the indwelling sin of his heart, to which his experience
of grace has made him keenly sensitive.   The flesh lusteth
against the Spirit and the Spirit against the flesh.   The law
of grace in the mind warreth against the law of sin in the members.   The two are essentially contrary, the one to the other.
Now the one, and now the other, gains the ascendency.   In
this unceasing and bitter conflict his peace departs, and his
heart becomes a prey to anxiety; his feelings are expressed
by one suffering from the same cause: "O wretched man
that I am! who shall deliver me from the body of this death?"
The power of the gospel provisions of grace to cheer and
comfort in the midst of this experience is discovered in the
expression of joyous thankfulness which immediately follows
that sad complaint: "I thank God through Jesus Christ our
Lord."   These two contrasted expressions bring to light
again the paradox of the Christian joy in the midst of the
Christian suffering.   The realization of the stubborn strength
of his inward sin is a perpetual source of anxiety, but the
realization of the gracious provisions of the covenant, and
the assurance of complete ultimate victory, are just as
powerful to conquer fear and to inspire the cheerfulness of
assured hope.

One of those great provisions is revealed in the gospel
doctrine of the Holy Spirit.   His work in the human heart
is so delineated in the record as to provide amply for the

joy and peace of the believing sinner, no matter how much
he may be troubled by the consciousness of his own infirmity
and his habitual sinfulness. The Holy Spirit is represented
as "dwelling" in every regenerate soul. He undertakes to
sanctify it. All its state is fully known to him before he
undertakes this work. He is fully acquainted from the beginning with all its weakness, and with all its wickedness. His
omniscient eye has foreseen all the future sins which will
emerge out of this inward pollution. He completely appre-
ciates each and all of these things, all of this habitual tendency to sin, at their full significance. No future expression
of its evil will ever take him by surprise, or show him an
element of provocation which is new or strange to him. Yet,
in full view of all this mass of pollution fully foreseen and
fully appreciated, he nevertheless deliberately enters into
that unholy soul as into his own home and workshop. He
is not a mere transient visitor, "a traveler that turneth aside
to tarry but a night." He enters, too, for the very purpose
of subduing the evils into which he goes. He enters under
a covenant pledge to make good the promise to the believing
sinner, "Sin shall not have dominion over you."

He is bound by high treaty obligations to do this work—a
work which he fully understands to be the conquest of the
very sins which breed the misery of the saintly soul. He
knows, too, that under the mysterious, but wise, appointment
of the divine Saviour his work will not be completed until
the close of the natural life. He is, therefore, not discouraged by the protracted struggle of the law of sin. That slow
progress in overcoming the evil in the heart, which brings
such pain and discouragement to the believer himself,
does not move or disturb him. Calm and unmoved he
keeps place in the very citadel of the soul, and, not discouraged by the perpetual turmoil and insurrection of sin, by
the unholy thoughts, the turbulent passions, the ungodly impulses, which are forever warring against his holy control,

he works even according to his own wise and loving will at his appointed task.   Yet further: the Holy Spirit is not only under the bond of the covenant of grace to make good the promise to the faith of the believer himself, but he well knows how the honor of the whole Godhead is involved in the full, firm, and successful discharge of his function as the sanctifier of the saints.   All the persons of the Trinity are pledged to this work.   Jesus, the Son, by his very name is pledged to be a Saviour from sin.   He is no Saviour at all unless he does save from sin.   Salvation in sin is a contradiction in terms.   To save from sin was the very end and purpose for which he came—for which he died.   If this end is defeated, all his work comes to nothing.   The eternal counsel of the Father was to do this very thing, and if it is not done, his counsel is brought to nought.   His highest and most cherished plans, his greatest glory, would be demolished.

But further still: the hope of believers is encouraged, and their anxieties legitimately subdued, by the fact that the Holy Spirit is represented in the doctrine of the Scriptures as animated, not merely by an intense fidelity to his trust, but by an infinite delight in his work.   The love of the Spirit is emphatically asserted, and what he loves he delights to do.   He loves to help a soul oppressed with sin.   He is prompt to answer every appeal.   He rejoices to win battles against Satan.   His title as the Comforter proves his joy in doing all his glorious work.   Such are some of the leading features in the Scripture doctrine of the Spirit.

Now, it is obvious that the antidote to the discouragement, anxieties, and fears of the believer, growing out of the consciousness of the strength and stubbornness, the incessant presence, and the perpetual activity, of his own inward sin, is here plainly revealed in this doctrine of the grace of the Holy Ghost.   When, pained and terrified by the incessant and stubborn outgrowth of his remaining depravity, he dreads the departure of the Holy Spirit, leaving him to himself, let him take hold on the truth taught him in this doctrine of the Spirit. The Spirit never leaves him. He may hide his presence, under provocation, but never abandons his work. The Spirit never grows indifferent. The Spirit never loses patience. The Spirit never forfeits his covenant fidelity, or his zeal for the honor of God. He never ceases to delight in his work. He is always the Paraclete of the saints, and always comes when called; no honest sigh for his presence, no earnest cry to him, is ever unheeded. If such are the functions of the Holy Ghost in the economy of redemption, that provision which secures a special grant and special gifts of the Spirit to every believer is a blessing absolutely inestimable.

CHAPTER II.

GIFT OF A PECULIAR KNOWLEDGE OR INTUITION TO BELIEVERS.

"That the God of our Lord Jesus Christ, the Father of glory, may give unto you the spirit of wisdom and revelation in the knowledge of him: the eyes of your understanding being enlightened."—*Paul to the Ephesians.*

THE passage of which these words are a part settles the fact that there is a special gift of the Holy Spirit to believers subsequent to their faith and the initial processes of their salvation. The defects in the Christian experience, the anxieties, the weaknesses, the fluctuations of hope, the sins, and the trials of believers, illustrate strongly the need of this gift, and the value of it when given. To secure the benefits of the grant it must be known, suitably esteemed, and put to use. So long as Christians are either ignorant of it, or fail to value and turn it to account in their systematic experimental employment of it, it will not produce its effects, and the old chronic state of crippled hope and imperfect comfort will prevail. This sort of imperfection is positively contrary to God's explicit will; he commands his servants to "rejoice in the Lord always." It is no compliment to the grace he has provided and revealed to their faith, that they should go all their lifetime subject to bondage. He requires them to enter and "stand fast in the liberty with which Christ has made them free." That liberty is something more than freedom from the yoke of that cumbersome and costly ceremonial ritual which Peter declared neither they nor their fathers were able to bear. It is freedom from the condemnation and the liabilities of sin; from its power and pollution in the soul; from the fear of death. From all these evils they are delivered by the redemption which is in Christ. Those, then, on whom that redemption has taken effect—which is only another description of all who believe—are required to do justice to the grace which has wrought such inexpressible benefits for them, and to rejoice in hope of the glory of God. "The joy of the Lord" is said to be "their strength"; and if the want of strength in his servants is an injury to his cause and a discount to his glory, then strength is their duty as well as their personal privilege; and if joy is their strength, it is as much their duty and privilege to be joyful as it is to be strong. Assuredly, if all Christians were as happy as it is their duty to be, there would be no resisting the spread of a faith so visibly rich in power and blessing. To secure this joy and energy, and to break down the anxieties and discouragements to which they are opposed, is the object of this special gift of the Holy Spirit, and the special gifts which he brings to believers. To aid us in turning this wonder of benignant grace to account, let us scrutinize the value of this great gift, and the gifts which follow and flow from it:

1. The value of the gift is conspicuously displayed in the nature of the gift: *it is the Holy Ghost himself.* The distinction is rooted, in the nature of the case, between the gift of the Spirit and the gifts which he bestows when given; we must, therefore, consider them separately and in succession. Obviously, the great Author of all the special gifts is himself the greatest of them all. It is the Holy Spirit, a person, not an influence, a being capable of sympathy, capable of approach and appeal, capable of assuming the responsibilities of a covenant, and the execution of a task. It is very wonderful to observe how, in this whole matter of redemption, the infinite God puts himself forward as the only agent, as well as the final object, of that deliverance for lost men which he has undertaken. The original purpose was his; the execution was his; the effectual application of it to individual

souls was his, and his only. Nothing entering into the effective work to be done is delegated to any inferior being. Angels are employed, but only as ministering spirits; men are employed, but as mere instrumental and secondary agents; ordinances are employed, but their effectual influence is due only to the concurrence of divine energy. The whole tenor of the gospel teaching is, that "salvation is of the Lord," and all trust in any other person or thing is rigorously inhibited. This grand conception of dealing only with God in all that concerns an effective hope in matters spiritual, is due not merely to the natural impossibility of salvation being achieved by any other means or power, but to a design to meet a particular fact in the condition of a sinning soul. It is designed to restore man to his natural relations to God, to train him from the start to replace the divine being in his proper relations to his creature. Those relations were dislocated by the apostasy of mankind. Man grew to be without God in the world; he remembered God and was troubled; and as the result of his studied attempts to get rid of the oppressive conception, it resulted that God was not in all his thoughts. The very idea of a Deity became a nuisance to be abated. The consequence was the practical extinction of the concept; no attention was paid to the exiled King; no use was seen for him; no appeal was made to him, recognizing the original loving and friendly relations between the parties. Now, the great gospel system of restoration begins its restorative processes at this point, and never ceases to work at the reconstruction of the direct relation between God and man. Hence, all the thoughts of the returning sinner are trained immediately upon God as the only Saviour and source of hope. All that enters into the matter of salvation is to be looked and sought for from him. Back of all human instrumentalities, beyond all the ordinances, though appointed by divine authority, the eye is taught to look for God himself.

So far as the efficient energy is concerned, God is always in
the forefront, nay, above and apart from means. Means are
appointed to serve inferior ends, and can never be safely
abandoned, but salvation is of the Lord himself. He, and
he alone, is the Saviour. What is to be done, he does; what
is to be given, he gives, whether pardon, or life, or guidance,
or comfort; all is to be sought from him. Most wonderful
of all, he makes himself the great gift which he bestows on
his returning rebel. Nothing less is deemed worthy of his
divine dignity to bestow, or suitable to the grand nature and
the ineffable necessities of his redeemed creature. He knows
that nothing less than something infinite can satisfy a nature
ever reaching beyond all present good, however good it may
be; ever insatiable in the headlong stretch of its immortal
aspirations. Made to be satisfied in God only, the very
structure of an immortal, ever-progressive being determines
the only satisfaction for it in the illimitable resources of the
Infinite. The gracious Lord also knows that in the awful
stress and straitness into which sin has brought his unhappy
creature, no power less than divine can save him. Therefore
it is that in every phase and part of the great redemption
God gives himself to the work.

Hence, God the Son came into the world to pay down the
needful ransom on the cross. Hence, God the Father gives
himself as the Father and the everlasting, satisfying portion of
his redeemed people. Hence, the Holy Ghost is given to
encounter all the inward mischief which sin has wrought in
the soul itself, to regenerate the unregenerate sinner and
make him in this regard a child of God, and when so
quickened into genuine spiritual life, to take up his abode in
him, and by special gifts of himself and from himself, to conduct the work he has begun until he triumphantly presents
the rescued sinning soul, without spot or blemish or any such
thing, in the presence of the Father's glory. No human
conception or words can begin to adequately express the

intrinsic worth of this gift of the Holy Spirit. Having given the Son to redeem the lost, and himself to be the Father and the satisfying portion of saved sinners, the rich Lord of the universe had only one more gift of equal value to bestow, and he gives this when he gives the Holy Ghost. Heaven's gorgeous treasure-house has nothing like it to give. The Spirit is a person, a living, intelligent, and powerful being, not a mere influence, however valuable, but a person exerting an influence, capable of action, varied according to the necessities of the soul with which, and in which, he dwells, capable of loving affections, able to receive appeals, able to hear and answer the calls made to him. His work is unceasing; it is not a brief but transcendent enterprise, like the Son's in bearing the sins of the world in his own body on the tree, but the constant work of an indweller in the soul and in the church, ending only with the completed purification of the one, and the final triumph of the other. He is the Paraclete, which means, "the one called to our help," always ready to aid, always on the watch, always effective in his interference. To one engaged in any enterprise of difficulty or danger, nothing could be more of a comfort or encouragement than to have and to know that he has always an assistance ready and powerful which he can call to his side at any moment, and can rely upon as all-sufficient for every emergency. Such is the gift of the Holy Spirit to every believer—a person capable of all personal sensibilities and acts; a divine person infinite in loving-kindness, in wisdom, and in power. No adequate conception can be formed of its value.

2. The value of the gift of the Holy Ghost is illustrated *by the manner in which he is given.* The marvelous doctrine of the indwelling of the Holy Ghost is a plain assertion of the word of God. The Messiah thus asserts it: "And I will pray the Father and he shall give you another Comforter," (Paraclete), "that he may abide with you forever: even the Spirit of truth; whom the world cannot receive, because it

seeth him not, neither knoweth him; but ye know him: *for he dwelleth with you, and shall be in you.*" According to these clear words he is a person, designated by the terms of personality, but a person who shall not only dwell with the disciple as a companion in his home, but as an occupant dwelling in himself. To many this wonderful statement is as utter foolishness as it was to the Greeks. But if the omnipresence of God is true, as it must be of all necessary being, and assures us of his pervading all things in space as well as all space itself without taint or stain, there is nothing more credible than his special presence in a human soul as the preservative power which is to secure its integrity and its peace. On the contrary, the want of his presence would present the real difficulty. Pervading all things to preserve their being, he pervades the regenerate soul to preserve its regenerate life. The only difference is, not in the fact of his presence, but in the purpose to be accomplished, and in the mode of its manifestation. Mysterious as the fact of the indwelling of the Spirit may be, if the word of God assures it, it is nothing but repudiation of that record as the word of God to deny the fact or cavil at its credibility. In this wonderful doctrine the Christian sees the guarantee of his safety. If a strong man keeps his house, it cannot be plundered unless a stronger than he shall bind the guardian who keeps it. Who is stronger than God, the Holy Spirit? In every hour of bitter temptation and conscious personal weakness, the Christian may remember the indwelling of the Spirit, and take courage. All fear is legitimately and logically conquered when faith realizes who is on guard. Into every Christian soul he enters to abide, and when bulwarked by his infinite love, pity, patience, faithfulness, and power, every such soul is entitled to rejoice in hope.

3. The value of the gift of the Holy Spirit to believers is shown in his taking up his indwelling in the regenerate heart

under a positive covenant engagement to accomplish its complete deliverance from the power and stain of sin. He enters to make good the promise to faith, "He that believeth shall be saved"; "sin shall not have dominion over you." There is no salvation except a salvation from sin. The object of the Spirit is identical with that desire which is the most constant and intense in the regenerate heart, deliverance from sin. Without this inward cleansing the whole work of redemption would be nullified. The pledge of the Spirit is to make it good. Solemn covenant engagements bind strongly on all good and honorable human minds; what can be conceived more powerful, or as affording a stronger ground of confidence and hope, than the covenant pledge of the Father, Son, and Holy Ghost?

4. The value of the gift of the Holy Spirit is illustrated *by the objects for which he is given.* In general terms, his design is to subdue the sin in the soul—that energy of evil which is its shame, its peril, its disease, and its death—and to *infuse holiness*—that energy of goodness which is its glory, its safety, its health, and its life. He works on all powers and principles of the human spirit, on every energy of the intellect, and every affection of the heart. He seals, anoints, guards, comforts, certifies, upholds, and edifies the favored soul into which he enters. But in the passage at the head of this chapter the apostle singles out one function of the Holy Spirit, and makes it the special object of his prayer for the Christians of Ephesus, and afterwards specifies three objects on which he desired the exertion of this function. As this special function and these objects of its exercise enter largely into the conquest of the anxieties and imperfections of Christian experience, the particular consideration of them will advance the object which we have in view.

The special function of the Holy Spirit alluded to is his *illuminating influence* on the understanding. By this gift the believer is enabled to comprehend more and more fully the great truths of the gospel. He is called "the Spirit of wisdom and revelation in the knowledge of him." The personal pronoun points to the person of the sacred Trinity just mentioned before, "the God and Father of our Lord Jesus Christ." This fact presents us with the first noticeable point in the declaration made, and that is, that it is the knowledge of *the Father*, as distinguished from the knowledge of the Son, which the apostle prays that the Ephesians might receive. The knowledge of the Son is all-important, and is equally to be sought at the hands of the Spirit; it is expressly stated, "He will take of the things of Christ and will show them unto us." But in this prayer of Paul, it is the knowledge of the Father and of his relations to the saints which is sought as an object of the guidance of the Holy Ghost.

The second noticeable point is *the kind of knowledge* of the Father which is sought for the Ephesian saints. It is not simply the information concerning the Father given in the Scriptures inspired by the Holy Ghost. The church at Ephesus already had that knowldege, if not yet in the written New Testament complete, yet certainly in the instructions of the apostles. Paul's prayer was not that they might have the word of God. Neither was he praying that they might be *inspired* in the sense in which he was inspired; it was a knowledge to be given to them simply as saints, as those who had believed, and in whose heart the love of the brethren demonstrated a regeneration already accomplished. This knowledge, then, was distinct and different, both from the knowledge given in the Scriptures and from the inspiration of the apostles. It is said in one place in the sacred record, that the natural man receiveth not the things of the Spirit of God, neither can he know them, because they are spiritually discerned. This spiritual apprehension is repudiated by many as a mystery incomprehensible and incredible, a mere dream of fanaticism unworthy of rational acceptance.

But so far from this being true it is only an example in the spiritual sphere of what is true in every sphere of nature, and in every line of human employment. There are two kinds of knowledge which every human understanding may have of things. There are two kinds of discernment, one depending merely on the untrained energies of the natural organs of perception, the other, on a previous training and discipline of faculty, and the mental quality and capacity conveyed by that training. Of this latter class take an instance in the sphere of music: two persons may hear with equal chances a piece executed by a great master; both may discern and enjoy the general impression of the melody, but only one of them has the musical training which will enable the discernment of the actual skill and genius involved in the performance; for these can be only musically discerned. There is a quality in the mind of the one which is not in the other. Two men may investigate a line of policy adopted by a civil legislature; one, a merchant or manufacturer, may see the effects on the productions and trade of the country, for they discern all things commercially; the other, a statesman of deeper and broader views, may see in addition to its effects on trade and production its effects on the well-being of the consuming classes, on their moral character, on their personal happiness, and on their patriotic affections. These things are only discernible through the high and just civil wisdom of a true statesman; they are politically discerned. It is notorious in human experience that the view of men and things is governed by the feelings of the heart towards them—love producing one judgment and dislike another.

Of the first class of instances, the two radically different kinds of knowledge of the same identical thing, the enumeration could be easily extended to the degree of tediousness. We do assuredly know that the reason why one tree bears peaches, and another apples is in the nature of the trees, but what that nature in either of them is, or what is the

difference in that nature, no one can tell. But suppose one
could penetrate that secret, and clearly comprehend the
exact nature of the trees, he would only know what all knew
before, that the nature of the trees was different. He would
know the same thing, but his knowledge would be different
from the knowledge of other men. A man may know that
an orange is a delightful fruit before he tastes it; but when
he tastes it he knows the very same fact, but his knowledge
would be very different. The knowledge that fire will burn
may be certain without touching it, but the same fact may be
known, but with a kind of knowledge very different, by touching it. Is it needful to multiply instances? In the line of
these analogies why should any one doubt that there should
be an intellectual knowledge of religious truth, and a different
kind of spiritual knowledge of the very same truth, the one
knowledge making him acquainted with the fact that there
is such truth, and with its intellectual limitations and relations; the other, with its deep and true significance—its
moral weight—its profound appeal to the whole affections of
the soul. It is absolutely certain as a matter of fact in a
human experience, without assignable bounds to its extent,
that there is such a difference in the apprehension of the
gospel of the Lord Jesus in all the distinct truths embraced
in the system. One man may know and honestly believe
the fact that God so loved the world as to send his Son to
redeem it, and that now salvation is offered to all men
through him, yet he sees nothing in these ideas to move
his feelings or to induce him to action. His knowledge of
the glad tidings of great joy brings no joy to him; he remains
unmoved and uncheered by it. His knowledge does not
place before his mind the real nature and significance of the
grand ideas he so coolly contemplates. He has had no adequate previous sense of his own need of the remedies of infinite
grace, and there is no quality conferred by this previous
discipline on his understanding to enable him to appreciate

them.   But another man, who apprehends his personal need
of an effectual relief, may so see into the real nature and
significance of the gospel remedies that he catches the joy
that is in them; he realizes that his sin may be forgiven
him; his knowledge now acquaints him with the power that
is in these glorious conceptions.   It is *this kind of knowledge*
which Paul prays may be given by the spirit of wisdom and
revelation to the Ephesian Christians; not the *inspiration* of
an apostle to give a fresh measure of truth; not the truth
already given in the Scriptures; but a true intuition of the
truth already given.   It was a knowledge through feeling,
and producing higher measures of it.

Yet a further discrimination must be made.   These saints
at Ephesus already had a degree of this kind of knowledge;
they had been led by it to the faith which had saved them;
it had developed in them a distinctive mark of the regenerate heart—the love of the brethren.   But Paul knew
that further measures of the grace which had first led them
to taste the sweetness and power of the gospel was necessary to lead them through the whole course of their saintly
career into larger and ever-progressive realizations of this
rich experience of gospel grace.   He knew the trials before
them; he knew the anxieties and sorrows they had to encounter, and the constant consequent need of the illumination which
first led them to peace.   He knew, too, there was a vast scale
of degrees and possible progress in that glorious species of
knowledge of which they had already partaken in a certain
precious measure.   They might not know, or at least *effectively* apprehend, that the covenant provided a *gift of the Holy
Spirit for believers,* to bestow rich degrees of this same kind
of knowledge, leading them steadily into deeper and higher
views of the same old glorious truths.   He reveals and em-
phasizes this wonderful truth and prays that the saints of
Ephesus may receive this gift, and illustrates its use in dealing with all gospel truth by seeking its application to three

truths which he specifies as entering far into the comfort of all believers. It is fit for us in these modern days of the kingdom to accept decisively the consolatory fact involved in this history. If this precious gift was practicable for the Ephesian Christians, it is practicable for all believers, it is available for us. The manifestation of the Spirit is given to every one who believes that he may profit withal. To take of the things of Christ and show them unto us, to open our understandings that we may truly understand the Scriptures, to enable us to spiritually discern the things which can only be spiritually discerned is the very function of the Spirit to which Paul refers as the spirit of wisdom and revelation in the knowledge of God *given to believers*. Not only is there no presumption in all saints hoping, and like Paul praying, for this gift for ourselves and others, but there will be a grave delinquency *in not doing it*.

It may be well to recur to the first of the two points which are conspicuous in the passage heading this chapter, for some explanation of its meaning. Why does Paul lay emphasis on the knowledge of the Father as distinguished from the knowledge of the Son, and especially desire it for the Christians of Ephesus? To the natural apprehensions of the human heart God appears only as the Creator, the sovereign Lord, Lawgiver, and Judge of all the earth. The consciousness of sin enforces these overawing conceptions. Consequently he only appears in the form and attitudes of one to be feared to the degree of dread. There is a solid foundation for these views; they are confirmed by the Scriptures. Out of Christ he is unequivocally said to be a consuming fire. He is angry with the wicked every day. He loves his law, because it is the eternal dictate of all rightness; and his law is universally violated. He hates evil, and evil is eagerly pursued by the perverted human heart as the choice road to enjoyment. He loves holiness and all righteousness, and both are repudiated in the practices of the natural man. He has made no

secret of his requirements; he has revealed his law in conscience and in his word; he has thoroughly engaged his authority to restrain, and his veracity to punish, sin: but all in
vain: his authority is repudiated, his menaces are despised.
His necessary attitude under such a state of things, unqualified by any provisions of grace, must be that of righteous
anger, and resolution to punish. It is, in fact, precisely the
very attitude ascribed to him by the conscious guilt and fears
of a conscious transgressor. To know God in these unqualified natural relations, as determined by the sin of the creature, is to have a knowledge which can only carry terror and
despair. Any knowledge of him which is attractive must
proceed on an entire change in these threatening relations.
It is the very essence of the gladness of the gospel tidings
that this change has been effected. It was the very change
wrought by the redemption work of the Son. He undertook
to pay the claims of the law and justice of the Father, repre-
senting in that wonderful covenant the dignity of the whole
Godhead. He undertook to remove every obstacle out of
the way to the free exercise of the Father's grace. Conceiving this done, obviously the whole state of the case as between the sinner and the insulted majesty of the divine government is altered. Conceiving a real redemption accomplished, the necessary result would be, *first*, that all penalties
would be remitted, and all danger removed; and *second*, that
all the favor needful to secure the purchased blessings and
to insure the welfare of the redeemed would be made absolutely certain. The effects of transgression would be removed, some, instantly;. all, in the progress and issue of
events. That effect of sin which had procured the just
displeasure of Almighty God, and placed him in the attitude
of a Judge certain to condemn, is among those which are
instantly qualified. The other effect, which had been to
alienate the feelings of the offending creature, and to fill the
heart with apprehension and terror, is also instantly removed.

In the same class of speedy and accomplished effects are many which affect the relations and feelings of God as well as the redeemed creature. God is reconciled to man, as well as man to God. The relation of a Judge is changed to the relation of a Father. Righteous anger gives place to infinite kindness. The resolve to punish gives way to the resolve to save. The obligation to inflict evil for evil gives way to the obligation to do justice to the Redeemer by showing favor to the ungodly for whom he has intervened. The whole attitude of God in the person of the Father has been so completely and so benignantly altered, that to know him in these new relations has become a source of boundless peace and joy. It is not at all difficult now to understand why Paul desired the believers at Ephesus to know with an intense realizing discernment the God and Father of their Saviour Christ. For he was now their Father also. He had ceased to be their angry law-giver; he had been reconciled to them. He was no longer their Judge; he had committed all judgment to the Son—their own loved Saviour—their own elder brother. They are his Son's by adoption, as well as by regenerating grace. Instead of anger in his holy heart towards them, he is giving way to the impulses of his own infinite loving nature—moving like the great tides of the sea. This mighty change in the relations of God the Father rests on a basis which secures all its blessed effects unalterable forever; it is wholly grounded on the accomplished work of the Son of God. If it rested on human will or works it would be constantly liable to be overthrown; the relations of God would fluctuate between their old and their new character; and no comfortable assurance could be connected with them. Where there is no certainty in the future, hope is annihilated; for rational hope is the expectation of a future good surely given but not yet possessed. All else is vague presumption or expectation without a warrant.

We have seen* that in the distribution of the work of sal-

---

*Page 230

vation among the persons of the Trinity, the Father gives
himself not only to be the Father, but the satisfying portion
of the soul.   Nothing else can satisfy it.   Heaven as a mere
locality, glorious in its gold and pearl and matchless splendor,
can never do it, although the well-being of man is seriously
conditioned on his local circumstances.   The conversation
and society of angels, and the spirits of the just made perfect, will be ennobling and delightful, but they cannot satisfy
a soul, although the satisfaction of a human heart is largely
dependent on his companionships.   The human spirit was
made to find rest in God; it cannot find it in anything else.
It crowns the wonderful benignity of the grace revealed to us,
and completes the perfection of the basis for the hope and
comfort of the believer, to be assured that God the Father, in
all the infinite resources of his infinite being and excellence,
is revealed and assured as the ultimate portion and satisfaction of every redeemed soul.   These two grand endowments,
the Fatherhood and apportionment of God, constituted the
chief reasons why Paul wanted the saints at Ephesus to become acquainted with the God and Father of our Lord Jesus
Christ   To know him as such, to know him in all the relations in which the redemption of Christ has placed him, is
everlasting life; for this is eternal life, to know him and Jesus
Christ whom he has sent.   This true realizing knowledge of
God is not merely to know, but to love him with a supreme
affection, to obey him with loving regard to all his command-
ments, and to rejoice in him always.   Thus to know the
Father, and the Son, and the Holy Spirit, is to rise superior
to all fear and sorrow at all times, for it discloses the Christian basis for the hope which is full of immortality.

CHAPTER III.

GIFT OF KNOWLEDGE OF THREE PARTICULAR TRUTHS TO BELIEVERS.

"That ye may know what is the hope of his calling, and what the riches of the glory of his inheritance in the saints, and what is the exceeding greatness of his power to us-ward who believe, according to the working of his mighty power."—*Paul to the Ephesians.*

THE apostle specifies three distinct forms of truth on which he prayed that that gift of the Holy Spirit, that realizing and intimate knowledge, might be employed, about which we spoke in the preceding chapter. He prays that the Christians of Ephesus might know, as a man knows the sweetness of a fruit when he actually tastes it—*first*, the real nature of the hope which sprang out of their calling; *second*, the glorious riches of God's inheritance in them; and *third*, the greatness of that divine power which stood guard over their security. The two last of this triplicate of truths bear a logical relation to the first, and all three are thus bound up together. The inheritance of God in his saints, and the might of his power, are the guarantees of the hope of their calling. Their calling is his act; the ownership of them is in him; and the power is his own which secures his possession. Let us endeavor to get fair hold of each of these truths into which the gift of the Spirit may guide us.

1. What is *the hope of the calling* which God claims as *his own?* The first thing to be settled is, the nature of this calling. It is evidently a calling which has an effectual and essential connection with the hope of believers, with the inheritance of God in them, and with the power which secures the safety of those who are his property. It is something different from that general invitation and call to repentance

and faith which is made indiscriminately to all persons to
whom the proclamation can be made.   That call often fails
in effect.   But this is a calling altogether distinct from that
ineffectual invitation; it is an effectual and saving call.   Such
a call is plainly asserted in such words as these: "Not many
wise men, not many mighty, not many noble are called";
and "whom he called, them he also justified."   All the
mighty and noble are called in the universal invitation; not
many of them are called with the other species of calling.
All who are called by the one are justified; none who are
only called with the other are justified.   The one call only
makes known the will of God; the calling which he specially
claims as *his* secures obedience to it.   The distinction, though
sometimes confounded, is radical and all-important.

The *hope* of this calling is the hope produced and assured
by this calling.   This hope may be considered under two
aspects: it may be considered with reference to its *objects*,
the things which are hoped for; or with reference to the
nature, the period, and the effects of the hope itself.   It is
evident, however, that the latter aspect of it is the one which
was in the mind of the apostle at this time; for it is viewed
in its immediate connection with the calling in which it originates, and as an immediate outgrowth of it.   The *objects* of
this hope are, for the most part at least, distant, unseen,
glorious beyond measure, but not realized on the instant; all
the objects of true hope are in some part of the future.   It
is certainly, then, the nature and immediate effects of hope
which are brought up for consideration in connection with
that calling and its legal consequences, which takes immediate effect.   It follows, then, that there is in this hope a
present and immediately available antidote to the present
cares and anxieties of believers.   As such it is repeatedly
explained and recommended in the Scriptures; and as such
we shall seek to develop it now, in the eager desire to see
the life of at least some of God's children in these days of

trial brightened with more comfort, and their strength increased by more joy in the Lord.

One noticeable thing in the teaching of the Scriptures about Christian hope is that it is positively required of the people of God. "Let Israel hope in the Lord." "Why art thou cast down, O my soul; and why art thou disquieted in me? hope thou in God; for I shall yet praise him for the help of his countenance." These are specimens of the Old Testament requirements. Paul gives an instance of the requisitions of the New Testament, when he says, "We desire that every one of you do shew the same diligence to the full assurance of hope unto the end." If the Lord has bound himself by two immutable things—his *promise* and his *oath* to perform it—in which it was impossible for him to lie, in order that those might have strong consolation who have fled for refuge to the hope set before them, it certainly cannot be a matter of indifference to him whether that consolation is realized or not in the actual experience of his servants. They are commanded to "rejoice in the Lord always." It is in fact a gross injustice to the salvation of God to hold it as practically incompetent to cheer and comfort the heart in which his grace is reigning. Hope is therefore required of every one of them.

Another peculiarity of Christian hope is that it *is designed to be exercised*, and therefore it is practically available *now*, in the present life of the believer. It is intended to distribute its comforting influences where they are most needed. To remit its exercise and the strength and comfort which it brings to the future life, is really to destroy it altogether as *hope;* for hope that is seen is not hope; for what a man seeth, why doth he yet hope for it? In the future, the objects of hope are already in possession, and the functions of hope are so far forth brought to an end. Hope is the effect of things which are surely given, but not yet obtained, and is intended for the present comfort of the future possessor. If there is no certainty in the future possession—no assurance in the gift given—no reliability in the promise and the maker of the promise, no real hope can exist; nothing but vague and uncertain expectation can emerge. But if the grant and title are sure, hope is warranted and requirable, and when exercised will throw its comforts strongly all along the progress from the pledge to the possession. Every Christian therefore is required to hope and rejoice always; it is not the choice privilege of a few, but the duty and privilege of all believers. A Christian without hope, then, is not only living below his privilege, but in violation of his duty; and on both of these accounts is grieving the great loving heart of his God and Saviour.

Another point about this hope of God's calling refers to *the basis* on which it rests, not its primary basis, which is the work of the Redeemer, but the secondary basis, which connects it with the *first*. This secondary or instrumental foundation of hope is two-fold—*faith* and *experience*. If one gives a promise of some future gift to another, faith in that promise, and in him who makes it, will be instantly followed by the hope of obtaining what is promised. If the faith is strong, the hope will be strong; if the faith is weak, the hope will be weak; if the faith vacillates between strength and weakness, the hope will vacillate. *Faith*, therefore, is clearly, in part at least, the foundation and instrumental cause of *hope*. But now, suppose the promise is actually fulfilled in part, and a part is still left to be fulfilled, the partial fulfilment will create an additional confidence and hope of receiving the remainder. In this case *experience* worketh hope; it thus becomes a part of the basis of hope by strengthening faith, by adding the assurance of *fact* to the assurance of truth in the promise and the promiser. It vindicates and strengthens faith by the fulfilment of promise, and so breeds hope. As faith is the natural and obligatory demand of all truth and of all trustworthy invitations to confidence, hope is equally demanded, because it is the natural and logical consequent of the faith which is rightfully required.

In addition to these secondary foundations of hope, it rests on *a great primary basis*, which gives all its force to the secondary bases of faith and experience. If faith has no solid ground to rest upon, it is incapable of creating confidence, and so incapable of producing hope. If the solid ground exists, and there is no faith in it, it will produce no hope. On the contrary, if there is no solid basis, the faith in it will be spurious, and the hope produced by it will be illusive. The two must co-exist, the solid ground and the real faith in it, in order to secure a reliable hope. If one make a promise of a future gift to another, faith in the promise will yield hope, but only on the condition, not only that the maker of the promise is reliable in his integrity, but is unquestionably able to do as he has promised. The basis of hope, then, is not merely faith as the secondary ground of it, but the integrity, willingness, and ability of the promiser as the original basis of the faith which produces hope. This primary basis is that which justifies faith, and thus vindicates the hope it produces. The grand primary foundation of Christian hope, then, is the whole official work of Christ as the Redeemer of lost men, and the pledge of the divine veracity that it not only is effective to save, but that whosoever accepts and relies upon it, shall be saved. To this great ground of confidence and hope it is that faith looks; it is this which creates confidence; it is this which originates experience. It is this to which the whole attention of a soul seeking safety and peace should be directed. To turn the thoughts within to see if there is faith in the heart, to ransack consciousness and memory to discover an experience which may warrant hope, is to divert attention from the primary basis that grounds both faith and hope, to the secondary basis which merely mediates and conveys the virtue of the only real ground of both. Such an investigation begins its search at an intermediate point, and to withdraw the attention from what lies back of faith, and warrants and mediately produces it. In this overlooked ground of faith and hope *the work and personal power* of the Saviour himself are either of them to be found.

Just here we discover the great practical mistake of believers which produces that chronic state of uneasiness and anxiety which is the shame and the peril of the heirs of grace. They look only to their faith and experience for comfort; the aim of their self-examination is solely to certify faith and experience, and until satisfied with these they refuse to be comforted, or to indulge any hope. The desire to certify faith and hope is altogether right; self-examination is an undoubted duty. But the exception lies against the mode in which the scrutiny is made. To know that we confide in a thing, the natural order of thought which ought to regulate the inquiry is, to fix attention on the thing first, and then to look at the mental exercises about it. A traveler on a public highway comes to a bridge; he does not pause at the bridge-head and turn his thoughts inward on his own mind to study whether he has confidence in the bridge; he looks outward to the bridge itself; he knows that confidence in the bridge is to be bred by the bridge itself. As he inspects the bridge and finds it strongly built, his faith in the structure comes without notice into his feelings. Common sense will tell every man that such is the method by which confidence of safe advance on his journey is to be elicited, and not by a curious inward search of his own mind to see if he has faith in the bridge. No wonder a similar method of self-examination results in disappointment to the believer. No wonder hope eludes their search; for they ignore the very thing which breeds faith and hope, and yet expect both apart from the ground on which they grow. The procedure is as unequivocally foolish as for a man to look for a crop without looking for it on the soil on which it grows. It is as silly as to look for intellectual results apart from any intelligence, or for sensations of health apart from a sound condition of the bodily organs. Let us learn this lesson of Christian faith and hope, and look for them in the order in which grace has ordained them to come. We are saved by faith in the Son of God, and not by faith in our faith. Let us understan.l that the faith and the experience of grace we so eagerly seek to certify are to be found not in themselves or in any isolated position in our minds, but in connection with that great truth which is the primary basis of faith, experience, and the hope they yield—that Jesus is the Son of God, mighty to save. Let us correct this blunder in our Christian life and accept with a clear apprehension the great gospel doctrine that faith comes by hearing, and thus knowing, the truth as it is in Jesus. Faith is all-important, but only because it brings to Christ, in whom alone the power to save is found. There is no scriptural warrant for putting faith in the place of that redemption and that Redeemer in whom we are required to trust. Our faith at its best is too feeble, too fluctuating, too easily shaken, to form the primary basis of a stable and robust hope. It is indispensable to all rational hope, and eminently to a hope full of assurance—at once staunch and full of comfort—that it be founded on something more effective and more durable than any human faith, no matter how true and noble it may be.

Another, and a better, ground of both faith and hope, is furnished in the gospel of the grace of God. It is the finished work of the Saviour himself. It needs no addition to complete its virtue; it is already complete. It meets every conceivable or possible emergency in the condition of a sinner, past, present, or to come. That extinction of hope that follows sin in the believer is a gross discount of the power of the atoning blood. If every sin of the believer is properly followed by the extinction of hope, no hope is possible to him; for he is continually coming short in his obedience. Only presumptuous sinning is entitled to overcloud his hope, and that no longer than repentance won by a fresh resort to the cleansing blood is exercised. The true attitude of the Christian when he sins is to go instantly to the throne of grace with a prompt confession of his sin, and an instant and fresh appeal to the power of the atonement and the grace of the great High Priest. Who can estimate adequately the power of that remedy which we are assured takes away all sin? Who can gauge the power of divine blood? Who can exhaust the reach of a righteousness which God has wrought out? The whole salvation is the salvation of God. The torment of sin in the conscience is that God is rightfully offended; but if God himself is revealed as the deliverer from sin, who is entitled to gainsay it, or refuse to apply to him in his character as a Saviour? If God be for us, who can be against us? If we are commanded to hope in God as a Saviour from sin, where is the warrant for losing hope just because we have sinned? It is said that we encourage sin by this freedom of grace in forgiveness. Cannot God's own deliverance from sin be relied upon, not only to secure pardon but to secure repentance? Cannot he freely forgive, and yet govern; pardon, and yet purify; relax penalty, and yet secure obedience? All that is provided for in the covenant of grace. All who believe are kept by the power of God through faith unto eternal life. The integrity of the weakest is secured; for it is explicitly declared that God is able to make him stand. As already said, every emergency is provided for in a way to warrant the positive pledge, he that believeth shall be saved.

As the whole length and breadth and depth and height of the Christian ground of hope is more perfectly apprehended, the more fully is it seen to warrant a hope that is unspeakable and full of glory. Is it not a shame to mistrust in any direction a salvation by God himself? The blood of Christ secures pardon for all sin; his indwelling Spirit secures deliverance from its dominion; his righteousness, an assured title to eternal life. No greatness of human guilt can overcome the power of the atonement; no strength of personal wickedness can defy the control of his life-giving power. All the provisions needful to a full deliverance from sin are embraced in the covenant executed by the Son, and have been ratified by the veracity of the Father. They are guarded by his power; they are supported by his whole circle of moral attributes; they are executed by his Spirit; they are bound up with his glory. They are as reliable as his throne. They are guaranteed by his very life, for he says, "Because I live, ye shall live also." He won the power to save by the sacrifice of his life once; he has pawned it a second time to insure its application to every believing soul. It is impossible to give an exhaustive statement of the guarantees of the great Christian ground of hope. The infinite love of the Father, the dying love of the Son, the indwelling love of the Spirit, and the infinite power of the Triune God, all enter into them. If any basis for hope, a hope full of immortality, can be conceived by any stretch of human thought, it is overpassed by the actual securities of the gospel covenant. With such a basis for hope there is no excuse for any sinning soul to go burdened with fear,—no sinner to remain in his sin,—no believer to live without rejoicing in the Lord always.

The last characteristic of the hope of God's calling which we cite is its capacity *for coëxisting* with all the changes in the Christian career. With whatever change of circumstance, with whatever trial, with whatever condition of life, with whatever form of death, this hope may exist. Every believer may rejoice in the Lord always. It is not necessary that he should escape trouble in any form; he may rejoice in spite of all. Age may not yield its infirmities; bereavement may not receive back its dead; poverty may not relax its severities; death may refuse to turn back the head of his pale horse, or to blunt the point of his fatal dart; yet the hope of the calling of God may coëxist with all, and triumph over all. It can cheer the common roadway of ordinary life, animate the labors of men, sweeten the charms of domestic life, color the beauty of nature with new delight, and over all the ills that flesh is heir to can exert a subduing influence. Its practical value is inestimable. Such is the hope of God's calling.

2. The second of these truths on which Paul desired the improved spiritual discernment of the Ephesian Christians should be exerted, is the *inheritance of God in the saints*. This truth and the one associated with it are cited from their bearing on the hope of the calling of God. Both logically bear on it and confirm it.

It is to be noted that this inheritance is not the inheritance of the saints in God, but his inheritance in the saints. They also do have an inheritance in God, for they are joint heirs with Christ in an inheritance which is described in noble words as incorruptible, undefiled, and that fadeth not away. This inheritance is sometimes confounded with the one here mentioned; but this is the inheritance of God in the saints. The terms used in description of this inheritance are cumulative and very powerful in expression; it is called "the riches of the glory of his inheritance," that is, the glorious riches or wealth of this inheritance, a form of expression which carries, with all the power of the rich Greek tongue, the idea of the infinite worth of God's inheritance in the saints. The expression itself, *inheritance of God*, is very peculiar. An inheritance is a possession not originally one's own, derived to him by the death of another. The singularity of God's inheriting a possession is grounded on the fact that, as the creator of all things, he had an original proprietary right in all things. His inheriting anything implies a change in his original relations to it. Such, in point of fact, was the state of the case with his creature man. Man as his creature, was his by absolute right; but man had re-

belled, renounced his claims, thrown off his authority and
yielded himself to another master. The effect of this was
that man had become lost to God. The penal claims of violated law had taken possession of him, and while the right
of God in his creature had not been abolished, the claims of
justice had rendered it no longer possible for God to show
him favor, apart from the consideration of an adequate redemption from the demands of his insulted government. If
such a policy was practicable and permissible, then his right
to bless his lost creature and regain his lost property in him
was possible. It is the very essence of the gospel that the
Son of God did undertake this wonderful enterprise of redeeming the lost human race, and by actually accomplishing
it, restored the practical ownership of the Father in his lost
creature. Once lost, but now redeemed by the Son, the
restored right of the Father possesses that distinctive feature
of an inheritance which consists in something not one's own,
derived and bestowed by another. Inasmuch as the Son of
God had to accomplish the redemption by the sacrifice of
his life, the other element of an inheritance, *derivation
through death*, appears in God's inheritance in the saints,
and his restored right becomes an inheritance in the strictest
sense of the term.

The value, the peculiar and surprising value, which this
inherited possession has in the eyes of the Father is strikingly presented in the strong cumulative terms in which it is
described. It is "a glory" of an inheritance. It is a veri-
table wealth of glory as an inheritance. The language carries
the notion of estimated worth to its highest expression; it
describes the most valued of all his possessions. God is
rich; he owns all things; the wide universe is all his own.
The stars and suns, all the riches of inventive wisdom and
power infinite in degree, are his; the splendor of heaven and
the rainbow-circled throne are his; the glorious angels, with
their princely dominions and personal gifts, are all his; but

the real wealth of the glory of his vast possession is this inheritance obtained by the unparalleled work and out-poured blood of his Son. This is the great reason why the possession is so precious: it was bought for him by the death of his only-begotten and well-beloved Son. The saints are identified with this infinitely beloved being; they are *his* friends; they are *his* brethren; they are *his* loved ones; they are the purchase of *his* priceless blood, the acquisition of *his* mighty and victorious struggle with the awful conditions of human redemption. That contention is the wonder of the universe, the unequaled and splendid mystery of all the counsels of God. Is it wonderful that God should value an acquisition obtained by such mysterious humiliation, agony, and death on the part of his own Son? A band of marauders swoop down on the flocks and herds of a great pastoral chief; his gallant son pursues the robbers, and by wonderful displays of valor and conduct rescues the property and restores it to his father; and as the restored flock is driven back on the paternal meadows, the heroic youth is borne back to his father's house pale with many a gaping wound. Is it at all wonderful that the father should set a higher value on the rescued herd than ever before? So with the inheritance of God in his saints; there is a blood-mark on every one of them; that mark is the blood of his Son, and wherever he sees it he counts it richer than all the jewels of his crown. The parallel only conveys a faint shadow of the real case; for the inheritance of God was won by a far more desperate adventure than a combat with robbers of the desert, and by a far more trying sacrifice of his glorious Son. All of God's other works were accomplished by the word of his power. A long preparation, amazing transformations, years of effort, and awful agonies of strained almightiness were necessary to accomplish this. No wonder he values its results.

Another reason of the extraordinary value placed on the

inheritance of God is, the relation it sustains to his Son's glory. That glory is indissolubly bound up with these saints; if they are not saved, all his wonderful redemptive work is an absolute failure. What the Almighty wills, simply resolves to accomplish, will be accomplished. Who can stay his hand? What he executes by any formal and deliberate preparation to accomplish, gives to us a higher impression of the certainty of its production. But what had to be done by such preliminary conditions as those involved in the redemption of sinners: the descent of the eternal Son from his throne; the assumption of human nature; the humiliation; the want; the suffering; the implacable hostility; the shame; the scourging; the spitting; the agony of crucifixion; the death—all these give us an assurance, which beggars all human or creature conception, that what all this was done for will surely be accomplished. Failure after all this is inconceivable. But if it could happen it would extinguish the glory of the beloved Son; it would nullify his heroic endeavor; it would render his infinite zeal of love abortive; it would extinguish the awful virtue of his blood, and turn the highest counsels of the only wise and omnipotent God into foolishness. If the hope of the believer in Jesus is so bound up with the glory of the Son, no higher guarantee of the assurance of that hope could possibly be given. The actual measure of the value of God's inheritance in the saints is the length and breadth and depth and height of the glory of the eternal Son and the esteem which the eternal Father feels for it.

The value of the saints in the Father's eyes is also enhanced by their relation to the glory of the Holy Ghost. He undertakes to deliver them from the power and the inward stain of their sin. He gives them the germ of the eternal life in the beginning; he takes up his abode in them for a period avowedly perpetual; he guides the whole process of their purification; he guards their integrity. If all this should be baffled ana defeated, the glory of the Spirit would be extinguished.   The glory of the Father would be equally shattered.   The whole scheme of redemption was his; its execution involved to him the cost of his Son's humiliation, and the contact of his Spirit for ages with the pollutions of the hearts he purifies.   Besides these awful considerations, his character is illustrated in this wonderful enterprise as it is in no other work of his hands.   In every other work he has done, his attributes of wisdom, power, holiness, justice, and truth are displayed in their normal forms and along the natural lines of their exercise; they are manifested singly or in combinations limited by the object in view.   But in the plan of redemption they are exhibited in a combination and degree without a parallel in the history of the universe But more than this: in this grand enterprise alone, among all the multiplied works of his hands, is there any disclosure of that sweetest and most marvelous attribute of his nature, the existence of which was unknown to the most profound student of his glorious character among the angels of his presence, that attribute which is worn to tatters in man's ungrateful ears—*his grace*—his free and boundless love for unholy creatures.   But all the counsel of God, all his sacrifice in giving up his Son to redeem and his Spirit to sanctify, all the marvels of his wisdom, holiness, goodness, justice and power would be nullified, if the subjects of the whole grand endeavor should fail to receive any effectual benefit from it.   Nay, grace, the newly discovered attribute, will appear to be powerless of all abiding good effects.   The issue would be the ruin of the glory of the Spirit and the glory of the Father, equally with that of the glory of the Son.   Can we wonder that an inheritance, which effectually forestalls, and which only can forestall, such inestimable mischiefs as these, should be esteemed and valued beyond all things else?

But there are other less imposing, but yet powerful, considerations that enter and enhance the value of God's inheritance in the saints. They are valued from their attachment to the Son of his love. That Christ is precious to the hearts of his saints is one of the infallible marks of genuine saintship. They are valued by the Father for this affection to his Son, and for all it leads them to endure and do for the Son's sake. Their glorious struggles to obey him, their resistance to his enemies, their devotion to his great cause, their self-denial, their suffering, their tears, their trust in him, their weary but patient waiting, all because of their fidelity and love to him, intensify the Father's value for them. This value is also enhanced by the great ends God designs to accomplish by them. He has matched these frail and faulty creatures against the enormous numbers and the mighty combination and strength of the powers of darkness. He sends them out as his shepherd with a sling to confront the armed giant of the infernal hierarchy. By their weak hands he intends to save the lost world of guilty immortals, to pull down and grind to powder the mighty ramparts of the satanic kingdom, and to establish on an unchanging basis the splendor of his Son's triumphant kingdom. They are to judge the world as the assessors of the royal Judge at the last day. They are probably to be the occasion by which the spread of sin in the future is to be stayed in the universe of God. They are the joint heirs with his Son, and will reign with him forever and ever. If these grand ends in the counsel of God can be defeated, then may the hope of the saints be confounded. This is the value in the Father's eyes of his inheritance in the saints. Now the inference may be fairly drawn from this inheritance, in its bearing on the hope of his people: If God has actually such an inheritance in them, are they not entitled to hope? The foundation of it is stronger than the mountains. Is not therefore the absence of hope in the heart of saints a reproach as well as a calamity, a mystery of weakness towards themselves, a miracle of injustice towards God?

3. The sure hope of those who have been called of God is confirmed, even beyond these enormous guarantees, by a consideration of similar power. The third truth on which the apostle desired the improved spiritual intuitions of the Ephesian Christians to be exercised was "*the exceeding greatness of his power to us-ward who believe.*" The discernment of this power would develop and confirm the hope of their calling, because it was the second guarantee of this hope. The power of the Almighty God could surely certify anything it undertook to do. Such is the apostle's reasoning. The full energy of accumulated expression is used to convey an idea of this awful force. It is described as "the exceeding greatness of his power." The original Greek words are even more expressive: they speak of it as "the might of the energy of his power," or, in other phrase, "the energy of his power in its might, in the uttermost of its strength." The words express the full energy of the power that is in the Almighty God. They carry the notion that all the power that is in the Infinite God is pledged to guarantee the hope of every believer. The full weight of this expression cannot be brought out until we compare it with a fact, and that is, that in all the works of God he has never put forth more than a part of his power. The grandest exertion of it has been made in the several departments of the work of redemption, but his full energy has never been taxed to the uttermost of infinite power. Already, in every believer a single instance of his peculiar and distinctive divine energy has been displayed in their new creation by the power of the Holy Spirit. Similar exercises of it attend the development of this germ of eternal life to its final perfection, and is all-sufficient to effect both. It is said to be the same power employed in raising our Lord from the dead. It was not exhausted in either of these marvelous works, the raising of a dead soul to spiritual life, and of a dead Christ to the resurrection life; it still abides undiminished and undimin-

ishable. This one part or portion of the almighty power is sufficient to give an unimpeachable guarantee to the hope of God's calling and the expectation of his saints; it has been already exemplified and demonstrated. Yet the strong phrases of the inspired apostle assure us that, beyond this actually exerted and sufficient power, the whole residuary mass of power in the boundless energies of the Almighty God is pledged to secure the hope of his calling and the integrity of his inheritance. If all the power inherent in a being whose every quality is stamped with the impress of absolute infinity, can secure a hope, then the hope of his calling is assured. Assurance can rise no higher. The great inheritance of God through the death of his Son and the limitless greatness of his power are the two great buttresses of the Christian hope. What can undermine it? If such is the safety of every believer, and such the real security of his hope, even of the weakest who has received the explicit assurance that "God is able to make him stand," what ought to be the hope even of the weakest? Hope has no sphere except in the future; it deals only with the future; and if the future is assured, what can lawfully interfere with the hope *and the present comfort* of his saints? If their hope is defective, it does injustice to the ground on which it is based; it ought to be commensurate with it. Let us hearken to the gracious command: Give all diligence to reach the full assurance of hope to the end. The hope in the heart ought always to be adjusted to the ground of hope in the covenant.

CHAPTER IV.

THE SEALING OF THE SPIRIT.

"In whom also, after that ye believed, ye were sealed with that Holy Spirit of promise."—*Paul to the Ephesians.*

ALL continuous work must be performed by a succession of special acts. The work of the Holy Spirit in the purification of believers is accomplished by such a succession. Abiding always in the regenerate soul, he discharges his covenant engagements by repeated exertions of his power, in a series of acts differing each from the other, though all are connected as parts of a whole, and each is productive of progressive effect on the grand purpose of them all. These special acts of the Spirit are sampled in the *witness* of the Spirit, in the *anointing* of the Spirit, and in the action alluded to in the passage at the head of this chapter, *the sealing* of the Spirit. Each of these actions has *a general* and *a special* significance, as will be illustrated hereafter. A *seal* is a symbol of expression, an inarticulate sign to which a certain meaning, or a certain number of meanings, has been attached by a conventional or arbitrary appointment. The use of the seal has been a custom among all nations of any advancement in civilization, and among barbarous or semi-civilized tribes. The signet, or seal, was in use from an early period, at least as early as the time of Judah the son of Jacob. It was common among the kings as well as the private persons of the oriental nations, and has descended to modern nations in the usages of law and commerce, and as the personal signatures of individual men. Among the ancients the seal was often worn also as a personal ornament as well as an instrument of business, generally as a ring upon the finger, and sometimes as a bracelet upon the arm. This use of the seal also continues in modern times. No special form was essential to the uses of a seal; it might be of any form and with any device graven upon it. The actual purpose of the symbol might be different, being more or less extensive as determined by custom, by the law of the land, or by the determination of individual will. A seal of extreme simplicity of form might be made to carry almost any wealth of meaning. The connection between the sign and the thing signified being purely conventional, or a matter of voluntary arrangement, it is obvious that either one or any number of meanings might be attached to it. The seal was often rich in significance. It was used to *grant authority, to give a commission, to delegate power.* Thus Ahasuerus, the Persian king, took his ring from his finger and gave it to Haman, the son of Hammedatha, when he authorized the destruction of the captive Jews. It was used to attest *instruments of writing,* commissions, covenants, and contracts, as in the case of Jeremiah the prophet, when he bought the field in Anathoth, of Hanameel, his uncle's son. It was used for the purpose of *confirming and giving assurance,* as when Abraham received the sign of circumcision, *as a seal* of the righteousness of the faith which he had, being yet uncircumcised. It was used as a *medium of proof, or a testimony,* as when Paul appealed to the converts under his preaching as the seal of his apostleship. It was used as a *certificate of trustworthiness* in a ground of confidence and *a pledge of safety to those* who relied upon it, as when the foundation of God is said to stand sure, having this seal, the Lord knoweth them that are his; and when Satan is cast into the bottomless pit, and a seal is set upon him for a thousand years. Finally, it was used to *secure secrecy,* as when John in Patmos saw a book sealed with seven seals. While there is no definite room to assert that the seal of the Spirit is designed to carry all these meanings, yet certainly the use of the word *seal*, to describe a sanctifying act of the Holy Ghost, would be altogether misleading, if it was not to be construed as carrying some of the most important of them at least. In one place the sealing of the Spirit is indicated in general terms as the confirmation of the hope of believers, as when we are told not to grieve the Holy Spirit, whereby we are sealed unto the day of redemption. In more than one place the sealing of the Spirit is identified with the earnest of the Spirit, as *a general pledge of safety* to the believer. This is, then, the *general* significance of the seal of the Holy Ghost. But there is a special significance, as we shall see, not absolutely identical with the earnest, but going somewhat beyond it, not so much designed to give assurance of safety as to keep our minds in the love of God and in the comfort of the Holy Ghost. It is this special influence in giving stability to all the mental exercises of the believer which has so important and powerful a bearing on the hope and peace of the saint in this present life. It is to this special energy of grace, then, that we wish to turn attention. What does the sealing of the Spirit under this aspect signify?

1. We remark, then, as preliminary, that it is a work of the Spirit peculiar to souls already in the faith. Some of his gracious work is done in unbelievers in order to lead them to the exercise of faith; but this sealing work is not; it is distinctly said that the sealing with the Holy Spirit of promise took place "after ye believed."

2. Neither is it to be confounded with *regeneration*. Regeneration is done in the unregenerate soul, and in order to regenerate and change the heart. The prayer of Paul for the increase of grace in the Ephesians proceeded on the previous recognition of their faith in Jesus, and their love to all the saints. This faith and love to the brethren are recognized marks of a soul already regenerate. The *sealing* of the Spirit, then, was to be done in the regenerate soul. This

also indicates a distinction between the seal and the earnest of the Holy Ghost: the earnest is given in regeneration, the sealing, in its special significance, after it.

3. Nor is the sealing of the Spirit to be confounded with *sanctification* in general. Sanctification is a term that embraces the whole progressive work of subduing the inward energy of sin in the soul, and inbreeding the graces of holiness in the place of it. The sealing is one of many special acts of gracious energy by which this long, progressive work is accomplished. It is no more to be confounded with the general work it is designed to accomplish, than the *witness* of the Spirit, or the *intercession* of ihe Spirit, or the *bringing to mind* of the Spirit. All of them are *special* acts by which the general work is accomplished—specific and separate manifestations of the Spirit's influence by which he carries out his great covenanted work, but are to be distinguished from it, although connected with it. What, then, is the nature of the special significance of the sealing of the Holy Ghost?

4. This question may be answered in the light of a testimony of Scripture, and of a Christian experience common to every believer, and really not unknown to some unregenerate persons, who have been to a certain extent under the influence of the Holy Ghost, and who have found out, by what may prove a fatal experience, how frail and evanescent are spiritual impressions in an unholy soul. The Bible recognizes this tendency to fade out in both classes, the regenerate and the unregenerate. It speaks of a goodness which is like the morning clouds and the early dew. It exhorts believers to stand fast in the liberty with which Christ has made them free, and to keep themselves in the love of God. The universal experience of Christians illustrates the need of these exhortations, and for the sealing of the Spirit. They know how frail are their richest spiritual apprehensions of the truth, their warmest and most comfortable frames of feeling, their most ardent aspirations, their firmest resolves. They

know how easily the spirit of prayer dies out, how quickly clear and joyful apprehensions of the doctrines of grace, and the promises of the covenant, die away, how soon the most spiritual frames of feeling perish. All this they know by an experience too definite to be mistaken, too sorrowful to be denied. They tremble under it; they thus learn to mistrust their hope; they are often led by it to discount all their claims to Christian character, and they are thus emptied of comfort. It is obvious that the relief for this would be an influence to counteract this evanescent character of spiritual apprehensions, and to give *stability* to the various exercises of the Christian feelings which delight so much by their presence, and grieve so much by their fleeting and unstable hold on the heart. The old hymn which has voiced the experience of so many modern followers of Christ represents exactly the felt want and the recognized relief:*

"Prone to wander, Lord, I feel it:
Prone to leave the God I love:
Here's my heart, Lord, take and seal it;
Seal it from thy courts above."

As the need is for some more stable and abiding form to the experiences of grace, the cure is to be found *in the sealing* of the Spirit. The nature of this sealing, then, in its special significance, is plain enough: it is an act of the Spirit's influence, giving *stability and strength* to all the exercises of the renewed soul, and thus adding clearness to the evidences of regeneration, giving force and definiteness to the doctrines and precepts of the word, infusing vigor into hope, multiplying comfort, and bestowing firmness and endurance on the zeal of the soul, and on all the energies of conduct. It is an action of the Holy Spirit assuring and adding vigor to all his work in the heart, giving more definite, stable, and abiding form to all the graces, the germ of which

---

*Philip of Maberley's "Love of the Spirit."

he has implanted in regeneration. It is done in pursuance of his covenant engagements, with a view to the more effective advancement of his work of sanctifying the believer. The *sealing* of the Spirit is an all-important part of his official action. It is not only, in one sense at least, essential to the discharge of the functions assigned to him in the covenant of grace, but it is indispensable to the comfort and the highest usefulness of the souls he has undertaken to purify. The joy of the Lord is their strength. This will appear under the following statements.

5. The Spirit *seals and gives permanence to the desire of the regenerate soul for the salvation of God.* He originally creates this desire in the unconverted heart, awakens the conscience, alarms the fears, overcomes the mad resistance which always meets it and animates it, until the sinner has been made willing in the day of his power. But for this gracious action of the Spirit on the will, the sinning soul would surely accomplish its own ruin. In this treatment of the unconverted soul we have an image of the sealing power of the Spirit dealing with the will of the saint. The resemblance is maintained along the line of a general direction; but a difference is obvious. He acts on the will of both classes of men—in the one to implant a desire, in the other to stimulate and confirm a desire already implanted; in the one it is an act of pure grace sovereignly exerted, in the other it is an act of grace under covenant, sovereignly determining time and measure of relief, yet faithful to covenant obligations freely and sovereignly assumed. A seal is a symbol confirmatory of all the pledges in the covenant or contract sealed. To the unconverted God has not come under any covenant pledge, and may, therefore, at any time previous to the exercise of faith withdraw the Spirit, and give the resisting sinner up to his own devices. But as soon as he believes, the whole case is changed. God has graciously pledged himself to save the sinner who believes, and as soon as he believes

God comes under covenant; he is bound by his own gracious pledge. He now undertakes to absolutely save; but he undertakes to do it without violating the nature of the being he has taken in hand. He rigorously respects all the laws of his being. As man is a creature of reason and will, God saves him in full recognition of both. He saves, not against his will, but through it; he makes the sinner willing; he awakens his desires, and then complies with them. This desire has to be kept alive in the heart, and made to lead in the whole progress of the sanctifying work down to its triumphant conclusion. As is the *desire* of the regenerate soul, so is the progress of his purification. Around this central point in the mighty struggle the whole contention between the powers of darkness and the powers of grace is concentrated. To extinguish the desire of spiritual good, all the agencies hostile to the salvation of the soul are directed; to sustain and increase it is the aim of all the agencies friendly to that grand purpose. It is the pivotal point of the whole case. Satan knows that he cannot coërce a soul contrary to its own will, and his whole strength is put forth to misguide the will, and to make him the voluntary agent of his own destruction. God equally respects the freedom of the creature, and grace seeks to save him through his own will. That awful faculty of free will, at once the glory and the peril of a moral agent, is the vital centre of the whole mighty battle. It is, therefore, always surrounded with dangerous influences. The remaining depravity in a regenerate soul, that law of sin in the members which is always contending with the new law of grace in the mind, is always subtly eating at the *desire* of the soul. The world and all its seductions are perpetually adjusted to awaken *other desires* to supersede the desire of grace. The mighty art and craft of the tempter and his trained legions of seducers are all converged about this one point. Here, too, the contending forces of the glorious covenant concentrate their strength, and in no particular is the

wonderful energy of divine grace more wonderfully displayed
than in keeping the desire of eternal life burning, unextin-
guished by all the tremendous forces brought to bear on its extinction.　Ah! it is not like the love-light of the Hindoo maiden
set afloat as the dusk settles down on the smooth waters
of the sacred Ganges and under the still air of an Indian
summer evening.　It is a point of slender flame, no bigger
than the blaze of a candle, set afloat on the wild waves of
the tempest-ridden seas.　The mad waters are lashing at it;
the winds are blowing a hurricane upon it; it is amazing
that it lives for a moment.　But, strange to see and strange
to say, clear, shining through the darkness and the storm;
now riding on the crest of the billows; now buried in the
belly of the deep, that slender flame floats unharmed.　It
has been sealed by the Holy Ghost, and in that impervious
casing of covenanted grace it will ride out the tempest, safe
and inextinguishable.　Christians are sometimes tempted to
hard thoughts of God because he does not respond more
promptly to their desires after grace; but that desire itself is
proof of the living energy of grace within them; this alone
ought to comfort them.　Those in whose breasts the desire
for God's salvation lives steadily, even though somewhat
feebly, as the years pass, know something at least of the
sealing of the Spirit.　The stronger and more eager, the
more constant and abiding in its eagerness, this desire is,
the more clear becomes the evidence of the sealing of the
Spirit.　Without his perpetual touch the desire would have
perished in the heart of an apostle.　Often fluctuating, often
feeble, sometimes apparently extinct, it is nevertheless indestructible, because it has been sealed by the Holy Ghost.
This living desire, sealed thus by the energy of the Spirit, will
always lead to the higher energy of volition corresponding
with it, the sealed purpose and determination to seek
actively for the favor of God.　Often, under discouragements
and serious trials of faith, failures to realize specific hopes,

or to attain the measure of comfort we desire, there is strong temptation to construe ourselves as altogether mistaken in our confidence and hope, and thus to abandon hope and effort altogether. If our hearts were not sealed by the Spirit that hour of trial would be apt to prevail; but when, in spite of discouragement, the *desire* still breeds and animates the *purpose* to seek on, and if need be perish seeking for mercy, it shows the sealing of the Spirit. Believers have ample reason to thank God for this gift of his grace to his children.

6. *The Spirit also seals our sense and feeling of our spiritual necessities.* The intuitions of sin and the sense of guiltiness and personal pollution, which spring up under the convicting energies of the Holy Ghost, are always painful; the mingled feeling of dread and shame is well-nigh unbearable. Nature shrinks under it, and an effort to throw it off is inevitable. Even in the experience of the Christian, who has desired and prayed for these deepened intuitions of his personal sin, there is need for caution and self-restraint when his prayer is answered, and this quickened sense of his criminality is upon him. He needs to have his desire for them, and his faith in their value to him, sealed by the Spirit. Under the impulse of natural reluctance to suffer, and under the constant, secret repulsion of the law of sin remaining in him, a silent resistance will be set up which needs constant watchfulness and a steady effort to overcome. Otherwise, the painful but wholesome apprehensions will begin to fade out, and the Christian soul returns to a certain normal condition of feeling, partially sensible of the criminal nature of his sin, yet so imperfectly apprehensive of it as to leave room for many a grave and haunting fear lest these needful intuitions of sin should be fatally defective. It is obvious how these clear and strong apprehensions of spiritual necessities would exert a profound modifying influence upon character and on all the gracious experiences of the soul, if

they were sealed and made stable in the heart.   They would
lead to a deeper repentance; to a more profound humility;
to a more eager clinging to Christ as the Saviour; to a richer
ultimate development of all the graces of a purified heart.   It
is very sure, that if the Holy Spirit did not seal the perception and feeling of spiritual want, they would speedily die
out altogether.   All who have this abiding and prevalent,
even though fluctuating and feeble, apprehension of their
spiritual wants, are not entirely without some evidence of
the sealing of the Spirit in their hearts.

7. *The sealing work of the Holy Ghost also embraces the
great doctrines of the covenant,* and so affects the sense and
spiritual discernment of their real significance as to bring
out their intrinsic power to impress the human heart.   Nothing is more unintelligible to a certain class of minds than the
esteem placed by others on the doctrines of the gospel.   To
them they are mere intellectual combinations of certain mysterious and unpractical ideas, in no way different from mere
metaphysical or speculative theories; both are assigned to
the same class of intellectual productions to which all such
theories are asserted to belong.   To them the zeal for doctrinal accuracy is nothing more than zeal for precision in
idea where it is of no particular importance whether accuracy or inaccuracy prevails.   The conception is wholly erroneous.   A Christian doctrine is no mere combination of mere
ideas; it is a verbal description of a great fact.   Accuracy
and completeness in the conception of facts is recognized as
a matter of supreme importance in these days of scientific
investigation, and the verbal description of a fact is recognized as only relatively important to the fact it describes.
The verbal description of a great work of engineering is entirely subordinate to *the thing* which is described.   The doctrinal statements and expositions of the Christian teachers
are mere descriptions of great things, some accomplished already, and some yet to be accomplished.   The doctrine of

the resurrection is a mere verbal statement of a great fact in the future history of the human race. The doctrine of the atonement is the verbal account of a grand enterprise accomplished in order to bear on the sins of mankind. The doctrine of the kingdom of Christ is a mere verbal delineation of the force and ascendency of a kingdom now and yet to be as completely a matter of fact in the history of the world as the kingdom of England or the empire of Germany. The blunder in the conception of doctrine is gross and inexcusable. The explanation shows that there is an immeasurable *power* in the Christian doctrine. The doctrine of a divine Saviour and the redeeming energy of his blood is the only possible source of a sound hope and comfort to a mind really awake to just conceptions of sin. But as soon as the notion of an effectual atonement takes hold of the heart pierced and pained by a sense of guilt, it will at once reveal its antidotal power. Peace will spread its white wings over the disturbed soul, and it will rejoice in God the Saviour.

This instance samples the influence of the Christian doctrine when apprehended by the intimate knowledge Paul desired for the Ephesians. But, alas, how soon the sweet vision passes! The Saviour found is far too often like the Saviour seen after the resurrection, at the supper-table in Emmaus—revealed in the breaking of bread, and satisfying one spell of hunger, and then vanishing away. How glorious would be the blessing of a sealed and stable vision of a divine Saviour! How sweet are even these passing apprehensions of the unsearchable riches, the freedom, the completeness, the exact adjustments to human need of the great salvation. Fleeting as they are they abide in memory like a sweet spring morning, and often exert a commanding influence for a half-century of time. But, alas, they commonly vanish soon, like a sunset glory of crimson and gold sinking into the grey dusk of twilight, and often into the darkness of night. How happy if they could only be sealed by the

Spirit into some stable dwelling in the rejoicing soul! That effect is possible to every believer, to enable him to obey the command to rejoice in the Lord always; for the Spirit does *seal* the vision of a Saviour and his great salvation; and if more sought as a sealing power he would do more of his *sealing* work. In like manner, he seals the view of the plan of salvation. How clear and simple, how complete and satisfactory, the way of life seemed in the first hour of a living faith! How easy it was to believe! How simple faith appeared to be! How completely it lost sight of itself, and how fully it was satisfied with Christ! It wanted no other ground of trust; he was enough! Yet how quickly this happy mood passed away! How mysterious faith grew to be! What struggles, vain struggles, to get back to the same state of mind! What a blessing it would be to have that view of Christ, faith, and the plan of salvation *sealed* and stamped with a more stable hold in the heart! Do we not begin to see how precious is the sealing of the Holy Ghost?

8. This will appear still more forcibly when we consider him *as the sealer of the promises.* These promises are in themselves both great and precious. When faith takes proper hold upon them they lift the burden of all earthly care; they soothe sorrow; they quell regrets; they open boundless prospects of permanent and invaluable possessions to the heirs of God. Yet how poor is the effect they generally have! Any trial of faith in them, any apparent failure to realize them according to our own notions of what the fulfilment ought to be—in the time, place, or substance of that fulfilment—seems to empty them of all meaning, and turn them into mockeries of our misery instead of stable elements of our comfort. Nay, in trials of faith which are really severe, when the providences of God seem to deny his words, how precious then would be the sealing of the promises in our hearts, and the enablement of faith to stand steadfast on the bare word of the Lord, coupled with a full trust *in him*

as well as in *his promises*. The promises are often fulfilled
when they seem for a time to be denied. Our Lord prayed
to be delivered, and was delivered from what he feared; yet
through all the needful trial he had to go. His faith did
not fail, though the cup did not pass. Deliverance may
come after an evil happens; it may be arrested as well as
prevented. The denial of a petition is often the prelude to
its answer, or the grant of a better equivalent. God does
not engage to answer all prayers of his people according to
the literal tenor of their petitions, for their prayers are often
diametrically opposed, and this would introduce utter confusion. Unlimited answers to all human petitions would make
the discretion of man, and not the wisdom of God, the ruling
power in the administration of the universe. He will not
give a stone for bread, and Christians may be often asking
for a scorpion, when they think they are asking for an egg.
He wants them to trust himself as well as his words. On
the other hand, he does not wish us to construe his promises as empty of all meaning and encouragement to pray
because he reserves the discretion of answering some petitions in his own hands. No, after all deductions are made,
the promises stand; they are great and precious; they warrant steadfast and unflinching prayer; they warrant unfailing
expectations of a certain class of blessings; they encourage
hope for many others. Every prayer of faith offered according to the written will of God is sure of some answer, in
some manner. There will be a large percentage of literal
answers to bold and patient, ardent and submissive pleading
of the promises. No doubt one reason why Christians are
timid in pleading the promises is that their insight is too
feeble to disclose the real meaning of the promises. It is
certain that we are commanded to come boldly to the throne
of grace. It is certain that great boldness of faith is com-
mended. The promises are like checks written in invisible
ink, plain when brought under the warmth of quickened

affections, but unseen in the common light and heat of day. When they open their sense to the healthy spiritual mind, they are full of power and great consolation. If they were only opened and sealed in the heart by the Holy Ghost, there would be no impediment to their free effects on the soul; no trial would shake our confidence in them; no misconception of them would empty them of their enormous power to stimulate energy in obedience, and to fill the heart with the sunrise splendor of an immortal hope.

9. *The Spirit seals the spirit of prayer.* As God has appointed prayer and promised to answer it, it is necessary that man should be adjusted to the work. There must be a spirit or frame of mind suitable to the priceless ordinance. This spirit of prayer embodies a lively confidence in the instrumentality adjusted to the real force that is in it. As it is not for God's honor to appoint an ordinance, and then turn it to shame by making it powerless, so the true spirit of prayer will be adjusted to this reliability in it. When the spirit of prayer fills the soul, it will become eager, ardent, intense in desire, resolute in action, patient in supplication, and steadfast in faith. With this spirit there will be, not only *power* in prayer, but confident and unpresuming expectations of answers to prayer. The gift of such a spirit, and it is one of the gifts of the Holy Spirit to believers, is an absolutely priceless grant. Yet how seldom it emerges in the experience of the Christian! How few of them are acquainted with the rapture of the exalted frame born of strong desire and confident expectation! How few ever realize the sense of power with a faithful God which grows out of this spirit of prayer exalted to some of its higher degrees! Yet this is not exclusively the privilege of a few favored saints; it is warranted in the covenant to any who will seek for it, however it may be confined in fact to the few who turn the privilege to account. It is not unfrequently given, but it is not cherished and preserved, and

generally proves to be only a passing mood, leaving often unutterable sense of loss, and yearning for its return. But it does not come, for it is not sealed by the Spirit. He is neglected in his sealing office, and the soul is left enfeebled and desolate. But he can stereotype the spirit of prayer in the heart, and is more ready to do all his gracious offices in the Christian soul than earthly parents are to give good gifts to their children. This sealing blessing is one of the Spirit's gifts to believers.

10. *In like manner the Spirit seals the evidences of conversion in the renewed heart.* How often do these appear dim and doubtful even in a heart truly regenerate! At some rare times they are clear and full of comfort; it is frequently the case that the soul has to look back from a period of confusion to a clearer manifestation in the distant past. Just as David once did when his soul was cast down within him; his only resource was to look back and recall the deliverance and the joy that came to him when he was in the land of Jordan and of the Hermonites, in the hill Mizar. This policy is never long satisfactory, nor is it always safe. The comfort of the believer ought always to be sought directly in Christ the Lord, and only subordinately in anything else, no matter how lawful. It would often be well for the believer, instead of worrying over the effort to spell out the meaning of signs which have lost color and definite outline, to go at once, as at the first, to the feet of Jesus, and appeal to the help of the Paraclete for sin, and to the Paraclete for the inward struggle. The atoning blood of the one will always give peace. The other can bear witness with our spirits that we are children of God, quicken the evidences in us and add his testimony to them, and then *seal* the witness of both in the heart.

11. The Spirit, in a word, *seals all the energies of grace of every kind, the affections, emotions, principles, and all the other vital driving forces of the regenerate soul.* Zeal and

real energy, real joy, and a living delight in all the service of God, appear sometimes in the experience of the average believer, and then there is always life in his work, and happy feelings even in hard and self-denying labor. But when it passes off it leaves a spirit behind it which makes every duty a burden, every sacrifice a grief, and every energy an exhausted force. But a steady and ardent energy can be infused into all the graces of the new man by the sealing of the Spirit. All the principles of obedience can be made staunch and resolute; every impulse can be turned to useful account, and every affection be drawn out into pure and high development by this gift to believers.

12. *Lastly, the Spirit seals the hope of heaven in the regenerate heart;* and can so quicken and seal it in its improved condition as to make it produce its legitimate effects on the hope and the happiness of the Christian in this life. The hope of heaven is in every saint, but it exerts an influence so maimed and impoverished as to be even grotesquely out of proportion to the intrinsic power of the object on which it is exercised. Heaven expresses the very highest embodiment of glory, honor, and eternal life. A real and well-founded hope of entering into such supreme conditions of blessedness has a natural tendency to breed not merely comfort, but joy and exultation in the highest possible degree. But this tendency is generally disabled of its effects in the experience of the great bulk of regenerate men. Even when the character of Christian is fairly claimed, and although it is confessed that every Christian soul will assuredly go into the mansions of the blessed dead, yet as soon as such a soul is challenged to actually rise to the height of its great and acknowledged expectations, it falters and trembles, and often passes over into the contrary mood of actual despondency. In this state of mind, even heaven becomes a depressing thought, and the pilgrim of grace, on his way straight into the golden gates, goes forward with his head wrapped in mourning weeds, his

eyes wet with tears, and his heart full of pain. His whole mental state is in a false condition, unworthy of his hopes, cruel to himself, and dishonoring to his Saviour. If the blessed sealing influence of the Holy Spirit could be brought to bear on the hope of heaven, all this would be changed. The transition into glory would never so alter its natural effect as to become a depressing influence; all earthly cares would be transfigured, and heaven, as the covenanted and sealed home of the soul, would throw down upon the shadows and the dark places of the earthly pilgrimage the sweet and mellow splendor of the Paradise of God. To enjoy habitually the hope of heaven, it is necessary to seek for the sealing of the Spirit. It is a gift to believers beyond conception in value.

It is plain that all Christians of every age, at all times and under all circumstances, need the sealing office of the Holy Ghost. The tendency of all the Christian frames and exercises, under the present conditions of existence, is to fade out; they need always to be confirmed and strengthened. The convictions or intuitive apprehension and sense of sin; the discernment of the grace of God in its unsearchable riches; the fatherhood of God; the love of the Spirit; the grace of the Son; suitable views of doctrinal truth; resolutions of more fidelity in service; the perception of need in ourselves and others; the communion of saints; interest in the souls of particular persons and in the conversion of the world; desires after holiness and efficiency in service—all these are subject to this tendency to fade out, and need the sealing of the Spirit. It is specially needed by the aged Christian as the world goes more and more to decay for him, and the realities of eternity bulk larger on his vision. It is specially needed by all in times of affliction. It is one of the most precious of the gifts of the Spirit to believers.

CHAPTER V.

THE UNCTION OF THE SPIRIT.

"But ye have an unction from the Holy One, and ye know all things."
—*John.*

THESE words describe another of the series of special acts by which the Holy Spirit carries out his general work of purifying the covenanted soul. Each of these acts, or certainly some of the more prominent members of the series, seem to have a general and a special significance. The Holy Ghost is given as a general seal, pledge, or security that the promises to faith will be redeemed; and in this view of it it is identical with the *earnest* of the Spirit; yet there is a special sealing which is designed to give stability to the various exercises of the renewed heart. The *witness* of the Spirit has a general significance, because the gift of the Holy Ghost in regeneration is a proof of saving grace in the soul; yet this is different from that special testimony which is borne concurrently with the testimony of the believer's own spirit in proving his sonship. It is equally true in reference to the action called the *unction* of the Spirit; it, too, has a general and special significance. The general grant of the Holy Spirit to renew the heart is spoken of as *an outpouring of the Spirit, and an anointing of the Spirit.* The expression is a figurative one, drawn from the practice of pouring oil on the head of one chosen to an office, or consecrated to a particular service. Oil was thus used as the official sign of setting apart to the office of king, priest, prophet, and captain of the host among the ancient Jews. It was thus figuratively transferred to the vocabulary of the gospel system in order to express different impressions made by the grant and the gifts of the Holy Spirit. The general

significance of the unction of the Spirit was this general setting apart or consecration to the service of God. But the
act of anointing with oil did not only carry *a certain significance* in meaning, but *made a certain impression.* The meaning of the act was one thing, the impression of the act was
another, and the act itself was different from both. Nor will
we be able to gain a full conception of the action as a whole
unless we distinguish between the mere act which was transitory, and the more abiding intention of the act and the more
abiding impression which it made. In the physical anointing with oil there was included the pouring out of the material, the purpose to be served by it, and the effect on the
person of the individual anointed. In the anointing of the
Spirit there is the *agency* applied, which is the Spirit himself; *the purpose* to be gained—consecration to the general
or some special service of God; and *the impression* made on
the heart and spirit of the anointed man to fit him for that
service. This *inward impression* is *the special significance* in
the unction of the Holy Ghost. In the sealing action of the
sanctifier there is a similar distinction between the seal and
the impression which it makes on one side, and the purpose to be secured on the other. As, then, the sealing of
the Spirit is more than a general confirmatory grant or earnest, and implies also a special inward influence, giving stability to the frames and exercises of the Christian experience; as the witness of the Spirit is more than a general
proof or testimony from the work of the Holy Ghost, but is
also a special testimony about that work, giving assurance of
personal salvation, so the unction of the Spirit is a special,
consecrating influence, not only for the purpose of setting
apart for service, but for conveying a special personal fitness
to do the work or endure the trial.

Yet a further discrimination must be made. This unction
is said to be attended with a peculiar effect on the *powers* of
spiritual discernment: "Ye have an unction from the Holy

One, and ye know all things." A similar effect is exerted on
the power of spiritual intuition in regeneration. Is, then,
this peculiar unction of the Spirit to be identified with regeneration, or, if not, in what does its power on the energies
of spiritual discernment differ from that of regenerating
grace? That the unction of the Spirit is not to be confounded with regeneration may be inferred from a number
of circumstances. It is inferable from the fact that regeneration, with its effect on the spiritual vision, can occur *but
once*, and its effect on the vision is to create the power to see,
where no such power existed before; but the oil of joy for
mourning may be *repeatedly applied*, and its effect on the
vision is simply to heal disorders which have impeded a
vision already existing, but diseased and disordered. It is
inferable from the fact that this unction is always attended
with strong and rejoicing spiritual apprehensions, "Ye know
all things"; whereas in regeneration only a percentage of its
subjects see very clearly at the period of regeneration, and
frequently "see men as trees walking." It is inferable from
the fact disclosed in the experience of Christians universally,
that after the grant of spiritual vision in regeneration there
is many a spell of distressing darkness, showing disorder in
the granted vision, and the need of subsequent healing influences from the same loving and healing Spirit. The eyes of
the saint have to be anointed with eye-salve that they may
see many a time after the power of vision has been conferred
upon them. It may be inferred from the allusions of John
in the context of the passage at the head of this chapter; he
evidently teaches that the unction, with its greatly improved
powers of spiritual knowledge, was in those who possessed
the grace of regeneration; they were already saints, and this
abiding condition of advanced intuition was superinduced
upon previous gifts. Moreover, the exhortation of this same
John, in Revelation, to the church of Laodicea, to "anoint
their eyes with eye-salve that they may see," implies the

same distinction. The church was in a state of extraordinary declension; they are described as neither cold nor hot; not warm with vigorous spiritual life, nor yet cold in spiritual death. They were in utter spiritual darkness; but it was the difference between eyes entirely blind and eyes diseased, bandaged closely, and confined in a darkened room. They could see no more than if they were actually without eyesight, and they needed an eye-salve which was never used to give sight to the blind, but only to heal disorders which prevented the use of a sight which was actually in possession. It is not warrantable to confound the unction of the Spirit, and its effect on the organs of spiritual perception, with regeneration and its effect on the same organ when merely diseased. Regeneration creates the power of vision in eyes totally blind; the unction heals its diseases when given, and enables it to see clearly. This discrimination has not been uselessly made. It brings before the troubled Christian, tried by long spells of imperfect spiritual discernment, the knowledge of a remedy not confined to the instant and unrepeatable act of regeneration, whose effects his own experience shows are not able to keep him in rejoicing views of the truth, but a remedy capable of *repeated and continuous operation*. The saints of God would be in a bad condition indeed, if no steady sanctifying grace was provided for them, and they were only left to the one impulse given in regeneration.

But this is not all that is important to be said in order to lead up to a clear conception of this precious influence of the Holy Spirit. The unction is not to be confounded with sanctification in general any more than with regeneration. It is one of the actions of the Spirit by which he carries forward the work of sanctification, but is not to be identified absolutely with it. It is always connected with it and designed to promote it, but is yet to be distinguished from it. There is a practical use for the distinction, inasmuch as the peculiar

nature of the unction is so attractive, while its effects are so
purifying that it invites activity in seeking, more than some
other means of sanctification which may be equally effective,
yet not so pleasing.   The graces and gifts of sanctification
may grow in darkness and pain; they always grow with conscious joy and freedom in their growth under the unction of
the Spirit.   Trial and suffering, though commonly the conditions of growth in grace, and to be welcomed as such, are,
nevertheless, not the only conditions of it.   This will be apparent as soon as we conceive the real nature of the unction
or inward impression made by the special anointing of the
Holy Ghost.   This unction may be thus described: it is a
special act of gracious energy on the part of the indwelling
Spirit, by which he so softens and clears up the heart of the
saint that all the exercises of his graces, faith, hope, penitence,
long-suffering, joy, and gentleness—in a word, all the energies determined in him by regenerating grace—become free,
sweet, definite, clear, and full of a delightful energy.   The impression is analogous to the softening and soothing influence
of a perfumed oil on the skin.   The progress in sanctification is always delightful under the unction of the Spirit, because it always brings clearness to vision, warmth and sweetness to the affections, fervency and great tenderness to
prayer, great submission and great boldness to faith, great
ardor to hope, great keenness and pitying softness to zeal—
in a word, this wonderful grace of the Holy One infuses
fresh degrees of happy influence into all the energies of the
regenerate soul, and causes all its graces to grow with a delightful freedom.   Under this action a certain fervor of
saintly consecration appears *in the character;* a certain holy
ardor and tenderness *in the prayers;* a certain eagerness and
tender solicitude *in the zeal;* a certain loving energy *in the
conduct;* a certain loving and spiritual elevation in the whole
manifested spirit of the anointed man.   Many a truly regenerate and painfully sanctified child of God never reaches,—

apparently, at least,—the sweet blessing of the Spirit's unction. Yet it is a blessing which, however distinct from the
common experience of average Christians, is within reach of
them all. With this conception of what is meant by this
unction from the Holy One, let us consider some of its characteristic signs and some of its significant effects.

1. The first detail in reference to this gift which we encounter in the teaching of the Scriptures about it, is *its effect
on the spiritual vision of the regenerate soul.* "Ye have an
unction from the Holy One, and ye know all things." We
have already seen that this is not the original creation of
this capacity of spiritual vision; this is given in regeneration. It is the improvement of a power of vision already
given, healing its diseases and giving vigor to its perceptions.
The Holy Spirit was promised to those who were already
his disciples, after the death of our Lord, "that he might take
of the things of Christ and show them unto them." This
was not designed to furnish them with the inspiration peculiar to the twelve, but to lead their dull apprehensions into
the full apprehension of the truths they already knew, and
of those which should afterwards be taught them. The gift
of inspiration was only necessary to them officially; the gift
of understanding was equally essential to all other Christians. It is the uniform teaching of the word of God, that
the necessary effect of sin is to destroy spiritual life and all
its particular manifestations—the power of spiritual perception among others. The natural man knoweth not the
things of the Spirit of God, for they are spiritually discerned. Consequently a certain measure of the Spirit's influence is indispensable to enable a man to·see enough of
these things of the Spirit to be saved at all. But he may be
enabled to see enough of his sin to repent, and enough of
Christ to trust in him, and yet be far from "knowing all
things."

His spiritual life may be real and yet feeble; his spiritual life may be restored, and yet be weak in degree, and vacillating in exercise. It is a possible and an intensely desirable thing to have this real, yet feeble, power of discernment made strong, clear, and stable in its energy. A high degree of this improved condition is what is meant by the expression "knowing all things." It certainly does not mean what it literally says; it does not confer omniscience, and make the man a god; it is only to be construed as conferring a greatly improved capacity of spiritual intuition. Only this, but what an inexpressibly sweet and glorious blessing is this only gift! What a blessing is the power of physical vision, that glorious energy which unseals to us all the vast riches of the visible creation and their innumerable relations to the safety and comfort of life! None can appreciate it like the blind, who walk in one long-continued midnight, or the old, whose decay of sight, and whose memory of better days only brings out the more pathetically the losses involved in the decline of nature. But even more sorrowful, for greater losses are involved, is that spiritual blindness which shuts out entirely the revelations which lead to eternal life, or that incompetent discernment of these truths, which excludes their full power to lift the soul to the level of its promised expectations, and cheer it with all the riches of the heirship of God. The believer is measurably aware of this loss to him. What grief comes to him from imperfect vision! He sees dimly, but he sees enough to know the treasure which remains unseen in its full glory. He sees enough of his faith to hope it is the true fruit of the Spirit, but not enough to be unpresumptuously certain. He hardly knows whether he sees sin aright, or the plan of salvation, or the nature of repentance, or faith, or love, or hope. From this state of mind come all the anxieties of an unassured hope. He sees plainly that there are great defects in his views, and he knows not but what they may be fatal defects. He longs for clearness of vision. He knows that the Saviour of sinners is entitled to his best affections; he longs so to love him; he is grieved and pained that he cannot love him as he ought to love him, and as he longs to love him. But, alas! his vision is so imperfect, he does not know whether he sees Christ as he wants to see him, or loves him as he desires to love him. It is a piteous case. How piteous is the condition of a blind husband and father, longing to see the dear faces of wife and children, yet cannot see them! He loves them, and the love in his heart is the very thing which gives poignancy to the sorrow of his disabled vision. Assuredly the heart that grieves because it cannot see Jesus, and do justice to his claims on the affections, does love him to a certain degree; but this dim and feeble eyesight in the lovers of the Lord robs them of infinite riches. They are surrounded by the unsearchable treasures of grace divine. An atonement full of power to give peace to conscience is before his eyes; but he cannot see it, or sees it so dimly that its power to remove his burden is shorn away, and he walks on bearing the intolerable load. Grace sufficient to secure him a sure entrance into eternal life is pledged to him, but he sees it too imperfectly to receive it into his weary heart. The infinite love of God, the rich and full provisions of the covenant, the great and precious promises, the glorious doctrines, and the entrancing prospects of the gospel stand round him like radiant angels fresh from the empyrean heavens, but his dim eyes grope over the splendid company. A traveler with imperfect vision is passing through a landscape, charming with forest and field; bright glancing streams are gliding through orchards and meadows, sweet with bloom and verdure; fair human homes are here and there dotting the landscape, and the cattle are browsing knee-deep in the lush grass; but the dim-eyed traveler sees nothing, and his heart receives no pleasure from all this wealth of beauty. He sees a little immediately about him, and in this he is better off than one who comes behind him totally sightless and dog-led through

an endless night.   But worse—far worse than either—is the
soul, whether altogether blind or seeing but dimly, which
passes through the sweet landscape of covenanted grace and
sees nothing, or nothing clearly.   That unction of the Spirit
which would enable the weak-eyed saint to see the things of
Christ as they really are would be an inestimable blessing.
In this precious function of the Holy One there is a real
remedy for this robbery by blindness and diseased vision of
the peace and joy which are the rightful heritage of every
believer.

2. Taking up the clue furnished by the metaphor of the
text, we can advance further in the conception of the significance and value of the unction of the Holy Spirit.   *It
brings comfort.*   It has long been a favorite luxury of the
Eastern people to qualify the effects of their hot and exhaust-
ing climate by the use of oil as a cosmetic and lubricant of
the skin.   The surface of the body, parched and dried by
the appalling heat, could find no comfort equal to that produced by the cooling and softening influence of friction with
a soft and perfumed oil.   The unction of the Spirit produces
an analogous effect.   Let it be borne in mind that it is an
influence peculiar to the regenerate soul.   In one stage of
its experiences every such soul learns something, be it more
or less, but something of the comfort of forgiven sin, something of the peace of a yielding and subdued will.   But a
change is always impending, and when it comes, and the
long struggle of the spiritual warfare with unbelief and the
law of sin in the members takes the place of the former experiences of faith and submission, the contrast is specially
painful.   As the struggle goes on, the heat and weariness
seem to grow more and more unbearable.   If, now, in this
crisis, a restorative could be applied to the fainting spirit of
the faithful soldier; if the sweet vision of the rest and peace
of the past, and in a higher and more enduring measure

could be restored, it is easy to understand the comfort which the unction of the Spirit will bring.

The gospel is intrinsically full of joy; it is glad tidings of great joy; it is a flowing and full fountain of peace and hope. It only fails to reveal this priceless energy because the eyes are too dim to see it. This gladness of the gospel is powerful enough to assert its glorious energy in triumph over any form or degree of human grief, if only suitably comprehended. But the eyes of the believer are so often weak with watching, or dim with long and bitter weeping, that they cannot see it. When the eve-salve of the Holy Spirit touches these injured organs they begin to know the things of Christ, and as the gracious influence strengthens the vision more and yet more, they begin to "know all things." When guilt tortures conscience, the discernment of the real meaning and power of the great atonement will bring comfort. When the consciousness of the real evil of a sinful heart afflicts, the vision of God's strong and firmly covenanted grace will give comfort. When a sense of personal weakness comes along with a quickened apprehension of the awful weight of the issues to be determined, the vision of the Saviour's absolute ability to save to the uttermost will bring comfort. The unction of the Spirit, giving clearness to the eyesight and softening the stony habit of the heart, cannot fail to flood the rejoicing soul with a current of joy and peace. No soul so lifted into spiritual elevation of pious affections can ever be unhappy. *To be spiritually minded is life and peace.*

3. Another effect of the physical unction with the rich, perfumed oils of the East was *a restoration of strength, vigor, and efficiency for any kind of work.* The tired and heat-baked muscles were relaxed; the sinews were suppled; the oil sank to the bones, and lubricated the joints. A sense of renewed vigor floated through the nerves, and the refreshed and reinvigorated man was again ready for work or travel,

for the toils of the field or the camp, or the more desperate
exertions of pitched battle. Even so the unction of the
Spirit renews the energy of the saints of God, for "the joy
of the Lord is their strength,"—their strength to do and to
suffer his will. Paralysis of Christian energy often comes
with the decay of Christian joy,—certainly and always damage to the best exertions of Christian energy. A stern fidelity
may keep up a steady endeavor in a time of darkness and
the eclipse of hope, and it is a noble display of faith and
firmness when it does; but, nevertheless, the joy of the Lord
is the best equipment of his servants to serve him. A Christian soul, clear and bright with the unction of the Spirit, will
undertake any allotted work with a vigor of joyous energy
which will cower before no difficulty or peril. It will endure
any trial without rebellion, or fainting in patience or in hope.

4. As the result of this strengthening influence, the unction
of the Spirit will *not only increase usefulness, but it will* add
to the enjoyment and right use of other lawful and pleasing
things. The regenerate soul is pronounced by the Master
himself to be the salt of the earth. By prayer, by instruct-
ing in the knowledge of the truth, by holy example, and by
faithful use of appointed means, its useful and preservative
influence goes out for the benefit of the world. This influence will be healthful and effective in proportion to the
degree of the grace that is in him. When the regenerate
soul itself is suffering under any kind of spiritual impediment,
its power for good is proportionably limited. But when the
freedom and clearness which spring from the special unction of the Spirit are infusing its joyous health and vigor
through all the powers and graces of the regenerate nature,
its influence for good is redoubled. When the prayers it
offers are full of the unction of intense desire and ardent
filial confidence in the promises and in the Saviour, they
will have more power to prevail with God. When zeal is
full of fervor, tempered with reverence towards God, and

with the tenderness of a real sympathy for sinners, the persuasions employed will have a pathos and a melting force which cannot come from a regenerate soul not under this unction from on high. In every species of effort for the spread of the kingdom, the improved conditions of personal efficiency springing from the unction of the Spirit will tell wonderfully on the usefulness of the servant of Christ. Yet another effect will follow: this joyous sunshine in the soul will shed an additional brightness of enjoyment over every other lawful source of delight. The days will be brighter; the rest of sleep will be sweeter; the flowers will bloom with more beauty; every joyous thing will be more joyous. Sweet prospects, sweet birds, and sweet flowers, instead of losing, will yield a richer sweetness to the anointed and rejoicing soul.

5. The unction of the Spirit *also exerts a beautifying influence*. The friction of the perfumed oil on the toil and heat-disfigured countenance restored its charms, not less than its energy and strength, when applied to the whole body. There is nothing ever seen in this strange world so beautiful as a human spirit full of the gracious cheerfulness and the tender sympathies of a regenerate heart under the unction of the Holy Ghost. Unregenerate men are often unattracted, nay, frequently, positively repelled, by the manifestations of Christian character. The type of piety is so low as not to furnish a steady control of the conduct—not to govern the temper, or to master the selfishness, or to animate the benevolent sympathies sufficiently to give a pleasing impression of real goodness. But under the unction from the Holy One there is an irresistible attraction developed in the character. The disposition grows so sweet and sunny, the temper so placid under provocation, the sympathies so quick and strong towards joy or sorrow, the judgments so charitable, the integrity so irresistibly trustworthy, the hand so generous, the heart so good, as to create a subduing charm

even on ungodly men, and they will often say of such an anointed soul, "Would God I could be just such another!" But in the eyes of the saints, in the view of the angels, in the sight of a redeeming God rejoicing in the rich results of his redeeming grace, the loveliness of such a soul is sweeter than the flowers of Eden—more beautiful than the splendors of a morning in Paradise. It is, in truth, a miniature image of God's own beauty. The grant of such grace on the part of the loving Lord of the covenant is, in one of its aspects, like Mary's act when she broke the alabaster box of ointment on the head of Jesus—the token of a love stronger than death.

6. The design and consequent effect of this unction of the Spirit is somewhat varied, but under every variation exhibits the one uniform and high value to be attached to all of its effects. In some cases it follows the example of the sister of Lazarus just mentioned: it is an *anointment for burial.* This rich gift of the Spirit to believers is sometimes the prelude to the added blessing—admission to heaven. It betokens in such cases a death of unutterable triumph. Happy is he who is anointed for his burial by the unction of the Spirit. But in many other cases, perhaps in the most of them, it follows more closely the analogy of the physical unction with the consecrated oil, from which its name is taken. Instead of an anointing for burial, it is an unction consecrating to some office to be actively discharged in this world. When the sacred oil was poured out on the head of one man, it set him apart as king over Israel; when poured on the head of another, it consecrated him as a priest of the sanctuary; on the head of another, it made him captain of the Lord's host; and when poured on the head of another, it separated him as a prophet to proclaim the message of Jehovah to the princes and people of his covenant. No doubt it is now given sometimes to call and qualify particular persons to do a particular work of exemplary importance; but wherever it

is given, it is only giving in those cases full, practical effect
to a consecration which is really common and obligatory on
all believers without exception. The saints are all consecrated souls; they are all appointed to be prophets, priests,
and kings unto God. They may fail to realize their appointment to these grand functions, but they are nevertheless so
appointed. The failure to develop functions so assigned, or
the development of them on a scale so low as to obscure
their real dignity and importance, cannot possibly abolish
the functions assigned, or abate the obligation worthily to
discharge them. They bind, although not recognized; they
bind on every believer, under all possible changes of circumstance. Every regenerate soul is bound to be a prophet
for God, to declare his will and make known his truth. He
is bound to be a priest unto the Lord, consecrated to his
service, offering sacrifices of holy self-denial, and making
perpetual intercessions that his kingdom may come. He is
bound to be a king unto God, ruling his own soul into obedience and submission to all the divine will; and fighting unto
the death, if need be, against his enemies, the world, the
flesh, and the devil. This is the duty of all believers; but
they who receive the unction of the Spirit, alone, to any
practical or proper extent, comply with it. But when the
consecrating oil of the anointing Spirit falls on the soul,
filling it with the clearness, warmth, ardor, and joyous tenderness of the unction of the Holy Ghost, then the prophets
do begin to declare the will of the Lord; the priests to make
sacrifices, and to offer prevailing intercessions; the kings to
combat his enemies, and the captains of the host to lead
forth his armies to conquer the world. Then his priests are
more glorious in the graces of the Spirit than Aaron in his
snow-white linen robes and his breast-plate glowing with
jewels. Then his prophets are greater in the truths they
teach, and in the influence they wield, than the long-haired
prophet on the banks of Jordan; or Isaiah, as he outvied

Homer in his magnificent poetry; or Elijah, when he confronted the apostate king and his apostate people on the slopes of Carmel. Then his kings are more glorious than David in his armor on the field of Helam, or Solomon blazing in silk and gold on the throne of peacocks and lions. The unction of the Spirit carries a dignity and a grace, a power and a comfort, a beauty and a universal blessedness, which can be gained from no other source, and can be matched in worth by no other value. It fills the mind with clear light, because it purges the visual energy with a "euphrasy and rue" of nobler virtue than the gardens of earth ever grew. It fills the heart with holy and rejoicing affections toward God and man. It kindles hope, until it rises like a column on which the sacred fires burn in imperishable brightness. It nerves the will with a heroic ardor. It fills the soul with intense desires, and with staunch and unpresumptuous confidence of their fulfilment. It breathes out in prayers full of tenderness and pathetic solicitude; full of faith and trustful love. It guides the conduct with a pure zeal into all the mazes of a full and loving obedience. It moulds the whole character of the anointed man into a beautiful combination of serious pathos and exulting joy. It paints God on the soul.

CHAPTER VI.

THE WITNESS OF THE SPIRIT.

"The Spirit itself beareth witness with our spirit, that we are the children of God."—*Paul to the Romans.*

THE witness of the Spirit, like the sealing and the unction of the Spirit, has a general and a special significance. Like them, too, the. most marked interest of this action lies in its special manifestation. In its general sense, it refers to what the Spirit has done; in its special sense, it refers to a certain testimony borne by the Spirit to what he has done. The one refers to a work; the other, to a certificate or deposition concerning it. The work of the Holy Spirit, in regeneration and sanctification, is that which inwardly makes a child of God, and is, therefore, a testimony or proof of sonship. But inasmuch as there is an essential difference between a thing and a testimony in reference to it, there is a difference between the regenerating and sanctifying influences of the Spirit, on the one side, and the witness of the Spirit on the other. The witness of the Spirit, as described in the text of the chapter, is evidently a testimony to something already done, and consequently cannot be confounded with it. The Spirit testifies to sonship, and this implies the previous existence of it. The sonship of the believer is twofold: the legal relation created by adoption, and the personal change created by regeneration. The act of adoption changes the legal status of a servant into the legal status of a son. Regeneration makes the personal change, which the change of the legal status has rendered necessary, and alters the affections and feelings of a rebellious servant into those of a son in full affection and friendship with a father. This is the correlation between regeneration and adoption, in making sinners into sons or children of God. But *the witness* of the Spirit is something which comes after the grace of regeneration and the grace of adoption have done their work, and *certifies it.* We are, then, to understand by the witness of the Spirit a certain peculiar influence of the Holy Ghost, subsequent to his first saving work in the soul, giving assurance of its reality, and thus of all the glorious results which accompany and flow from it. The subject suggests for inquiry these particulars: *what is the nature of this peculiar testimony; on what conditions it is given in the soul; on what features of sonship it is exercised; and what are the effects produced by it?*

1. *What, then, is the nature of this witness of the Holy Spirit?* As distinct and different from regenerating grace, and, by consequence, from all the antecedent and successive manifestations connected with it, and as it is a testimony to sonship, the following discriminations may lead us forward to some conception of what it means. The teaching of the Scriptures in reference to it seems to settle these points. *First,* It is a proving or certifying influence altogether. *Second,* It is said to be *with our spirits.* This implies that it is a testimony borne *within the mind,* not communicated to the mind from without. It is not an audible or visible sign transmitted from some external source, like those voices and visions, which, in the old prophetic periods, signalized and proved a communication from God. *Third,* This further suggests, that the direct or immediate object of this witness is that *form* of sonship which is registered in the mind; that is, to sonship as determined by regeneration. *Fourth,* The expression *with our spirits* implies something more than a simple *internal operation;* it implies *an energy put forth in connection with another energy acting at the same time.* It is an energy of the Holy Ghost, coöperating with a certain co-existent and concurrent energy of our own spirits. The co-existent testimony of two witnesses upon the same point

to be proved implies *activity in both*; the exercise of two
distinct energies, either directly or indirectly proceeding from
intelligence and will.   These four points furnish the guiding
lines to the nature and operation of the witness of the
Spirit.   It is a testimony to sonship, a testimony within the
mind, and consequently directly to that inward or subjective
sonship wrought by regeneration, and indirectly to the legal
sonship determined by adoption.   It is a testimony of the
Holy Ghost, and a testimony of our own spirits at the same
time.   The witness of the Spirit, then, may be defined as a
*certain clear and enlivening influence of the Holy Ghost,
shining on the effects and evidences of regeneration as they
appear in the exercise of these graces in a Christian heart*, so
as to make them clear and certain in the consciousness.

The fact that the witness of the Spirit is not borne separately from the operations of the mind, bearing witness to
the same point and at the same time, is a material item in
the consideration of this subject.   The witness of the Spirit
rests upon the witness of our spirits as its basis.   As the
witness of the Spirit is to the effects and evidences of regeneration, those effects and evidences must not only exist, but
their existence must be disclosed by some degree of activity.
The testimony of the Holy Ghost could not be given to
things not existent or not discoverable.   An illustration may
be found in the connection of the text.   The verse immediately preceding it is a description of the filial feeling in a
regenerate human heart: "For ye have not received the
spirit of bondage again to fear; but ye have received the
Spirit of adoption, whereby we cry, Abba, Father."   Then
follows the assertion: "The Spirit beareth witness with our
spirit, that we are the children of God."   It is evident that
the existence of this filial spirit is the basis on which the
witness of the Spirit to sonship is founded.   His sweet and
exhilarating testimony comes at the same time, and in concurrent movement with the activity of the filial feeling.   This

is a sample of the whole operation of the Spirit as a witness. He gives the graces, and excites them to activity, and then so illumines them as to give a joyful assurance of a true sonship. The witness of the Spirit is, therefore, in the order of things, dependent on the activity of our spiritual graces. His witness to faith implies the existence and activity of faith. His witness to love implies the existence and activity of love. He witnesses the worth and value of obedience when obedience is rendered. It becomes very clear, then, that the witness of the Spirit is not to be expected in a careless course of Christian living, or in a stupefied condition of the Christian graces. It is clear, that when Christians desire and pray for this wonderful grace, the witness of the infallible Spirit of God to the reality of their spiritual graces, they need not expect it when those graces are paralyzed. Our spirits must also testify; his witness is borne along with the witness of our own spirits, and not without or independent of them.

It may be said, if the testimony of our spirits, the evidence of our own exercised graces, is present in the mind, we may infer the fact of our sonship from the facts in our consciousness, and will therefore need no special additional testimony from the Holy Ghost. But this ungrateful inference is barred by several decisive considerations. The sacred record evidently implies the truth of both the coördinated testimonies; it does not discount the truth or value of the witness of our spirits; but while it yields that testimony both true and valuable, it still asserts the inexpressible worth of the coördinate testimony of the Holy Spirit. That value is vindicated by the following several facts:

First, It is vindicated by the unquestionable fact in the history of the human mind, that feeling will not always obey the dictates of the understanding. A conclusion may be calmly reached by a process of reasoning, and yet no special exhilaration of feeling may follow it. It is possible, then, that even in cases where the evidences of regeneration are definite enough to warrant a strong inference as to the reality of the regenerate sonship, it will not follow by any means that the inference can be drawn with any special or noticeable measure of comfort. This is by no means an uncommon case. Old and experienced Christians are well aware, that while their judgments are reasonably content with the evidences of their hope, the feeling of decisive comfort in viewing those evidences is not always by any means proportionate to the strength of the convictions of their understanding. They know they are as dependent on the influences of the Holy Ghost for the ability to draw the inference comfortably to themselves, as they are for the appearance of the evidence in their consciousness. They may have a calm, rational, and scriptural conviction from the proof they see in themselves, and yet be far from finding any special joy or comfort, either in the facts or in the inference which they warrant. Their own spirits are testifying in such a case, but the Holy Ghost is not testifying with them. The value of his testimony under such circumstances is obvious enough.

Second, It is also vindicated by the fact, that oftentimes the testimony of our own spirits to the reality of our regenerate sonship, even when intrinsically very strong in proving power, is of such a sort as to bring obscurity upon the very fact which they prove. Strong intuitions of sin, though demonstrative of gracious influence in saving measure, are almost sure for a time to obscure hope, and, it may be, break it down altogether. Afflictions, which are often proofs of sonship according to Paul in Hebrews, sometimes have the same effect. If in such cases the witness of the Spirit, shining clear on the submissive exercises of a tried regenerate soul, and aiding the apprehension of the evidences of the nature of the trial, should coöperate with the struggling heart, all this added sorrow from darkness and self-sus-

picion would pass away.   The value of his testimony is undoubted.

Third, The value of the Spirit's testimony is vindicated
also in all that large class of cases in which the evidences of
regeneration are not very definitely outlined in the consciousness.   We have hitherto proceeded on the supposition
that these evidences were clear and strong, and endeavored
to show the value of the Spirit's witness, even where the
testimony of our own spirits was clear or powerful.   But in
the majority of cases this is not true.   The bulk of mankind
are not very efficient students and judges of mental phenomena, and the perplexity of many Christians in judging
the significance of their own exercises is not at all wonderful.
If, now, these feeble and obscurely outlined evidences are
yet exercised under the concurrent testimony of the Holy
Ghost, their true significance will be brought to view.   The
witness of the Spirit is not dependent on the existence and
exertion of strongly marked graces; it is dependent on the
existence and exertion of the graces whether strong or weak.
It is even more needed where the graces are weak, and when
these are rightly brought into play it may be as truly expected as where the witness of our spirits is more definitely
given.   The value of the Spirit's witness in this class of
cases, which probably includes the bulk of believers, is very
clear.   Its value in all its applications does not admit of a
doubt.

2. From this connection between the testimonial exercise
of the graces in our own spirits and the witness of the Holy
Ghost, we may infer the answer to the question, *on what conditions* this rejoicing testimony may be expected to rise in
the soul?   As it is dependent on the gracious activities of
our own spirits, the conditions of its appearance are just the
conditions which invite any other special favor of God.
Intense desire, resolute purpose, patient and persevering
prayer, careful living, unselfish zeal and devotion in God's

service, resistance to temptation and the overcoming of all evil impulses of thought or feeling, cultivation of every Christian sensibility, steadfast and trustful use of the means of grace—these are the conditions of success in seeking special manifestation of divine favor, and for the witness of the Spirit among others. When these conditions are brought into play, they will necessarily place the activities of our own spirits in the state to receive the concurrent energies of the Holy Ghost bearing his witness that we are the children of God. Pain is as good a proof of life as pleasure, though not so agreeable a demonstration; and consequently the motions of our spirits in spiritual suffering may lay the foundation for his testimony just as truly as the more agreeable motions created by activity in obedience, or the happier conditions of the pleasure-giving graces. To the question, On what conditions the witness of the Spirit may be expected? we answer, it may be expected when the activity of our own spirits in the exercise of any Christian grace or graces—graces of action or suffering—is brought into exercise. To have the witness of the Spirit to our faith or love, our faith and love must be in exercise. To have the witness of the Spirit to our patience and submission, our patience and submission must be in exercise. It is only with our spirits that his testimony is borne. To expect this gracious certifying influence to bear on any one grace, or on the reality of our piety as a whole, when our granted gifts are lying dormant, is unscriptural and not to be expected. Only on those general and special conditions on which any special favor, or any general advancement in the divine life may be looked for, is the witness of the Spirit to be anticipated.

It is a compulsory conclusion from this view of the subject, that this doctrine of the special witness of the Holy Spirit to the regenerate sonship of the believer lays no foundation for any fanatical or enthusiastic claims to special testimonies of acceptance with God, apart from godly obedience, and the personal experience of the ordinary sanctifying influences and gifts of the Holy Ghost. The test, "by their fruits ye shall know them," is to be applied to every enthusiast laying claim to special communications with God, as well as to every claimant of the Christian character. If the life and conduct are not such as to show the energy of sanctifying grace, operating on the springs of action within, no claims to the special testimonials of the Spirit can possibly assert themselves, simply because the witness of the Spirit is nothing more than his certificate of graces existing and active in the human spirit. It is also clear that this priceless gift of the indwelling Spirit to the believer, like all other expressions of divine favor, is not so placed as to give encouragement to idleness, presumption, or personal indifference about the gift, but just the contrary. This peculiar certifying or demonstrative influence, bringing out into clear and definite shape the graces of the renewed heart, graces which are often, even when substantially sound, so obscurely outlined in the consciousness as to create an anxious uncertainty, is obviously a blessing of inexpressible value.

3. It will not be difficult now to answer the third question touching the witness of the Spirit, *on what points or characteristic features of sonship* it is exerted in giving its delightful solution of spiritual difficulties? It may be noted that its bearing on the legal sonship created by adopting grace is altogether indirect, but no less important on that account.

The sonship of the believer is created by two distinct factors: the *legal sonship* determined by adoption into the family of God, affecting the relation of the believer to the law, and raising him from the position of a servant to the position of a son; and the *personal sonship* determined by regeneration, affecting the personal character and consciousness of the believer, and altering the affections and principles of his nature from those of a rebellious and hostile servant to those of an obedient and affectionate son. The proof of the legal sonship depends upon the prior manifestations of the regenerate sonship, and consequently the witness of the Spirit to the legal sonship is indirect, being mediated through his witness to the personal sonship. The witness of the Spirit, being within us, is directly concerned only with the evidences of regenerate sonship as they appear in the gifts and graces of regenerating grace. The answer to the question, on what features of sonship the testimony of the Spirit is employed is, that it is employed on every factor entering into sonship, indirectly on the sonship of adoption, and directly on every characteristic feeling and distinctive mark of a regenerate heart. It illuminates and brings out clearly the true nature of every feeling and affection, every hope and fear, every joy and sorrow, every fruit of the Spirit, every characteristic pain or pleasure, desire or aversion, of the regenerate nature. It illuminates the love of Christ, which is a mark of the renewed heart, and enables us to discriminate the mere veneration of a heroic example from the love which in a sin-stricken soul springs from apprehending him as the Lamb of God whose blood cleanseth from all sin. It illuminates the word of God, and discriminates the love of the Scripture on account of its high intellectual merits, and the love of it for the truth which sanctifies unto eternal life. It illuminates the love of the kingdom, and discriminates the affections of a mere partisan from the affections which see in the church the chosen instrument for the deliverance of a dying world.

The method of seeking the gracious testimony of the Spirit to the sonship of any individual soul is, to bring the particular graces into earnest, practical use, and seek in the use of the appointed ways for the influence of the Spirit to test their real character. There is a percentage of the feelings created by regenerating grace, and consequently demonstrative of a saving work, which are prevailingly painful. Saving intuitions of sin in the life, and sin in the heart are always distressing. The witness of the Spirit is so generally and truly regarded as a source of joy and comfort, that it is seldom thought of in connection with these painful experiences; his aid is not sought to enable a just discrimination of them; his testimony to penitence and *the characteristic* sorrows of the regenerate nature is not delivered; and this is probably one reason why the strange and touching paradox of Paul is so infrequently realized—*rejoicing in tribulation*— why there is so much suffering without any concurrent comfort among Christians. These sufferings are often in themselves the highest proofs of sonship; *the nature* of the affliction, as when we groan under the tyrannies of an unholy heart, and share in the spiritual trials of Christian souls, is full of testimonial power. In addition to this, not only the nature of the affliction sometimes, but the mental and spiritual exercises determined by any kind of affliction are frequently of clear testimony to the reality of sonship. If we endure chastening, God dealeth with us as sons. The submission, patience, and unfaltering confidence in God's wisdom and goodness, awakened by the touch of some deep and irreparable sorrow, are demonstrative proofs of regenerate sonship. Nay, more, the very feelings of resistance and rebellion against the chastening will of God may carry proof of the same grace ; they carry it, when they excite the disgust and horror of the heart, and rouse up a weeping and agonized, but resolute and persistent resistance to such impeachments of the divine administration. But it is not easy, it is often impossible, for a Christian soul, under the strain and stress of this species of trial, to interpret them aright. Their spirits are bearing witness, but so bearing it, yielding testimony in such a shape, as to obscure its own significance and the real conclusion which it warrants and requires. Like a lighthouse on a stormy night, so covered by the rushing sea that all is dark although the light is burning.

But if now the Spirit could be found bearing witness with their spirits, and interpreting the true nature of the testimony whose very vigor has marred their hope, all this would be changed. The light burning under the water-covered lamp would be seen and known to be truly kindled, though its beams are arrested for a time. The subjects of the witness of the Spirit, being all the elements of sonship, afford a wide field for the employment of this illuminating grace, and the sonship of particular individuals may be demonstrated on many varying points. Any Christian perplexed to understand the complicated expression of his own religious state can have all his puzzles brought to a restful conclusion by seeking in the right way the witness of the Spirit.

4. The last question raised touching *the results* of the witness of the Spirit is easily answered. The object of the testimony is to prove sonship, and this object is always gained. The assurance of hope is always a happy issue. As the witness of the Spirit works out its general demonstration by testifying to a variety of particular graces which establish it, the resulting effects will present a great variety in their appearance. The Spirit may shine upon the graces bred by affliction, and prove his point with a peculiar combination of grief and comfort as the result. He may shine upon the perceptions and emotions leading to repentance, and prove his point by a similar combination of mixed emotions growing out of sin, analogous to those growing out of afflictions. He may shine upon a manifested exercise of love and holy consecration, and prove his point through a wonderful evolution of holy and rejoicing affections brought out into strong relief. The witness of the Spirit may thus produce widely varying appearances in the experience of different saints, but they all tend to one grand and joyful conclusion—proving them all to be the sons of God by the unimpeachable witness of the Holy Ghost. To each, no matter how different may have been the special basis of the demonstration

in the activities of his own spirit, that demonstration brings
the inexpressibly precious assurance of eternal life. The
witness of the Spirit is to be relied upon absolutely. He
does not deceive; he certifies no grace which is not true;
he creates no hope which can be disappointed. A modest
construction of his hope is wise, when a man's own spirit is
alone bearing testimony. The causes of a possible misguidance are so many and so powerful; the just discrimination of consciousness is so difficult, even to very keen and
practiced students of mental phenomena, and the bulk of
mankind is so incompetent to judge; the experience of the
vast majority of average Christians is so defective in sharp-
ness and precision of outline,—it is by no means easy for our
spirits to bear effective testimony. But where the witness of
the Holy Spirit is borne along with a testimony intrinsically
defective, where the sonship is yet real, all hesitation is out
of place, and instead of a dictate of prudence, becomes a folly
and a sin. The witness of the Spirit yields absolute assurance; his testimony to his own work, to the graces implanted
by his own hand, is resistless by the most self-mistrustful
and self-jealous of timid souls. The faith of the heart, certified by the witness of the Spirit, will become like the purged
vision of the proto-martyr Stephen, and amid the confusion
of the spiritual warfare will be able to see clearly into the
very throne-room of heaven. Hope will spring high into the
future, as the eagle strains his grand flight upward. Assurance of eternal life, peace of conscience, unfailing faith, and
joy in the Holy Ghost are the results of the witness of the
Spirit.

CHAPTER VII.

THE EARNEST OF THE SPIRIT.

"Who also hath given unto us the earnest of the Spirit."—*Paul to the Corinthians.*

A N "earnest" was a *part* of a thing promised or pledged
by contract, given at the present time as an assurance,
pledge, or security, that the whole would be transferred at
some period in the future. The *design* of the earnest was to
secure the future, and thus to lay a reliable foundation for
hope and confidence. The earnest given was also the pledge
that the future balance to be paid should be of the very same
kind with the earnest given. An earnest in a handful of the
soil was the pledge that a land sale was assured of completion; an earnest paid in money was a pledge of the balance
in money; an earnest of silk or jewels, a pledge of a fuller
payment in the same materials. Thus the earnest served
two purposes: it guaranteed the debt, and defined the
material in which it was to be paid. Thus a contract to pay
a certain sum of money was unalterably ratified and confirmed by the gift or transfer of a sum of it, large or small,
in the presence of witnesses. This immediate payment was
called an earnest of the debt. When land was sold, the
seller took a handful of the soil and gave it to the buyer as
an earnest of the sale, and after this action nothing could
bar the right of the purchaser; he had received his "earnest."
A striking sample of an earnest was found in the offering of
the *first-fruits*, as they were called, on one of the three grand
yearly feasts among the ancient Jews—the feast of Pentecost. It occurred just at the time when the harvest was
ready to be gathered. All Israel was collected in Jerusalem
for a whole week of rejoicing and festive worship. On an

appointed day, a delegation of priests, followed by multitudes of people, rejoicing with song and shout and attitudes of delight, went out of the city to the nearest grain-fields, cut down a few sheaves of the crop, and brought them to the temple amid the wildest demonstrations of public joy. The sheaves were then solemnly offered in grateful worship to the Lord of the harvest. They were the earnest of the harvest, a pledge of bread again given to Israel for another year. The grain was then threshed from the offered sheaves, immediately ground into flour, baked into bread, and in this form re-offered before the altar and consumed in the sacred fires. Until the first-fruits of the harvest were thus presented before the great Giver of all, no one in all Israel could reap his grain, or turn it into bread. This unloosing of the restrictions of the law was another cause of joy added to the general assurance of bread, which made the presentation of the first-fruits the occasion of the exhibition of the public joy so strikingly exhibited at the feast of Pentecost. These first-fruits gave occasion to a noble use of a metaphor by Paul to illustrate the introduction of believers into the church of God, from the example of the patriarchs, and the resurrection of Christ as the proof and assurance of the resurrection of the human race at large. "If the first-fruit be holy, the lump is also holy." That is, the faith of the patriarchs, and their introduction by means of it into the covenant and kingdom of God, was the pledge and assurance of the same privileges to their descendants on the same conditions. "Now is Christ risen . . . and become the first-fruits of them that slept." "Christ the first-fruits; afterward they that are Christ's at his coming." In both cases the idea is the same, assurance for many in the future from the example of a few or of one in the present or the past. The reception of the patriarchs into covenant relations on account of their faith was the earnest of the acceptance of their posterity where they should believe. The resurrection of Jesus of Nazareth is the earnest of the resurrection of the whole human family.

The Holy Spirit considered as an earnest presents us with the inquiries: what is the particular work of the Spirit which constitutes him an earnest, and gives the pledge of the future involved in an earnest; what is the full significance of this earnest of the Spirit; what are the things of which the Spirit is an earnest; and what are the logical and practical results of this earnest of the Spirit when given?

1. The first inquiry to be settled is, *what is that work of the Holy Spirit which makes him an earnest*, and carries with it that precious pledge and assurance of the future which it is the very nature and design of an earnest to convey? Much of the preliminary work of the Spirit in the human heart carries no pledge of any future work to be done by him. All the exercises of the heart, awakened by his dealings with an unconverted soul, are of this description. He awakens, and to a certain degree, convinces of sin before conversion; but only too many lamentable instances prove that he is free to yield, if he pleases, to the resistance he invariably encounters. But the unqualified promise of salvation to faith introduces a new condition of things when faith is exercised. Then the soul enters into the covenant of the Lord; the pledge of actual salvation into which he has entered takes full effect. Faith is *the fruit of the Spirit*, and the gift of faith is the work of the Holy Ghost, which constitutes him an earnest with all its glorious assurances of the future. The gift of faith is only an expression of a broader gift which enables its exercise, and reveals the mode in which it is given, the impartation of the germ of spiritual life, and of all the particular spiritual graces, faith, hope, love, contrition, and others which grow out of this germ. Life must exist before the acts of life can be put forth; but, inasmuch as regeneration is that energy of the Holy Ghost which gives this life, and makes a sinner personally a son

or child of God, it is in itself a demonstration of sonship, an earnest and a full pledge of eternal life, a perfect assurance of the future. Regeneration and the faith which it enables *close the covenant* of infinite love, and assure its fulfilment. Previous to the work of the Spirit in granting faith and repentance—both the expressions of the new heart; one towards the Saviour, the other towards sin—his work in the heart carries no pledge and gives no security. But repentance and faith are the terms on which the pledge of salvation to the uttermost takes effect, and therefore regeneration, which inevitably grounds and issues in these terms, carries with it the earnest and pledge of eternal life. All those special acts of the Spirit subsequent to regeneration, the special forms of the grace of sealing, unction, and witness, constitute special manifestations of the earnest of the Spirit, and bring out its power of assurance into stronger lights. But he who has received the gift of regenerating grace, although he may never have enjoyed the favor and comfort of the higher and more marked forms of sealing, unction, and witness, has, nevertheless, received the Spirit *as an earnest*. All the special acts of the Holy Ghost subsequent to regeneration, and designed to carry out the progressive work of sanctification, only renew the impression, embellish, illuminate, and develop the power to comfort in the earnest given in regeneration, but the earnest itself is irrevocably given in regeneration itself. Consequently, every regenerate soul, however unacquainted with the subsequent peculiar favors of the Comforter, does, nevertheless, possess the Spirit as an earnest of eternal life. However feebly, if yet truly developed in the soul, repentance and faith are proofs of a regenerate heart, and a regenerate heart is proof of the earnest of the purchased possession. The simple evidences of changed affections towards God and his manifested will, even though never followed by the higher and more inspiring special gifts of the blessed Paraclete, do, nevertheless, reveal him in propor-

tion to their own clearness as the earnest and sure pledge
of all the grand ultimate glory of eternal life.

2. To appreciate the real value of the earnest of the Spirit
as given to every regenerate soul, let us look at the second
question suggested: *What is the full significance of this
earnest?* It is all that any earnest ever was on any subject.
The earnest given in payment of a debt guaranteed its
payment. It was a full confession and acceptance of the
obligation to pay the whole amount. No question as to the
binding force of the unpaid part of the debt could ever be
raised when the grant or payment of the earnest money had
passed. No plea in any court could set aside a claim based
upon an earnest. No dispute about a land-title could ever
be raised when the actual gift of a handful of the soil from
the seller to the buyer could be proved. No doubt could
remain that the fields stood covered with the vegetable gold
of the ripened harvest, when the officials of the temple, in
their snowy robes, bore the first-fruit sheaves, lifted high to
view, along the crowded streets of Jerusalem, and up into
the courts of the Lord's house. There was no room left for
doubt. The earnest was given; it was palpable to the eyes
of all, and none could hesitate to accept the assurance of
the earnest; all knew that bread for the coming year was
already given to Israel, already waved on the harvest
fields.

As in matters of trade the earnest money avowed beyond
recall the obligation to pay the debt, so does the earnest of
the Spirit; God under covenant is in debt to his own honor
to save the soul that has accepted his own terms. The gift
of the Spirit in regeneration is the earnest of that debt, the
beginning of its payment, the certain pledge of its ultimate
redemption. The golden sheaf of faith is pledge that the
whole golden harvest of saving grace is already provided.

An earnest was a *proof* as well as a *security*. It settled the
point for which it was given. It settled the obligation of debt,

the title to land, and the assurance of harvest. The earnest of
the Spirit in like manner settles the question of personal salvation; it is salvation already begun—salvation in part accomplished. . It is demonstrative proof of sonship, that personal
sonship which carries and certifies the legal sonship. No matter if a heart weary with struggle, and sick with doubt and hope
deferred, can take no comfort in evidences of grace which
satisfy others touching his state—evidences that would satisfy himself about the state of others—yet, if those evidences
appear in the tests given in the Scriptures, the proof is
demonstrative. Such evidences of conversion do not create
mere presumptions, or establish a mere scale of probabilities; they create an absolute certainty; they prove that an
earnest has been given. That dread of sin, that grief for its
prevalent power over the heart and life, that yearning after
purity, that longing for Christ, that perpetual and welcome
presence of God in all the thoughts, that delight and comfort in the ordinances, cannot be mistaken; they prove the
earnest of the Spirit, and the earnest of the Spirit proves the
actual beginning and the certain title to eternal life.

But, further, *an earnest was a part of an indivisible whole*,
and he who possesses it has that assurance of ultimately
possessing the whole which springs from *actually possessing
a part*. The angler who has drawn the head of a fish above
water knows that he also possesses the remainder of its
body, although unseen as yet in the water. The rich man
who is lifting a bag of gold out of his treasury, and already
sees the top of it, knows he is drawing up the whole as well
as the part which is in sight. The miner who is drawing up
a chain from the dark depths of a mine knows he is lifting
the unseen parts of the chain as well as the parts which are
seen. So he who has the earnest of the Spirit need not
simply or merely hope without assurance; he need not comfort himself with mere probabilities, which may be truly
called high and reasonable, but are only probabilities after

all. If he has an earnest, he is in an actual though partial possession; a possession actual and real, although only in part. He has the earnest money in his hands, and although the coins may look worn, battered and unsightly, they are true money of the realm, and bind the payment of the rich balance in the end. He grasps the handful of the sacred soil, which carries the title to the land. He waves the golden sheaves cut from the field thick with the wide-spreading crop—an actual part of the priceless harvest. He who has an earnest has an actual possession.

Yet, further, an earnest is not only an actual part of the whole in actual possession, but this part is given as *a pledge, a legally designed and effective security* of the as yet unpossessed remainder. It is easy to conceive a part given without any reference to any other portion of the thing given; the granted part standing simply for itself. But supposing the law connected the part with the whole, and required the part to be given for the express purpose of securing the whole, then the law would secure the whole by the grant of the part. This was the intent and the effect of an earnest under the law or binding custom of the old Jews. The earnest, then, not only secured the *right and title* to the thing conveyed, but secured a provision to make it good. It provided security for the unpaid balance. It is easy to conceive a part of a promised sum as actually paid, yet carrying no assurance of the payment of the balance. The balance and main part of the debt may therefore fail from the bankruptcy or fraud of the debtor. But if the law required that when the earnest money was paid, the remaining part of the debt should be absolutely provided for by a sufficient security, then the earnest would not only carry the title, but provide for securing it. The earnest would carry assurance for the future. The handful of soil may be conceived as given, and yet the seller as afterwards regretting the sale, and endeavoring to prevent the transfer; but if the law of the land had definitely decreed that the earnest handful should carry an unrepealable and actual conveyance; although immediate possession be not given, the sale stands beyond impeachment. The *whole* is as certain as the *part;* for that is the designed and legal effect of the part actually given. The whole public power of the Commonwealth guarantees the final possession to the purchaser. The earnest carries all with it, conveying not only title, but security for the future payment; it is a positive and universal pledge covering all contingences, giving absolute assurance, forestalling all resistance and extinguishing all doubt.

But this is not all the effect of the earnest in accomplishing that part of its design which consists in the guarantee of a debt. As a positive pledge and seal of assurance, expressed by a thing given at the present time, is designed chiefly to affect the future, and by securing the future to extinguish fear, to enkindle hope strong and ardent, and thus *not merely to secure the property of the receiver of the assurance, but his peace of mind.* This view of the gracious design of the earnest of the Spirit is of inexpressible importance to the believer. *The grand aim of the earnest was to secure the future.* The grand source of anxiety to the saint is *for the future.* However measurably content with the present, his fears for the future are the main causes of his anxieties now. He dreads the facts in the future, temptation, sin, his own weakness, death, judgment, the presence of the scenery of the life to come, the face of the angels, the unveiled glory of God's almightiness. *The future is the sphere of the grand passions, hope and fear* in the human heart. Both seem to be indelible instincts of a nature conditioned inexorably to emerge *into the future.* They are apparently imperishable indexes of immortality; signs fixed in the inextinguishable consciousness of a being essentially conditioned to live forever; buoys floating in ceaseless agitation, yet fixed and stable on the tumultuous

motions of a deathless nature. The domination of the
future is supreme. No matter what may be the conditions
of existence at present, whether prosperous or adverse, the
eyes of the human spirit are always bent upon the future.
If the future is uncertain or menacing, even a prosperous
present is marred of its enjoyment. If the future can be
assured as fortunate, even a trying present is lightened of
its burden, and a happy present is doubled of its blessedness. The future is equally powerful over the past; the
only thing which will heal the wounds of an unhappy past is
the assurance of a happy future. To secure the future, then,
is the grand demand of the human soul. But to do this with
its full effects the future must be assured, absolutely assured.
To create mere possibilities of good in the future; to create
mere probabilities, however high and rational, will only answer a qualified purpose; will only qualify fear and kindle
hope to a certain extent. Even this partial establishment
of hope is valuable to a certain degree; but it cannot bring
solid peace. The human heart, oppressed by its experiences
in the past and its fears for the future, will cling to any
fragment of hope, even when insecurely based, and in the
words of the suffering Idumean possibly, "be confounded
because it had hoped." To induce a real, restful, and enduring hope the future must be assured, absolutely assured,
on a basis which cannot be shaken or mistrusted. To give
such an assurance of the future is the very end and purpose
of an earnest in every various kind of business in which it
is used. The earnest of the Spirit gives this assurance of
the future in all that enters into the matter of salvation.
He who is in possession of an earnest is not only in possession of a present and actual part of a value, but is also
in possession of an assurance of the future. He who is
in possession of the earnest of the Holy Ghost is in possession of a sealed security of all the privileges of the sons of
God, not only for the present, but for all the future. That

future is eternal; it is pregnant with countless and illimitable changes; but in all the vast scale there is one thing which defies the power of change—the sonship guaranteed by the earnest of the Spirit. This lays a sure and unpresumptuous foundation for a genuine Christian hope. Without it there is no sure basis for hope, and hope can only be a vague, vacillating, unassured, unconsolatory presumption. But upon it hope can kindle its beacon fires until they rise high in the vaulted skies, amid the thickest darkness of this earthly scene.

3. To enable us to appreciate still more fully the value of the Spirit as an earnest of the purchased possession, we must find an answer to the third suggested question: *what are the things or blessings of which the Spirit is an earnest?* To this the reply must be made in the most comprehensive terms, the earnest of the Spirit guarantees all the blessings of redeeming grace. But to follow the suggestions of Scripture in their specializing of these blessings, we may first notice that the earnest *gives assurance of a positive period of a full redemption.* "Grieve not the Holy Spirit of God, whereby ye are sealed unto the day of redemption." "Now he which establisheth us with you in Christ, and hath anointed us, is God; who hath also sealed us, and given the earnest of the Spirit in our hearts." "In whom also, after that ye believed, ye were sealed with that Holy Spirit of promise, which is the earnest of our inheritance until the redemption of the purchased possession, unto the praise of his glory." The seal of the Spirit, as we have seen, has its general as well as its special significance. Under its special significance it refers to a special influence of the Spirit, giving a special degree of stability and staunchness to the exercises of the regenerate soul. In this sense it implies regeneration, and is distinct from it. In its general sense it carries the general significance of confirmation or security, and in this sense it is coincident with one of the chief sig-

nifications of the earnest of the Spirit. For this reason it is sometimes employed in the sacred record as identical, or at least a term interchangeable with earnest. It is so used in one of the passages just quoted. One glorious thing which is sealed and assured by the earnest of the Spirit is *a fixed and certain day or period of complete redemption.* A lost soul is sealed to a day of perdition, that is, it is assuredly bound over to certain destruction when the time arrives. A saved soul is bound over *to a day,* or as that day is fixed for one part of that redemption, to-wit, the resurrection of the body *to the day of redemption.* Redemption is a purchased deliverance; the term carries both notions, deliverance and deliverance by purchase, which grounds it in moral right, and thus adds to its certainty. Redemption from sin is such a deliverance from sin and all its deadly issues, from its power and its pollution, its hazards and its pains. This includes the whole man, soul and body; sin has involved both, and both are involved in the redemption from sin. This redemption is only begun in the forgiveness of sin, which removes the danger of its penalties, and in regeneration, which partially breaks its power and initiates the purgation of its pollution. But the redeemed soul is still left, for a time, to the conflict with the remainders of evil in the heart, and to the disciplinary sufferings necessary to the process of purification. But *the day of redemption* will put an end to all this conflict and all this distress. It will put an end both to sin and suffering. In other words, the day of redemption means the day of deliverance to the soul from all the evils which are peculiar to the soul as distinguished from the body. But as sin has involved the body and subjected it to disease, deformity, and death, to all the evils of physical nature, the day of redemption is the day of deliverance also to the body. It involves deliverance from all the evils possible to the body itself, and from all the evils in the world to which man is related through his body. It implies a total

change in the existing conditions of human life.   The day of
redemption is the period of full release from all the ills to
which flesh is heir.   It is the period of serene and sinless
peace for soul and body.   It is the time of release from all
care, all fear, all pain, all sickness, as well as from all pangs
of conscience and from all sin.   Nay, as sin has brought
death into the world, and the body dies, or is dead because of
sin, the day of redemption is the day of resurrection to the
body.   It is the time when the awful and apparently complete and unreversible victory of death shall be reversed,
when the graves shall give back their dead, and the rejoicing
heavens shall be filled with the rescued victims of sin and
death.   The day of redemption means a changed earth, a sinless and happy human family, souls and bodies redeemed from
the power of the curse, and fixed in eternal freedom from all
evil, and from all fear or hazard of it.   Such is the day of
redemption of which the Spirit is the earnest, and as such
the absolute seal and assurance.   When given as an earnest
in the gift of regeneration and faith, the Spirit breaks the
power of sin and delivers from it in part, and this part
given is the assurance of the grant of a deliverance which is
complete, embracing soul and body, and enduring forevermore.

In the second place, the earnest of the Spirit assures
another thing inexpressibly glorious: *it assures heaven to the
regenerate soul.*   This is one consummate end and object of
the earnest given.   The record testifies that the earnest of
the inheritance is given to serve until the actual redemption
of the purchased possession.   There must needs be an outcome, both in *locality and character*, to the forces and process
of redemption.   Man as a being of limited and localized
nature must have some particular place in which to exist.
He cannot be in two places at once, and must therefore have
some one place to be.   The redemption from sin and suffering necessitates a place where the conditions of sinless and

unsuffering existence are established. The Holy Scriptures reveal such a place as the final habitation of the just made perfect, and while designating it under various forms and names, principally describe it under the name *heaven*. Heaven then, in part at least, is a *locality*. But the earnest of the Spirit which is given in regeneration is designed to affect personal character, to create a holy nature, and thus to transform and perfect finally a moral change of an unholy nature. As an earnest of heaven, then, as a part of an answerable whole, the earnest of the Spirit proves that heaven is *a character* as well as a locality, and discloses the striking fact that the characteristic spirit of heaven is to be found, and is only to be found in the spirit, temper, and affections developed in regeneration. Under both of these aspects of locality and character, heaven is represented in the word of God as a place and state of existence inexpressibly glorious. Under its delineations of it as a local habitation, it represents it under the figure of a city, on the banks of a river, bordered with parks of noble fruit-bearing trees, built of jewels and gold, crowded with the mansions of the saints, within whose mighty walls no temple is seen thrusting its steeples and towers over the masses of its buildings, because the whole place is one consecrated scene of holy service, over whose glowing structures no sunlight falls, on whose streets no pale moonbeam ever gleams on the thick-trodden gold, "embossed and ingrained with celestial roses," where no night ever lets down its raven curtains to wrap the splendor in a passing gloom, where no sickness ever disturbs any home, no tears ever moisten any cheek, no species of evil ever darkens the serene and cloudless peace of the blest inhabitants. It has never entered into the heart of man to conceive the splendor of heaven as a place; its local coloring beggars description.

Still more powerless is human thought to conceive the higher range of the spiritual and mental blessedness which

God has prepared for those that love him. We only know that the same essential principles of obedience; the same feelings of love, gratitude, reverence, and delighted communion; the same confidence in the love of the Father, Son, and Spirit; the same delight in prayer and praise, in the word and worship of God; the same love to all who love him and bear his image—in a word, all the graces which are planted in germ in the regenerate soul by regenerating grace, which is the earnest of the Spirit, will be seen in heaven. These graces when exercised here, not only reveal the moral beauty of spiritual holiness, but fill the heart with joy and peace. They also work another noble effect: they add fresh strength to the holy habit of mind from which they spring. All these results of spiritual graces, happiness, and growing strength, will be seen in heaven, and constitute its highest blessedness. The only difference will be a difference of degree, not of essential nature. Here the graces are weak, and often intermit their exercise, and the necessary result is that their happy effects are proportionally weak and infrequent. There the graces are strong and perfect; they never intermit their energy; and the happy effects are answerable in power and permanence. Oh! blessed object assured by the earnest of the Spirit—heaven—the home of an endless and perfected peace; the eternal dwelling-place of joy inexpressible and full of glory; the immovable kingdom of holiness which is the health of the immortal mind!

Yet more, the earnest of the Spirit insures another blessing inexpressibly important from its instrumental bearing on all the high, ultimate issues of the promised redemption; it insures all the intermediate gifts of grace which are necessary to secure the glorious result. An issue may be made contingent on any number of procuring causes. As a matter of course, to guarantee absolutely the attainment of the end, it will be indispensable to guarantee the successful procurement of each procuring cause. If this can be done, the end, though conditioned and contingent, may be absolutely assured. Many procuring secondary causes are linked with the grand end certified by the earnest of the Holy Ghost. Faith, repentance, holy service of many kinds, prayer, self-denial, and consecrated devotion all bear upon the end, and without them the end cannot be gained. But when the earnest of the Spirit guarantees the end, it guarantees the means; the assurance of the end is the assurance of the means. No end dependent upon procuring agencies can be guaranteed except by the guarantee of the agencies with which it has been linked by the law. But grace all-sufficient is irrevocably pledged in giving the earnest of the Spirit; the grand executive guarantee is given in that wonderful gift. The Father becomes the covenanted and treaty-bound Father of his adopted and regenerated sons. The Son rejoices to be the covenanted and treaty-bound Saviour of his trustful children. The Spirit becomes the covenanted and treaty-bound Paraclete of every saint whose sanctity he undertakes to achieve. Grace all-sufficient is pledged by the earnest of the Spirit. The declaration is positive concerning even the weak of the covenanted host: "He shall be holden up, for God is able to make him stand."

4. The answer to the *fourth question, touching the effects of the earnest of the Spirit when developed in the consciousness*, will complete our view of the value of this gift.

In the first place, the earnest of the Spirit reveals to us *the nature of heaven*, as it had already done *the fact* of such a place and state. It discloses its characteristic spirit, its fundamental quality in the great controlling trait of spiritual holiness. It thus reveals the insufficiency of all religious qualifications for entry into that glorious citizenship, except those which are rooted in a regenerate nature. In the earnest a part is always given as a sample of the whole. In regeneration the germ of holiness is implanted, and all the graces, which are "the fruit of the Spirit," are the outgrowths of this germ, the results of the earnest. These fruits are the characteristic marks of the earnest part, and are, therefore, the characteristic marks of the guaranteed whole. Heaven is thus revealed to us in its essential nature as love, joy, peace, long-suffering, gentleness, goodness, faith, meekness, temperance. Every manifestation, then, of these graces is a proof of participation in the spirit of heaven, and consequently of a fitness for it. All the affections, all the works, all the characteristic exercises of a regenerate heart are *assurances of heaven*. They prove *a title* to it by proving a fitness for it; for the earnest is a pledge as well as a sample. No proof could be more irresistible of the absolute necessity of a regenerate and holy heart; heaven will be no heaven without it. As a locality it would be of all places the most oppressive, without the spirit which is congenial to it. How sweet is the assurance of heaven given to the humble believer by the earnest of the Spirit! It assures him that his humble graces, however feebly developed, carry the guarantees of his personal part in the heaven of the just; they are the earnest of that glorious whole, a part, a pledge, a sample, a proof, a certificate which is made by the law of the institution to carry absolute assurance of that of which it is established as an earnest.

Another effect designed to be the issue of an earnest, and effected by it in proportion to the clearness of its own realization, is *hope*. It will yield hope by its mastery of the future on a scale of degrees rising in combination with the witness of the Spirit to full and abiding assurance of personal salvation. The earnest always carries the assurance in fact, but is not always suitably apprehended in the mind, and therefore does not always yield the effect of the truth which it certifies. But when no obstruction in the mind impedes its power, it will create in the consciousness the assurance which it carries in itself. The earnest unimpeded will breed a hope full of immortality. Another effect is *comfort and peace of mind;* assurance of the future logically grounds comfort, and when truly apprehended inevitably breeds it. Another effect is *strength*—strength to do and to suffer; to exert activity; to develop patience; to deny self, and to serve others; to overcome evil, and to walk worthy of the Lord in all pleasing. It creates absolute *safety.*

5. The crowning blessing in the earnest of the Spirit *is the earnest given,* which is the loving and most Holy Spirit himself. It was noted in the beginning of this exposition that an earnest accomplished two purposes: it secured a debt, and defined the material in which it was to be paid. The earnest as a part of a whole was a specimen of the whole, a sample of that which was promised. An earnest paid in a handful of soil indicated a payment in land; an earnest paid in gold pledged a full payment in gold; an earnest in silk or jewels, a larger transfer of the same rich materials. But an earnest given of the Holy Spirit of God is positively the highest of all gifts. It is the richest of all the blessings in the hands of the rich Lord of the universe. Having given his Son to redeem, and himself to be the Father and Portion of his people, he had only one more gift of equal value to bestow. When this was given it completed the grand gift of his whole self to his redeemed creature. In point of actual fact, the gift of the Spirit as an earnest carries with it the gift of the Son as a Saviour, and the gift of the Father in all the blessedness of his glorious restored fatherhood. But the gift of the Spirit as an earnest, a part as a sample and pledge of a whole, raises our hopes and conceptions into a region where they are confused and lost in the immeasurable prospect of glory, honor, and immortal life. Even as a mere earnest, a mere fragment of the good to come, the grace of the ever-blessed Spirit is literally infinite. He is given in all his infinite power and wisdom and goodness; the riches, the freedom, and the tenderness of his patient and pitying love, as he dwells in the human

heart, and struggles to subdue its evils, are positively unsearchable. Even as a mere earnest, he is the richest gift in the treasury of heaven. What the whole is, of which such a gift is only a part, no tongue can tell. It suggests gifts of the Spirit in the long sweep of a blest eternity granted endlessly, in forms no mortal mind can conceive, no mortal tongue can even begin to describe. The Spirit as an earnest of the purchased possession guarantees eternal life to all to whom he is so given.

CHAPTER VIII.

THE LEADING OF THE SPIRIT.

"For as many as are led by the Spirit of God, they are the sons of God."—*Paul to the Romans.*

ALL parts of the work of grace in the human heart are adjusted to all those destructive effects of sin which it is designed to remove, and, at the same time, it is adjusted to the essential nature of the being in whom the gracious energy is to be exerted. Man is essentially an active being; active in all the processes of his intellectual nature, in all the affections of his will, and in all the actions of his conduct. This activity is essential and unalterable; it abides, no matter what changes take place in the moral complexion of his energies; he is active in holiness, if his moral quality is holy; he is active in evil, if his moral nature is evil; he is active in both good and evil, if his moral nature is under a progressive and unfinished process of redemption from sin. All his active energies have been affected by moral evil, and the enterprise of redeeming him from sin necessarily requires the delivering influence to be exerted upon them all. This influence must be exerted in accordance with the essential nature of each one of the energies he undertakes to purify and govern; he exerts no compulsory power in the sense of actual force; he does not overbear or oppress any energy with which he deals; he does not interfere with the native and essential quality of any one of them all. As in the witness of the Spirit, it is a testimony borne with an influence concurrently exerted along with a similar testimonial activity of the human spirit, to prove sonship to God. In the inspiration of the Scriptures, the influence of the Spirit is so ex-

erted along with the activity of the human spirit employed,
that the peculiar mental quality of the instrument is impressed upon the message delivered, as well as the higher
stamp of the higher intelligence engaged.   This rule is regarded in all the dealings of grace with the unregenerate
and regenerate soul.   This influence, thus limited when exerted on the positive activities of the human energies, is
what is meant *by the leading of the Spirit.*   As these energies are deadened by the influence of sin, they need a stimulating influence of saving grace.   As they are enfeebled,
they need a communication of vigor, sufficient to bring them
up to their appointed work.   As they are affected both by
ignorance and blindness, they need an enlightening and a
guiding influence.   As in themselves active, this guidance,
instruction, and quickening is to be exerted in the way of
leading them in the search, and not by way of force or com-
pulsion.   Leading implies a corresponding and cotempora-
neous motion.   The leading of a little child implies some
movement on the part of the child; the guidance of a blind
man implies movement on his part.   In the leading of the
Spirit, as in all the motions of delivering grace, the essential
nature of man is respected, and while grace is always efficacious to accomplish its purposes,.it always works in accord
with the law of the nature it deals with.   *The leading of the
Spirit, then, we understand to be the influence which he exerts
in guiding all the active powers of the man to the right discharge of all his appointed functions.*

Leading may be accomplished in several ways.   It may
be accomplished by going before and showing the way, as
where a guide is employed to lead an army through an unknown country, or a stranger along unknown paths.   It may
be accomplished by taking hold of the hand of a little child,
or by supporting the strength of a blind or feeble person
unable to go safely without the aid of positive contact with
more available strength and vision.   It may be accomplished

by a glance of the eye, or a gesture of the hand, when the
needed direction is more properly given by a silent sign than
by open command.   It may be accomplished, finally, as the
commander of an army leads his forces by determining and
commanding all their movements.   These differing forms or
degrees of leadership are determined in part by the nature
of that which is to be guided, or by the greater or less
degree of the necessity for guidance.   In like manner the
leading of the Spirit may take a variety of forms, according
to the varying necessities of those whom he leads.   A shepherd will carry the lambs in his bosom, and gently lead those
which are with young, but he will walk before an adult flock
with more unhesitating and less restrained decision.   As
when training untrained sheep, he will keep closer and more
constantly with them, and use more decisive measures to
train them, he will guide the flock when trained, by mere
gestures or calls from a distance, and with less, because
now unnecessary, painstaking and solicitous management.
Just so with the leadership of the Spirit.   He will guide the
young, the feeble, the weary, and the sorrowful with more
direct and tender communications of his grace.   He will
guide the wayward, untrained, and disobedient with severity
if needful.   He will guide the experienced and veteran subjects of his grace with the glance of his eye, and find it
sufficient.   These are the general characteristics of the leading of the Spirit.   But to become more specific:

1. As the Spirit leads all the activities of the human soul,
the intellect, the will, and the outward conduct, he leads the
understanding into the knowledge of the truth as God has
revealed it.   He does this not merely as having given the
revelation of the Scriptures, but when that record is given,
he is equally necessary to guide into the knowledge of the
truth revealed in it.   This he does in two ways, yielding
each a different kind of knowledge: one giving a more or less
accurate intellectual discernment of the truth revealed, and

necessary to soundness and orthodoxy of religious opinion; the other giving that spiritual apprehension of the true significance of truths already known and avowed, which is necessary to personal salvation.

Touching the first of these two kinds of knowledge, the right intellectual apprehension of the truth in the Bible, the leading of the Spirit is always necessary, and can never be ignored or neglected without a serious hazard of departing from the faith. The truths of the Bible are like the truths of any broad system, somewhat subject to accident. Lord Bacon says: "There is something accidental in the knowing of all truth." A dozen men may look at a field, or a house, or a tree, and each one will see something in it which, the others do not see. That which leads each one to see what he sees and the others do not see is what Bacon means by the accidental in knowledge. A hundred thinkers before his day had seen and appreciated the principle of induction from observed facts, which that great thinker established as the basis of that grand philosophy of fruit, as he called it, which has resulted in all the wonderful discoveries and inventions of modern times. In fact, every human being from the age of infancy to maturity of years and reason has acted consciously or unconsciously upon the principle. But Bacon saw something in it which no one else had ever seen in it before, and hence the wonderfully controlling and fruitful use which he made of it. His insight of it is a sample of his maxim touching the accidental in thought. It is so with the truth of the Bible. One interpreter will be absorbed by one truth as he sees it, and fails to see how it is qualified by another truth as seen by another interpreter. Hence he disputes the existence of the truth he does not see, or apprehends it as inconsistent with the truth he does see. This is one mode in which men of equal abilities and equal goodness will be found holding different creeds, all based upon the Scriptures. There is yet another cause involving more of moral responsibility than the one just illustrated, which results in this same division of sentiment. The human heart affected by sin has a profound influence on the views of the understanding; the transparent glass, colored with red or gold, will give its own colors to whatever is seen through it. From these two causes we may see the necessity for the leadership of the Spirit as a guide even to the intellectual knowledge of the truth. His guidance is all-important to control that accidental quality in knowing which leads one to apprehend a force of truth in an idea which another does not see in it. His guidance is all-important in controlling those regulating colors which are transfused through the whole field of the intellect by the moral tastes and affections which fill the heart. No body of Christians in any branch of the church are ever safe from the danger of departing from their creed, when they cease to recognize the perpetual necessity of the leading of the Spirit. The great Protestant formula asserted against the assumption of power in the Roman Catholic Church to decide all issues of Christian truth by authority—the Bible alone is the religion of Protestants—is true in one sense and not true in another. It is true in affirming that all revealed truth is contained in the Bible, and that it is to be found nowhere else; it is true in asserting the right of all men to search the Scriptures, because they are one of the means of grace appointed of God to lead to salvation. But it is not true, if taken to exclude the necessity of the Spirit to lead the individual mind in the search of the Scriptures. The great principle of evangelical Protestant Christianity is two-fold in form: the Bible, alone, as the text-book of faith, and the leadership of the Spirit as the principal teacher. The wreck of the Presbyterian creed in Geneva a century ago, and in Holland at the present time, resulting in the shameless expulsion of all real adherents to that creed which has been accepted by all the agents in this cruel tergiversation, is a striking proof of the perpetual need of the leading of the Spirit in retaining even the intellectual knowledge and hold of the truth.

This leadership is all the more necessary to that other species of the knowledge of the truth which alone yields its saving benefit. This form of apprehending the truth is that which is alluded to by Paul, when he speaks of it as "spiritually discerned." The natural man cannot so discern it. This species of intuition is a gift of the Holy Ghost, and to gain it his leadership is indispensable. The assertion of this form of knowledge is considered mystical by some, and positively fanatical by others, but it is as purely rational and common-sense a distinction as the difference which exists in the knowledge that fire will burn in one who is actually feeling it burn, and one who is not feeling it, but simply knows that it will burn. It is the simple difference between the knowledge which is lodged in the understanding and memory, and that knowledge which exists in a felt experience or in an existing consciousness. In the one, the knowledge is the simple apprehension of a truth; in the other, it is a living intuition of the real force and meaning of it. Sin apprehended in the one form of knowledge may be fully received as a theoretical evil of enormous magnitude; but this apprehension of it will lead to no personal concern on account of it. Sin apprehended in the other form of knowledge will be felt as a personal implication in guilt and danger, and will lead at once to intense personal solicitude on account of it. Christ apprehended under the one form of knowledge may be truly accepted as a Saviour of men, as a mere truth of history; apprehended under the other form of knowledge he will be received as a Saviour, personally accepted and trusted. One may know that the view from the top of a mountain is surpassingly beautiful; one who actually stands upon its summit actually sees what the other merely knows, but does not see. The difference in the two forms of knowledge is neither mystical nor fanatical. It is the office of the Holy Spirit to take of the things of Christ and show them unto us. Under this species of living intuition all that grand grace which makes the gospel glad tidings of great joy can only be apprehended under his leading of our powers of perception. David prayed, "Lead me in thy truth, and teach me"; and if any man ever hopes to be furnished with that intuitive insight into the truth, which is the saving knowledge of Christ, he must make the same prayer in all earnestness and patient waiting upon God. If any Christian ever hopes to reach any high or joyous views of the greatness and perfect adaptation of gospel grace to his own and the souls of others, he must seek the special leading of the Spirit. Let it be remembered that leading implies activity and movement on the part of the led, as well as on the part of the leader. He who seeks to rise into these high and exhilarating views of the gladness of the gospel must give himself to the effort to comprehend them, while he appeals at the same time to the leadership of the Spirit to guide him into adequate conceptions. When the Spirit is leading the intellectual activities of the soul, whether in the intellectual or spiritual apprehension of the truth, he requires the concurrent activity of the intellectual and spiritual intuitions of the soul. He leads, but does not carry; he stimulates, aids, gives needful help, and demands the resolute forth-putting of all our powers, and the active use of all his previous gifts. He rewards no indifference; he warrants no idleness; he pays no premium on spiritual laziness. The rewards of clear and steadfast vision, the real apprehension of what he leads us to see of the greatness of the glad gospel of grace, will be an infinite recompense of all the labor and self-denial which conducts us up on this spiritual Pisgah, and opens to our view the wide, rich landscape over which it looks.

The Spirit also leads the energies of affection in the regenerate heart, as well as the activities of the intellect, and thus proves sonship. All those affections are his gift; they are implanted in regeneration. They are established then in germ; in an infant, but indestructible form; they are the bulb-roots of an eternal life. But they are dependent on the same gracious agent who implanted them to lead them into light on the surface, and to guide the spreading of their ever-increasing stem and branches. This familiar truth, the constant and never intermitted dependence of the regenerate soul on the living grace of God for the health and growth of its graces, is not apprehended as it should be. It ought to be used with a sharp and definite application every day of the Christian's sojourn in this scene of preparation. In the sad consciousness of feeble, it may be of invisible, growth in any grace of faith, hope, patience, gentleness, fervor of sympathy, gratitude or zeal, the first step to be taken is an instant appeal to and for the leadership of the Spirit; he is always ready; the Father is always ready; more ready to give his Holy Spirit to them that ask him, than earthly parents are to give good gifts unto their children. The Saviour, the great High Priest, never abdicates his loving priestly function, and is always ready to intercede for the grant of the Spirit. Nor shall we ever grasp the real strength of the case until we are able to do justice to the Spirit himself; until our conceptions of the love of the Spirit, his delight in his work, the unsearchable depth of the freeness and fulness of his grace, are suitably enlarged. He solicits our appeal to him; he is ready to lead us forward; he is waiting to be gracious. He delights to stir up the soul to a genuine hunger after spiritual blessings. He delights in kindling the spirit of intense desire in the heart—that spirit of prayer which will cry day and night at the throne of grace. He likes to strengthen faith, to develop love, to make staunch the spirit of obedience, to put down selfishness, to waken those wide sympathies for lost men which lead to self-denial and ardent efforts to save them. He delights to spread joy and peace in the soul, and to fill it with the brightness of the sweet spring morning of a revived and animated piety. But he calls upon us to let him lead us. He calls upon us to show our desires for these rich spiritual blessings, and he works at the death-like torpor of our worldliness that he may lead us forward to the needful activities of spiritual desire, in order that through these activities he may lead us further still into richer and more abundant grace.

There is nothing in our relation to the leading of the Spirit to make us think, when we are in a state of conscious spiritual torpor that we must wait for a special motion on his part before we begin to call upon him. The written law is a perpetual prescription and definition of our duty; any desire, however feeble, to come up to the discharge of it shows the first tender leading touch of the Holy Spirit on our hearts. All affections which are led out in the heart by the Holy Spirit will conform to the characteristics of true spiritual affections laid down in the word of God. All false or fanatical religious affections; fierce and uncharitable zeal; the disposition to coerce; the eagerness which overruns prudence and breaks conformity to prescribed duty; all disregard of decency and order in the worship of God, are not led out by the Spirit of God. They consequently do not prove sonship, while those which are led by the Spirit are unquestionable proofs of it. If, then, there is any motion of desire for the improvement of any one or all the affections of a regenerate heart, let us remember and resort to the leadership of the Holy Ghost. No matter how feeble, and consequently how doubtful, the affection itself, or the impulse to better it may be, apply to the Spirit to guide it right and lead it forward. As the shepherd led gently the feeble ones of the flock, so the Spirit of all grace will not despise the weakest of motions towards himself, and the ends he is working to gain. He will not quench the smoking flax; nor break the bruised reed. He will lead if the Christian soul will follow.

The impulse to follow is itself from him, and he will not despise his own gift or mar the purpose for which he gives it. We may appeal to him to give us the impulse, to lead it forward through every degree of desire to fixed purpose, to replenish all the energies he excites, and ever steadily to lead onward from resolve to attainment, and from one attainment to another, until thus growing in grace we arrive at the stature of full-grown men in Christ Jesus. We are never straitened in his offices any more than we are in the grace of the Son, or in the infinite fatherly affections of the Father. If we are straitened at all, we are straitened only in our own souls. If any Christian heart is oppressed with the state of his own graces, and longs for better things, that longing is proof that the Spirit is *leading*—drawing him by the hand, and pointing to the sunshine on the distant hills, and saying, Come, let us go out of these dark, chilly spots on the narrow way, into a higher and more cheering place. Let him lead you; it is always safe to go wherever he shows the way.

3. The leading of the Spirit extends to the actions of the regenerate child of God also. Action is the final and irreversible expression of all moral energy, good or bad. It begins with desire; it ripens into positive volition or determined purpose; and at every stage of manifested will before it passes over into action, it is capable of change; its direction may be altered. But when it passes into action it is fixed forever; and the responsibility which has accompanied every previous expression of will is carried to its highest expression by reaching its final and unalterable form. For these two reasons, the fixation of the fact, and the development of responsibility into its highest and immutable shape by the actual doing of an act, it becomes of the last importance that all positive actions should be well guided and determined. Actions in the course of coming into being often need good and effectual aid and guidance, in order to secure their being so performed as to meet and accomplish the end for which

they are done. The leading of the Spirit, then, as made available in all our conduct, is a blessing inexpressibly great and valuable. It may be looked and asked for in everything which may rightfully be done. In all the duties of life, no matter how purely secular the matter of the duty may be, we may seek for it; for *duty* is only another name for the will and law of God. We have no right to do anything which we cannot ask God to help us do, and to bless us in doing. Where the Spirit leads we may safely go, and where we may go the Spirit may lead. All that we may lawfully omit or refuse to do, we may seek the leading of the Spirit in so refusing; and if we cannot ask him to lead and sanction our negative action, we have no right to refuse to act. No omission of any duty, no evasion of any just obligation, can possibly be led by the Holy Ghost. All acts, of whatever kind, in which he may lead, will be wisely done, and will bear the scrutiny of the final Judge.

All such acts will determine a responsibility which may be safely encountered. All the results and consequences legitimately attributable to such acts will be sound and wholesome in themselves and need not be dreaded. To any mind suitably impressed with the awfulness of accomplished facts, with the unchangeableness of the facts themselves, with the uncontrollableness of their influences, with the indelible nature of the responsibility they create, this covenanted provision of the Holy Spirit as an available leader in action constitutes one of the richest provisions made in the covenant of grace. As such we may seek his guidance in every stage of the action, in the original contemplation of it, in the determinate purpose to attempt it, in devising the means to effect it, in the execution of the act itself, and in securing the happy consequences that flow from it. It is a glorious privilege to have such a guide and helper. We only forfeit our right to seek and expect his leading when the action is faulty in itself, in the motives which actuate it, or in the unhappy consequences which inevitably flow out of the act itself, or may be perverted out of it by the weak in faith when needlessly done. We have no right to seek or expect his guidance in any weak or foolish action, the test of which as such is to be found in the principles or precepts of the written word, and not in the mere prejudices or passions of the natural mind. These remarks define the leadership of the Spirit in the personal actions of individual men; but it is equally available and equally necessary to safety in the public actions of organized bodies, and especially of the church of God. Statesmen and legislators, the rulers and counsellors of all organic bodies of every sort, are not independent of divine counsel, nor released from the obligation to seek it. This is always recognized earnestly in times of public calamity. A celebrated Swedish statesman once sent his son on a tour of travel through various countries and courts of Europe, not merely for the purpose of giving a liberal finish to his education, but especially that he might see with what a small amount of wisdom the world was governed. The need of divine guidance in this dearth of foresight is obvious. The very same defect is to be seen in the courts and councils of the church. These courts are composed of men with all the deficiencies which attach to the wisest, and those which more seriously attach to those who are not the wisest; and while consultation and the comparison of views will be pretty sure to raise the counsel taken higher than the wisdom of the average individual member, it will not naturally rise above the level of the controlling minds.

The history of the church in its best development is full of proofs of the necessity for a perpetual and wise leading influence within and over its best human counsels. It is an inexpressible blessing that the leading of the Spirit is available to the courts and parliaments of the kingdom. This guiding influence is a totally different thing from that claim to infallible guidance which is the distinction and disgrace of the great Roman apostasy. It is analogous in character with his leadership of individual men, with no more and no less of infallibility in it, effective to secure salvation, yet giving no guarantee of universal doctrinal correctness of religious opinion. There may be true Christians, yet holding different views of points not essential to personal salvation. The pledge to them is guidance into the truth necessary to save them, not into absolute completeness and inerrancy in the knowledge of all the truth revealed. In like manner there may be safe guidance in the counsels and testimonies of the organized church, without absolute and universal infallibility. In all the parliaments of the church human energies are in motion as well as the leading of the Spirit, and will stand accountable for the mistakes that may be mingled with conclusions on the whole sound and salutary. Though not securing infallible accuracy and wisdom, the influences of the Spirit are available for invaluable results in the councils of the kingdom. Every combined effort of any particular congregation, or of any part of it, ought to recognize, with earnest and patient application for his aid, the leadership of the Spirit. Otherwise, such a practical declaration of independence of his assistance will be apt to result in disappointment or absolute failure. His leading in anything, whether of individual or organized action, gives the best securities possible; it shows he is taking part in it. With such a leader, and just in proportion to the fulness of his intervention, there will be comfortable assurance of right and safe guidance, and of an answerable success.

CHAPTER IX.

THE INTERCESSION OF THE SPIRIT.

"Likewise the Spirit also helpeth our infirmities; for we know not what we should pray for as we ought; but the Spirit itself maketh intercession for us with groanings which cannot be uttered."—*Paul to the Romans.*

INTERCESSION is a leading element in prayer, and often stands for the whole of it. Strictly construed, it is that part of prayer in which he who prays offers petitions for others than himself. It is an interposition, a mediation or going-between, in which one asks favor for persons or interests distinct from himself, or his own immediate concerns. It is a part of the duty of prayer as it is defined for us in the word of God; while permitted and commanded to pray for ourselves we are required to pray for others. Intercession is not only a part of ordinary prayer, but one of the grand functions of an official priesthood; and one of the sweetest and most encouraging aspects in which our Lord is presented to our confidence, is that in which he is represented as praying for us at the Father's throne. Christ is commonly recognized as a being to be prayed to, but is not so fully recognized as a praying being himself, praying for us. This priestly intercession of the great High Priest is the combination in his prayers of a plea of his own official work, with a petition grounded upon it, that the favor of the Father may be bestowed on those for whom he prays. The Holy Spirit is also an intercessor for us; but his intercession differs from both the intercession of the great Priest of the covenant, and the ordinary prayers of the human petitioner. Originating in the same grace as the intervention of the Mediator, and aiming at the same gracious end, it is not a plea based upon what he has done for us, but a present work

334

done in us. Unlike the priest in the heavenly sanctuary,
and unlike the human petitioner, who both present their
personal petitions in their own persons, he does not offer his
own petitions in his own person, nor appear directly before
the throne. His intercession is indirect; he exerts an influence upon us to enable us to pray aright, to show us our
need, to kindle our desires, and to enable us to pray in faith.
His influence is thus all-powerful in securing answers to
prayer. His intervention in prayer is all-important; without
it we not only pray without effect, but our prayers become
fresh forms of offence, and constitute a new reason why they
should *not* be answered. We must "pray in the Spirit."

The teaching of the apostle is very plain; he unequivocally
says: "We know not what to pray for as we ought"; and it
is on that very account, and to prevent the disappointment
which would grow out of misguided and incompetent prayers,
that the Spirit is given to help our infirmities, and to make
intercession for us "with groanings which cannot be uttered."
He is consequently called the Spirit of grace and supplications. This control over the prayers of men is one of the
chief functions assigned him in the economy of redemption.
One passage assigns to him the control over the *matter* of all
acceptable prayer. The *manner* of acceptable prayer, the
earnestness, the reverence, the patience, and the confiding
spirit, is equally dependent upon him; for we know not how
we should pray, any more than we know what we should
pray for as we ought. Christ taught, saying: "After this
manner, therefore, pray ye"; but the influence of the Spirit
is necessary, after we are intellectually instructed by the
lessons and examples set forth in the Scriptures touching
the manner of prayer, to enable us actually to pray after this
manner. We are equally taught by the word of God *what*
we should pray for; we are then informed of the real necessities of our souls; yet we are dependent on the Holy Spirit
to enable us to see and realize these wants in our own con-

sciousness and as a part of our own personal states before we can really feel the need, and so really pray for the supply of the want. The Father must be worshipped in spirit and in truth. Prayer must embody genuine activities of our whole spiritual being, genuine mental apprehensions of our real case, and genuine desires of our hearts for the relief that is needful. To enable us to offer true and heartfelt petitions from sin and danger, it is not enough to know the bare fact of our being sinners, and therefore in peril of violated law, because it has been stated to us; we must know it in our consciousness. The awakening and convicting influences of the Holy Ghost are indispensable to give this conscious, personal knowledge. He must open the understanding to see, and touch the heart that we may feel, or else we shall never be able to pray as we ought. This is the general ground on which our dependence on the Spirit as the Spirit of grace and supplication is rested in the Scriptures. But to be more specific, let us look first, at the *matter* of prayer as the Spirit controls it, and then at the *manner* of it as developed by him.

1. The *matter* of all prayer suitable to fallen beings is defined for us in the word of God. All our necessities are there explained, all our privileges and warranted hopes are there described. The whole state of case of a moral and responsible agent who has sinned against God is expounded. The effect of sin in determining guilt, depravity, and danger is explained. His exposure to temptation; his peril under it; his weakness to resist it; his utter inability to deliver himself from his sin; his subtle and invincible aversion to be really saved and separated from the sin he loves so well—all these are exposed to view. The way of relief provided for him, and all its exquisite adjustments to his condition, are made known to him. His privileges under the covenant, his duties, and the provisions made to enable him to discharge them, are revealed. Under such instruction developed in

the Scriptures, and in the preaching of the gospel, it is altogether possible for a man to have a general and well-defined
intellectual knowledge of his spiritual condition on the same
terms and in the same way in which he may gain any other
kind of knowledge on any other subject, and without any
special influence of the Spirit.   But this knowledge, remaining in this form will do him no good; it will awaken no sensibility, kindle no desire, determine no purpose, excite to no
action.   It will lie in the mind as *mere knowledge,* and, remaining so, will only heighten the danger by increasing responsibility without doing any saving good whatever.   It will not
lead to prayer at all; the mind will not recognize the need of
prayer, because it does not personally recognize any want
nor feel any desire to supply it.   These items of knowledge
touching the spiritual condition determined in every transgressor by his sin must pass into consciousness; they must
be known to be true in the realized experience of personal
standing as well as in the Bible.   They must be recognized
as facts as well as mere *ideas,* as personal qualities as well
as general characteristics of human nature, or prayer, genuine prayer, is impossible.   Here, then, is the first necessity
for the influences of the Spirit; and the change of mere abstract intellectual knowledge into personal convictions is the
first preliminary work of the Spirit *as intercessor.*   He begins to teach man the secret of prayer by opening his eyes
to see his real wants.   He is in danger, but he does not see
it; all looks safe and full of hope; and he goes on careless
and gay-spirited, as one who treads a flower-strewed, but
rotten bridge over some awful chasm, unnoticed and disregarded in view of the apparently safe and beautiful pass-
age-way over it.   When the Spirit begins his work as intercessor he reveals the danger; and this is called *the awakening* of the Spirit.   But the transgressor is not merely in
danger; he is guilty; he has sinned, and sin necessarily
involves *criminality* as well as danger; but the sinner is as

blind to this feature of his condition as he was to the other. Consequently, although allowing in a general way, as a mere abstract, but by no means pressing or poignant personal truth, that he is a sinner, he is not moved by it. He is conscious of much rectitude; his motives are good; his impulses are generous; his principles are honorable; his sympathies are kindly; his tastes are refined; his personal and social affections are amiable; and he feels that on the whole he is a good man. His ways are clean in his own eyes. He does not see any sin, but a good deal of righteousness in his whole character. God is to him a mere idea, true, indeed, and important in its bearings on the laws and interests of society, but a mere abstraction, not a living person with claims to personal affections, to gratitude for kindness, to love for his personal excellencies, to reverence for his infinite greatness, and to obedience on account of his sacred right to command. He is conscious of some uneasiness and fear towards God at times; but as a rule God is not in all his thoughts; he lives without him and feels no need of him or his favor. Death and the transit into another life seem to be immeasurably far off, and are never realized as certain events in the personal future. No real prayer can come from a soul in such a state; the only prayer possible to it is a mere formal offering, a duty done under some sentimental view of a social propriety, or possibly of a general and ill-defined personal relation, whose claims can be fully satisfied by a formal and occasional recognition of them. But when the Spirit begins his work as intercessor he opens the mind to the consciousness of *sin* to a greater or less degree; he convinces of sin and righteousness and judgment to come; and this office is called *the conviction* of the Spirit. This conviction may exist on a scale of degrees running up from a low and feeble intuition of personal criminality to the most awful and tragical apprehensions of personal guiltiness. But whatever may be the degree of this conviction, when it comes to such a soul as we have just described, as clean in his own eyes, all is now changed. His easy self-complacence is now gone; he has become conscious of sin. His feeling of self-righteousness, though not exterminated altogether, has received a deadly wound, and leaves the field of consciousness to be occupied by strange apprehensions of personal criminality walking hand in hand with menacing apprehensions of personal danger. The feelings are now roused in proportion to the energies of the awakening and convictive influences exerted; fears begin to fly abroad; anxieties as to the future begin to emerge. Then a different kind of prayer from that easy formal offering just alluded to will begin to stir in the soul. A cry, selfish, and as such impure, but startling in its earnestness, will begin to rise in the silence of the heart. Remorse, or a selfish repentance, what the apostle calls the sorrow of the world that worketh death, begins to work, and effectually disposes of the easy and complacent state of the unawakened and self-righteous heart. The praying now done is often even tragically eager and importunate. But this sorrow of the world is not the genuine repentance which brings pardon and safety. Flashes of self-righteous feeling will now and then break out of the cloud of conviction and remorse—a feeling that God ought to show mercy, and is either unjust, unkind, or unfaithful to his word, if he does not show it. Bitter, rebellious, hard, and blaspheming thoughts now come thronging to the front, and aggravate well-nigh to madness the partial consciousness of sin, and the more effective sense of danger which exasperate the struggle of the stricken heart. Prayer will then come in good earnest; the last trace of indifference vanishes; and a cry comes up as out of the belly of hell. But it is not yet the prayer that the prayer of a guilty soul, seeking the mercy and grace of an offended God, ought to be; it will still be fierce, complaining, bitterly anxious, yet bitterly rebellious.

Then the Spirit leads forward, and if he never does this, all
is lost. Up to this point, we see only the effects of the
awakening and conviction that precede regeneration and
true repentance. The repentance so far developed, although
it may rise to even a tragical degree of remorse, though often
fatally misconstrued as the repentance which is unto life, is,
nevertheless, all selfish, mere remorse and sorrow of the
world which is unto death. All may stop here, and short of
eternal life; the remorseful soul may go back to receive a
double damnation in the end. But if the Holy Spirit in his
work as intercessor leads forward, and begins to teach how
to pray as we ought, he will give a deeper and truer view of
sin than that which breeds this passionate but unavailing
kind of remorseful praying. He opens the eyes to see how
wicked this state of feeling, and this kind of praying really
are. He makes us see more fully what sin really is—a thing
that justly forfeits the favor of God—that justly exposes to
his wrath. He fills the heart with the feeling that it *deserves* to
be rejected, that it hangs suspended simply on *the grace*, the
sovereign and distinguishing grace of God, that it can neither
by its own strength comply with the terms on which pardon is
promised, nor compel God to enable the soul to comply with
it. Then the proud heart becomes humbled; it is content
to submit to God; it becomes willing for God to determine
the case; and as the Spirit leads still forward it begins to
trust God to determine it safely for him. Then comes the
broad and joyful apprehension that salvation is really the
free gift of God; that faith and repentance, "true belief
and true repentance, every grace that brings us nigh," are
all his free and gracious gifts. In this altered and most
happy mood, the prayer that comes from this advanced work
of the Spirit as intercessor is wholly altered; it becomes
humble and hopeful supplication: sin is *confessed;* God is
felt to be injured by it; the plea for mercy looks away from
self and all that self has been trying to do to obtain mercy,

and joyfully apprehends that mercy is free; that grace is all-sufficient; that Jehovah, Jesus, is himself the Saviour of sinners. The Holy Spirit has at last taught the soul what to pray for, and how to pray as it ought. The way in which he does it is by a successive and progressive opening of the eyes to see the *real condition and necessities of the soul.*

2. The Spirit maketh intercession for us and teaches us to pray as we ought, *by enkindling and controlling the desires of the heart.* Prayer is the offering up of our desires unto God, and the nature and the force of the prayer will be determined by the nature and the energy of the desires embodied in it. If the desires are selfish, the prayer will be selfish; if the desires are holy, the prayer will be holy; if the desires are feeble, the prayer will be feeble; and if the desires are strong and intense, the prayer will wear the same characteristics. It is obvious, then, that the desires must be controlled, if the prayer is to be regulated. Nothing can more powerfully illustrate the necessity for the Spirit as an intercessor to indite our petitions for us than this essential fact in the nature of prayer. The human heart is full of evil; its affections have been corrupted by sin; and no true or honest desire after a holy salvation can spring up in it unless the Holy Spirit gives it. There needs no special influence of the Spirit to make men willing to escape the penal consequences of sin, except, perhaps, in cases of extraordinary depravity; the natural principles of hope and fear will ensure that result. Selfishness will determine desire in all matters in which self is concerned, whether in view of danger or the bitter power in sin itself to create sorrow. A man may be terribly oppressed by a sin, by the power of a destructive, sinful habit, or by the strength of an evil impulse, and yet be purely selfish in it. He is oppressed because he feels he is injured by it; yet that feeling of dread towards his sin may have no more moral merit in it than a man's anxiety to be rid of toothache or neuralgia.

A man may selfishly desire to be holy, not because he likes it, for if he likes it he himself is holy and not selfish; but because holiness conditions heaven, and he knows that without it he cannot see God.   This fact is enough to make us all pause and ponder with intense self-scrutiny the state of our hearts; even the most mature and veteran of regenerate souls may well be startled into watchfulness when the deceitfulness of the heart is brought into remembrance.   Are our desires after the salvation of God what they ought to be? Are our prayers, after all, only embodiments of selfishness? If not altogether so, may there not be an element of selfishness in them, which may possibly account, in part at least, for so many defeats in prayer?   May not our very desire for the salvation of sinners be tainted with selfishness, as when we desire it to gratify a partisan attachment to our own church, and outshine a sister denomination?   If our desires are substantially sound, are they truly regulated in degree? Are they strong enough to overcome our reluctance, our laziness, our love of money, our pride, our resentments, our love of ease and self-indulgence?   These questions may make us set more value on the Spirit as an intercessor; for he can remove all defects in our desires, and thus elevate the character and increase the power of our prayers.   It is right that we should seek with all earnestness our own salvation; the desire to escape the penalty of sin is a desire altogether legitimate, and the distinct consciousness of such a desire does by no means *per se* discount the integrity of our wish to be saved.   But is this the only reason why we seek for grace?   Is there not something in the very essence of sin, a criminality in its nature, that, independent of its penal hazards, would make every right heart revolt at it, and rejoice to be delivered from it?   But surely, however trying may be the perplexity created by the effort to discriminate justly the mixture of motive in our religious experience, it is a matter of infinite comfort to know that the Spirit in his intercessory work takes charge of the desires of his own people, and insures so much of a pure element in them as to make their prayers effective. He regulates the degrees as well as the nature of these desires; and those groanings which cannot be uttered are simply the strong yearnings of a regenerate soul after spiritual advancements, for which it longs intensely, although unable to give adequate expression to the desire, or adequate description to the blessings desired.

3. The Spirit makes intercession for the saints, and thus teaches them to pray as they ought by regulating *the motives* with which they pray. These often hinder the answer of prayer; we ask and receive not, because we ask amiss, that we may consume it upon our lusts, that is to say, in a generalized form of expression, that we may serve selfish ends; for example, when we pray for the salvation of sinners that we may get credit, that our church may be praised, that our anxieties for particular persons may be eased. Also when we pray for the gift of the Holy Spirit that we may be assured of our personal salvation merely to have less trouble. Also when we ask for this blessing or that, that we may be spared some trial, or may gratify some prejudice, or win some advantage. All these motives terminate on self, and damage the efficiency of prayer. Yet a certain regard to self wellbeing is right, and the subtle mixture of allowable and unallowable self-regard is hard for us to discriminate or manage, and makes the intercessory function of the blessed Spirit in regulating the motives and spirit of our prayers all the more precious. To him we ought incessantly to refer all our motives and desires, that he may control them. A jealous watch upon our apparently most holy and religious acts is wise; for without his gracious influence we cannot think a thought or indulge a desire which is not in some way more or less tainted by the unholy mind and the unholy heart from which they spring. He makes intercession for us according to the will of God. Our guide in prayer is the

written word, and whatever object is warranted by the precepts, examples, or general instruction of the word, we may pray for boldly under the guidance of the Spirit of grace and supplications.

4. The Spirit teaches us to pray by opening the way of acceptance to our understandings, and enabling the exercise of faith. Faith is his gift, and, when given, its exercise ought always to be under his guidance. We always need his illumination on the plan of salvation. Now it is so plain and clear, and Christ as a Saviour seems so completely sufficient, we are filled with peace. Then a cloud sweeps over all, and the whole way of salvation becomes as mysterious as it seemed when we were first struggling to understand and embrace it. Sometimes the promises do so flush with a hidden glory of priceless value, and seem so great and precious, we feel as if we had come into possession of a talisman richer than the magic formula in the Eastern story, which unlocked the chambers of the earth's hidden wealth, and laid the vast masses of ruby and diamond open to the eye. Then the inner glory of them seems to die out, and we gaze on them as on blank orders for an infinite treasure, and they become empty of all power to strengthen or comfort us. It is expressly said, if we pray not in faith, let no man expect anything of God. Those words often sound like a knell of hope; yet they invite us to trust in a living love and power back of the promises, and as worthy of our confidence as the promises themselves, though they do challenge our trust on a basis stronger than the pillowed firmament—the truth of the stainless and infinite God. How sweet to know that the Spirit, as the Spirit of grace and supplication, is also the giver of faith! How sweet to know when we are perplexed how to handle the promises; how to confide in them; how far to expect and when to look for their fulfilment; for what objects to plead them; how to be kept from any abuse of them, in the way of presumption on the one side, or of too

little expectation on the other; how sweet to know that the Spirit may guide our petitions, as well as give the faith which lays hold on the sure words of promise! He opens to us the significance of the priesthood of Christ, and unseals that glorious refuge of a sinful and sin-oppressed soul, the sacrifice and the interceding prayers which give assurance of forgiveness. The intercessions of the Spirit carry the gift of faith in the Saviour, and secure all the pledges of the covenant.

5. The Spirit teaches us what to pray for by opening up to us *the significance and the mighty power of the pleas by which we may urge our petitions.* We often feel as if we would give anything for a plea so powerful as to secure what we ask. The pleas which are given us are the most powerful which even the vast power of the infinite God could give. They are pleas whose acceptance is pledged to our faith beforehand. They are never pleaded in vain. If they fail in securing the very thing we *ask*, it is due to some misuse upon our own part, and the security against that misuse is the intercession of the Spirit. They never fail in securing the very thing which we *need*. He always intercedes according to the will of God; and every petition which he creates in the soul goes into the censer of the great High Priest, and is offered with his endorsement before the throne, and him the Father heareth always. Look at some of the pleas which are given us to plead in prayer. The plea of the blood of Jesus; who can estimate its power? It has shaken the kingdom of darkness until its vast foundation stones are split wide open, and the awful structure is tottering to its fall. It has quenched the wrath of God against a sinning world. It has redeemed millions upon millions of immortal sinning souls. It has loosened the bonds of law and justice which bound the arm of God's almightiness, and set it free to work for the redemption of the world. It has impoverished hell; it has enriched heaven a thousand-fold; it moves the

Father's heart as no other power ever has or can move it, it has moved his just wrath out of the way and given place to the free movement of his infinite grace to sinners; it will ground a sure hope of pardon and eternal life, more fully than the solid earth would ground the gossamer weight of a bee's wing. Then take the plea of the love of God—the fatherhood of the Father, the love of the Son, and the grace of the Holy Spirit—what a plea is this! Unexhausted by all that it has done for the salvation of man, that wonderful love which originated, executed, and now applies the wonderful provisions of the covenant, still stands back of all this executed wealth of mercy, as mighty, as free, as solicitous to bless, as before its glorious achievement was done, undiminished and undiminishable! The appeal to a loving human heart is always full of power; yet it may fail. An appeal to the love of the Father, Son, and Holy Ghost is measured in its strength by the infinite tenderness to which it appeals. Who can estimate the power of the plea in the love of God! There is yet another plea to support our petitions, in *the glory of God.* Once only possible of manifestation in the upholding of righteous law and in the punishment of evil doers, his wisdom has worked with such infinite reach of skilful contrivance, that now both his personal glory, and the honor of his law, can be actually magnified in the eternal salvation of sinning creatures. If there was any demand involved in the plea for pardon, for any eclipse of the glory of God, there could not be and there ought not to be any power in the plea; but so far from this, his glory, which is nothing but the display of his infinite excellence, is great in the salvation of sinners; made greater than in any display of it ever made, or that can ever be made. We ask no sacrifice of feeling or right on the part of God, when we plead for pardon now; on the contrary, we ask God to magnify his glory, to do a thing which carries with it the achievement of another result in which the whole Godhood finds an infinite and most

worthy delight. When the Spirit, interceding in us, opens
up the power of the great gospel pleas, the vilest of sinners
may well feel bold in coming to the throne of grace, as he is
commanded and exhorted to do. Covered with the spotless
robe of the Lord's own righteousness, he can venture
nearer to the intolerable splendor of the throne of God
than the most favored angel in the ranks of the heavenly
hierarchy.

6. The Spirit as an intercessor in us gives stability to our
desires, patience to our waiting, assurance to our petitions,
and joy to our anticipations of sure answers to our prayers.
The indulgence of strong and ardent desires for any length-
ened period of time is wearisome to human weakness, and if
left to our own protection and support, unaided by grace,
would certainly soon wear out. There is infinite comfort in
the thought that he who gives these needful elements of prevailing prayer can sustain them in our weak hearts. Our
patience in waiting for answers to prayer is apt to weary and
pass over into fretfulness and unbelief; he can make us rest
in the Lord, and wait patiently for him. Left to ourselves
to pray unaided, our prayers could give no assurance except
of failure; his petitions kindled in us, the Son will assuredly
endorse, the Father will assuredly answer. His intercession
is a fountain of joy as well as of strength in the offering of
prayers.

7. This control of the matter of our prayers will also control the *manner* of them. They will become reverent, child-
like in humility and freedom, intensely solicitous, yet full of
submission, persistent in spite of discouragements designed
to test faith, patience, and sincerity of desire, full of confidence without presumption, full of joy, full of hope. Prayers
are often offered in a manner which unerringly indicates that
the interceding Spirit has nothing, or but little, to do with
them. Coldness and formality, studied rhetoric, pride of
elegance and grace, censorious reflections, impudent famil-

iarity, often mistaken for child-like simplicity, any atom of
the Pharisaic spirit, absence of avowed dependence on the
Mediator, the presence of avowed dependence on Virgin or
saint, or store of churchly merit, all give token of the absence
of the Spirit in his office as an intercessor. Every prayer
in which he has no share is sure of rejection, not only as a
failure to pray aright, but as a fresh offence in an aggravated form. It is, perhaps, safer to sin in sin's own livery
than to assume the livery of the King to do dishonor to his
crown.

8. It will be a fit close to this attempt to delineate a precious
function of the Holy Spirit, to lay emphasis on the free, loving
disposition and the never-failing readiness of our gracious
Intercessor to help our infirmities. He delights in his work;
he is always in reach; the freedom of our access to his loving
presence and to his gracious influences is absolute. The
merits of our Saviour are not more constantly and freely
open to our acceptance than the influences of the Spirit.
The Father is more willing to give the Holy Ghost to them
that ask him, than earthly parents are to give good gifts
unto their children. The Spirit is just as ready to be given
as the Father is to give him. His infinite loving-kindness,
his tender pity for lost souls, his delight in executing the
great covenant of mercy, all utter a welcome of surpassing
tenderness to all who would seek his aid.

One more remark, and we are done. The absolute dependence of a lost soul and of a saved soul during the
process of its inward deliverance may be, and often is, felt as a
discouragement; but never except under an entire misapprehension of both its design and its appropriate effects. So
far from any legitimate discouragement, even to an uncove-
nanted and an unsaved sinner, it is just the opposite; for it
gives him the only possible chance for him to be saved.
Whenever this feeling of discouragement springs up in view
of our dependence on this gracious helper, we may be sure

it is an illegitimate view, to be repudiated at once. His purpose in all his dealings with the saints is to help their infirmities, to prevent the failure of their hopes, to secure the answer to their prayers, to prosper their work, and to assure their reward. His boundless tender love and his official functions are so full, so free of access, so glowing in the welcome that they offer to every soul in search of help and healing, that as no thought can compass the excelling mystery of his grace, no word can tell it.

CHAPTER X.

THE COMFORT OF THE SPIRIT.

"And I will pray the Father, and he shall give you another Comforter, that he may abide with you forever; even the Spirit of truth; whom the world cannot receive, because it seeth him not, neither knoweth him; but ye know him; for he dwelleth with you, and shall be in you."—*John in his Gospel.*

THESE words of Jesus were spoken to the disciples in that wonderful talk he made the night he was betrayed. He had at last made them understand what they had hitherto been so reluctant to believe, that his plainest statements seem to have no effect whatever. But now they did comprehend that he was to die, and they were overwhelmed with despondency. Their notions of the Messiah of Israel, at first in no way different from the universal notions of their countrymen, had been greatly modified by the Master's teaching, but were still full of error and confusion. The idea that Messiah was to die had never entered their minds, and having accepted Jesus as the Prince of Israel, the conception of his death seemed to be a mental impossibility. They had learned to rely upon his protection with such absolute confidence in his astonishing power; they had looked so confidently to be indemnified for the prejudice and loss of caste they had encountered by adhering to him, by high preferment in the kingdom they expected him to set up, that now the assurance of his death threw down their castles in the air and filled them with confusion. They had felt so secure, so completely emancipated from the fear of death, sickness, and bodily want, that ungovernable sorrow now filled their hearts. All their hopes were crushed by this unexpected blow. The words of the Messiah in this last pathetic and powerful

address—the most remarkable dying address ever delivered—
were all directed to qualify this state of feeling, and the
principal ground of comfort he unveiled before them was the
promised gift of that Comforter who was to take his place as
the guide, the strength, the universal helper in all the necessities of those who had looked hitherto to his visible presence for all they needed. He was to be emphatically the
Paraclete, which is the literal translation of the word rendered Comforter in our English Bible. The name Paraclete
is composed of two words, which literally mean "the one
called to," expressing the notion of one called to our side
for help in every emergency. No greater comfort can be
given to one engaged in any difficult or dangerous enterprise than to have a reliable assistant who can always be
called upon for efficient assistance at all times. The name
Comforter, then, given to the great Paraclete of the Christian covenant, is not altogether inappropriate; yet it is
defective in that it seems to confine his function to the
one specific service of giving consolation, whereas the
comfort really comes from the far broader sense of the
title as the universal helper of the saint in all the emergencies of his life and work. Inasmuch, however, as
the specific service of a comfort-giver is a true function of
the Spirit as a Paraclete, it will be entirely allowable to give
special consideration to that part of his work, more especially
as attention has been and will be still further during our
discussion, called to other specific modes in which the blessed
Paraclete discharges his glorious and many-sided office. He
was designated in connection with his promised consolation
as "the Spirit of truth." This title intimates, what is also
expressly stated, that he would do his work as a Comforter
by "leading them into the truth." He was to be a specially
valuable helper, because, unlike the visible Saviour with
whom they had lived only for a time, he was "to abide with
them forever." He was to prove an assured reliance for

them, not because he would be always accessible to them at some one place where they might not always find it convenient to resort to him; but, far higher and more effective privilege than that, he should "dwell with them," and better still, he should "be in them." These are the three general and yet discriminated modes in which his work as the Comforter should be done.

1. The word *comfort* carries the notion of a peculiar modification of enjoyment. It does not convey the conception of enjoyment in as high a degree as the terms happiness or pleasure; but it does carry the notion of more stability and substantial endurance than the word pleasure, and an equal measure of this more lasting property with the word happiness. But the principal differentiating feature which distinguishes comfort from other forms of enjoyment is its antithesis and relation to evil or pain. A holy angel may be said to be happy or to enjoy special seasons of pleasure, but he can hardly be said to be comfortable, because he is never subject to pain or distress. Comfort is a form of enjoyment which emerges when pain or distress is qualified by some concurrent alleviation, or is followed by relief, or when an impending or possible evil is effectively qualified in its stroke or absolutely prevented. Comfort, therefore, is on this account the more adapted and the more practicable to the conditions of existence in this world, because evil in ten thousand forms is perpetually threatening or actually preying upon human peace. *To comfort*, then, is to infuse a certain substantial element of enjoyment into a heart and life assailed, and constantly assailable with evil. The end and purpose of the Spirit as a Comforter is not directly a purpose to purify, but to promote enjoyment. His ultimate purpose in all his special acts is to carry out the pledge to the believer to deliver him from sin; to purify the heart and infuse holiness into the whole nature of the man. But all his special acts of sealing, unction, witness, leading, and

interceding have a special end directly in view, while all lead indirectly and ultimately to the general end of sanctification. The special direct end of the comfort of the Spirit is to comfort a sufferer. God is love, and he delighteth in enjoyment for its own sake, as one of the ends which his benevolent nature delights to accomplish. The Spirit delights in all his work, and he delights in comforting. The very purpose is to comfort, to infuse an element of peace into the regenerate soul, either as actually suffering, or as threatened with some coming sorrow, a form of future trial which will, of course, afflict in advance of its actual advent. The office of the Spirit as a Comforter is not only a distinct part of his work, but from its very nature, from the very end and purpose it has in view, is specially adapted to our conditions of existence. As a distinct aim and function of his office, and as an important and distinguished branch of it, so much so as to give him a distinctive title as the Comforter, he may be applied to as such; comfort as such may be sought for; and his consolations expected, in compliance with the terms on which all his gracious acts are promised. An unhappy Christian, though truly a child of the covenant, is not only living below his privileges, but in a breach of his duty. God has provided to comfort him, and commanded him to rejoice in the Lord always. Such a Christian is doing scant justice to the benignant Spirit whose official business is to comfort him, and who takes infinite delight in doing it.

2. The sources of comfort employed by the Holy Ghost are varied by the evils which it is designed to qualify. To comfort one who is blind he must be enabled to see, or be furnished with aids which may, partially at least, make up for the trying deficiency. To comfort one who is weak, he must be strengthened, or help must be found for him. To comfort one who is afraid, his fears must be qualified or removed. To comfort one in distress, some source of easement must be found. Comfort must be adjusted to the evil

it confronts.   The great comprehensive sources of comfort
to creatures conditioned as men are universally in this world,
or as the regenerate soul is in this scene of his progressive
sanctification, may be, not exhaustively, classified in the following forms: Deliverance from present evil, or a guarantee
against its worst results.   Security from evil yet to come;
from it altogether, or from its worst results.   The effects of
past evil prevented of its worst or its most lasting consequences.   Present evil accompanied by compensating agencies.   Sure grounds of confidence and hope furnished.   Rich
resources supplied, and available help in every emergency,
and assurance of their continuance.   Certain and valuable
future advantages as the reward of fidelity, and the assurance of their continuance when gained.   The reliable pledge
of a final, full, and unalterable deliverance out of the state
and possibility of all evil whatever, and the assurance of
all good attainable for all eternity.   These are among the
sources of comfort which are employed by the Spirit in
doing his blest work of cheering the saints in the trials of
their earthly pilgrimage.   He unfolds some of these comforts *by what he teaches; some by what he does; some by what
he imparts, and some by what he guarantees to their hopes.*

3. The Comforter whom Jesus promised to send is immediately distinguished as "the Spirit of truth."   This designation at once leads us to the conception that his work as a
comforter is to be done *by his teaching us the truth.*   This
is more clearly set forth than in a mere inference from a
distinctive name.   In an after part of his discourse our Lord
distinctly says: "The Comforter, which is the Holy Ghost,
whom the Father will send in my name, he shall teach you
all things, and bring all things to your remembrance, whatsoever I have said unto you."   This teaching as it applies
to the apostles, and other apostolic men, secured their inspiration in preparing the great standards of the Christian
faith.   As it applies to believers generally, it refers to that

influence exerted on the individual mind by which it is enabled to understand and realize the true force and meaning of the truth set forth in the inspired record. As the nature of this distinctive kind of knowledge has already been set forth in its contrast to a mere intellectual knowledge, it is needless to repeat it here. It then appeared to be a species of insight of the truth due entirely to the influence of the Spirit, by which the real sense and force of the truth was brought out, with an effect upon the feelings as well as on the intelligence—an effect suitable to the kind of truth thus apprehended. Alarming truth is thus made to really awaken alarm, and cheering truth to awaken joy. It is in this way the Spirit comforts *by his teaching :* he opens the sense and power of the glorious, glad, and comforting truths of the gospel, and through a lively faith in them unlooses their gladdening influences on the comforted soul. The gospel is in itself, in its essential nature, "glad tidings of great joy." It proclaims peace on earth and good-will to men. All its grand doctrines are full of delight. It filled heaven with rejoicing in anticipation of its enterprise, and sent some vast cohort of the heavenly host down upon the plains of Bethlehem on the night of the Saviour's birth, and in their unmastered exultation caused them to break through the veil which shuts out the sights and sounds of the upper sphere from the dwellers on the earth. No human soul has ever caught its real meaning without experiencing some degree of the joy and comfort which it carries in its bosom. It brings to view the grand truth that sin can now be pardoned through the work of the Redeemer; and whenever a human heart, oppressed with the consciousness of its sin, can grasp this one truth in its full meaning *it will be comforted.*

As comfort stands related to an evil in the qualification or conquest of which this form of enjoyment emerges, the Spirit comforts under the pressure of sin by unveiling the significance and the power of the atoning blood. Until he does unveil it, the poor, trembling soul, sick with its guilt and mortal fears, will stand gazing on the glorious redemption price without a solitary conception of its power to help him out of his troubles. It will seem as empty of significance as the cold, confused outlines of the figures stamped upon a porcelain lamp-shade, even although the strongest rays of the sunlight are poured upon them on the outside. That poor, sin-stricken heart will weary itself pitifully in the endeavor to see what others tell him there is of power in the remedy to subdue his pain. But now let the Holy Spirit assume his work as a comforter by his teaching, and then, like the lamp-shade when the lamp is kindled within and the flame brings out the hidden forms which lay in a confused and indiscriminate mass under the strongest sunlight, so, under the secret teaching of the Comforter, the gladness of the gospel to a lost sinner reveals itself, and the soul is filled with comfort. The promised Spirit has taken that one thing of Christ and showed it unto him. What is true of the soul in its earlier experiences is measurably true of regenerate souls to the end of their pilgrimage. Often to them the blood of Christ seems to lose its significance, and lay down its power. The cause of this appearance is the same, and the remedy is the same; the cause is dimness of eye-sight; the remedy is the teaching of the Comforter. What is true of this one grand truth, the blood of atonement, is equally true of all the glorious truths of the covenant. They are all inconceivably rich in meaning, and in their assurance of advantage to the sinners of the human race. But their power to cheer the human heart depends upon the teaching of the Spirit of truth in his work as a comforter. God designs to bring back his wandering creatures to direct intercourse with himself, and even the system of truth revealed for human redemption is not allowed to interfere with their dependence on him. They are sent first to the truth, and then back of it to a living Saviour to reveal its saving power. The great and precious promises without this shining of the Spirit within them, are like checks drawn for countless wealth, filled out plainly, but the vital signature written in invisible ink; they disclose no meaning; they exhibit no power to give content until the vitalizing heat of the Holy Spirit is brought to bear upon them, and then the draft and signature of a faithful God become visible.

The promises of the covenant cover all the emergencies in the career of a saint. There are pledges of grace for life and for death; for the time of joy and the time of sorrow; for supplies suited to the day; for guidance; for control; for needed aid; for every contingency. But they are all empty of power; they are changed into mockeries of felt necessity, unless the Spirit shine within them. Tempted believers, in the season of hot battle with some great trial of faith and patience, are often sorely vexed with the promises; they are so different apparently from what they seemed to be, and prove so powerless when they are most needed, the temptation is suggested strongly to throw them away as practically useless. To do this would be a fearful sin; it would be to charge God with folly and unfaithfulness; it would be to make him a liar; it would be to charge him with trifling with the hopes he has raised. The difficulty is in ourselves, not in him; in our unbelief, not in his unfaithfulness; in our want of insight, not in his truth. What is needed is the inward illumination of the Comforter teaching us to see the truth as it is and as we ought to receive it. In all such trials of faith it is well to meet the temptation at the threshold; to say what is true, the fault is in ourselves, and to make up the issue squarely in our mind; these promises are true; they do mean something; they are full of a great and precious significance. The reason why they seem otherwise is in me and in my sin, and I will not yield one inch to the suggestion that God is either false or trifling. I will trust thy words, O spotless Christ! Help thou mine unbelief,

O Comforter of thy people! Then in the happy moment when the gracious Spirit of truth assumes his office of Comforter, and shines in our hearts, and fills the darkened promises with his holy light, we shall be able *to see* as well as to know that the fault was in us, and that the promises were all the time full of a significance which deserved our confidence, and were inexpressibly rich in comfort.

So likewise the Spirit comforts by unveiling *the love of the Son;* that infinite and unwasting fountain of tender pity which led him to go through all the fearful conditions of redemption, and which still flows in infinite and undiminishable strength and fervor in the heart of the great High Priest. We are apt to regard the love of Christ as having done its work when he passed out of sight into the blue vault over Olivet, having made a wonderful display on a brief theatre which closed up with its closing scenes. But that same great love which led him from the manger to the cross is still beating in his bosom. It is as keen in the administration as it was in the achievement of redemption. The appeal of the living sinner is not merely to a great by-gone and finished work of a dead Redeemer, but also to a living love and a living power in a living Saviour; to a love as much more tender and vehement than the warmest of mere human and Christian sympathies as his infinite heart is more capacious of the generous affection. When the Spirit teaches from within the truth concerning the love of Jesus our priest, as he ever lives to intercede for us, it will bring all the comfort involved in a true priesthood to a sinful soul, and all that is involved in the love of a friend at court, and that friend the King's own Son.

In like manner the Spirit governs our apprehensions of *the love of the Father.* In our ignorance and narrowness of view the Father even when reconciled to us in the Son still seems to stand in the background, still the representative of the rights of the crown imperial, the offended majesty of heaven, to be adored at a distance and feared; but he does not receive credit for the infinite and brooding love of a Father's heart. Yet that is his name, his chosen designation. In his loving kindness the whole scheme of redemption took its rise. He had to require the satisfaction which the Son rendered; but it was his proposal that it should be done in order to secure the end in view. Now that it has been done, no restrictive regard to law and justice dams back the rushing tides of a Father's infinite love. He is all a Father now, yearning over his rebellious and unhappy creatures, yearning to draw them back to a Father's tenderness and protecting care. Ah! when the Spirit teaches us the glorious truth of the Fatherhood of God, no words can portray its comfort. All our dark and troubled apprehensions of him as the offended King and Lawgiver and Disposer of events, give way to the loving confidence of the filial feeling, and we are able to say, Abba, Father, with inexpressible peace.

In like manner the Spirit, when he would comfort us, teaches in the same way of realized spiritual apprehension *the truth concerning himself and his love for souls.* When it is said, "He shall not speak of himself," it is not meant that he would say nothing about himself. It means that he would not speak merely by his own authority or teach truths given by himself alone. He was to take of the things of Christ, things said and done by the Son, and, therefore, marked out beforehand for the narration of the Spirit. While the Holy Ghost does not speak much concerning his own share in the work of salvation, relatively to what he says of the work of the Son, yet he does speak enough of most precious revelations concerning his own work and offices to carry infinite comfort to a heart truly apprehending what he declares. One mighty element of this consoling truth is what he reveals concerning *the love of the Spirit.* We are ready* enough to give him credit for his faithfulness and his power

---

*Phillip's Preface.

in doing his official work, but are slow to recognize his loving delight in it.   It is easy to see and admire that somewhat stern fidelity, as it seems to some, and the masterful
strength with which he dwells amid the awful corruptions,
the serpents, the devils, and the unclean birds of an unholy
heart, and keeps the stronghold against the strong man,
Satan.   But in this view of his faithfulness and power we
are apt to lose sight of his infinite and tender love, his delight in his work, his infinite sweet complacency in holding
the fort, and with incessant and tender touch deadening and
wearing out the dread evils which he finds in his dreadful
habitation.   He delights to be trusted ; he delights to be appealed to ; he delights to put forth his mighty hand when the
cry of the tried soul comes up to him for help ; he delights to
infuse his might into the weak human arm and enable it to
drive the dread archangel back.   Who can measure the unsearchable riches of the love of the Spirit?   As he unveils
this love to the rejoicing apprehension of the saint, comfort,
deep and rich, will flow into the trembling heart, and it will
be comforted in its Almighty Guardian.

4. But the Spirit comforts not only by what he teaches,
but by what he does, by a positive exertion of his power, by
a positive indulgence of his gracious kindness in positive
actions.   All his inward teaching is done through a preliminary act on the soul.   The heart stands face to face with the
glorious facts of redemption, but it does not see them.   As a
blind man turns his sightless eyeballs up toward the starry
vault, and rolls them in vain to see the splendor of the
sidereal fires, so the sinner seeks in vain to see the glory of
redeeming grace.   To give that blind man even a glimpse,
still more a steady vision of the glory of the night sky, some
power of vision must be infused into his piteous, defective
eyes.   An act of power must precede the vision, and the joy
and comfort which it brings.   It is so with the energy of the
Spirit in the soul.   One of the modes of the Comforter

pointed out by the Saviour at the table of the Passover and his newly appointed supper, was *the dwelling of the Spirit with* the saint. He is in the house with him always. His dwelling there is no idle occupancy of a chimney corner; he is no old and helpless incumbent of a space by the household fire and in the household life. He is an active member of the family; he is a leader in its business; he acts continually in its interest. He guides; he governs; he stimulates to action; he rebukes; he rouses to vigilance; and he comforts and cheers the garrison of the hell-beleaguered heart. He is a soldier; the word of God is his sword, and he fights in the fore-front of every assault upon the walls. His active presence is an inexpressible comfort to the weary and often fear-stricken soldier of the cross. When he can realize who it is that is animating and guiding the strife he is comforted, his strength and courage are renewed. Like the knight in the romance when fighting with unparalleled skill and courage against three redoubtable champions at once, and felt that in spite of all his matchless valor he must go down, he suddenly heard the battle-cry of the lion-hearted king rushing to the rescue, and felt the assurance of victory return to his sinking heart, so the Christian soul renews its hopes under the active exertions of the Holy Spirit. It is a glorious encouragement to know that the blessed Comforter is able to infuse his consolations by the positive exercise of his infinite energies for that very purpose.

5. Yet another mode in which the Comforter imparts his comfort, as Jesus pointed out, arises from his positive indwelling in the very soul of the individual saint: "*He shall be in you.*" Not only shall he dwell in the same household and take part in its activities; not only shall he occupy the same fortress and take part in its defence; but, best security of all, he shall actually be in every soul that believes, and thus be even a nearer and a more effective help and security than as a member of the household dwelling with them. He

is in them thus for a double purpose, not only to impart to them all they need of wisdom, holiness, love, strength, and watchful energy, but also to guarantee the safety of the house and fortress even when men sleep. He is the strong man keeping his goods; a stronger than he must bind him before his goods can be spoiled. He is in them on no idle or fruitless errand; he is there to carry out the pledge of the Redeemer to the believing soul, *sin shall not have dominion over you.* He is there to impart holiness, to give grace according to the day, to bestow wisdom, patience, and courage, to sanctify and comfort in affliction, to erase the image of Satan, to impress the image of God, to conquer the unholy passions, and to fill the soul with all the fruits of the Spirit. His intimate indwelling is the guarantee of safety to the saint. Satan is mighty, but he cannot overcome and lead captive out of a rescued and regenerate human soul the Spirit of the living God, the Comforter, Guide, and Protector of all his people.

6. The Holy Spirit as a Comforter is a power practically available and in reach of every Christian. He may be sought as such; but he must be sought with all prayer and supplication, with watchful diligence in all duty, and in avoidance of all sin, if we hope to realize his influence in this sweet branch of his official work. The Father is more ready to give the Holy Spirit to do all his gracious work to them that ask him, than earthly parents are to give good gifts to their children. To give comfort is one great branch of his office under the covenant; he delights to do it, and consequently there is no excuse for an unhappy Christian. Let him seek the Comforter.

CHAPTER XI.

THE SPIRIT AS A REMINDER.

"And bring all things to your remembrance, whatsoever I have said unto you."—*John in his Gospel.*

1. THESE words instruct us touching another function and special action of the Holy Spirit which is of inestimable service to a fallen being, his influence *on the memory* in keeping the man alive to the great interests of his spiritual concerns. The reactionary effect of all positive sin on all the affections of the heart and all the powers of the mind constitutes, perhaps, the most remarkable, and certainly one of the most lamentable, of all the results of sin. Each sinful transient act leaves a permanent record and memorial of itself on the nature of the sinning agent. It deepens the inward depravity of the moral nature. It pollutes the fountain of moral energy more and more, and renders it more capable and certain of producing other transient acts of sin, each of which reacts in deepening the stain upon the soul. Thus there is an incessant mutual action and reaction going on between sin and depravity, leading to an endless increase of both. There is an awful reality in the phrase which describes every sinner as lost.

The effect of this depraved condition of the moral nature is displayed upon every faculty of the intellectual nature, not less' than upon the moral department of the soul itself. The affections of the heart exert an influence directly upon the perceptive faculties, and regulate the judgments which they form. This is the great source of errors in religion; they are always rooted in the disorders of the will, affecting the views of the understanding. The effect is not only misleading, but enfeebling on the general energy of the intellect, by affecting the justness of perception in each of its particular faculties. The very fact of its being misled shows the injury to its strength and its capacity of just discernment. That wide-spread ignorance and blindness of understanding which appears in the shocking and almost incredible degradation of barbarous tribes of the human race is the outcome of long periods of unrestrained moral iniquities. The whole structure of the mental nature in man has suffered and will always suffer from the effects of sin.

The faculty of memory has not escaped this desolating influence. It has shared conspicuously in it; it has become treacherous in receiving and holding the principles of duty and truth; it has become slackened and limp in its grasp upon religious ideas and impressions. It is easy to forget God. Impressions made by the truth are like the morning cloud and the early dew. Thoughts of eternity, responsibility, sin, and the awful issues of transgression are soon forgotten. This is just as true of memories, strong and vigorous, as it is of feebler specimens of the faculty. The same cause operates the same effect. That is directly due in all cases to the feelings of the heart. The feelings are opposed, intensely opposed, to the entertainment of these conceptions. Men remember God and are troubled, and in seeking relief from the trouble, the only relief which seems practicable, at least the only one which seems agreeable, is to make war on memory and to endeavor to forget. This state of reluctance in the will to entertain thoughts made unpleasing by the consciousness of guilt works out its relief and also its retribution upon this all-important faculty of the mind. Memory not only yields up its unpleasant presentments, but becomes less and less capable of making them; it grows incompetent on its spiritual side; it becomes feeble and treacherous of spiritual impressions. Hence line upon line, and precept upon precept is necessary to give truth a chance to do its work; and when much resistance is made, and the soul becomes skilful from long practice in evading the influence and in erasing the impressions of the truth, neither the line upon line nor the most vivid and powerful representations will make any more impression than writing on water, or wounding the invisible air with the stroke of a sabre. The final stage is when Ephraim is let alone altogether; the memory becomes utterly incompetent to retain any impression of religious ideas, and the great gospel of grace is as completely blotted out, so far as that unhappy mind is concerned, as if every page of the Bible had become blank, and God had recalled the offers of his mercy. Such a soul has by an elaborate and diligently sustained effort made itself a heathen; the most barbarous idolater in all heathendom is not more completely without the gospel of grace.

The awful danger of these effects of sin upon the memory springs from the fact that *the truth* is the necessary instrument both in the conversion of the sinner and in the sanctification of the saint. The one is begotten to spiritual life by the gospel; the other is sanctified by the truth. Consequently, whoever neglects the truth discounts his own hope of salvation. Whatever Christian seeks for growth and comfort, and neglects to keep his mind busy and imbued with the truth, is following a visionary hope. He who diligently endeavors to erase the impression of the truth from his mind is striving with special energy to blot out his own hope of salvation. He is like the lunatic drawing a keen razor across the jugular vein to see how close he can cut and not kill. Memory as the faculty by which truth is received from the understanding to serve all the high purposes of truth, carries heaven and hell in its grasp. It carries all the influences of the glorious gospel; all the chances of salvation to a sinner; all the opportunities of growth and comfort to a Christian; all the benefits of the work of Christ and the offices of the Holy Spirit; all the interests of the church; all the usefulness of life; all the consolations of death; all the experiences of grace; all the comfort of affliction; all success in the spiritual warfare; all the issues of the endless state beyond the grave; memory carries all these immeasurable interests because it carries or refuses to carry the truth which conditions and controls them. It is a lesson which can never be learned too soon, or fixed in a conviction too powerful, that while we are dependent on the efficacious grace of God in the whole matter of salvation, we are equally dependent on the active and constant handling of the truth, because the Spirit does his work through the truth as his instrument. Our energy and fidelity are provided for and called into play at every step and in every process of the redemption of grace, from the beginning to the triumphant conclusion within the gates of heaven, as well as the grace which alone can make that energy effectual.

The necessity and the value of the Holy Spirit in the office set forth in the text of this chapter is manifest. His relation to the sin-weakened memory is here brought to view, and suggests to our investigation the modes in which his healing influence on the injured faculty is exerted, and the inexpressible benefits determined by it.

1. The first great benefit which the Holy Spirit achieved for the church and the world, both for the regenerate and unregenerate human soul, by his work on the human memory, was displayed in the construction of the Scriptures. No doubt the words of the text had primary reference to the recall of all that Jesus had spoken and taught in the presence of the twelve apostles. But for his supernatural control of their memories much that Jesus had said would never have been reported at all; much would have been misrepresented with a perfect integrity of purpose; much would have been colored and changed by unconscious prepossessions; and all would have been defective, not only in certainty, but in authority. But it was too wisely ordered for such hazards to

be encountered. The Holy Spirit was put in charge of the memories of those commissioned to record the teachings of the Nazarene, and thus to furnish so much of the great permanent standards of the Christian system as the human memory was to be concerned in supplying. They wrote as they were moved by the Holy Ghost, and the church has the assurance in this part of the relation of the Spirit to the human memory that all of our Lord's personal history, instructions, and works, which were needful to the salvation of the world, have been wisely selected and reliably transmitted. He brought to memory in the chosen writers all that infinite wisdom selected to be recorded; he gave a perfect guarantee against error in misapprehension and misstatement; he stamped the whole with the divine authority by his own relation to the record. One grand department of his work of inspiration was in his influence upon memory; and if there is any value in the Scriptures; any guidance for the sinner; any gracious effect on the heart of the saint; any consolation in the glad tidings of great joy, it is due in an important measure to the relation of the Holy Spirit to the faculty of memory. As we know that these things were written that men might believe in Jesus, and believing, have life through his name, we can see in this one effect of the Spirit's power over memory a benefit absolutely beyond any adequate esteem.

2. But this relation of the Spirit to human memory comes nearer to the person of every man, and exerts a more direct and personal influence for his benefit. To this it is due that the sinner is kept at all awake to his spiritual relations and interests. To this it is due that the moral nature of the heathen is kept sufficiently alive to allow of the influence of the moral conceptions necessary to the constitution of civil society, and the discharge of its functions. It is due to this that any thought or concern for his own personal relations to God, for the forgiveness of his sins, or for his interest in

the great salvation, ever makes any impression on any sinner under the preaching of the gospel, or ever abides for ever so transient a period in his mind. The thoughts are absorbed by the scenes and interests of this life. Any recognition of the fact of another life, or of the principles which will control well-being to man in passing into it, is the result of some act of memory, or some suggestion to the understanding from without. For the most part, so far as these ideas are concerned, in the vast bulk of mankind memory is practically paralyzed. Perhaps the most extraordinary manifestation of this strange scene of human existence here in the world, as it appears to the intelligences of the sphere of existence beyond it, is the amazing insensibility of the teeming and energetic masses of mankind to what is before them. There is a wonderful force and precision in the Scripture teaching which represents men as *asleep;* the ordinary states of consciousness very strongly resemble the physical condition of somnambulism. To the angels of God, and especially to the disembodied spirits of men who have themselves passed from under the shadows and the stupor into the clear light beyond, this state of the memory is the wonder of wonders. For this insensibility is in a great degree due to the state of the memory, although that is itself due to other influences below it. The facts of the case are all admitted; death is fully recognized as the separation of soul and body, and a transfer into another state of conscious existence; but there is a prevailing insensibility to the facts; they do not abide in the mind, or disclose the power that is in them. If this state of things is not broken up it will, of course, continue to the end, and induce all the fatal consequences attached to the folly. Men are truly in a deep sleep so far as these great interests are concerned. Rouse them up by ever so eager and passionate a remonstrance, and they sink back at once into the same stupor. Nay, rouse them to a degree that will make them solicitous and lead them to some good measure of activity, and unless the same gracious Spirit who first broke their slumber shall continue to maintain the impression, it will only require a very brief contact with the living interests of this world to sweep it away, and the great interests of the future will again fade out of sight. No lesson is more important to be learned by the sin-sick and stupefied souls of men than this: that all their impressions of spiritual things, no matter how vivid and stimulating to hope, fear and activity they may be, are absolutely dependent on the influences of the Holy Spirit to keep them alive and operative in the mind. What is true in this respect of the sinner before regeneration is in its measure true of the soul after regeneration. The Holy Paraclete must keep his watchful hand on the springs of memory at every stage of the process of sanctification through the truth, or the memory will lapse and discharge its precious freight, on a scale of completeness measured exactly by the energy of the Spirit's influence on the faculty. No human wit or watchfulness can, in its own strength, resist the evasive influences which are brought to bear to rob the soul of the truth which leads to life.

3. These original movements in the series of acts by which the Holy Spirit leads from spiritual death to spiritual life, are mediated through that part of the truth called the law. He takes of that part of the things of Christ and shows the sinner his *danger*. He has been before instructed as to the peril which his sin has superinduced. He does not question the fact; for he is aware that God in nature, as well as in Scripture, imposes penalties for violated law; but he is in a condition of entire forgetfulness of a part of the fact which he theoretically admits, and that is the *urgency* of the admitted peril. When the Spirit brings that to mind it becomes impossible for him to remain in the same state of cheerful indifference. His sleep is broken; he is *awakened*,

to use the technical term employed to describe this rousing of the perceptions and memory, to the full significance of a fact which was both known and acknowledged before. Then the value of the Spirit's influence on the memory gives another proof of its worth. The soul had been fully instructed that sin not only involved the sinner in danger, but in *criminality*, and made him guilty in the sense of blameworthiness as well as of exposure. But this sort of knowledge of the iniquity of sin made no impression; he did not see or care for it. Nay, it is possible, and frequently the case in point of fact, that the sense of danger may exist, and produce only feelings of rage against God, because there is no concurrent sense of deserving to be in danger. The memory of this part of the truth is in abeyance. But as the Spirit quickens the memory to recall, and the understanding to grasp, this feature of the case, a new modification of feeling comes into play. The Spirit takes of the penalties of the law to awaken to danger; he takes of the precept, the excellent substance and matter of the law, to produce intuitions of the nature of sin. The worth of the lesson in both cannot be fully conceived. Forgetfulness of the divine law will be followed in both saint and sinner by consequences eminently disastrous. It leads to the obscuring, and thus to the neglect of duty; it leads to false moral ideas touching both right and wrong; it leads to false principles impelling to action, and to false rules for guiding it; it leads to incompetent and false views of sin, and thus to false repentance, or prevents it altogether; it leads to false conceptions of the divine authority, and obscures the supreme nature of all his claims Forgetfulness of obligation leads to every species of transgression. An influence on the memory which will keep it at all alive to the significance and the claims of the divine law is immeasurably valuable to a being whose mental states tend perpetually towards insensibility and stupor.

4. This same tendency continues to exist to a greater or

less degree in the regenerate soul. It is one of the effects of sin, and sin, though its power is broken by regenerating grace, still abides in the soul, and exerts a degree of all its tendencies as before. There is a conflict at once begun, which never ceases until the final triumph of the law of grace over the law of sin. From the deadly influence of this re-mainder of indwelling sin upon the memory of the Christian soul, springs a large proportion of his spiritual trials and his spiritual disasters. From the Spirit's influence on the memory springs a large proportion of his spiritual comforts and his spiritual usefulness. As the Holy Ghost leads the awakened and convicted sinner forward, he takes of the sav-ing offices, work, and love of Christ, and shows them to the agitated soul. Then he receives and rests upon the Saviour for salvation. He is full of peace; Christ is at last under-stood and trusted; joy animates the discharge of duty, and nerves the struggle with sin. The plan of salvation shines glorious in its simplicity and complete adaptations. Faith appears so easy and so effective. This happy frame con-tinues for a time; but, alas! it soon passes; and now the whole scene is changed. All becomes obscure and difficult. Faith becomes as much of a mystery as before it revealed its power in the heart. The tried soul wonders what has be-come of all its sweet views, and its blest contentment. In vain the effort to recall them; but in that dear shape in which it once appeared no struggle can bring it back.

> What peaceful hours I once enjoyed!
> How sweet their memory still!
> But they have left an aching void
> The world can never fill.

But now let the Holy Spirit touch the springs of memory with an effective touch, and these blessed things of Christ are restored again. They had vanished through some dis-astrous change in the affections; from some neglect, from some positive faultiness; and the return comes through the

Spirit's touch, memory, and the powers allied with it; or sometimes this process may be reversed, and the heart quickened by new views of the truth as it is in Jesus; new in some aspects, though familiar in others. The touch of the Spirit on the memory often brings back melting and rejoicing views of the great High Priest, the Prophet, and King of the covenant. When the real significance of the priesthood of Christ is opened up by the clear shining of the Holy Ghost on some clear exposition of the power of his blood, the efficacy of his priestly prayers, and the subduing charm of his priestly tenderness towards sinners, then the way of escape unseals its sufficiency so as to banish every fear, and fill the heart with joy. The very memory of such an apprehension of the truth is sweet and full of comfort long after it has passed away in the smoke and strife of many a succeeding battle. David remembered the hill Mizar as the scene of some such rich experience. But the actual restoration of them to the full experience of the heart and memory is unsurpassed in consoling power. It is no small enhancement of the Spirit's value to the Christian soul that he can at will retouch these memories of a favored past, and cause them to renew in a favored present the joy of bygone grace. He can take of all the gracious things of Christ and show them unto us, either by giving us new views of the old glory, or by bringing them back upon the memory in all the charm of their original delight. He thus sometimes brings back in a time of conflict or deep distress some particular truth, some promise, some warning, some passage of Scripture just suited to the emergency. The word of God is the sword of the Spirit; the weapon by which he makes war on all kinds of spiritual evil. A memory stored with the words of Holy Writ is an arsenal well stocked with the arms of the holy warfare. While it would be presumption to expect the Holy Ghost to give any new revelation for the benefit of any one of his saints, however beloved, it is not presumption, but imperative duty, to expect and seek him to quicken memory, and bring up out of its mysterious depths some truth of the word he has already given, suited to an emergency of sorrow or temptation. He may be appealed to to rouse the memory of sweet promises, when the shades of death are thickening over a dying saint, or when a dread emergency is lifting its horrid head across the pathway of a living saint. The offices of the Spirit himself are very gracious and very powerful; these, too, are subject to his quickening influences on our dull apprehensions. When he said that he would not speak of himself, we have already seen he did not mean to declare he would not teach anything at all of himself, either in the Scriptures or in the hearts of his people. He has said enough of his own loving spirit and gracious offices to awaken intense gratitude in those who apprehend his grace. The very riches and vehement glory of that grace are enough to oppress our feeble powers of conceiving and retaining them. But he can show us his glory in proportions suited to our capacity; and we all might be far wealthier than we are in these rich apprehensions of the love of the Spirit if we would set ourselves to seek his gifts more freely. He can take of his own glorious grace, as well as of the unsearchable riches of Christ and the father-hood of the eternal Father, and show unto us many a hidden mine of infinite grace in each and all of them.

The spirit of prayer is also powerfully controlled by the influence of the Spirit upon the memory. It is often amazing to see how quickly our own apprehensions of our own abiding spiritual necessities fade out from our minds. A keen state of eager yearning will sometimes seem to vanish in an hour. Deep feeling of spiritual destitution will quickly give way to a sort of despairing hardness. Ardent solicitude for others, longings for the well-being of the church, and for the salvation of sinners, will give way like the fast-changing colors of a sunset. The feeling of obligation, as well as the desire to pray for others, for the spread of the kingdom, for the revival of religion in a particular community, or the salvation of particular persons, is subject to this rapid and portentous vicissitude. Our forgetfulness of such things would soon become dangerously complete if it were not for the work of the Spirit as a reminder. He keeps the regenerate soul alive to its own necessities and its duties, far enough as to secure something like habitual solicitude to be at peace with God, the habitual use of the means of grace, and the reputable discharge of appointed duties. The point in which his gracious influence upon memory allows of great advancement, subject largely to the saint's own desires and faithful efforts, is in this relation between his sympathies and the wants of others. He can quicken this habitual, but low-toned and comparatively inactive recollection of the spiritual wants of others into a spirit of keen appreciation, leading to intense desire and to energy of action. Such an influence would be an incalculable blessing to the regenerate soul itself, and to all the interests which can be affected by his faith, his prayers, and his active labor—a blessing which would strongly illustrate the value of the Spirit as a reminder. Without it no sinner would ever know the saving force of the truth he has learned, never appreciate danger or remedy, never be able to form a just judgment of the value of the life that now is compared with the value of that which is to come; never comprehend his position under the law and government of God, nor under his grace. Without it the Christian, though once acquainted with his necessities, would soon lose sight of them. Though once made to rejoice in the apprehension of Christ as a Saviour, he would soon lose the sweetness and joy of that glorious vision. The whole gospel would die out of the apprehension of the church; the very intellectual knowledge of Christian truth would perish, as more than one grand melancholy example in its history has proved. The doctrines of the covenant would lose their priceless meaning; prayer would vanish into a thin, unreal observance; God himself would pass into a mere abstraction; the promises would become blank checks in invisible writing, which no flame of fire, no cunning of artful science, could restore to vision. The glorious gospel would be turned into a legendary tale, and the golden gates of the eternal city, far-shining in the distant clouds, would die before the longing eyes of the saints, under the rushing darkness of despairing hope, like the rubied clouds on the vault of evening perish under the gray shadows of the fast-coming night.

But the truth stands; it will not perish from the view of a dying world. The Spirit will keep all the precious words of the Redeemer in remembrance. This gracious pledge was not fulfilled and then antiquated and thrown out of service when the writers of the sacred books had, under the hand of the Holy Ghost, recalled the words and acts of the Messiah, and fixed them in an imperishable record. That pledge is still a working truth for the encouragement of every sinner and for the comfort of every saint. To the one he can still bring back the healthful knowledge of his sin in order that he may repent, and still bestow the healthful knowledge of the way of life that he may believe. To the other he can renew all their past experiences of grace, and lead them forward to still richer and higher realizations of the great salvation. He can restore and vivify the spirit of faith and the spirit of prayer. He can illumine the promises until they glow with a richer wealth than a king's ransom. He can make and keep the watchful soul of a believer all alive to its duties and its dangers, its wants and its resources, its privileges and its endless glory. He can do a mighty work for a lost world and a struggling church by bringing into a living remembrance all the words the great Giver of eternal life has spoken, and all the great deeds he has done.

CHAPTER XII.

THE LOVE OF THE SPIRIT.

"Now I beseech you, brethren, for the Lord Jesus Christ's sake, and for the love of the Spirit, that ye strive together with me in your prayers to God for me."—*Paul to the Romans.*

THE absolute dependence of a sinner for regeneration, and of the regenerate soul for the exercise, the comfort, and the availability of his regenerate gifts, on the influences of the Holy Ghost, will be taken as something of a discouragement unless guarded from misapprehension of the real truth involved in the case. The sinner frequently makes it an excuse for his idleness, and his refusal to use the means of grace. It is often cited by the enemies of the evangelical faith of Christians, as an argument against the doctrine of grace, that it cuts the nerves of energy and logically discounts the value of all human effort. But this objection in the mouth of a sinner only lies in his mind so long as his view of his own necessities is dull and incompetent. Just let his mind wake up to the real nature of the facts in the case; let him realize the peril of his position; and he will no longer make his dependence on the Spirit an excuse for inaction. Nay, more, just in proportion as his own efforts fail to give him relief, and he feels his need of help, he will only be all the more solicitous to gain any help he can find. He then finds out that his dependence on the Spirit, so far from warranting his inactivity, was the very thing to rouse him to action by placing help in his reach when his own exertions had failed. The difference in the matter is, that in the first case he did not understand his dependence, nor realize his own infirmity, and in the advanced portion of his experience he did fully comprehend both. The objection in the lips of a speculative opponent of the doctrine of grace springs from the same root—the ignorance of the real necessities of a sinful soul. When he denies the dependence of such a soul on the influences of the Spirit, he consistently denies the actual ruin of a fallen moral nature. As long as this is done, no matter by whom or on what pretext, there is no prospect of a gospel salvation.

The same feeling is sometimes found measurably discouraging the Christian. Whenever it does, it is due to careless living, and the consequent darkening of the gospel ideas before eyes dimmed by sin. The influence of the Spirit is the very provision made in the covenant to give success to prayer, to develop the whole series of the regenerate graces, and to unseal the gladness and comfort of the gospel; and, therefore, instead of being a discouragement to the feeble or back-slidden Christian, is the very thing which warrants him to hope, and animates him to energy in seeking for the restoration of his peace. It is equally advantageous to the eager and watchful Christian, yearning after stronger graces and more assured hope; for if the Spirit was not available for his help in seeking these ends, it would be vain to desire or expect them. To break down all this feeling of discouragement, and to replace it by the feeling properly excited by the offices of the Holy Ghost, we design to open one single consideration, which in itself alone is sufficient to accomplish this purpose, and to lead both the regenerate and the unregenerate soul to find encouragement instead of discouragement in their dependence on the Holy Ghost. We pass by the consideration of the official work assigned to him in the economy of redemption, and his zeal for the glory of the Godhead; we pass all references to his power or his faithfulness, although all these are powerful inducements to confide in him. We simply fix attention on *the love of the Spirit;* his infinite and tender *personal affections* towards the sinners of the human race; his great pity and compassion towards the victims of their sin; his delight in his work of bringing them to pardon, to peace, to the rest of heaven, and to the whole manifestation of the unsearchable riches, the freedom, and the resolute tenacity of his grace towards them.

1. Love is the emphatic attribute of God; it is that quality in his character which under one of its manifestations leads him to distribute good, not for any increase to his own blessedness, already perfect, but simply to widen the range of happiness in other beings beside himself. This attribute is so masterly an element in his infinitely complete being that it defines his nature and gives him his name, "*God is love.*" It was this which prompted him to create; it was, at least, one of his ends; it is this that regulates his whole plan of creation, his whole policy of administration. Like all his other attributes, it is literally infinite in its strength, in its tenderness, in its patience, in its bounteous fertility, in its eagerness to bless. The large-hearted spirit of a benevolent man is a noble quality. The love in the heart of a great angel is a still higher form of the sweet and magnanimous feeling. As you rise in the conception of intellectual and moral being, this quality, an essential constituent of moral excellence, expands proportionally on the view. But in God it exists in the highest degree it can possibly reach; love cannot exist, nor any other conceivable excellence, in a higher or more perfect form than it exists in God; in him it is literally infinite. This lovely quality in him overpasses every conceivable or possible modification of it in any other being, actual or possible, as far as the infinite passes beyond the finite. God is love, and the Spirit is God; and our first step in the effort to form some notion of the love of the Spirit places us face to face with the fact that love in its illimitable and divine degree is his intrinsic, essential, and unchangeable attribute.

2. The love of God takes on its most wonderful and peculiar form in its application to *sinners*. He is infinitely holy;

a sinner is a being morally polluted. To him this pollution
is an essential horror and disgust. He is infinitely just; a
sinner as a breaker of law is criminal, a being on whom
justice has a claim, a claim to punish his criminal conduct;
and God is bound by eternal rightness to do justice, no
matter what justice may demand. Yet the loving-kindness
of the just and holy one goes out upon sinners. The
impulse is altogether what the impulse of love always is, to
do them good. The instinctive feeling which springs up in
a sinning soul is dread of God, because he is just, a being
whose judgment must be graduated by the nature of the fact
before him, and who must therefore seek to requite an evil
with a result naturally and justly answerable to it. Such a
result is necessarily the opposite of a benefit to the transgressor. This seems to present an issue on which a collision
ensues between his love seeking a benefit to the sinner and
his justice prohibiting it. But when the love of God takes
on that peculiar modification which is called *grace*, the very
thing which distinguishes it from every other modification of
divine benignity is *sin*. How it could be brought into harmony with the claims of justice and holiness is the great
wonder in the divine nature. This is that, as then, unknown
and inconceivable mystery in the just and holy one, whose
sudden display in the day of Adam's fall confounded the
murderous archangel, and filled all heaven with wonder and
delight. That God should love sinners and let loose on
them all the tides of that infinite quality in his nature—on
those who were an offence to his holiness, and the objects of
his inflexibly righteous and true justice—this was the mystery
of mysteries. Yet it was done, and it was so done that no
claim of justice was sacrificed, no demand of holiness failed
of full contentment. The redemption from the claims of justice
was committed to the love of the Son; and we know how a
dying Saviour redeemed us from the curse of the law, by being
made a curse for us. The redemption from the inward power

and pollution of sin in the soul was committed to the love of the Spirit. The love of the Father shone glorious in the proposal and contrivance of the whole wondrous plan. The grand sum of all the marvelous policy was this wonderful assurance to sinners of the human family, that the *love* of the whole Godhead, the love of the Father, the love of the Son, and the love of Spirit, *the whole energy of an infinite attribute of love*, was now turned loose, free from every restraint, armed with infinite power, and fully supported by infinite holiness, justice, and truth, to walk all the wards of the sin-sick soul, to save sinners at its own will. The love of the Son, the Paraclete for sin, confronts* the miseries of guilt; the love of the Spirit, the Paraclete for all inward wants, confronts all the weakness and the wickedness in the soul. If, therefore, any sinner, seeking for peace and assured safety, is discouraged by the strength of the evil within him, and is dreaming of first accomplishing some preliminary purification within himself ere he will be fit to ground any appeal for help, let him endeavor to take in the meaning of the offices and the loving-tenderness of the Holy Spirit, who has charge of that work. It is only necessary to appeal to his power as the agent of the royal Saviour. If, therefore, any discouraged Christian, oppressed by conscious sins; by unbelief; by a hard heart; by a quick temper; by an unmastered over-eagerness after worldly good; by *any sin*, is yet anxious to overcome these faults, let him not dream that he must wait to get the better of them before he applies for the grace of the Spirit; let him come at once for the grace to overcome them. If any eager Christian soul, sick of the infirmities, the weak graces, the mutilated comforts, the ineffective prayers, the whole imperfect service of his low and feeble spiritual development, desires to attain unto better things, let him at once renew his courage, and appeal to the Comforter. His infinite and most tender love has been put in charge of

---

* 1 John ii. 1.

all the inward work needful to the healing of a sinful soul.

3. The love of the Spirit is displayed in a more or less effective way, literally *upon all sinners* in restraining the natural growth of their depravity and in thus limiting the desolating effects of it. He exerts a restraint upon every heathen soul, sufficient at least to preserve the moral element in human nature from being utterly eclipsed, and to make society, civilization, domestic life, and civil law possible. Sin is a powerful energy; it works towards all its natural results with a swift, relentless determination. It corrupts and breaks the force of the instinctive moral sentiments; it inflames the passions; it pollutes the whole nature of the sinning actor. Through this evil influence on himself it affects all the relations of the man—his social, domestic, business, and political relations. A certain amount of good moral sentiments, a sense of moral obligation, a perception of truth, honor, and justice, are necessary to bind the social structure together and make it workable, to make homes possible and trade possible, and all the interchanges and connections between men possible. But for the secret restraints of the Holy Spirit sin would have long ago broken up all human associations, and not only ruined civilization, but swept the human race from the face of the earth in the torrents of their own vices and crimes. To the love of the Spirit it is due that any man enjoys every benefit, every joy, every right, every comfort which the old and vast heathen peoples have ever possessed. To it it is due that there is such a thing as a respectable man, a being with any effective moral ideas, to be found anywhere. He alone prevents the utter depravation and ruin of the moral element in human nature, and preserves the mighty interests which are conditioned upon its preservation in some sufficient degree of serviceable working order.

4. The love of the Spirit is still more wonderfully displayed in his dealings *with sinners generally under the gospel*

dispensation. The two great agencies in the conversion of sinners are, *the truth* revealed in the gospel, and the concurrent influences of the Holy Spirit. The truth alone is powerless to save; the Spirit, as a rule, only operates in connection with the truth. But wherever the truth comes the Spirit comes. Wherever the truth is neglected or repudiated the Spirit ceases to strive. But on whatever ear the truth falls the Spirit makes his way into the conscience and the heart. If he ever suspends his influence in connection with the truth, it is because the truth has been abused, and his own incitements to obey it have been presumptuously resisted. The glad tidings never fell on the ear of harlot, or gambler, or thief, or murderer, that the Holy Spirit did not enter, or endeavor to enter, the darkened and crime-haunted heart. He is always resisted, met at the threshold and rudely rebuffed. Satan and his satellites, viewless and unsuspected, are always leading on the unholy soul, quickening its evil impulses, stimulating its passions, obscuring the influence of healthful views, laying snares for the willing feet, mocking at suggestions of danger. Gaily the victim advances, seeing nothing but pleasant things in his lawless career. But the loving Spirit steps across his path, and lays his gentle hand on the deluded wanderer. Instantly blows are struck at him. The tempting angels put forth all their skill and cunning. The poor foolish lover of his own wild will pulls back from the loving hand of the Deliverer. But he will not yield; he makes his way in; and there, amid the darkness and the stench of excited carnal passions, his resolute tenderness, for days, and weeks, and months, and sometimes for years together, struggles for a foothold. Sometimes he will yield and go his way; sometimes to return and renew the conflict; and only at the last will he take his final flight, and abandon Ephraim to his idols. What a scene is this conflict of the Holy Spirit with the unholy passions of a human heart and the watchful angels of the abyss! What

wickedness on one side; what grace on the other! What
infinite love; what sweet pity; what eager compassion; what
heroic patience; what resolute fortitude; what divine loving-
kindness, does the love of the Spirit yield in this strife with
and for an unconverted sinner! Yet this he shows in greater
or less degree to every sinner to whom the gospel message
comes. He shows it even to those who, he knows, will fight
him to the bitter end. He shows the infinite love of his sweet
compassion, not only to those who will yield to him, but to
those who will go on in their sins, and down into the pit at
last. No words can tell the tale of the love of the Spirit,
even to the most unholy and reckless of disobedient men.

5. But the love of the Spirit takes on its sweetest and
most charming form in his dealings with those whom he
resolves to regenerate and save. All without exception resist
him; some he abandons to their own devices after a long
and desperate conflict; but some he determines to conquer.
Not because they are better or more worthy, but solely because of his own sovereign and distinguishing grace, because
for reasons in his own wise and sovereign counsels his love
burns for them into a higher and an intenser flame! He
puts forth his strength; he rouses their fears, and intensifies
their convictions of their sin until resistance is overmastered.
He teaches them to pray in passionate earnestness; he makes
them keenly desire his aid now, and to find the way to
Christ. He gives them experimental knowledge of their own
perversity, blindness, hardness of heart, and their helplessness in the dreadful strait. He keeps them under lights
which reveal the delusions under which they have hitherto
lived and acted. He overwhelms them by such a consciousness of their guilt, danger, and need of a Saviour, as to prepare them to appreciate the deliverance and the Deliverer
offered to them. He breaks down all their self-righteous
excuses. He then makes plain the way of salvation; he
leads them to Jesus; he gives them the faith which is the fruit

of the Spirit, and they pass within the muniments of the covenant of life. This act of regeneration is the first step in this peculiar manifestation of the love of the Spirit to the saints. Now comes the highest and most impressive of all its wonderful displays. It is called the *indwelling* of the Holy Ghost. It is always shown to every regenerate soul; it is begun in the act of regeneration which opens the way to his permanent occupation of the soul now pledged to eternal life by the act of faith in the Saviour. Until then his entry into the unholy heart, and his contact with all its pollutions, has been at will, not under the bond of any covenant engagement, most freely entered, most binding when made. He was free to leave as he was to enter before the terms of mercy were closed. The offer is, Believe, and thou shalt be saved; and when the regenerate soul puts forth the act of faith the covenant is closed, and that happy spirit stands in new and invincible relations with the Father, the Son, and the Holy Ghost. The promise to faith is a pledge of an absolute salvation, a salvation from sin as well as from its consequences. Its sacred assurance is, *Sin shall not have dominion over you.* This is not a pledge that all sin shall be destroyed at once and the soul made perfectly holy. If that were so, there would be no place for the peculiar display of the love of the Spirit to the saints; for he would then have a holy and a pleasant place to occupy. The promise secures a full conquest over all sin in the end, but only that sin shall not be master in the progress towards the end. Sin shall not have dominion; but this implies that sin shall still have a standing, and exert an influence, until the end of the natural life puts a period to the presence and the mischiefs of moral evil.

It will be impossible for us to appreciate suitably the unsearchable love of the Holy Spirit as involved in his indwelling in the saints, until we can form some conception of the state of a regenerate soul, in which the law of grace in the mind is perpetually confronted by the law of sin in the members. It is a scene of conflict, not of peace; a scene of evil as well as good, for the grace given is living grace, and the remaining sin is real sin, a power broken, but not destroyed; weakened, but still formidable; wounded, but still capable of long and desperate strife even against the Spirit of the living God. Into that chequered scene in every regenerate heart that holy agent enters to make good the pledge of the covenant, sin shall not have the mastery. He enters it not as a wayfarer who turneth to tarry but a night. He enters it to dwell there; he enters it as his home; he enters it as his workshop, the chosen place where his wonderful achievements are to be accomplished. He enters it under a covenant promise, more durable than the everlasting hills, to stay there and never to abandon it, until his work is done and the covenant with the believer is fulfilled. If he left, all would be undone. But the bond and security of his holding his place is the strongest that can be conceived; the faithfulness and the pledged veracity and honor of the whole Godhood, Father, Son, and Spirit. His love and zeal rejoice to confirm the grand guarantees of the covenant and the divine integrity. The very throne and life of the sovereign and immortal God stand not on a firmer basis, or under a more absolute assurance, than the permanence of the Spirit's indwelling in the regenerate human heart. But to appreciate the love, the faithfulness, and the delight of the Spirit in his work, we must comprehend the place where he dwells, and the nature of his activity in it. As already said, the power of sin is broken, but the evil still abides. It is there, with all the elements and particular evils which sin involves, just as it was before. The lusts of the eye and the pride of life still linger, weakened, but not destroyed; the new law is infused, a new energy is created in opposition to these evils, and a perpetual collision is inaugurated. But sin is still there, and sin is an infinite offence to a holy being, even when lying quiet and inactive; it is far more so when stirred into activity. Just as a foul pool shows nauseous to sight, and emits its odors slowly and faintly when in repose, but becomes far more offensive to eye and nostril when stirred out of its stillness. The Holy Spirit goes into a regenerate heart to dwell in the midst of sin, in habitual presence, and often in fierce activity. The Scripture symbols of a sinful heart are absolutely fearful: darkness, stony hardness, a cage of unclean birds, a den of serpents, a lonely cottage in the stillness of a desert, within whose swept and garnished walls, eight devils, supreme in wickedness, are holding an infernal revel, and making the midnight wilderness hideous with their appalling and malicious glee. This is the home of the Holy Spirit. By his side within the dreadful walls that "new man" he has created in Christ Jesus stands confronting the awful array in the armed attitude of watchful war—war to the belt-knife. See the pale, resolute face of the spiritual man, crossed often by pangs of mortal fear, or wrenched with agony at some sly serpent bite, or pierced by some devil's poisoned arrow or fiery dart, or anon stupefied and stiffened by some foul blast of air, or the touch of some foul wing, as the unclean birds slip through the shadows. Ah! can he win; can he come safe out of such a scene? Look at the grand figure at his side. The Spirit of the living God is dwelling with him and is in him; he is on guard. He is sitting in the fixed posture of one who has come to stay. He kindles a gentle light, which qualifies the murky darkness, and shows the lurking figures of the hostile forces. His glorious face beams with serene peace, and kindles with infinite loving tenderness, as he supplies all needed strength and comfort to the tried and wearied soldier at his side. Now and then his mighty hand is stretched forth, and a stroke of sword or hammer falls on some over-insolent intruder, and at the touch the devils crouch and whine, the ser-

pents writhe and twist, and the foul birds droop wing or
slumber.   Now and then he pours a fresher and a stronger
grant of grace into his weary charge, and then songs in the
night ring cheerily in the beleaguered fortress of the regenerate soul.   So it goes until the end; but the victory
is assured by the presence of the divine indwelling Spirit.
In one sense his perils are great; in another his safety is
absolute.   In one sense his trials are awful; in another his
blessedness is unspeakable.   His danger is in himself; for
these vultures, serpents, and devils, which the poverty of
human thought and words compel us to represent as in him,
but distinct from him, are his own unholy energies and passions.   His safety is in the blood and righteousness of Jesus,
in the fatherhood and faithfulness of the Father, and in the
presence and love of the Holy Ghost.   But this scene of the
Spirit on guard in a regenerate heart compels the question,
if the righteous scarcely be saved, where shall the ungodly
and sinner appear?   The same awful company are in his
heart, but no indwelling Spirit of grace is found there to
oppose and subdue the deadly mischief.   The answer to the
question asked can only be, they will appear the ruined
victims of the infernal garrison; they will appear on the left
hand of the judgment throne; they will appear in the long
line of the devil's captives, moving down to the iron gates;
they will appear in the final scene riding on the waves of the
lake of fire; for they have grieved and repelled the Holy
Spirit, and he did not dwell in them.   But his victorious
love will finally exterminate the birds, and serpents, and
devils of an unholy heart, and the soul, delivered by the
love of the Spirit, will appear on the right hand of the
Judge, on the highway to the gates of pearl, in the long
procession of the King's ransomed, and on the sweet fields
by the river of life forever.   All their fitness for this high
destiny will be due to the love of the Spirit; their title to
it, to the love of the Son; their opportunity for gaining both

title and fitness, to the love of the Father. Salvation is all of grace.

6. The love of the Spirit is also powerfully illustrated by that *delight* in all his official work, in all its general and special acts in the regenerate soul, which is assured by that love itself. Love delights in its own exercises and its own offices. It would seem that such a constant dwelling in such a devil-haunted cottage in a wilderness, as we have just described, might afford room for the exhibition of the faithfulness and power of the Holy Spirit, but could hardly allow of his finding any delight in it. Perhaps this will account for the general recognition of the fidelity and strength of the Spirit, and the equally general scanty recognition of his love, the unspeakable tenderness and freedom of his grace.* But we are emphatically assured of his love; and this certifies that his *delight* in fulfilling the will and counsel of the Godhead in his work in the saints is fully equal to the delight which the Son found in doing his part, and the Father in his. Although the Holy Comforter finds an amount of offence, which no mortal mind can conceive, in the pollutions of a soul only partially purified, yet, in spite of all, his loving heart finds an infinite complacency and delight in the work which he enters that heart to do. He is there on a mission of cleansing and healing; and he delights to do it. He is there to accomplish the grandest enterprise of the counsels of God; and he delights to accomplish it. He is there to defeat the malignant counsels of the kingdom of darkness; and he delights to do it. He is there to save millions of immortal spirits from an unimaginable ruin for eternal ages; and he glories in the mighty undertaking. He delights in the exercise of his glorious energies, in the indulgence of his infinite tenderness, in every part and specialty of his glorious office. He delights to awaken and arrest sinners as they are dancing along, devil-led, on the primrose path to the ever-

---

* Phillip of Maberly.

lasting bonfire. He delights in raising the dead soul to life by his regenerating grace, as Jesus delighted his own sad, loving heart in raising Lazarus, and in turning the sorrows of the Bethany home, which he loved so dearly, into songs of rejoicing. He delights in teaching the dim eyes of his children to see all the things of Christ. He rejoices to seal, anoint, testify, lead, intercede, and give the earnest of the Spirit. He delights in all his work. He is never idle; never reluctant; never churlish in doing it. He is the Comforter, and delights in comforting; he is the universal Paraclete of his people, and delights for them to call him to their side in any of their times of need.

The love of the Spirit gives the full assurance of the *absolute freedom and completeness of our access to the gracious influences of the Spirit.* It is just as free an access as we have to the unsearchable riches of the love and redemption work of the Saviour himself. The symbols of both are the wide, free winds of heaven, sweeping every inch of ground in a continent, stirring every leaf in the forests, and every blade of grass in the fields; and second, the water, covering two-thirds or more of the planet in its oceans, piercing every section with its running streams, every nook in wood or mountain with its springs and falling rains, and entering as a principal factor into the composition of well-nigh everything that exists—vegetable, mineral, or animal. These are the symbols of the love and free grace of the blessed Spirit. This love on his part stands side by side with the command of the Father, and the pleading love of the Son, and unites with these in giving the grand assurance to every needy sinner, and especially to every yearning Christian heart, touching that wide and welcome privilege they have to appeal for any grant of faith, hope, clear vision, holy affections, of guidance, strength, patience, love, comfort, for any grace they may need. No regenerate sinner need want for any comfort in life or death; no unregenerate sinner need stay in the peril or bond of his sin for a single hour, since we all have such free access to the power and the tender love of the Spirit. That love is so marked with every high and winning quality of love in its infinite and unsurpassable form; it is a love so distinguished by its tenderness, by its infinite sweetness, by its grand energy, by its absolute fidelity and trustworthiness, by its tender, unweariable patience, by its wise and resolute faithfulness to every interest entrusted to it, by its zeal and fervor, by its boundless power, by its delight in all its work, by its complacency in all its glorious results—that there is really no excuse for any poverty or slackness of either strength or comfort in the gifts of the Spirit. He is so necessary to us, to our trust in the Son, to our confidence in the Father, to our reliance on himself; he is so essential to our success in prayer, to our understanding and compliance with the terms of mercy, to the guarantees of our hope, to the soundness of our graces; he is so important to our safety in temptation, to our comfort in affliction, to our satisfaction in life, to our usefulness in service, to our support in death; in a word, so vast and absolute is our dependence on the influences of the Holy Ghost that we need every possible encouragement to go to him. That encouragement is given by this wonderful love of the Spirit in as complete a degree as need be hoped or desired. Infinite love, and infinite delight in his work, discount all fear of refusal in appealing for his grace.

CHAPTER XIII.

THE SPIRIT IN PUBLIC WORSHIP.

"For we are the circumcision, which worship God in the spirit, and rejoice in Christ Jesus, and have no confidence in the flesh."—*Paul to the Philippians.*

THE worship of God in private and in public, as it is prescribed in the Scriptures, requires our active attention always to the two grand divisions into which the service has been divided: the visible or tangible instruments to be used, and the effective power which is to be appealed to in the use of these instruments. In considering the worship of God and the surest means of benefit from it, it is necessary to recognize the outward ordinances as the only authorized method of our approaching him, and the only means by which we may expect his favor in benefits to ourselves. This dictates due care to have the ordinances as exactly conformed to the requirements of the law as it is possible to secure them. It is also indispensable to apprehend clearly, and then to act practically, on this knowledge of the correlated Scripture doctrine of the only agent and efficacious power by which the divinely-appointed ordinances can be made effectual. There can be no acceptable worship except in the use of those ordinances and actions in employing them which God himself has appointed. No man, or organized body of men, has a right to invent any action for the worship of God, and to challenge his blessing on the use of it. He would lay himself open to the cutting question, "Who hath required this at your hand, to tread my courts" therewith? Every earthly monarch claims the right to settle the etiquette of his own court, the dress and acts of homage and ceremony by which strangers and his own servants are to

391

approach the royal presence. To alter those prescriptions for others entirely different, or to make changes by addition or subtraction in the prescribed forms, would be considered an invasion of the king's right, and a personal affront to his majesty. Much more has the King of kings the right to order the etiquette of his court, and the acts by which he would be approached. His ordinances must be observed, as nearly as possible, according to his own prescriptions, without additions to or subtractions from them. But the teaching of the Scriptures is unequivocally clear, that even the ordinances appointed of God have no power in themselves alone to work the needful effects on the soul of the worshipper, unless accompanied by the efficacious influences of the Holy Spirit. The gospel must come, not in word only, but in demonstration of the Spirit and of power. Our present object, however, is not to illustrate the general doctrine of the relation of the Spirit to the ordinances of worship and the means of grace, but the particular doctrine of his relation to the public worship of God in the regular assemblies of the people for Sabbath service. The assertion of the text is, that one characteristic mark of a true believer is that he "worships God in the spirit." This includes all kinds of worship, whether secret, social, or public, whether in the use of prayer, or praise, or preaching, or sacraments, or any other ordinance. The presence and the exerted influence of the Spirit is essential to the right and profitable use of them all. The special presence of the Holy Ghost, then, in the public assemblies for divine worship, *is a fact* certified to us in the word of God. The expression used by our Lord in reference to the Holy Spirit, "he dwelleth with you and shall be in you," points to a distinction, which, perhaps, cannot be fully understood in its complete, actual application. But it evidently implies both a dwelling with and a dwelling in the believer. The dwelling with has been applied, and with obvious propriety, to the presence of the

Spirit in assemblies for worship, considered as wholes, as companies, or bodies, associated according to the divine requirement.   His dwelling in has been stated, in contrast, as his presence in the soul of every individual worshipper, as the guide and animating influence of his personal feelings. The expressions do unquestionably embrace also a perpetual presence with and in the believer at all times, and not merely in connection with public worship.   But as bearing on the matter of worship, the distinction evidently points to a presence with, and yet outside the worshipper, and also to a distinct presence of the Spirit within the worshipper as the guide of his spirit in worshipping.   We have no fear of being far from the truth in saying that one of the meanings of these remarkable phrases refers directly to the presence of the Spirit in the assemblies for worship.   He is no doubt a perpetual presence around as well as within the individual Christian.   But he is also a perpetual presence in every Christian assembly.   This last is the particular truth that invites our attention now:

1. The first question which excites notice is, what is meant by this presence of the Holy Ghost in the Christian assembly?   There is a sense in which he is necessarily present in such assemblies.   He is God, and God is everywhere present.   But in this sense he is present in a drinking or a gambling saloon as truly as in a church.   In this sense his presence in an assembly for worship signifies no more than it signifies in the depths of an impenetrable forest, or in the cave of a mountain, or in the solitudes of a desert.   In this sense, also, the Father and the Son are equally present. The presence of the Spirit in the Christian assembly must mean something more than this natural and necessary determination of his omnipresence.   The analogy of similar conceptions of the divine presence may guide to the meaning.   Although the divine being is everywhere present, he is frequently spoken of in the Scriptures as "coming," com-

ing to a place or to a person, and for different purposes:
"The Lord came down upon Mount Sinai." "The Lord
came down to see the city and the tower of Babel." "The
Lord met him and sought to kill him." "He cometh to
judge the earth." It is obvious that all these forms of expression about a being, naturally everywhere present, simply
mean some peculiar manifestation of his presence for different purposes, and the nature of the purpose in each case
gives its peculiar coloring to the coming or presence which
it qualifies. Thus when he comes in judgment, it is God
manifesting himself in the actual infliction, or in his official
announcement of his purpose to inflict his judicial ven-
geance. When he comes or is present as the God of peace
and love, he manifests himself in the grant of peace and in
the expressions of his tender mercies. From these analogous
forms of expressions it is safe to conclude that the peculiar
presence of the Holy Spirit in the Christian assemblies is
the manifestation of that blessed agent in all the relations
which he sustains to the worship of the church, and in such
acts as he pleases to perform in the progress of the service.
As God he is the object of the worship offered; but his peculiar relations to the worship, determined by the great covenant of salvation, present him prominently as the animating
and guiding influence which controls the worship, and enables its offering in an acceptable manner.

It becomes clear, then, that the first in the official order
of divine worship is the Holy Spirit, who enables the worshipper to offer his service in faith to the Son, who, as official priest, offers it to the Father. This priority, of course,
implies no precedence of dignity or honor, but merely indicates the appointed official relation to the worship to be
offered. The first of the three sacred and mysterious persons of the Godhead in meeting his worshippers is the Holy
Spirit of God. The Christian dispensation is emphatically
called "the dispensation of the Spirit"; it is so called from

the declared prominence given in the gospel to his part in the work of salvation. The Spirit meets the worshipper to prepare his approach, to enable him to exercise faith in the Saviour, and thus through the mediation of the Son, realized and secured in its gracious functions by faith, to approach the Father, and to call him Abba, in acceptable worship. To enable the worship of the Father through the Son, the Spirit takes the lead in the worship of the saints. No ordinance has any effective spiritual power, except as the Spirit gives it. No worshipper's heart is ever in a proper frame for worship, except as the Spirit gives it. Without faith it is impossible to please God, and there is no true faith except that which is the fruit of the Spirit. The great fact, then, which is presented to us in this doctrine of the relation of the Holy Spirit to the worship of the Christian assemblies, is one of very high and solemn significance, a fact that ought to be fruitful of constant and profound practical effects on all who assemble for divine worship. That fact is, that the Lord is in his holy temple, in a peculiar posture, waiting to meet them. The Holy Ghost is pervading every sanctuary where the assembly meets to worship the Father through the Son. How striking the conception when we fully master it! How solemn the thought! To what searching inspection is the heart of every worshipper about to be subjected! The effects which this grand Christian doctrine ought to produce on the whole bearing and demeanor of those who come into the presence, and challenge his special attention by assuming the attitude and character of a worshipper, are so obviously those dictated by the immediate presence of such a being; they are so manifold in form, yet so strongly demanded by the fact, that it would hardly seem necessary to specify them.

2. It dictates that there should always be some suitable preparation of the thoughts and feelings before we leave our homes to attend public worship. We are going to meet the

Holy Ghost.   If we were going to meet a king or any great person by his own invitation or command in his own palace, our anxiety would be keenly roused as to the propriety of our own demeanor in his presence.   We should anxiously acquaint ourselves with the rules of etiquette to be observed. We should have our minds thoroughly purged of all listless-ness and indifference.   We should be solicitous to do nothing to forfeit his regard, or spoil our own welcome.   If we went to solicit some favor or advantage for ourselves or others, we should prepare for the best presentment of our cause, and seek carefully to avoid everything which might hinder our success.   To go into the special presence of the Holy Spirit without any recognition of it at all, with our minds in the same general attitude as if we were going into some secular assembly, with no feeling of reverence, with no quickened sense of obligation to wait before him in a suit-able frame of feeling, is to offend the obtrusive proprieties of the position.   To confound an assembly for the worship of Almighty God with an assembly to listen to a lecture on art or a political address, is to annihilate the spirit and the con-ception of worship altogether.   How keenly does this con-demn the prevailing spirit of our attendance on public worship.   This utter practical ignoring of the radical idea of divine worship, and construing it as a mere Sunday assembly of the people, warranted by custom, but of no vital signifi-cance, is altogether sufficient to account for the chronic un-fruitfulness of ordinary Christian worship.   No wonder the Spirit withholds his influences, and the ordinances are powerless, when his presence and the necessity for it in every Christian assembly for worship is so completely dis-counted.   Let us fill our minds with the thought that we are going to meet the Holy Ghost whenever we come to the sanctuary, and come with some suitable frame of thought and feeling.   It is as incongruous in itself, and far more so in the degree of its impropriety, to come unprepared than to

come with studied or careless indifference into the presence
of a king.

3. A suitable, that is to say, a serious and even solemn
impression that the Holy Ghost is in the house waiting for
us, would change much in the demeanor of the people before
the actual commencement of divine worship. They would
have little or no inclination to gather together and exchange
all sorts of ideas while waiting for the service to begin. A
quiet grasp of friendly hands, a brief inquiry after mutual
welfare, an expression of sympathy for an existing affliction,
the necessary exchange of thought about church affairs, reduced to briefest proportions, would precede a prompt
entry into the sacred house. A diligent preparation of mind
to enter into the impending service, before and after entering, would become a prevailing and instinctive habit. The
custom of lingering in protracted talks about all manner of
secular things, even after the signal for service has been
given, would become a thing of the past, and the disturbance
of the actual worship by the sound of the late-comers hurrying
to their places would soon be unknown. Listlessness and
inattention, careless conversation in the house as well as out
of it, would be abolished. The sentiment that the Holy
Ghost was in the house, ready to search every heart to see
what and how much desire was there for his blessing, and
waiting to bestow his grace on all who really wanted it, would
soon put an end to all this censurable carelessness. Our
whole view of entering into the sanctuary would be powerfully modified by the grand thought of his holy presence,
and all our behavior would be adjusted to it. Sleeping
during the service, the study of costumes, and the critical
observation of our fellow-worshippers, would be swallowed
up by our proper conception of the presence of the Holy
Ghost in the sanctuaries of Christian worship.

4. The proper recognition of the presence of the Spirit in
the sanctuary would suitably control that most difficult and

dangerous question of dress in the Christian assembly. A certain limited class of people are censurably careless about their appearance. Another, a much more extensive class, err on the opposite extreme, and seem to regard the temples of the most High God as the chief theatre on which to display the splendors of fashion and the taste of its devotees. No earthly king would be pleased with either of these species of display in his presence. A sloven would be probably shown to the door, and a rich parvenu who should refuse the court dress ordered by court fashions for the king's guests, and appear loaded with the ostentatious pomp of overgrown wealth, would scarcely meet with a warmer reception. Elaborate dressing in the sanctuaries of God is a serious spiritual snare. It absorbs the thoughts; it raises the frivolous passions; it distracts others; it excludes or deadens the impression of the truth, and indicates a mind as dead to the presence and purposes of the presiding Spirit as it would be in a saloon or a courthouse. A certain simple dignity and propriety of dress, alike distant from carelessness and ostentation, is alone suitable to the presence and aims of the Holy Ghost in the house of God.

5. The presence of the Spirit as the guide and animating energy of the worship of the church ought to qualify profoundly all our use of the ordinances. These instruments are appointed of God in order that man, the worshipper, may be assured that his action in the use of these instruments is acceptable to him. The ordinances are, as it were, trysting-places where the soul that seeks may find God. This meeting with God in the ordinances ought always to be definitely recognized whenever we use them. It would be a fruitful thought every time we employed any ordinance in public or private worship—prayer, reading Scripture, praise, sacrament—if we should formally remind ourselves that we are going to meet the Holy Ghost that he may lead us into the presence of the Father through the Son. These ordinances

are not only instruments of worship towards God, but means of grace for ourselves. They are the acts which the King has prescribed by which we are authorized to approach him and obtain his favors. They can only be defeated by defective use. Their power will be increased by increased degrees of rightness in their use. The presence of the Holy Spirit properly dictates certain effects in the use of the ordinances. In the first place, it dictates *the use of all the ordinances*, not to all men indiscriminately, but only such of them as have been prescribed to certain classes of men. Some of them have been appointed to be used by unregenerate men in order to regenerate them. Others have been appointed for the use only of regenerate men in order to their growth in grace; and the limitation in the use is to be observed, as well as the use itself. Prayer, reading the Scriptures, and attending on the whole worship of the sanctuary, may be lawfully used by the worst of men. The sacrament of baptism as applicable to adults, and the sacrament of the supper, are only to be used by those who avow their faith and obligation to obey the Saviour. But no one, saint or sinner, has the right to decline the use of any ordinance which the law authorizes him to employ; for that authorization not only confers a privilege, but issues a command. It is an offence to the present and watchful Spirit to refuse to join in all those acts of worship which he has required to be used. Disobedience in his special presence is a special offence, and effectually discounts the prospect of his blessing.

In the second place, the presence of the Spirit *dictates*, not merely the use, *but the right use* of all the ordinances. There is a certain spirit or frame of feeling in which the law requires them to be employed. There is *a certain reverence* which is indispensable. To challenge the Holy Spirit of God to meet us in the act and ordinance which he himself has appointed for the purpose, involves the obligation to do it with a reverent frame of mind suitable to his majesty. To meet him before whom all angels bow in adoring awe, with no more concern than we would whistle up a dog or speak to a boot-black, is appalling irreverence. All our intuitions of moral propriety are shocked by disrespectful conduct in the presence of superior dignity; and we fear a very brief inspection of the frames of feeling in which we commonly appear in the sanctuary would disclose a most alarming want of reverence and godly awe in the worship of God.

In the third place, the presence and the purposes with which the Holy Ghost presides in the worship of the Christian assembly dictates the eager expectation of a blessing on the worshipper. "Open thy mouth wide, and I will fill it" is a command and a promise peculiarly adapted, and as such, designed for the public assemblies of believers. These ordinances of worship are not designed as mere empty forms. God is seeking not merely the homage which is due to himself, but he is seeking also the highest interests of his poor, sinful, and unhappy creatures. His appointed ordinances carry richer blessings, when rightly used, than all the valuables of the world put together. They ought to be employed, therefore, with an eager confidence in the grace they tender. They ought to be used with a lively desire and expectation, with an earnestness and vigor, an absorbed interest and occupation of thought and feeling, exclusive of all other thoughts and feelings, all other ideas and things.

In the fourth place, the presence of the Holy Spirit in the use of the ordinances determines also the spirit of joy and gladness in the public or private worship of God. The reverence due to his divine majesty does not in the least detract from the joy that is also legitimately due to his presence and the gracious purposes for which he is present. He is in the ordinances as the Paraclete, the one ready to be called to our side for the help of every worshipper. He is there for the purpose of taking the things of Christ and showing them unto us. He is there to unseal to our dull vision the gladness of the gospel. He is there to enable us to "serve the Lord with gladness." How shamefully has the spirit of joy been banished from the worship of God, the gracious! Any true or adequate apprehension of the Spirit's presence would make the worship of the sanctuary and the closet ring with delight. His presiding grace dictates a lively and loving expectation of joy and comfort in waiting upon him, an anticipation of realizing all the gracious ends of divine worship, comfort, and strength to saints, awakening and conversion to sinners.

In the fifth place, the presence of the Spirit in the public sanctuary dictates the keeping pure and entire all such ordinances as he has appointed, not taking anything away, not adding anything to them. It requires strict compliance with his given law concerning ordinances. The notion is entertained by certain sections of the Christian body, that the presence and influence of the Holy Spirit in the assembly of believers warrants any and every one to take the leadership of the worship when impressed with the belief that they are moved by the presiding power to do so. This notion is unfounded. If the Holy Ghost did so move, it would of course be right. But the presence of the Spirit is not designed to abolish the written laws he has ordained, but rather to secure their fulfilment. The words of Holy Writ are to be the guide of all acceptable worship; they order what is to be done; they affix every restriction, as well as impose every precept. The refusal to observe those restrictions, so far from being justified by his presence, is rather a demonstration of his absence.

In the last place, the right use of the ordinances, as determined by the presence of the Holy Ghost, *dictates always a look beyond the ordinances to the Spirit himself to give them efficacy.* To rest in the ordinances, though given by God himself, is to repudiate his own agency, which is alone efficacious. To attribute a mystic energy to the ordinances themselves, as many do, is to rely upon them, and to renounce all

dependence on God himself or on his grace back of the ordinances.   This is the grand central doctrine of Christianity,
that salvation is of the Lord, and that he alone can give the
increase, though even Paul may plant and Apollos water.
The presence of the Spirit confirms this doctrine; there
would be no need for his presence or the forth-putting of his
energy if the doctrine was false.   This living presence of the
Holy Ghost requires every worshipper, while using the instrumental means of grace, with all fervor and engagedness
of feeling, to construe them as they really are, *mere means,*
and to look beyond them to the power of the living Spirit,
who alone can give them any efficacious energy or saving
effects.   This is the vital difference between an evangelical
and a ritual religion.

This wonderful truth of the presence of the Spirit in the
Christian assembly ought to make us open our hearts, and
always keep the attitude of expectancy of a blessing and a
readiness to receive it.   Let it be distinctly marked and
remembered, that this official presence of the Spirit is constant, a regular incident of all regular public worship, and
not, as the course of events for many years has taught us to
construe it, as only the incident of special occasions, called
revivals.   If Christians would honor the Holy Spirit more in
his regular offices in public worship, and always keep themselves designedly amenable to his influence, both in the
sanctuary and out of it, there would be far more constant
and effective manifestations of his power and grace, both in
building up the saints and in the salvation of sinners, than is
to be seen now.   The long intervals of barrenness, the coldness and discomfort of Christians are due, in great measure,
to the well-nigh complete degree in which all divisions of
the church have lost the practical and adequate apprehension of the presence and the official designs of the Holy Ghost
as the presiding power in the Christian assembly for public
worship.

CHAPTER XIV.

THE PERSONALITY OF THE SPIRIT.

"The grace of our Lord Jesus Christ, and the love of God, and the communion of the Holy Ghost, be with you all."—*Paul to the Corinthians.*

THE lesson which we propose to draw from these words, and confirm by other testimonies from the word of God, is the proof of *the personality* of the Holy Spirit, and the infinitely important practical uses and consequences which flow from it. By the personality of the Spirit is meant, that he is a *person*, not a mere *quality*, a distinct existence having the qualities of a distinct person, and not a mere attribute or characteristic quality of another person. A *person* is different from a *mere thing*, not only in the possession of reason, moral quality, and a will colored by these attributes, but as possessed of a *consciousness* of these powers. The doctrine of the Trinity is the datum of the Scriptures alone. This is equally true of both elements of the doctrine—the *unity* of the Godhead, and the trinity of the persons in the Godhead. The history of the human race has shown an apparently irresistible tendency in the human mind to recognize the existence of many gods. The existence of good and evil in this strange world, the universal spread of both in some degrees, and the perpetual conflict between them, are more easily accounted for by supposing two or more hostile superior powers, than by ascribing them to the ordering of a single will. Accepting the unity of the divine nature, the unguided natural reason in man accepts it as excluding any qualifying conception of unity in Godhood. But the revelation in the Scriptures, in its progressive unfolding of the mysteries of the spiritual universe, has clearly taught that in the unity of the divine nature, not disturbing that unity, but in full consistency with it, there are mysterious and incomprehensible distinctions which lay the foundation for the ascription of names, titles, affections, and works to each of these distinctions. What the exact nature and mode of existence in these distinctions may be is not explained. The fact is asserted; the mode of its existence is left involved in impenetrable mystery. All attempts to understand and bring the fact under comprehensible forms of definition and statement are absolutely useless. For a man to spend time and energy in the attempt to comprehend what is absolutely incomprehensible is an absolute waste of both. In ten thousand things we are compelled to be content with the knowledge of *a fact*, and to remain in absolute ignorance of its nature, its origin, its method, and many other points connected with it. In reference to God, that mystery which encompasses all things without exception might have been expected to attach itself with extraordinary force to the conception of his being. His eternal and uncaused existence, his omnipresence, his self-subsistence, the whole circle of his attributes, confound our conceptions. Our minds are conditioned to conceive, and they cannot conceive beyond the conditions established for our thinking. But we can know facts which we cannot explain in many things essentially connected with them. If, then, God is declared to exist in a unity, embracing and not inconsistent with itself in allowing distinctions within that unity, it is a rational demand upon our confidence to *accept the fact* without resistance or an irrational attempt to define the mode of the fact. To a *finite* mind an *infinite* existence is simply *beyond* the conditions of its thinking, and consequently can only be known *as fact*, and not comprehended in anything in which the infinitude appears. If God is incomprehensible to us in his relation to time, space, and the law of causality, he may be also in relation to number. If incomprehensible in all his infinite attributes, why not in reference to the mode of his infinite being? If we can and do accept all other facts in his nature which are incomprehensible in their modes, why reject a single fact on the mere ground of incomprehensibility? If that circumstance warrants the rejection of one mysterious fact it would warrant the rejection of them all, and reduce us to absolute atheism, because we are not gods ourselves, because the thinking capacity of a finite and conditioned intellect must conform to the conditions of its own mental energy, and cannot transcend them. This lands us in absurdity. We are, then, content to accept the facts in the constitution of the divine nature as they are stated in the Bible, without making any attempt whatever to comprehend the nature or mode of the facts stated.

1. We do not propose to present the Scripture testimony to the doctrine of the Trinity as a whole, we merely state briefly the proof of the personality of the Spirit. The Holy Ghost is called by *separate personal names*. In the apostolic benediction he is associated with the Father and the Son, on the same level of dignity and authority, and discriminated, as they are discriminated from each other, *by a distinct and separate name*. If the name *Father* is intended to express a distinction from the Son, and the name *Son* to express a distinction from the Father, no matter what that distinction may actually be, then, unquestionably, the name *Holy Ghost* is intended to express a similar distinction from both the Father and the Son. Whatever the distinction may be, it is impliedly affirmed of the Spirit as it is of the Father and the Son. To make the distinction a personal one between the Father and the Son, and then to make the Spirit nothing but a mere quality or attribute of either or both of them, is to confound the passage with absurdity, and to arbitrarily change the signification of names which are indiscriminately applied to each distinction in the series. If the distinction is personal, as between the Father and the Son, it is personal as between the Holy Ghost, on the one side,

and the Father and the Son both on the other. The formula of baptism yields the same result. A distinct name, carrying the same distinction and implying the same dignity and authority, is there applied to the Spirit, as it is to the Father and the Son. The baptized person is consecrated by the ordinance to the service of the Holy Ghost, just as much, by the very same ordinance, by the very same words, with the very same meaning as he is to the service of the Father and the Son; to the service of each one of them as to the service of all of them. Personal names are ascribed to the Spirit, and emphatically the supremest of all names; he is called God, as when the unhappy Ananias and his wife are first said to have lied to the Holy Ghost, and then immediately after are said to have lied to God. He is called the "Holy Spirit," "the Spirit of grace," "the Spirit of holiness," "the good Spirit," "the Spirit of Christ," "the Spirit of the Lord," and absolutely "the Spirit." He is described as proceeding from the "Father and the Son," yet is emphatically called "the free Spirit" and "the eternal Spirit." These personal names are employed *in such connections* as to leave no doubt of their design to designate a person, and not a quality.

Personal attributes are ascribed to him. He is said to be holy, wise, good, active, powerful, eternal, and free. *Personal affections* are ascribed to him. He is said to be grieved, pleased, offended and tempted. A personal *will* is ascribed to him: "As they ministered unto the Lord, and fasted, the Holy Ghost said, Separate me Barnabas and Saul for the work whereunto I have called them." "Take heed therefore unto yourselves, and to all the flock, over the which the Holy Ghost hath made you overseers." *Personal actions* are ascribed to him. He is said to *teach*, to *strive*, to *comfort*, to *lead*, to *intercede*, to *bring to remembrance*, to *create*, to *regenerate*, to *search all things*, yea, even the deep things of God. He is said to *know*, to *choose*, to call men to particular acts of service, to guide and govern the church as a whole, and the souls of believers. He is called God, and the incommunicable and exclusive attributes of God are ascribed to him. If such qualities, names, affections, and positive actions do not *prove personality*, nothing can prove it. To attribute will, knowledge, capacity of feeling, choice, and action, to a mere abstract quality is absurd. A personal being only is capable of such things.

2. The personality of the Spirit is not a mere unproductive exactness of theological opinion; it is full of infinitely important practical uses. The Spirit is the great agent for applying the redemption purchased by Christ. He alone, under the arrangements of the covenant, can awaken and bring a sinner to seek for salvation. He alone can regenerate a carnal, and sanctify a regenerate, soul. Without his incessant concurrent action the ordinances are absolutely powerless. Without his aid no prayer will be answered, no grace can develop, no strength can be secured, no comfort can be enjoyed. If the Holy Spirit is a mere quality, conditioning all spiritual benefit and hope, it is clear that no special solicitude, attention or application need be, or can be directed to him. The only object of such feelings and acts will be the person who possesses and administers this quality. But if the Holy Spirit *is a person*, it is obvious that if any hope of his gracious offices is to be indulged he must be recognized as a person; he must be approached as a person; he must be conciliated as a person in every application made to him. Any attempt to misconstrue him, to deprive him of his personal character, or his personal rights, may be expected to result in the defeat of the objects for which the approach and appeal are made.

3. The first all-important and intensely practical inference from the personality of the Spirit is this necessity of approaching him as a person. This involves *the necessity of making this approach suitably to his personal character, to the*

glory of his qualities, and to the greatness of his divine majesty.
The very grace of the Holy Spirit, and the very freedom of
our access to him, symbolized by the wide air and the
abounding waters, has a tendency to lead our misguided
feelings into degrading and dangerous conceptions of his
influence and his gracious affections towards sinners. We
are so prone to the abuse of mercies, it tends to present
him to us rather as a quality or a provided influence, impersonal as the air, always accessible, creating no special
solicitude to enjoy it, incapable of offence or personal affections of any kind; and, therefore, a thing which may be neglected, made subject to our convenience, postponable without
hazard for other interests, just because of the width, con-
stancy, and patient energy of the blessed influence itself.
But the influence of the Spirit is the goodness and power
residing in *a personal will,* and while comparable to water,
or to the wide and free-flowing winds, on account of its
infinite strength and tenderness, and the freedom with which
it is offered to all who need its grace, nevertheless it is not
comparable to water or air in its insensibility to abusive
treatment. Water may be fouled and rendered unfit for
service; the free winds may be loaded with poisonous gases;
yet neither water nor air suffer, because they are not sensitive, because they are not persons. But the Holy Spirit is
a person; his wide, free grace is simply the intense and masterly affection of a personal will, infinite in its compassionate
and tender sensibilities. But this very fact that it is personal
love and kindness is proof of a personal control over its
direction and application. It may be checked by abuse; it
may be alienated by presumption; it may be directed upon
one and averted from another; it may distribute one degree
of its energy to one, and a greater or a less degree to another; it may be sought or despised; it may thus be granted
or denied. Sought aright there is every assurance of its
being granted; neglected or misused, it is assured of being

removed. It becomes evident, then, from the personality of the Spirit, that it is a matter of incalculable importance that all who seek his favor, whether sinners seeking grace to convert them, or saints seeking increase of grace, or any of his special acts for their benefit, must conform to the demands of his personal nature or to the conditions of his official interference. Humility, fervor, and absolute sincerity, reverence, patience, submission to his own times, terms, and measures in his gifts, and absolute confidence in his wisdom and grace in giving or withholding, are indispensable to success in seeking his favor.

There must be a *compliance with his known will.* He is God; he must be sought with unfeigned reverence. He is holy; sin must be renounced; for if we regard iniquity in our hearts he will not hear; if we come with cherished evil, fresh on our hands, he will despise our prayer. Isaiah explained why Israel was not heard, though they made many prayers: their hands were full of blood. The sinner, seeking the converting grace of the Spirit, must, at once, and in advance of obtaining it, put away his known sins. The drunkard must abandon his bottle, and the licentious his lust. He must abandon his prayerlessness, and begin to pray; he must give up his disregard of the Bible, and begin to read it. No matter what *the will* of the Spirit requires, there must be an effort to comply with it. This rule of action, determined by the personality of the Spirit, is equally applicable to the believer seeking growth and special graces; and doubtless the reason why so many prayers of the saints apparently and actually fail is, that the Holy Ghost, as the sole source of acceptable prayer, is not suitably recognized as such, and proper attention is not given to comply with his will.

The personality of the Spirit also determines another fact all-important to be recognized, and dealt with accordingly; that is, that the Holy Ghost *may be grieved and offended.* His influence is the only stay to the natural growth and

maturity of moral evil in the inward nature, and in the
visible conduct of all men. Left to themselves, the ruin
would soon become absolute and irretrievable. This evil is
an energy in the will of sinning agents. The conflict of the
Spirit is not with mere dead or fossilized habits, but with an
active, positive, persistent energy of personal will, seeking to
do evil, and to enjoy its results. Consequently, there is always
present in all the restraining and purifying conflicts of the
Holy Ghost an *element of provocation* to him of intense and ex-
asperating offence. It is a wonder he ever makes the struggle at all. It is no wonder he sometimes gives up the contest.
"My Spirit shall not always strive with man," said God, just
before the waters of the flood were turned loose on a world
of incorrigible sinners. There is such a thing as "grieving
the Spirit." There is such a thing as "quenching the
Spirit." There is such a thing as God saying, "Ephraim
is joined to idols; let him alone." No conception of the
work of the Holy Ghost is more full of power to warn
the presumptuous and overawe the scornful than this truth
of the personality of the Spirit and his consequent capability
of being offended. To guard the Holy Spirit from insult in
the near contact which his office involves with all the secret,
but to him undisguised, pollutions of a fallen soul, the Scriptures seem to have taken particular pains. They have surrounded him with certain vague, but menacing safe-guards,
which are appalling in their mysterious terrors. Blasphemy
against the Father and against the Son may be forgiven;
but blasphemy against the Holy Ghost hath never forgiveness. This offence to the Spirit, whatever it may be, is the
only sin which cannot be forgiven. It is not easy to discern
the reasons of this peculiar solicitude for the honor of the
Spirit, as compared with the honor of the Father and the
Son. It may be due to that close personal contact with the
sin in the soul, which his work demands of him. He comes
into the very midst of the infernal mob. The stench of the

unclean birds is in his nostril; the hiss of the serpents is in his ear; the insulting, malicious demeanor of the lurking fiends is in his eye. He is liable to peculiar violence, and he is guarded specially against it. His work also gives effect to all the provisions of the covenant. Without his work the counsels of the Father would fail; the whole work and sacrifice of the Son would come to nothing. To resist his work, then, is to resist all the work of the Father and the Son also. To do despite to the Spirit is to do despite to the whole Godhead; to resist the love of the Spirit is at the same time to resist the love of the rest of the sacred Trinity. Yet again, the Spirit's entrance into the unregenerate heart is a free accession to it. So far as man, the sinner, is concerned, his original entry is absolutely free, not under any covenant bond to him to do it or to repeat it. To resist it involves peculiar wickedness and peculiar foolhardiness. His free entry involves a peculiar personal kindness, and on this account resistance to it involves a peculiar ingratitude. Yet more, that hatred to God, which is the universal distinctive trait of the carnal mind, is peculiarly obnoxious to the Holy Spirit, inasmuch as being the immediate agent of applied grace he has to come into a closer contact with it. These reasons are more vaguely suggestive, than positively demonstrative, of the cause why the Spirit is so specially guarded against insult in the unholy human heart. But the fact is clear, however perplexing the reason of it may be. The nature of that sin against the Holy Ghost which is never to be forgiven is involved in an obscurity that creates a vague terror and makes us tread lightly, even at a distance, from the guarded shrine of the honor of the Spirit. Some have limited it to the form of the sin in which it first appeared, that is, in the blasphemous ascription of the Saviour's miracles to evil spirits. As they were done by the concurrent power of the Holy Spirit resting on his human energies, the ascription of them to a devilish agency was a direct and malignant

assault on the Holy Ghost, as well as on the Son. The
Pharisees, in order to break the force of the miracles, claimed
that they were done through a compact with the prince of the
devils, who had, therefore, given order to his subordinates
to obey the commands of the Nazarene. If the form of the
sin contained the essence of the sin, then the blasphemy
against the Holy Ghost was confined to the period of the
Saviour's personal life, and could not be committed afterwards. But it is a dangerous pulling down of the defences
of the Spirit, perhaps a dangerous making it easy to commit
the sin, to construe it in this manner. The essence of the
sin was probably different from the mere form of it as committed by the Pharisees. That malignant hatred to the doctrine
and the person of the Redeemer, which lay at the core of
Pharisees' blasphemy, has often appeared since; and this
feeling may involve the sin against the Spirit which hath
never forgiveness. The whole narrative of his history, and
the whole statement of his doctrines, have been given under
the superintendence of the Spirit; they are thus endorsed by
him; and to assail the record is to assail the Maker of it. If
hatred to Christ involved the outrage on the Spirit at first, it
is equally probable that the same malignant temper may
always involve it. The *personality* of the Spirit, involving as
it does a capability of offence, is thus shown to involve the
most solemn and impressive lesson in the whole revelation of
God concerning the sins of men, the lesson that there is *one
sin* which the blood of the Son cannot purge away, which
the infinite benignity of the Father cannot pardon.

4. The *personality* of the Spirit also determines his claim
to our confidence in his personal qualities and his personal
affections, as qualifying him for his great trust. No approach
or application to him can be expected to succeed which does
not do some justice to his fitness, to the qualities which ad-
just him to the work assigned to him. Equal justice must
be done to the affections which animate him and encourage

the appeal to his power. He has asserted both in the word
he has inspired, and confidence in his word will breed confidence in his fitness and his love. Want of confidence in
either lays no ground of hope or expectation of his favor.
His fitness and his loving-kindness are both grounded in his
personality. No one is qualified to deal with the strong and
complicated evils in a fallen nature, unless endowed with an
intelligence and a strength equal to the emergency. His
love is equally essential; his sympathy and readiness to help
are indispensable to make the appeal of a soul conscious of
its sin, hopeful, and persevering. Just in proportion as
justice is done to the loving heart of the Holy Ghost, and the
anxious mind of the seeker for grace can realize the infinite,
brooding tenderness of his grace, his delight in his work,
his pity, his patience, and the unsearchable freedom and
riches of his grace, just in this proportion will spring the joy
and comfort of a real hope and confidence of his blessing.
The personality of the Spirit also gives assurance touching
his *power to help us effectively.* There is great power in
impersonal agencies and energies; but they are not always
available. Even when under the direction of personal intelligence and will, they require the intervention of machinery
to render them effective in the use of the power that is in
them. If the Holy Ghost is a mere quality, and not a person, he is unfit to serve our uses. We are assailed by a
mighty personal intelligence; we ourselves are personal intelligences with all their changeable impulses; the evil to be
combatted in our nature resides in the living and shifting
energies of a personal will. A mere quality cannot help us,
because it exerts its force along certain fixed lines, and according to a certain fixed constitution in its own nature. It
is consequently unfit to cope with the infinitely various manifestations of a personal will, subject, in addition to its own
impulses, to the subtle temptations of personal wills outside
of its own proper sphere. But the personality of the Spirit

makes him a match for Satan and for man, in not only the degree of his power, but in the mode and adjustability of its exercise. It therefore lays the foundation for unlimited confidence in his teaching, in his guidance, in his protection, and in his control of all events and vicissitudes of the spiritual history and experience of those in whom he dwells. The personality of the Spirit teaches us to recognize and conform to *his determining will*. The changes in the religious experiences of regenerate souls are sometimes unaccountable in their apparent causes, and in the ends and purposes for which they are ordered. The changes which took place in Job's condition, outwardly and inwardly, must have appeared very strange to the people who knew him. They could not account for it. They knew nothing of the scene between God and Satan. They knew nothing of the grand lessons of instruction to all ages and generations of the world which God was intending to educe. Many similar cases of great affliction to good men have since occurred. The general purpose in all such cases is the purpose of all afflictions whatever; it is a spiritual profit, that we may be partakers of holiness, as Paul puts it. This is the proximate cause. A remoter cause is the determination of his own will in the sovereign Spirit; he determines to subject his loved pupil and subject to this sorrow, just as the Father subjected Job. It is the result of his sovereign will; but his will is never separate from reasons; the more sovereign the will the stronger the assurance of reasons, though known only to himself. Therefore an absolute trust in the wisdom and the love embodied in the will of the Holy Ghost in all spiritual trials, and the resolute and loyal determination to submit and conform to that will, is essential to peace and the highest profit under these spiritual trials. The assurance of the propriety of that unerring will which orders them is found in the infinitely perfect, personal qualities of the Holy Ghost; qualities which are guaranteed to us by his personality. To conceive the vicissitudes of Christian experience, however attributable to other causes as they always are, as in no sense due to the wise and faithful ordering of the indwelling Spirit, is to subject his people to the same bitter sorrow with which we recognize the trials of life, apart from the wise and gracious ordering of the Father in the sphere of providence. The control of *an unerring personal will* is essential to mental peace under both forms of trial. The personality of the Spirit holds high relations to the interests of his people under the vicissitudes of the spiritual life.

5. Lastly, the personality of the Spirit assures us of *his rights*, his own regard to them, and the danger of infringing them. He has a right to command; it is dangerous to disobey. He has a right to enter the heart of any sinner; it is dangerous to resist him. He has a right to convict of sin and to lead to the Saviour; it is perilous to refuse his enlightenment and to go where he leads the way. He has a right to confidence, to gratitude, to obedience; it is dangerous to deny him either of these claims. He has a right to reverent treatment, to be met freely in his gracious advances, to be loved and appealed to at all times and under all circumstances. He has a right to be recognized as a person, and dealt with as such in all the acts and offices in which he is appointed to execute the covenant of grace. Every sinner seeking pardon should deal with him as a person. Every Christian seeking for his seal, his unction, his witness, or his comforts should deal with him as a person. All should deal with him as a person endowed with his great and lovely attributes ought to be, as infinitely holy, wise, powerful, and full of gracious tenderness and love. The Holy Spirit is God, and has all the rights of the infinite and glorious Lord over all his own creatures, to their love and faithful service, world without end. To refuse him even the least of them all is to rob and repudiate him; than which nothing can be conceived more wicked or more dangerous, more insulting to him, or more ruinous to the creature.